Anthropology

AND THE POLITICS OF

Representation

Anthropology
AND THE POLITICS OF
Representation

Edited by Gabriela Vargas-Cetina

THE UNIVERSITY OF ALABAMA PRESS
Tuscaloosa, Alabama

Copyright © 2013
The University of Alabama Press
Tuscaloosa, Alabama 35487-0380
All rights reserved
Manufactured in the United States of America

Typeface:Caslon

Cover art: *Fieldnotes* by Megan Galaviz
Cover design: Gary Gore

∞

The paper on which this book is printed meets the minimum requirements of
American National Standard for Information Sciences—Permanence of Paper for
Printed Library Materials, ANSI Z39.48-1984.

Library of Congress Cataloging-in-Publication Data

Vargas-Cetina, Gabriela
Anthropology and the politics of representation / edited by Gabriela Vargas-Cetina.
p. cm.
Includes bibliographical references and index.
ISBN 978-0-8173-5717-7 (quality paper : alk. paper) — ISBN 978-0-8173-8624-5
(ebook)
1. Ethnology—Methodology. 2. Ethnology—Philosophy. 3. Representation
(Philosophy) 4. Political anthropology. I. Title.
GN345.V37 2013
305.8001—dc23

2012036141

Contents

Illustrations

Acknowledgments

We first started to work on this volume after some of us had participated in a series of articles, "Representations of Indigenousness," published between 2003 and 2004 in *Anthropology News,* the newsletter of the American Anthropological Association (AAA). Due to the success of the series, Susan Skomal, then director of AAA publications, suggested we put together a larger group and develop a book around the theme of representations in anthropology. Stacy Lathrop had coedited the series with me, and she helped me write the book project, put together a list of possible contributors, and edit the first rounds of chapters before she had to leave the project.

June Nash and Kay Warren have accompanied our project all along. They attended the group's meetings, pointed me to crucial references, sent me relevant materials, and discussed ideas with many of us, in person and by e-mail. Additionally, June was one of the contributors to the original *Anthropology News* series, and then she was the discussant at a 2004 AAA presidential session in Atlanta, where working versions of some chapters were originally presented. Kay discussed with us the themes and suggested possible book contributors; the current list of chapters and contributors reflects some of her suggestions.

Tracey Heatherington's chapter is adapted from *Wild Sardinia: Indigeneity and the Global Dreamtimes of Environmentalism,* a title published by Washington University Press (2010). The ideas and themes in Katie Glaskin's chapter have appeared in a different version in "Litigating Native Title: Anthropology in the Court," which appeared in *Dilemmas in Applied Native Title Anthropology in Australia,* edited by Toni Bauman and published by the Australian Institute of Aboriginal and Torres Strait Islander Studies (2010).

Editing a book, and especially a book that seeks to foster internal and external debate, is never easy. The Facultad de Ciencias Antropológicas at the

Autonomous University of Yucatan helped me find the time and the peace of mind to work on completing this book, first through a sabbatical leave in 2006 and 2007 and then through a diminished course load for one semester upon my return. Cornell University put at my disposal a plethora of resources for two consecutive years, first as a fellow enjoying the exciting and collegial space of the Society for the Humanities in 2006 and 2007, and then as a visiting professor in the Department of Music in 2007 and 2008. Thanks to Genny Negroe Sierra, Brett de Bary, Timothy Murray, Judith Peraino, Gissell Vargas, Roxana Chavarria, and all others who with kindness and warmth made these spaces and work periods possible.

Fred Gleach and Vilma Santiago-Irizarry were with me through the best and the hardest times. My parents, Eduardo Vargas Vargas and Rosa del Alba Cetina Quiñones, and my family in Valladolid and Merida were always supportive of my work. My husband and colleague, anthropologist Steffan Igor Ayora-Diaz, has discussed the volume's ideas with me from the beginning. I thank him for more help, support, and encouragement than it is possible to recount here.

Thanks to the anonymous reviewers for their excellent comments and suggestions. Thanks also to Joseph Powell and his staff at the University of Alabama Press, and especially to Karen Johnson, Joanna Jacobs, and Gary Gore. Thank you to Megan Galavitz for the beautiful art for the cover. Finally, I thank all the authors who participated in this project in all its different incarnations and stages. Special thanks to those who stayed on and worked with me to see it published.

Gabriela Vargas-Cetina

Anthropology
AND THE POLITICS OF
Representation

Introduction

Anthropology and the Politics of Representation

Gabriela Vargas-Cetina

Representation and the epistemological problems inherent to it are key anthropological problems of the twenty-first century. Local people everywhere feel betrayed by anthropology. Instead of studying identifiable, rooted communities, anthropologists have turned their attention to the rhetorical construction underpinning the very ideas and practices sustaining the experiences of rootedness. In the meantime, anthropologists' accounts, even when they pertain to places usually thought of as remote, are becoming just other discourses and texts among many focusing on the same groups and locations. Is anthropology still relevant in the twenty-first century? Should anthropologists engage in strategic essentialism? Should anthropologists support important local causes that cannot be backed up by the information they gather in the field? What are the implications of the different kinds of intimacy we develop during fieldwork?

Today, anthropologists systematically deconstruct local worldviews, including those in their own societies, while supporting local causes that are often based on some form of essentialization. In a world marked more than ever by the politics of identity, where access to resources is often predicated on establishing a clear membership in recognizable groups, anthropologists everywhere are showing the contingent construction of "truth" while taking sides in local struggles. How do we deal during fieldwork and in our academic production with all the conflicting angles affecting the politics of representation, including the description of local people and groups, of anthropology, and of the ethnographers themselves? Do anthropologists today keep our discipline's long-standing commitment to respect and promote cultural diversity while we try to keep our analytical and theoretical tools sharp?

This book brings together an international group of anthropologists, all reflecting on the epistemological, political, and personal implications of ethnography, the politics of representation, and anthropologists' engagement in identity politics. While in recent years this exercise has been undertaken at the theoretical and methodological level (for example, Bibeau and Corin 1995; Clifford 1988; Clifford and Marcus 1986; Jacorzynski 2006), here we look at our own representation practices, their contexts and effects, and describe our personal choices when it comes to self-involvement in local causes, or when through our academic views we choose to become involved in larger cultural and political issues. All of us are already established in the field in our home countries and abroad. The purpose of this book is not to bring new topics or completely new ethnographic cases to the fore, but to show the academic, political, personal, and performative processes inherent in our research and our writing. We all show how and why anthropology matters and will continue to have an important place alongside other sources and forms of representation, including the representation of local identities.

Issues and Politics in Anthropological Representation

In the twenty-first century, *anthropology*, which used to refer mainly to academic anthropology, has long exploded everywhere into *anthropologies* that stand in different positions in relation to academia, national governments, corporations, nonprofit organizations, and the "subjects" of anthropological inquiry (Diamond 1980; Field, this volume; M. Kirsch 2006; Lins Ribeiro and Escobar 2006; Yamashita, Bosco, and Eades 2004). Furthermore, as Johannes Fabian (2006, 2007, 5) brings to our attention, not only are former *subjects of* anthropology now subjects scrutinizing anthropologists, but even entire fields have sprung to compete with academic accounts in the very same fields. Popular psychology, popular history, naturopathic medicine, folk culture societies, and socially minded journalism produce competing interpretations of those subjects that used to be the privileged field of anthropology and other social sciences. This poses a new set of problems unknown to the early pioneers of our discipline and radicalizes the situation already described by the *Writing Culture* group (Clifford and Marcus 1986; Marcus and Fischer 1986) in terms of ethnography having to be placed alongside other versions and other forms of representation. Through the new connectivity afforded by twenty-first-century communications technologies, what anyone, including an anthropologist, publishes in the form of books, blogs, films, pictures, or videos is going to be only one version of the same or similar events: in the age of the Internet, competing representations are the order of the day. This makes it all the more important to highlight the possible relevance and limits inherent in anthropological representations.

Representation in anthropology has an important ethical dimension. Today local populations and groups often see themselves as having a common, collective identity. If the anthropologists see themselves as contributing to the betterment of people's lives, the choices, in terms of courses of action, are manifold. In some countries, as in Mexico and Russia, anthropology was used by national governments as a tool for social intervention. In Mexico, for example, anthropologists were in charge of development programs to turn Indians into Mexicans during much of the twentieth century (Caso et al. 1981; Favre 1996).

Many anthropologists have supported, and some continue to support, national governments and transnational agencies with their research, trying to further the goals of governance, rural development, and even war. The case of Arturo Warman, a prestigious anthropologist who was Mexican Secretary of Agrarian Reform between 1995 and 1999, is remarkable but only one among many others. Anthropologists have often occupied positions in national governments, councils and bureaucracies, or national armies and have worked for the World Bank, the International Monetary Fund, the United Nations, or similarly transnational institutions. As George Marcus (2007) eloquently put it during a talk he gave at the Autonomous University of Yucatan, these anthropologists have been trying to "secure a place from where to whisper in power's ear" so as to help shape a better world for everyone—or at least speak to key programs and decisions on national and international issues—while other anthropologists have fiercely opposed these choices.

Many anthropologists think our discipline should never side with those in power, and many believe it should actually side with those against or outside the margins of established powers. Some think that ours is a critical discipline meant to offer alternative points of view from those prevailing in current societies. Others think that our work should primarily further the causes and enhance the lives of the people with whom we work in the field, helping the advancement of respect for alternative views and ways of knowledge. Still others think anthropologists should help corporations achieve better organizational and efficiency results. Such disparate goals are related to the current fragmentation of anthropologists themselves along ethnic, political, and academic lines, and each group and subgroup within the discipline are not only intent on representing their field sites in specific ways, but also intent on representing anthropology as a discipline that does specific kinds of things—or doesn't. Thus, representation in anthropology and the representation of anthropology to academics and the general public continuously generate debates and rifts in our discipline.

In the 1980s anthropologists began to write about a representation crisis in anthropology and the human sciences in general (Marcus and Fischer 1986). Business as usual, in the form of ethnography, had to reckon with changed circumstances and perspectives, if our discipline was to survive and thrive in the upcoming century. There was no need anymore for anthropologists to act as representatives of indigenous or other peoples, who could perfectly well speak for themselves at home and beyond or hire the specialists they chose. Some activists had already proposed that anthropologists' portrayals were only harmful to native peoples (Cardinal 1969; Deloria 1969), but, in fact, already many anthropologists were natives, so that anthropologists' home societies, including North Atlantic ones, had also become the subject of *native* descriptions (Le Pichon and Caronia 1991; Gupta and Ferguson 1997; Vargas-Cetina 1999). Many pages were also dedicated to the matter of ethnographic authority and whether or not it was a bogus concept (Clifford 1986a, 1986b, 1988; Crapanzano 1986; Marcus and Cushman 1982; Pratt 1986; Sangren 1988; Tyler 1986).

The *representation crisis* turned out to be more a moment of reflection (and, yes, a very important one) than a true crisis of the discipline. It has now resulted in new representation standards, self-monitoring practices, a higher awareness of the diversity of perspectives within anthropology, and the understanding of the ethnographers as themselves cultural beings, whose views are always colored by personal and epistemological circumstances. Still, in terms of field methodology and the writing of reports and the publication of books and articles, many anthropologists continue to carry on their work in ways not too different from before the so-called culture wars of the 1980s. In fact, it can hardly be otherwise: writing, publishing, and (as some of the chapters in this collection explain) performing are among the most important tasks common to all anthropologists everywhere, and they are all forms of representation. At this point, what was called *postmodern anthropology,* now mostly identified as *interpretive anthropology,* is on its way to becoming a quasi-paradigm. Frederic W. Gleach reminds us here (see his chapter in this volume) that for all the criticism to the scientific paradigm, interpretive anthropology continues to share many of its assumptions. As Fabian (2007) has noted, anthropology is still marked by its Enlightenment beginnings, and it is doubtful that it will cease to be so. Authors in this collection have accepted the *crisis moment* critique and adopted the resulting consequences as part of their regular research strategies.

For the contributors to this book the question, then, is not whether we should or should not represent the people we encounter in the field, but what are the implications of those representations on those same people, on the public(s) they address, on ourselves as anthropologists and individuals, and on the direction(s) of the discipline as a whole. We all have been involved in meaningful relations with local people in those sites where we conduct research, have been involved at one time or another in local politics of representation, and have faced difficult choices in self- and alter-representation both in the field and beyond. Here we describe some of those dilemmas and why we are choosing or chose a particular ethnographic path.

Modes and Contexts of Representation

Given that anthropology is a representational discipline, in the sense of being based on meaningful depictions of the world, what are the implications of ethnography and anthropological theory in current cultural, social, and political contexts? In the twenty-first century, anthropology may or may not be relevant in particular settings and situations or for particular purposes, but it has been immensely significant in helping to create the global sociocultural context within which the representation of local and regional identity became crucial. Anthropology and anthropologists have been at the origin of social processes and movements related to the politics of difference, the fight for cultural rights, the social engineering programs based on understanding and representations of "cultures," and even the new process of cultural commoditization that John Comaroff and Jean Comaroff (2009) have written of in *Ethnicity, Inc.* Also, and very importantly, anthropologists have participated in the creation of tools to analyze and critique representations of cultural phenomena. It does not matter whether anthropologists generated these processes (which they probably did, at least in some cases) or gleaned them from their surrounding environments inside and outside the locations of their fieldwork: since the beginning of the twentieth century, anthropologists have been present for much of "the small history of the quotidian" and have witnessed, registered, archived, and then circulated under new guises those *petit recits* that may escape and challenge modernity's grand narratives (Lyotard 1984) or may become mythologies justifying precisely the irruption of those grand narratives into every corner of local life.

This book takes into account the new contexts of corporate capitalism, global communications, and trafficking that are now the background to all forms of scholarship (Castells 1996; Comaroff and Comaroff 2009; Lyotard 1984; Poster 1990). We follow other groups of anthropologists who have preceded us on this reflection path (see the chapters in Ayora-Diaz and Vargas-Cetina 2005a; Bibeau and Corin 1995; Clifford and Marcus 1986; Jacorzynski 2006; James, Hockey, and Dawson 1997; M. Kirsch 2006), but also look at how ethnographic representation has personal dimensions for each of us and immediate resonance in those places where we conduct fieldwork and often participate as regular members. There is no unified anthropology or a single anthropological *we* that can go unquestioned; but here we have chosen, as a group, to enter a collective, collegial conversation along a number of common themes, including the forms and place of representation in anthropology, the perceived relevance of anthropological perspectives to local groups and populations, the methodological and ethical quandaries stemming from personal and cultural intimacy, and the problems (and eventual solutions) posed to us by strategic essentialism as a political tool. The fact that we all see these as important problems in the discipline does not turn us into representatives of anthropology at large, but we believe that we have identified and spoken to key questions and issues that may be of use to other anthropologists too: What are the implications of anthropological representation? And what are the problems with each representational choice? While other authors have asked these same questions for the discipline as a whole, we have decided to respond ethnographically and personally.

In the past, anthropologists had free range to go and "study" natives in the colonies (internal and external) in order to describe them and so represent them before metropolitan audiences (Asad 1973; Clifford 1988). Representing other people(s) at the time implied at least four different types of activities: (1) documenting, for the anthropologist's private archives; (2) describing in articles and books, for a larger public; (3) exhibiting; and (4) speaking for them at public forums. Of course, in many instances anthropologists mixed two or more of these modalities, such as when they were in charge of accompanying "their natives" to meetings or to staged presentations, or when creating dioramas for museums that were meant to display representative figures of regular life among "natives" of the world (Ayora-Diaz 2000; Di Leonardo 1998; Kirshenblatt-Gimblett 1998); Ishi and Nisa are constant reminders of both the powers and the dangers of anthropological representation (T. Kroeber 1961; K. Kroeber and Kroeber 2003; Shostak 1981). These four modes of representation continue to inform anthropological practice today, even if in modified forms.

Describing implies organizing one's records into texts and other media that can be intelligible to one's audiences, and it continues to be a key aspect of ethnography. Exhibiting often implied, and now less so, the physical displacement not only of artifacts but also of *natives* to the metropolis, where they were put on display. Speaking for others often took, and sometimes still takes, the form of translation, whether between different languages or even between different dialects or sets of idioms within a single language. Along with writing and exhibiting, speaking for others has come under great scrutiny and criticism in the late twentieth and early twenty-first century. Regarding documenting, the discussions have mainly centered on fieldnotes and journals, which are the basis of most anthropological publications (see Sanjek 1990; Glaskin, this volume). In this book we have explored other aspects of the documentation process and the way it relates to local identities and to the place of the researcher in the shaping of the anthropological archive.

Marcus (1998) recalls the importance of private archives for anthropologists. These are the repositories of all the notes, photos, diagrams, newspaper clips, journals, videos, and sound recordings we gather during fieldwork. Personal archives are at the basis of all academic production in anthropology. As he points out, only in a few cases has a group of anthropologists decided to build and share a common archive over the years. Famous cases include the Harvard projects in Chiapas, Mexico (Vogt 1994), and in the Kalahari in Botswana, Namibia, and South Africa (Lee and Biesele 2002), but in most instances anthropologists usually share their private archives only with selected colleagues and their students.

Jacques Derrida (1995) tells us that the concept of *archive* has a double origin: an *arkon* was a guardian in whose house documents were deposited. These arkons had the right to interpret these documents in order to dictate the law, which emanated from the documents themselves. *Arkheion* was the very place where the documents were deposited, and the act of turning a house (the arkon's) into a repository of documents transformed that place from private to public. The existence of a place where the documents were and the authority of the arkons, then, came to be one and the same. We can see this double principle of documentation and authority in operation during anthropological representation since the archive is both the foundation and the result of anthropologists' ethnographic authority.

Anthropologists are collectors who build large personal archives through the years, which are the basis of their ethnographies and often continue to be important in their subsequent work and that of their students. Besides taking fieldnotes, photos, and sound recordings, most anthropologists rely on additional information gathered in libraries and archives. While today most anthropologists have accepted the subjective nature of ethnography, many of us (and certainly all of us represented in this book) believe that there is something that can be identified as methodological rigor and that the place and systematicness of the archive are paramount to it. The collection of live information that transforms into an archive of stored information is what makes it possible for us to move around information entries as if they were parts of a puzzle that will come together in a text. Archival authority (the *archontic* principle, in Derrida's conceptualization) is invoked when settling ethnographic disputes and also when anthropologists face different and often complicated, situations, including ethical dilemmas.

Authors in this volume also propose ways to improve the anthropological archive and, in doing so, improve crucial cultural records: Sergey Sokolovskiy and his colleagues used anthropological knowledge to improve data collection in the Russian census. Katie Glaskin tells us that the anthropological record can make a difference in land settlements involving native peoples in Australia. Beth A. Conklin points to the nonessentialist representation offered to us by contemporary native peoples, which could change the general perspective on native societies today. David Stoll believes that number and concept inflation should be kept in check because it can only harm the people who are left out of the recounting. Les W. Field proposes that anthropological research has to be read in historical perspective, against the background of the social and political contexts characterizing the time when it was carried out. All these authors are looking for ways to improve the recording and interpretation of our archives. The working assumption is that if we can find better ways to put the archive to use, fieldworkers will accomplish, in the end, better ethnographic representations. Against the constant accusation from the quantitative methodology camp that interpretive anthropology lacks rigor, we see here qualitative anthropologists committed to finding systematicness and comprehensiveness in their recording methods and representational practices. Taking the chapters in this collection as examples, it is possible to see how and why, in Michel Foucault's ([1978] 2000) sense, interpretive anthropology is also a disciplined form of anthropology and, along with academia in general, an instrument of, but also against, governmentality.

Ethnography in the form of monographs and academic articles has been the target of much analysis and deconstruction in the last decades. Many books have been dedicated specifically to this discussion (Asad 1973; Hymes [1969] 1974; Clifford 1998; Clifford and Marcus 1986; Gupta and Ferguson 1997; Marcus and Fischer 1986). One of the most debated aspects of anthropological writing in general continues to be the situational perspective of the researcher/writer since, at the time of writing the resulting text, the point of view of the anthropologist becomes the unifying perspective holding together the different sections of the book or ethnographically based article. While life is forever changing, texts fix that flow and turn it into artifacts, no matter how much multi-vocality they may contain. Much contemporary cultural anthropology, including the chapters of this book, necessarily addresses this particular conundrum.

In this collection authors engage in textual, intertextual, and contextual strategies of representation to show how our participation in local life informs our viewpoint, how our personal participation in events has some repercussions on those events themselves, and how our resulting texts are part of the larger field of textual and meta-textual representation. We have chosen to focus not on what anthropology does not do (and is not suited to do), such as faithfully mimicking life's flow, but on what it can do well and in useful ways, including providing the contexts and the political coordinates to the relative place of different positions and perspectives in our fieldwork sites and beyond.

Anthropology, as a modern academic discipline, emerged and consolidated itself in close relation with ethnographic museums where *exotic* artifacts and individuals were exhibited. Still today, the anthropology sections of important museums around the world employ hundreds of anthropologists specialized in creating exhibits out of everyday and ceremonial artifacts and from expressive culture recordings, and even re-creating everyday life activities in places close and afar. Many anthropology departments are also connected to university museums or, as at Cornell University, hold anthropology collections comprising material objects from around the world. From the nineteenth century on, a new scale of cultural exhibition has gained terrain; it transcends specific buildings and construes entire cities and nations as exhibits of local or national culture for the benefit of paying visitors—that is, tourists (see, for example, Bruner 2005; Kirshenblatt-Gimblett 1988). While in the past tourism was associated with individuals adapting to new environments, the Industrial Revolution brought about a process of turning tourist destinations into places to be consumed in ways that make sense to the visitors, and not necessarily to the locals (Bruner 2005; Löfgren 2002b). The projects Cultural Capital of Europe and Cultural Capital of the Americas are efforts in this direction. However, as Thomas M. Wilson discusses in this book, there are problems enlisting anthropologists' help for these kinds of representations. The representations of indigenousness described by Conklin in this book, however, hold greater promise for eventual involvement of anthropologists, native and otherwise, since they imply a more dynamic understanding of culture and local life than the marketing of some untroubled past.

Anthropologists have often chosen to speak for the natives. Today, people in many localities, including many who are or were at some point the *subjects* of ethnography, can very well represent themselves legally or hire experts who will represent them in ways they need. Still, cultural anthropologists continue to work on behalf of the local people they encounter in the field, often having to accept or deflect issues related to local forms and contexts of identity. Elizabeth Povinelli (2002) shows how contemporary multiculturalism imposes on Australian aborigines the impossible need to become authentic by showing that they belong in a clear, rather self-contained cultural universe, distant from Western life and values. Embodying and representing this identity, which anthropologists tend to now matter-of-factly deconstruct as historical and contingent, may become the difference between the continuation of a group's life or its disbandment and loss of resources and cultural patrimony. Jerome Levi and Bartholomew Dean (2003, 2–3) are aware of this problem, but they think that indigenous peoples have to become politically involved in national and international circles, even when that means risking the accusation of fake authenticity. Could there be a conceptual middle ground? Since essentialized identities are usually built on long-established cultural logics, some scholars are beginning to point at these logics as already essentialized differences that precede current efforts of political essentialism (E. Fischer 2001; Montejo 2005).

With time, colonized peoples have learned to describe and represent themselves both in "Metropolitanese" and in their own languages, for themselves and for outside audiences, in a world where the *inside* and the *outside* of localities and social groups are often impossible to discern (Ayora-Diaz and Vargas-Cetina 2005a; Comaroff and Comaroff 2009; DeHart 2010; M. Kirsch 2006; Ong 1987; Olwig 1993; Torres 1997; Tsing 2005). Anthropology was among those disciplines giving natives everywhere (including in their own hometowns and societies) powerful representational tools (Jackson and Warren 2005; Torgovnick 1990; M. Kirsch 2006). Today, anthropologists working with native corporations and in nongovernmental organizations (NGOs) are helping natives everywhere conceptualize themselves as shareholders and stakeholders in our common world (Comaroff and Comaroff 2009; Coumans 2011). David Maybury-Lewis and Rodolfo Stavenhagen are two anthropologists who, well aware of the pitfalls inherent in ethnic labels, chose to campaign in favor of the recognition of indigenous groups around the world as bearers of distinct cultures and collective rights. As Jean Jackson and Kay Warren (2005, 556–57) point out, "ethnographic practice that bridges inquiry, activism, and participatory approaches to the production of cultural knowledge raises complex questions, epistemological and ethical, answers to which are not exactly around the corner," but anthropologists who engage fully in the support of local causes and the call for international attention to them now do so with full awareness of these questions (see the chapters by Field, Glaskin, and Sokolovskiy in this book).

Structure of the Book

This book is divided into three parts: Identity Strategies, Decentering the Ethnographic Self, and Anthropology in Crucial Places. And there is an epilogue by June Nash. All chapters speak more or less to the same issues, but the arrangement highlights some of the main themes addressed by each author. In this introduction I have sketched the general issues that framed our work and discussions as a group.

In part 1, Identity Strategies, five anthropologists look at the place of representation in anthropology and draw very general conclusions related to the field as a whole. First, drawing on his own fieldwork and discussing his personal position on the representation debates, Les W. Field proposes that anthropological representation in anthropology will cease to be seen as a problem when the construction of most representations of local identity has been completed, since through a double historicization of anthropological theory and social movements we can see how they have influenced one another. The second chapter, by David Stoll, is an admonition against what he calls "scholarly inflation" in anthropological representation. Stoll worries that when representations become impregnable to analysis and criticism, someone at some point is going to have to pay for the resulting inflation. He places his experience as part of the Rigoberta Menchú controversy within a larger framework of academic anthropology as part of a moral economy. Both Field and Stoll address the current fragmentation of backgrounds and epistemological positions in anthropology as a whole and how this fragmentation often results in contesting representations of the same situations and contexts. Since they deal with these larger issues, their chapters are good at framing not only the first part, but also the rest of the book.

The three other chapters in part 1 are by Steffan Igor Ayora-Diaz, Beth A. Conklin, and Vilma Santiago-Irizarry. These authors address specific local cases of identity construction and contestation in Mexico (Ayora-Diaz and Conklin), Brazil (Conklin), and the United States (Conklin and Santiago-Irizarry). Like Field and Stoll before, these scholars are careful to place their own vantage point as part of their ethnography and show the place of contesting discourses that support distinct identity choices. Ayora-Diaz's chapter provides a good transition between the two preceding and the two subsequent ones, as he brings the issue of fragmentation to bear on the ethnographic contexts themselves. In postcolonial societies, he proposes, the current fragmentation of national forms of hegemony results in the search for recognition of regional and local cultures, which relate to regional and local power structures. Anthropological representation, he says, is always fragmentary precisely because local life is fragmented into so many power-jostling groups. He looks at the construction of Yucatecanness as different from Mexicanness through gastronomy and food consumption practices in Merida, Mexico, always attentive to the fact that gastronomy is a field where some social groups can silence others. In her chapter, Conklin addresses the issues posed by Po-

vinelli (2002), Levy and Dean (2003), and many others around the representations of indigenousness and authenticity. Through the examples of visual
representation politics among indigenous activists in Brazil, among Zapatista
guerrillas in Mexico, and in the Indian Arts and Culture Museum in Santa
Fe, Conklin sees a way out of essentialist politics relegating native peoples
to the past. Next, following a discussion through an electronic list over several years, Vilma Santiago-Irizarry looks at the self-identification of people
as Hispanic or Latino. She is careful to map her own engagement in these
discussions, documenting a process of strategic essentializing that emerged
through a Listserv conversation. Her chapter is the only one that specifically
relates interaction via the Internet to off-line ongoing debates.

In part 2, Decentering the Ethnographic Self, five authors analyze fieldwork and ethnographic writing. Anthropologists are systematically trained
to acknowledge the simultaneous coexistence of multiple epistemologies.
Even when anthropologists saw themselves as working among "savages," as
Lucien Lévy-Bruhl and Ernesto De Martino did, they tried to understand the
"primitive mentality" of those among whom they found themselves. Today
anthropologists are expected not only to recognize the many possible epistemologies as valid ones, but also to adapt themselves as much as possible to
different epistemic environments. One of the important results of this exercise in systematic relativity (which Fabian [2007] calls "necessary trans-
locality") is that the academic world where anthropologists practice as professionals or teach and publish as professors also reveals itself as necessarily
cultural and relatively arbitrary. The constant shifting between one and another set of principles for thinking and acceptable behavior, which very often is accompanied by a shift in languages or dialects, often makes the anthropologist wonder: Who am I, really? Am I the person who is seen and
represented as a professor or applied anthropologist in this particular life-
world, or the person who is at ease relaxing, working, bantering, or performing with my local friends and acquaintances somewhere? Can I continue to
be one and the other alternatively or at the same time and still, somehow, be
my own self? In this section we see that anthropologists can resort to an understanding of a decentered, compartmentalized, and even slippery self as
they move in and out of different situations and locations. While in the past
anthropologists were not expected to mind their doubts and self-questioning
in their resulting ethnographies, the reflexive demands of contemporary anthropology have made these self-negotiations very complex, as the chapters
in this section show.

Bernard C. Perley opens and appropriately frames the section with an engaging self-reflection on his predicament of being a native and an anthro-

pologist and having to "go native" and "go anthropologist" continuously during work and regular life. He proposes that the strength of anthropology as method lies precisely in the possibilities of seeing the world through what he calls epistemic slips—that is, to situate oneself continuously in more than one life-world. Timothy J. Smith, in turn, describes his experiences in the field as marked by something that almost looks like multiple personality disorder: although he introduced himself as "Tim the American journalist," he was given (notwithstanding his initial refusal) a new identity in rural Guatemala as "Mateo the Canadian journalist." Tim embraces his multiple identities, often accompanied by specific languages (English, Kaqchikel-Mayan, and Spanish), reasoning that our ability to see the world through multiple social personalities and their accompanying epistemologies can only make us better ethnographers and help us to understand, at least to some extent, radically different worldviews.

In the chapter following these two, I (Vargas-Cetina) analyze the predicament of the native anthropologist/local academic from a different angle, choosing to conceptualize the shifts in personality, lingo, and worldview as so many different performances. I see these performances, and my own awareness of them, as a way to create coeval, respectful relations in the field and better, more respectful ethnography that can be read along with the texts and the other cultural products that musicians and their patrons are producing on the same topics. Next, the chapter by Tracey Heatherington highlights the ethnographer's discomfort with emergent conflicts between two obligations of advocacy that are implicitly shouldered by environmental anthropologists: advocacy on behalf of one's host community and advocacy on behalf of nonhuman species and ecosystems at risk. She notes that where human-environmental conflicts, social conflicts, and embedded cultural racisms shape local contexts, the representation of culture and environment is fraught. She acknowledges structural marginality and global hierarchies of power while also supporting those local individuals and groups that are trying to curb violence, revitalize tradition, and design sound resource management systems, by contributing an honest portrayal of local environmental debates. The chapter by Frederic W. Gleach closes this section by analyzing fieldwork and the resulting representations in historical perspective. Through several case studies he traces the reception and flow of anthropological knowledge to locals, who then use it for their own ends. Gleach considers the ability we can develop to step outside ourselves and finds that not all anthropologists have followed through with the responsibilities such a shift in vantage point brings along. Through a series of fieldwork stories involving the encounter of anthropologists with members of North American First Nations, as well as his current work with a Puerto Rican former cabaret and movie star, he ponders whether academics pay due respect to those who supplied them with information, to conclude that sometimes theory is a bad thing if it is put before the interests of those who were kind enough to allow us to come into their lives and supplied us with valued information.

Part 3, Anthropology in Crucial Places, features chapters by Sergey Sokolovskiy, Katie Glaskin, and Thomas M. Wilson. Sokolovskiy, who is worried about the fate of the smallest ethnic minorities in Russia, undertook, with a group of his colleagues, the task to redo the categories under which the population of that country was counted in the 2002 census. Anthropology in Russia, he explains, is divided in two main schools of thought: the primordialists, who see ethnicity as natural and geographically rooted, and the constructivists, who see it as changing and contextual. While Sokolovskiy and his colleagues tried to create a census questionnaire that could capture the fleeting nature of ethnicity, the way in which the census was applied and interpreted only reenforced the essentialist view, so now the Russian population is seen as *more Russian* or *less Russian* according to their cultural background and the languages they speak, instead of, as the anthropologists in Sokolovskiy's group had hoped, fostering a better understanding of the way in which people choose to be included or excluded from ethnic categories. Katie Glaskin has also chosen to work within an institutional context outside academia, working with Indigenous Australians engaged in claims for native title. While she is aware of the dangers associated with the view of ethnicity as a fixed identity with clear cultural borders, native title is one of the few avenues for the recognition of Indigenous Australians' property rights in Australia today. In her chapter, she examines the testing of anthropological expertise in the court, particularly in relation to fieldwork methodology and fieldnotes, in a legal context in which much is at stake. This is a passionate, well-thought-out chapter where we see the anthropologist demanding more accurate documentation and more compassionate representations of people who are at the bottom of precisely those hierarchies of power so many of us discuss throughout the book.

The section ends with Wilson's recounting of what he sees as the failure of anthropology to represent itself adequately to the public in Northern Ireland. He was invited to participate, with a group of his students, in research that would support Belfast's bid for recognition as the 2008 European Capital of Culture in the United Kingdom. Wilson chronicles the failure of the bid and proposes that one of the problems was that the committee in charge of promoting Belfast as a cultural capital engaged in a "politics of timidity." These organizers ignored the many social and political tensions in the city instead of taking stock of the actual social dynamics extant citywide, which were clearly known to external Capital of Culture adjudicators. He believes that if anthropologists seek to contribute to public culture in the European Union or elsewhere, they should learn from this experience so that their possible contribution to crucial local projects is made more relevant.

An epilogue by June Nash closes the book by summarizing her view of paradigm shifts in anthropology through her own career and the place she sees for our current volume to occupy in the politics of representation debate. She affirms that, through our collective work, we are engaging with the challenges posed by earlier ethnographers who believed that good ethnography could bring crucial problems to light. She acknowledges the important impacts of the cultural critique school on today's ethnographic practices and kindly considers that our collective work in this volume is advancing an anthropology based on a collaborative exploration between anthropologists and the local people with whom we work.

As a group, in this volume we have tried to assess the theoretical, conceptual, analytical, and personal consequences of ethnographic representation at a time when it is impossible to skirt the political and personal implications of all anthropological work. Hopefully, we have pointed our questions and problems in useful directions and our work will generate many productive questions that can lead us and other anthropologists to reflect further on fieldwork, academia, and anthropology and the politics of representation.

I
Identity Strategies

I

Double Trouble

Implications of Historicizing Identity Discourses

Les W. Field

In this chapter, I will explore dynamic facets of the analysis of identity in both anthropological circles and indigenous communities. As a part of this discussion, I will describe my work with a federally unrecognized tribe in California, the Muwekma Ohlone of the San Francisco Bay area, among whom the last dozen years of change and growth have helped me and others in the tribe to clarify and explore many of the facets of identity. The major theme I will explore here centers upon historicizing the identity discourse in anthropology and in anthropology's engagement with the tribe with which I have been working.

As an anthropologist, I am interested in how anthropologists come to pay attention to particular aspects of the sociocultural milieu in which they are immersed? How do particular parameters—such as race, ethnicity, gender, and sexuality—come to be accepted as ones that are more important than others, as those to which new anthropological work should attend? These are historical at least as much as purely analytic issues within the discipline, I contend. With respect to the derivation of contemporary analysis of identity, I will argue, these histories are intricately intertwined with postwar social movements, and this chapter is placed within the elucidation of that relationship.

Identity—*Double Historicization* as Theoretical Means and Practical End

I have argued that both different sorts of anthropologists, on the one hand, and different sorts of movements and leaders of the so-called Fourth World (indigenous and aboriginal peoples; marginalized, stateless, subnational groups; nomads and foragers), on the other hand, are simultaneously engaged in debates over constructionist and essentialist forms of identity (Field 1999a). If this is the case, it becomes important, I think, to historically trace the manner in which discourses of identity such as race, ethnicity, gender, or sexuality became so ensconced and naturalized in anthropological work. That tracing involves a complex double historicization, if you will. Identity movements have their own histories, as any scholar or activist knows, and the ideas used and developed by such movements form a part of those histories. Ingrid Rowland's (2004) recent exegesis of aristocratic Tuscans' obsessive focus upon identity in the seventeenth century and how that obsession was projected upon the Etruscans of antiquity illustrates the value of acknowledging the multiple and dynamically mutable meanings of identity over the centuries. But analytic ideas in academic circles also have their histories, and those ideas are not separated, whether historically or conceptually, from the ideas that grow in and motivate social movements. This is hardly a groundbreaking observation, as Michael Kearney iterates: "[The] intellectual products of anthropology should be considered sociocultural artifacts, no different from any other cultural artifact that is situated within, and is the expression of, a particular sociocultural and political process; yet it is amazing that the history of anthropology is hardly ever approached with such a working assumption" (2004, 3).[1] Notwithstanding Kearney's insight, it may be unsurprising that anthropologists, like the great theorists who inspire much of their work, can seem to negate the historicity of their own production. While in *Capital* Karl Marx proposed an analysis of capitalism in dialogue with the English political economists (Adam Smith, David Ricardo, and Thomas Malthus), in *Socialism, Scientific and Utopian* and especially in *The Origins of the Family, Private Property, and the State,* he and Friedrich Engels represented their analysis as a science of history and, by implication, transcendental. Michel Foucault (in *The Order of Things* [1973], for example), who has inspired so much contemporary anthropological analysis, also seemed to place his analysis outside of the flow of history in a kind of meta-epistemic bubble.[2] Taking into consideration just these two seminal influences upon postwar anthropology, it is challenging to untangle the braided, woven histories of ideas, analysis, and activism refracted in the interdependent, relational development of identity discourses that dominate both social movements and the academy.

In anthropology, the understanding of identity, particularly of Fourth World and other minority groups, has transformed in significant ways during the twentieth century. In my own work, these transformations can be summarized, perhaps somewhat simplified, as a movement from a traits-based essentialism, crystallized in the ethnography of California Indians by Alfred Kroeber (1925), to Barthian analyses of identity as defined as much by boundaries and difference as by essential traits (see Barth [1969] 1998), to constructionist analyses aligned to Gramscian and Foucauldian conceptualizations of identity as shaped by power relations, the role of organic intellectuals, and the multiple meanings of resistance to local, national, and global economies (see Kate Crehan [2002] for Gramscian approaches in anthropology; see Foucault [(1978) 1990] for his analytic approach in something of a nutshell). It is important to name these broad periodizations because in using different analytic strategies contemporary anthropologists align themselves in very different ways with and against one another and the peoples with whom they work (Field 1999a).

While the way identity is configured in anthropological discourse has been changing, I would argue that the powerful place the identity discourse has come to occupy in anthropology required that parallel processes in the academy and among social movements become conflated. The recognition or understanding of that conflation has remained largely unconscious or submerged. One historical process was initiated by post–World War II civil rights movements in the United States and elsewhere, organized around rejection of long-standing discrimination, prejudice, and multiple forms of social violence based upon cultural constructions of difference, particularly phenotypically construed difference, and especially race and gender. As the wave of civil rights movements expanded around the world, these movements coalesced around subtler and more mutable forms of culturally construed difference, such as ethnicity, linguistically based peoplehoods, sexual identities, and other minority statuses.

The emergence of social movements hinging upon rejection of oppression via the elaboration, discovery, reassertion, and affirmation of these forms of difference, all of which constitute one form of what we call *identity*, coincided with the decline of class-based movements and of class as a form of social solidarity. Marxists had long argued that class consciousness offered the only cogent axis around which to organize opposition to the various forms of oppression characteristic of capitalist societies—forms of oppression that typically have included racism, sexism, and many toxic forms of ethnocentrism. Marxists promoted class consciousness precisely because their analysis underscored that organizing around class and only class created a social movement intended not to reform but rather to destroy and replace capitalism. The kinds of post-1960s civil rights movements organized around differences *other* than class, by and large and with some exceptions, did *not* seek to destroy and replace capitalism. But it would be simplistic hindsight inference to argue that this is *why* racial-, gender-, ethnic-, and sexuality-based civil rights movements were successful in organizing huge numbers of people in late twentieth-century capitalist societies while class-based movements were not. Moreover, many post-1960s anthropologists detected the manner in which the *"cultural construction* of indigenous identities . . . [is] *socially constituted* as actual class positions" (Kearney 2004, 319, his emphasis), with the implication that this might be the case for other ethnically and racially demarcated groups.

During and after the social mobilizations of the late 1960s, anthropologists working within the Marxian analytic tradition came to understand the identity-based social movements of the last half of the twentieth century with an increasingly sophisticated theoretical armature that developed in relation to the historical events shaping social movements outside of the academy. The widespread dissemination of Gramscian ideas in the 1970s and after helped to make sense of why non-class forms of oppression and exploitation became the catalysts for social movements (especially in R. Williams 1977); Foucauldian analysis helped to explain how systems of power in capitalist societies could accommodate such resistance while at the same time extinguishing their radical potential (i.e., Scott 1985; Trouillot 1995). These perspectives acknowledged the profoundly Marxian appreciation for the materiality of commodities, ideas, economics, and ideology in a multicultural world, expressed well by Alberto Melucci:

> Collective identity is an interactive and shared definition produced by several individuals and concerned with the orientations of action and the fields of opportunities and constraints in which the action takes place: by "interactive and shared" I mean a definition that must be conceived as a process, because it is constructed and negotiated through a repeated activation of the relationships that link individuals. The process of identity construction, adaptation and maintenance always has two aspects: the internal complexity of an actor (the plurality of orientations that characterizes him), and the actor's relationship with the environment (other actors, opportunities and constraints). (Quoted in Escobar 1992, 72)

The development of this theoretical scaffolding, with its insight into the construction of identities and identity-based movements in the last decades of the twentieth century, paralleling what went on in the social movements of this time, erupted into the history of the academic disciplines themselves with significant consequences.

In effect, just as the strength and scope of postwar human and civil rights social movements were cresting, anthropologists and other scholars came to emphasize the same vectors of identity that were congealing in those social movements—race, gender, ethnicity, and, a bit later on, sexuality—as sui generis analytic factors and forces. Many anthropologists (but certainly not all), among them those working with indigenous peoples (Moore 1987; also Sider 1993), distanced themselves from traits-based essentialism and were also ready to probe identity formations on levels deeper than the Barthian framework. Increasingly, and with the sort of postmodern angle popularized by Clifford (1988), anthropologists theorized such identity vectors as social constructions that mobilized essentialist tropes and discourses. Along with that insight came an emphatic focus upon a given set of identity vectors that ultimately became routine. Anthropologists were expected to engage the same parameters of identity—gender, race, ethnicity, and sexuality became canonical—in any ethnographic situation they encountered, even if the manifestations of social solidarities they observed might diverge from the scholarly expectation that the germane analytic parameters always be the same.[3] To the credit of anthropologists working this vein in the 1980s and afterward, the ways these parameters of identity combined and crosscut in the bodies and real lives of individuals and collectives became a persistent theme.

This routinization was certainly also intricately intertwined with changes among the individuals professionalizing as anthropologists. Many more people of color became anthropologists, many more individuals from other countries were trained as anthropologists in the United States and Europe, many, many more women were trained as anthropologists, and many more anthropologists openly stated their sexual minority status. During what has been periodized as the postmodern moment, it also became routine for anthropologists in the context of writing their texts to "reveal" their positioning with respect to their own identities, once again emphasizing, and perhaps reifying, the same set of vectors, often to the exclusion of others. In retrospect, it seems that during the 1980s and '90s it was the privileged, unmarked, *white* anthropological mainstream, much more than the growing corps of minority anthropologists, that expected that specifying a certain skin color, ethnicity, gender, or sexuality also implicitly marked the theoretical position of any anthropologist in question. Perhaps even more problematically with respect to work in and with indigenous communities, anthropological discourses of identity taking shape in the last two decades of the twentieth century took for granted that constructionist analyses of identity always and inevitably are corrosive to essentialist formulations of identity. This assumption was based on the a priori opposition between the putatively universal character of all groups' historical construction and the (assumed) universal desire for essentialized identities among all social groups (as in Hobsbawm

1987) that had also come to take parameters of race, ethnicity, gender, and, later, sexuality very much for granted.

By the mid-1990s, the routinization of the identity discourse in anthropological discourse and among anthropologists and the perceived polarization between essentialism and constructivism led to a real impasse in ethnographic research and on the written page. The angst and paralysis that often accompanied postmodern approaches obstructed a realization that a less dualistic approach to social constructions and cultural essences was necessary, because what anthropologists were really struggling with were the self-imposed limitations of their own binary concepts, not to mention the constraints posed by a priori categories of identity.

Jonathan Friedman, among others, considered the opposition between the universal historical construction of social groups, on the one hand, and social groups' universal desire for essentialized identities, on the other, as simply insoluble: "If one is engaged in 'negotiating culture,' that is, involved in the construal and interpretation of ethnographic or historical realities, then one is bound on a collision course with others for whom such realities are definitive. Culture is supremely negotiable for professional cultural experts, but for those whose identity depends on a particular configuration this is not the case. Identity is not negotiable" (1994, 140). Other anthropologists, such as Charles Hale (1994), proposed positions such as "strategic essentialism," which aligned them with then-current thinking among other more public intellectuals, often feminists or people of color (such as bell hooks [1990] and Gloria Anzaldúa [1987]). This hopeful solution allowed that the use of essentialist tropes by civil, human, and cultural rights movements might be contingent, open to creative construction for progressive political purposes, and less hinged upon far more problematic essentialist tropes such as blood and purity. The promise of such ideas notwithstanding, outside of the academy the conflicts dominating the mid-1990s onward, such as the dissolution of Yugoslavia, the direction the Israel–Palestine conflict took during the first few years of this new century, and the popularization of Christian and Islamic fundamentalisms, indicated that essentialist discourse provoked violence on a mass scale, even if it had become that much more openly strategic. These deployments of essentialism emphatically illustrated that this discourse, while offering the potential to reaffirm identities among oppressed minorities, also manifested as a central tool of bureaucratic systems of power, in a manner resonant with the ethnographic case I will describe in the next section.

Neither the opposition between constructivist and essentialist concepts of identity nor the dominant role played by four parameters of identity (race, ethnicity, gender, and sexuality), from which I have suggested the former binary opposition has elaborated, can be resolved purely on conceptual or analytic grounds by either anthropologists or the intellectuals or leaders of social movements. Resolution, if it is to take place, derives from the changing historical currents—the actual moving forward of different social groups through identity-forming processes and into other kinds of social and cultural processes, perhaps pulling along anthropologists who might be associated with these groups as well. Changes within the anthropological discipline with respect to the analysis of, or even obsession with, identity might follow such changes in the communities with which anthropologists work; or perhaps such changes might only affect limited or circumscribed groups within the overall discipline. New analytic directions in both social movements and anthropological analysis might be made possible only once the limitations of identity discourses are overcome.

Erasure, Identity, and What Came after for the Muwekma Ohlone

To illustrate these ideas, I will make use of over two decades of working collaboratively with the Muwekma Ohlone Tribe, the indigenous people whose ancestors aboriginally inhabited the entire San Francisco Bay Area (see Field et al. 1992; Leventhal et al. 1994; Field 2003). Certainly, there can be no people more righteously concerned with the issue of identity than Fourth World peoples who have been declared extinct, often by the *experts* themselves, anthropologists. The Muwekma Ohlone were thusly declared by no less a luminary then Alfred Kroeber in his tome, *The Handbook of the Indians of California* (1925). In my work as a tribal ethnohistorian, my task has been to recover documents, ethnographies, and other sorts of archival evidence, as well as to interview living Ohlone individuals in order to trace the social and cultural continuities that connect the contemporary tribal members to their history. *Naming* their identity was an extremely important issue in the early period of tribal reorganization, starting in the 1980s.

The native people of the San Francisco Bay Area had been known as Costanoans in both the anthropological literature (in Kroeber's work, for example) and popular media. This name exemplifies a particularly specious, if not absurd, example of the formation of ethnonyms: the Spanish called native peoples of this coastal region *costeños,* Anglos bastardized that to Costanos, and anthropologists scientized this misnomer as *Costanoans.* The term *Ohlone,* by contrast, derives from *Olchone,* the indigenous name of a particular village territory, whose people lived at the base of the San Francisco peninsula prior to contact with the Spanish in the late eighteenth century. The ethnonym *Ohlone* was apparently adopted by the native peoples of the region as a self-identification sometime in the last decades of the nineteenth century. *Ohlone* or sometimes *Ohlonean* was the term used by many of these native people to identify themselves on Bureau of Indian Affairs (BIA) census forms in the early decades of the twentieth century (Muwekma Ohlone Tribe 2002). So when the native families reorganized as a tribe in the 1980s in the first move to achieve federal recognition, distinguishing themselves as Ohlones, not Costanoans, was a central aspect of proclaiming and claiming their identity.

The Ohlones' concern with naming as one strategy for reclaiming identity and rejecting the erasure of their presence in their aboriginal territory also took advantage of the extensive fieldnotes John P. Harrington recorded among their grandparents and great-grandparents in the 1920s and '30s. Harrington had worked with the last individuals who spoke Chochenyo, the East Bay Ohlone language, and in his notes the contemporary Ohlone found the word *Muwekma,* meaning "the people." They resurrected the term, naming their reconstituted tribe the Muwekma Ohlone. These were hardly insignificant acts but played profoundly important roles in affirming the identity of individuals and families and in the coming together of these families once again as a functioning tribe. The investment the Ohlones made in elaborating their identity, from the late 1960s and into the 1970s and '80s, coincided with both the heyday of much more extensive racial, ethnic, gender, and sexual identity movements in the Bay Area and the enshrinement of identity discourses in anthropology and other social sciences. When the Red Power movement took control of Alcatraz Island in San Francisco Bay in 1970, the biggest personalities in the movement were Lakotas, Iroquois, and other Indians who were not from California. By that time already, a large percentage of Native Americans in the state had come from elsewhere or were the children of those who had done so, resettled in the Bay Area and the Los Angeles area because of federal relocation policies of the 1950s that constituted yet another stage in the attempt to assimilate Indians into the illusory melting pot. By the end of the century, non-Californian Native Americans had outnumbered California Indians by a wide margin. "Aren't they [California Indians] all extinct like Ishi?" one Lakota man asked me at the San Jose Indian Center in 1991, making me wonder how many Indians who were not from California tribes had also accepted the hegemonic extinction perspective that had originated with anthropologists.

This stage in the Ohlones' struggle—naming and owning a specific identity during the 1970s and '80s—shaped two processes of research and discovery that unfolded during the 1990s, both among the Ohlones and for the anthropologists like myself who worked with them. One process focused upon uncovering and understanding the manner in which federal, state, and local governments, popular media, and anthropologist experts had each in their own way carried out the work of extinction that had resulted in the commonsense notion that the Ohlone no longer existed. My colleagues in the tribe, other collaborating academics, and I called this arena of research "back from extinction" or the "politics of erasure." We found that the manner in which the Ohlone were made extinct derived from a complex, reciprocally confirming relationship between academic anthropological knowledge circulating in universities and published work, on the one hand, and bureaucratic policy that determined Indian status and which native groups were eligible for land purchases.

In the early twentieth century, the federal government sponsored a great deal of anthropological work through the Smithsonian Institution and its Bureau of American Ethnology (BAE), which was charged with the work of cataloging and classifying the nation's Indians and scientifically understanding their demise and assimilation, processes which were taken for granted (see Hinsley 1981, Field 2003). BAE publications and the knowledge within them directly inspired and guided many of the policies that the Bureau of Indian Affairs developed on reservations across the country. The hand of the BAE was not as clear in California as it was among the Plains tribes, the Pueblos of New Mexico, or elsewhere. Nevertheless, the delegitimation of California Indians like the Ohlone and their subsequent *disappearance* also resulted from a relationship between academic and bureaucratic knowledges about Indians, as the Ohlones' research uncovered.

In California, the traits-based criteria by which BAE and other early twentieth-century anthropologists evaluated the authenticity of native identities encountered the combined effects of Spanish, Mexican, and then American colonialisms. Kroeber and his students at Berkeley found that for many coastal peoples like the Ohlones, Indian identity as determined by distinctive traits, particularly language, ritual practices, material culture, and oral narratives, had become tangential. For these scholars, the lack or dwindling of such traits was isomorphic with the disappearance of Indian identity. Summary statements to that effect in Kroeber's handbook (1925) then influenced the purchase of land for Indian groups still extant in the 1920s and '30s, a period during which the federal government was intent upon resolving the problem of so-called homeless Indians in and around California's growing urban areas and was purchasing very modest acreages, known as *rancherias,* upon which those Indians were supposed to settle. As Kent Lightfoot (2005) has shown, there is a very close correspondence between the published statements about the various Indian groups in academic sources regarding their cultural status and the decisions made by federal and state bureaucrats over whether and which of these groups should be awarded rancheria lands. Lightfoot concludes, "If descendant communities in coastal California had not obtained a land base by the 1920s or 1930s, the chances of their receiving federal recognition were very slim" (2005, 239). In a closed circuit of reciprocating, commonsense knowledges, peoples such as the Ohlone, whom anthropologists considered extinct by the 1920s and who had therefore not received rancherias, were thus denied federal status and were logically of little interest to the growing numbers of anthropologists. "Berkeley anthropologists ignored, for the most part, Indians residing within [this] former domain of the Hispanic frontier" (Lightfoot 2005, 222).

The second process of research focused upon understanding the actual manner in which Ohlone families had maintained a sense of belonging to a particular people after the extinction sentence became a commonsense notion, and the lack of both federal recognition and tribal land and resources became an established fact of life early in the twentieth century. The information the tribe needed to understand what had occurred was both ethnographic—interviewing older people and coming to terms with individual life histories and experiences—and fueled by extensive archival and documentary research. Researchers working with the Ohlone (Field et al. 1992; Leventhal et al. 1994), and corroborated by Randall Milliken (1995) and Lightfoot (2005), found that in the central coastal area, the Spanish/Franciscan missions had precipitated the "structural collapse of local native societies" (Lightfoot 2005, 88). "The fragmentation of traditional native polities" in this region led to "the emergence of new kinds of social organizations, and the creation of Indian identities no longer tied to individual polities, but more to a specific mission community" (Lightfoot 2005, 198). This entire process, linked to massive demographic declines, resonates with similar processes elsewhere in the Americas, where cultural change and the effects of stigma, poverty, and oppression transformed but did not destroy Indian identities.[4] For the Ohlone, these new identities were "predicated on kin tied, social connections, political positions, and factional groups within neophyte [i.e., missionized] communities, [such that] native peoples were now identified by the missions where they were raised" (Lightfoot 2005, 202). Both before but especially since the time John Harrington wrote his thousands of pages of notes as he traveled up and down the length of coastal California, ample documentation shows how Indian peoples closely identified themselves with the missions where their ancestors had been interned (Harrington 1921–1939; Merriam 1967, for example). Since the 1940s, into the

1980s, '90s, and the new century, contemporary Ohlone have used the term *the families* to refer to their tribal identity (Muwekma Ohlone Tribe 2002).

In the late 1990s, the documentation and analysis of Ohlone social and cultural survival that I have described was almost entirely directed toward completing the acknowledgement petition for submission to the Bureau of Indian Affairs/Branch of Acknowledgement Research and, subsequently, responding to the BIA/BAR's negative determination of the Ohlone case. This research can be characterized as focused upon describing and substantiating Ohlone identity and, indeed, upon *proving* that the Ohlones were who they said they were. During this period, the tribal chair and council conducted a series of workshops for the membership that kept members informed about the progress of the petition by educating them about the volumes of data that had been amassed in defense of Ohlone identity. Over the course of 2000–2001, the workshops expanded their scope. Members began discussing their economic aspirations for the tribe, envisioning a role for tribal enterprises in public health, substance abuse treatment, and environmentally oriented technologies. At the impetus of a number of individuals in the tribe, research and social activities turned toward a language revivification program for their moribund language, Chochenyo. This project succeeded in many ways. Many younger people became more active on a more frequent basis in tribal affairs through their involvement with the language program. Chochenyo words began creeping into everyday conversations at the tribal headquarters and at the dinner tables of many tribal members. Some members became able to exchange quite a few sentences back and forth in their old language. The program also attracted the attention of prominent local linguists, such as Leanne Hinton at the University of California, Berkeley; and, consequently, Muwekma Ohlone language activists were being included in statewide language conferences and activities about which they had previously known little.

I understood the increasing prominence of the Chochenyo project as indicative of a more assertive and self-assured membership, less concerned about asserting identity in the face of extinction and more comfortable with exploring the ramifications of daily life as Ohlone people. But the immediate concern with proving identity had changed for the anthropologists as well. On behalf of the tribe, I turned my own attention to documenting and analyzing material culture collected by the first European explorers in the Bay Area, with the goal of elaborating a broad discussion of Ohlone cultural patrimony. This research took place against the backdrop of federal Native American Graves Protection and Repatriation Act (NAGPRA) legislation and California's own repatriation laws, with the expectation that in the not-too-distant future the tribe's petition would prevail and that the Ohlones' claim to and relationship with their material culture history would become increasingly important to the members. In the past ten years that relationship has become increasingly important; at the same time, the research I explored and wrote about (Field 2008) showed that the making of abalone regalia in the San Francisco Bay Area, for example, did not demarcate distinct tribal, linguistic, or ethnic identities but instead suggested a geographically extensive sharing of iconography and symbolism before the arrival of Europeans. Such a discussion defies the parametric certainties of the identity discourse in both academic and nonacademic circles in the last few decades.

This short resume of the last two decades of Ohlone chronology historicizes the significance of the identity discourse for this small tribe, as well as for anthropologists (such as myself) who have worked for and with them. This double historicization illustrates the way that the historical (re)construction of identity becomes the means to living what eventually become at least partially essentialized traits, suggesting that essentialism is the outcome of successful identity construction. These are therefore not opposed, dualistic concepts or processes, historically speaking, I would argue. In the Ohlone case, the focus upon asserting, proving, and defending identity through discursive elaboration seems not to have become a permanent and obsessive focus for either Ohlones or for their anthropologist colleagues. The identity discourse may therefore be understood as a historical phenomenon both substantively and theoretically, one that runs its course and then leads to other forms of political, cultural, and analytic work.

Conclusion

This discussion has emphasized the limitations and historical contingencies of essentialism, constructionism, and the dominant parameters of identity discourses that developed in anthropology and Fourth World social movements in the last half of the twentieth century and into the current century. To underscore this argument, I again draw attention to Kearney's work, which resuscitated the utility of Marxian analysis as he argued that "contrary to the impression given by much of the current fascination with identity and cultural studies, the emergence of Mixtec ethnicity at this moment is primarily a reflection of the underlying class dynamics that are at play in the transnational political economy in which Mixtecs are situated" (2004, 345). Kearney's insight was both analytic and historical. He pioneered both transnational fieldwork approaches and the training of Mixtec anthropologists during the period in which Mixtec agricultural workers became an increasingly large percentage of the workforce in California's hyper-capitalist monopoly agriculture, at the same time Mixtec ethnic identity was congealing in exile. The fact that ethnic identity once again marked class became apparent through the dialogue between Mixtec and non-Mixtec anthropologists who nimbly combined aspects of both essentialist and constructivist discourse.

Similarly, the federal recognition work redacted in the previous section illustrated a set of unique relationships around anthropological work that made both anthropologists and native peoples interlocutors in a shared and historically unfolding project. Joanne Rappaport's work (2005) also emphatically illustrates that identity discourse was an inescapable step in both the Nasa and pan-indigenous social movements in Cauca, Colombia, but this stage has been superseded by other struggles, strategies, and goals. These different studies show that while anthropologists are developing increasingly sophisticated approaches to indigenous communities, leaders and intellectuals in indigenous communities increasingly adapt anthropological methods and analyses to their own uses. Under such conditions, one should expect that the representation of identity, its parameters, and the dualism between constructivism and essentialism will change substantially and not primarily through theoretical innovation.

Based on the discussion in this chapter, a double historicization of identity discourses therefore requires recognition of complexly related forms of contingency: doubled sets of historical contingencies, if you will, that intertwine the discourse of identity and its accepted parameters in both the anthropological discipline and in social movements. Recognizing that a discourse of identity as an analytic tool has become routinized in scholarly approaches does *not* mean ignoring or minimizing identity discourses among the people with whom anthropologists work, much less diverting attention from the ways capitalist economies conjugate race, class, and gender to structure inequality. As an anthropologist I would therefore consider the historical contingency of parameters of identity in both my own analysis and among social movements with which I interact from perspectives that are simultaneously ontological (those parameters as they are accepted as substantively "real"), epistemological (those parameters as phenomenon about which knowledge can be produced), and methodological (those parameters as criteria around which research can be organized and represented).

Unprivileging a priori parameters of identity discourses and rejecting the dualism of constructivist versus essentialist approaches to identity is therefore the point of departure not of arrival. Multiple levels of collaboration between various scholars and various individuals in Fourth World social movements in ontological, epistemological, and methodological projects is, indeed, the condition for and the means to new representations of identity but will not determine those representations, each of which will be based, I would argue, upon new forms of contingency.

Notes

1. Patterson (2001) charts an interesting and detailed social history of anthropology in the United States that entails a significant sociology of anthropological knowledge as well.

2. Derrida (1974) historicized texts as cultural artifacts. Arguably, his work lets 1980s literary theory "off the hook," to some extent at least, with respect to the argument I have made here. But I myself would not make such an argument. Deconstruction, as practiced by Derrida and others, is primarily about reading and does not treat history in the manner I would like to. I am interested in pursuing the analysis of events, ideologies, personalities, systems of production and consumption, social and cultural movements, and such, through chains of real, and not only discursive, causality.

3. In many important instances class was also a central parameter of identity engaged by influential and brilliant theorists, such as Eric Wolf, June Nash, Donald Dunham, William Roseberry, and Paul Willis. At the same time, I would guess that because of its analytic complexity and the demands of deploying the concept theoretically, as well as because class was not at the forefront of the identity movements that erupted in the 1960s, class was frequently *not* foregrounded among the routinized parameters of identity discourse in anthropology.

4. For example, see Field 1999b and Gould 1998 for the case of Nicaragua; see Sider 1993 and Moore 1987 for other North American cases.

2

Strategic Essentialism, Scholarly Inflation, and Political Litmus Tests

The Moral Economy of Hyping the Contemporary Mayas

David Stoll

Our subject is the collision between deconstructive anthropology and in-digenous activism. James Clifford (1988) spotted it in the 1976 Mashpee trial—cultural anthropologists no longer believed in the reified definition of tribe and culture, which the Mashpees needed to prove their existence as a le-gally recognizable entity. Jean Jackson fine-tuned the question in 1989: How can we talk about the making of culture without making enemies? Jackson and Kay Warren (2002) have articulated the problem more recently: to de-fend land rights and other claims based on indigenous rights, indigenous lead-ers must define boundary and authenticity in ways that anthropologists have the knowledge to refute.

My own work illustrates the problem. In 1998 I published an investigation of the historical background of *I, Rigoberta Menchú* (Burgos-Debray 1984; Stoll 2008), the 1982 life story of the 1992 Nobel peace laureate. Like other Mayan youth orphaned by the counterinsurgency campaigns of the Guate-malan army, Rigoberta Menchú fled into the arms of the Guerrilla Army of the Poor (EGP). A year after she joined the EGP as a political cadre, the orga-nization sent her to Europe with a daunting assignment: to tell the story of her people. And she did, more eloquently than anyone had expected. But the way she made a splash was by turning her family and village into represen-tative Indians who suffer every conceivable form of oppression. It was quite a story—but not the same as her family's and village's. They had their own rather different stories, which I thought should also be heard.

So was I deconstructing an indigenous representation? Well, I decon-structed a particular one with a large and loyal audience. Many activists and academics presumed that Menchú's story represented Guatemala's indigenous population. In its most elemental form, as a story of persecution, exile, and eventual triumph, it was indeed one with which many Guatemalans identi-fied. But I did not deconstruct Menchú's story at this level; I corroborated it, and a decade later it is alive and well. What I deconstructed was her account of her family's situation before the war and how political violence started locally, because this is where her story diverged from that of neighbors and relatives.

Some Mayas were upset with me, including Menchú herself. Others were not. Some congratulated me for "telling the truth"—that is, publishing their side of the story. So I wasn't deconstructing *their* representations—I was con-textualizing a version that grew out of a particular person's exile to Mexico, her affiliation with a guerrilla organization, and her appeal to international audiences. Reducing the conflict to an anthropologist versus native people dodges the question: Which native people? Like any human population, na-tive people are not monolithic. They have diverging experiences, they have diverging interests, and they make contradictory claims. To assume that it is anti-Indian to question Menchú's version of events, or Zapatistas' claims to represent the people of Chiapas, or campaigns for Bureau of Indian Affairs recognition, or sovereignty/autonomy doctrine is to overestimate the repre-sentativity of your preferred bunch of indigenous people and ignore or dis-count others.

There is a simple reason to avoid idealizing indigenous people. When they don't live up to the imagery, the gap becomes yet another rationale for dis-counting them. The problem is not confined to tourists looking for barefoot philosophers in communion with nature. Yawning chasms between expecta-tion and outcome are also generated by trendy imagery about native people defending their culture (Friedlander 1975; Feinberg 2003), gardening the Amazon rainforest (Conklin and Graham 1995), and defying globalization (Pitarch 2004). In the case of the Mayas with whom I work, the Ixils of Gua-temala, they have been drafted into an array of roles, including men of maize rooted to their land, victory-or-death revolutionaries, victims of genocide, and accomplices to genocide because, on repeated occasions, a majority have voted for the former army dictator who committed genocide against them. Even the idea that Ixils are Mayas is fairly new to them—until reached by state education and Mayan activism, they thought Mayas were an earlier race who lived in caves and had six digits on each limb.

None of the roles that Ixils have played for outsiders is completely di-vorced from what they say, think, and do. There was a period in the late 1970s and early 1980s when a large number supported a revolutionary movement, and a smaller number stayed with it until the 1996 peace accords between the Guatemalan state and the Guatemalan National Revolutionary Union (URNG). But as interpreted by the now-ubiquitous nongovernmental organizations (NGOs), idealizations of the Mayas have become an ever-renewable rationale for coaxing Ixils into agendas of diminishing appeal. For anthropologists who have framed their work in terms of NGOs, this is no small problem.

Now that many of us are inclined to dismiss social science as an oppressive Western construct, we have little choice but to derive our mandate from the people with whom we work. A community, a set of victims, an elderly healer who has blessed our activities, an oppressed nation—any of these can serve as a source of authority for our research. But what if this group of people authorizing our research is constituted by the projection of our own desires? Even a community with a countable number of households in a single location can consist chiefly of wishful thinking—worse, Mayas who don't realize they are Mayas and vote for a person accused of genocide. Broadly speaking, this was the problem I raised in *Rigoberta Menchú and the Story of All Poor Guatemalans* (Stoll [1999] 2008). Even after perfect storms of postmodern theory, Menchú's academic admirers were enshrining her guerrilla-friendly version of events, at a time when most of Guatemala's indigenous population wanted nothing more to do with the guerrillas. And so Menchú became a heroic surrogate for her people, admired with greater intensity abroad than in Guatemala. When I documented the discrepancies between her story and the stories of other survivors, the rejoinder was that I must be an apologist for the Guatemalan army.

In the interest of a more constructive discussion, I suggest that we look at how we derive moral authority from indigenous people, and how indigenous people work up their own idea of moral authority, in terms of competing moral economies. E. P. Thompson (1975) and James Scott (1976) used moral economy to describe how peasants view their way of life, and measure right and wrong, in opposition to political economy, that is, the bourgeois rationales of agro-capitalism. Yet bourgeois elites have their own sense of right and wrong, their own moral economy. So, presumably, does any social group with a distinct sense of morality, which it produces through ritual exchange of some kind. What ritual produces is solidarity, credibility, and, in a political context, political capital. So, if religious ritual is like an economy with characteristic forms of production and exchange, moral economy is how people produce moral authority through certain kinds of symbolic exchange.

Like an economy, ritual systems can inflate (become more intensive) or deflate. The inflation and deflation of new religious cults is an example. So is the rise and fall of theoretical fashions in anthropology, in which we use theory as a competitive ritual. Theory as ritual determines who manages to claw upward on the shaky and crowded career ladder in our profession. Now that homage to the old high-god Science has lost its luster, offerings must instead be made to the revolution or popular struggle, to the Mayas, to resistance or counter-hegemony, or to the postcolonial critique. The lexicon shifts more rapidly than the structure of feeling behind it.

Gabriela Vargas-Cetina (2003) suggests that contemporary anthropology has divided our attention into two different streams of representation. We deconstruct essentialism while constructing new forms of advocacy that require us to re-essentialize native people and other subalterns. A useful way of capturing just how easy it is to move back and forth between deconstructing and essentializing is Gayatri Spivak's (1996, 214) term *strategic essentialism.* The strategy resides in shifting without acknowledgment, often behind a smokescreen of critical theory, and often without acknowledging the political objective that justifies the inconsistency. Consciously or unconsciously, the strategic essentialist builds theoretical defenses around preferred categories, pet concerns, and protégés while demonizing opponents and the unwelcome information they offer. Consciously or unconsciously, strategic essentialism amounts to a compact with one's allies or sponsors to exaggerate their numbers and representativity.

This is how political engagement and critical theory can encourage discourse about native people to inflate in self-serving ways. To illustrate, I will run through six issues facing anthropologists who work with the indigenous people of Guatemala and Mexico:

1. the representativity of the Guatemalan guerrillas;
2. the representativity of the Zapatista rebels in nearby Chiapas, Mexico;
3. the representativity of the Mayan movement;
4. whether Mayas are a majority of the Guatemalan population;
5. the death toll in the Guatemalan violence; and
6. whether the Guatemalan army's massacres of Mayas constituted genocide.

Each is *delicado* (politically sensitive) because discussion of the evidence can trigger accusations of being anti-indigenous from anthropologists who are not indigenous themselves. This is the giveaway that strategic essentialism is at work. Each issue has become a political litmus test, in the sense that skepticism is interpreted as a sign of betrayal. In political economy, inflation is a technique for passing the bill so that someone else will have to pay. If the parallel holds in the moral economy of politically engaged anthropology, someone pays for inflation here too. Could this someone include the supposed beneficiaries of our theorizing, indigenous people?

Six Examples of Scholarly Inflation

Our first issue is whether the Guatemalan guerrilla movement was an indigenous uprising against a military dictatorship that left no alternative but armed resistance. This was the version of events put out by the Guerrilla Army of the Poor and other organizations in the Guatemalan National Revolutionary Union (URNG). It was accepted by the international human rights movement, and it is still being advanced by scholars (Grandin 2004; Manz 2004; Wilkinson 2002) who win back-cover endorsements from the likes of Aryeh Neier, Isabel Allende, Carlos Fuentes, Rigoberta Menchú, and Jon Lee Anderson. Judging from the high praise, this is the version of events that human rights luminaries prefer.

Politics often require exaggerating one's representativity. In this case, the EGP's success in inflating its popular support convinced the army that it should slaughter entire villages of presumed supporters. But political inflation did not have only negative consequences. In 1982, the same year that the army destroyed most of the EGP's support among peasants, a twenty-two-year-old schoolgirl named Rigoberta Menchú turned the EGP's rhetorical claims into a compelling life story. Her version of events gave the insurgency a fascinating afterlife on a very different stage, that of international solidarity with the army's victims. The international legitimacy generated by *I, Rigoberta Menchú* is part of the reason why, in the 1990s, URNG exiles were able to use international support to enter peace talks with the Guatemalan government and win certain concessions.

Posterity will judge whether the 1996 peace accords were an important step in democratizing Guatemala. Implementing the agreement requires organized pressure from the intended beneficiaries among Guatemala's poor. This pressure has been less than expected because, despite their grandiose claims, the former guerrillas and their allies have little connection with the majority of the indigenous population. Most indigenous voters failed to turn out for the Consulta Popular, a constitutional referendum to demilitarize the country and establish equality for Mayan culture (K. Warren 2002). In the populations hit hardest by the war—Quiché, Huehuetenango, and Baja Verapaz Departments—Mayas have voted heavily for a former dictator, the retired general Efraín Ríos Montt, whom the human rights movement would like to indict for committing genocide in the same areas. Even when the national electorate turned against Ríos Montt's party in the 2003 election, indigenous voters in these same departments chose it to run most of their town halls. As for the ex-guerrilla coalition, it did so poorly that, having failed to win 5 percent of the vote, it has disappeared as a legally recognized party.

A similar investment in indigenous rebellion, resulting in another public relations bubble, occurred with the 1994 Zapatista insurgency in Chiapas, Mexico. Here media imagery of an indigenous Mayan uprising against the North American Free Trade Agreement elicited a wave of support from the Mexican and the international left. Many anthropologists were impressed by the contrast between the Zapatistas' military strength, which was minimal, and their remarkable symbolic resonance, and so they became known as the first cyber-guerrillas in history. Unfortunately, the Zapatistas also had more political strength in cyberspace than among the peasants they claimed to represent. Falling victim to their own propaganda, the Zapatistas voted down a favorable agreement they had just negotiated with the Mexican government. Then they boycotted a crucial national election and alienated most of their allies in the Mexican left.

The result was a rapid deflation of Zapatista political capital in Chiapas and the rest of Mexico, although not internationally, where interest remained high. Within a few years the Zapatistas were a faction surrounded not just by the Mexican military but by hostile peasants—the same peasants who they supposedly represented but who regarded them as authoritarian and disruptive (Hernández Castillo 2001; Legorreta Díaz 1999; Leyva Solano 2001; Moksnes 2004; Pitarch 2004; Van der Haar 2004, 104–5). As in Guatemala, a political movement that devised a successful ensemble of images for attracting international support did not fare well at home. Instead of achieving broader alliances, it shrank, leaving behind a reputation that some scholars (e.g., J. Nash 2001) continue to regard as the standard for evaluating work on the subject.

In Guatemala, meanwhile, another publicity bubble was inflating the Mayan movement. The movement was in gestation before NGOs came on the scene and its defense of indigenous rights deserves the support of anthropologists, but the very expression implies a representativity that is far from being achieved. One problem is that the people whom scholars and fund-raisers wish would identify themselves as Mayas often reject the label or prioritize other forms of identity. In Mexico, speakers of Yucatec Mayan usually reserve the Mayan label for their ancestors and prefer to identify themselves as mestizos (Hervik 2003). In Guatemala, indigenous people are starting to refer to themselves as Mayas, but many still prefer local forms of identity. The people most likely to invoke Mayan identity are urbanized, educated, and associated with NGOs (Adams and Bastos 2003, 282; Nelson 2004).

One of the anthropologists who did the most to promote the Mayan movement, Kay Warren (1998b, 188), argues that it should not be measured in terms of the number of people it can turn out for a protest. Street power is not the only measure of a movement—the upward percolation of Mayan professionals, businessmen, and politicians into previously closed spheres of Guatemalan society is also important. But if the Mayan movement represents the Mayas, why can't it ever demonstrate it? In view of how the Bolivian and Ecuadorian indigenous have mounted general strikes and toppled governments, the question is a fair one.

Now let's take the standard reference to Mayas as a substantial majority of the Guatemalan population—63 percent according to Jackson and Warren (2002, 36). Only if you count people whose connection is genetic, who rarely or never identify themselves as indigenous, can these claims be true. It is much safer to say that roughly half the Guatemalan population is indigenous.[1] Judging from the case studies analyzed by Richard Adams and Santiago Bastos (2003), the only safe approach is to never take indigenous identity for granted. According to Victor Montejo (2004, 237), who is writing specifically of his own Jakaltek Mayas but believes that all Mayan language groups face the same problem, "Ladinization happens mainly among youth who abandon their customs and traditions. Usually, they do not want to speak their Maya language, and they no longer consider themselves Maya, claiming a Ladino or Mestizo identity. They try to pass as Ladinos by denying their cultural heritage." Of the total Mayan population in Guatemala, "only 50–60 percent are actually speakers of the Mayan languages," according to Nora England (2003, 733), who is quoting the careful estimates of a team of Mayan linguists (Richards 2003, 44–88).

Next consider the death toll in Guatemalan political violence from 1962 to 1996. There have been three major efforts to collect all the available data. Building on earlier compilations by a human rights consortium (Ball, Kobrak, and Spirer 1999) and by the Catholic Church's Project for the Recuperation of Historical Memory (ODHAG 1998), the UN-sponsored Commission for Historical Clarification (CEH) registered a total of 42,275 victims. Of these, 23,671 were victims of arbitrary executions, and another 6,159 were victims of forced disappearance and are presumed dead. Thus, the CEH compiled a total of 29,830 countable dead people. From these and other data, "the CEH *estimates* [my emphasis] that the number of persons killed or disappeared as a result of the fratricidal confrontation reached a total of over 200,000" (CEH 1999). The CEH's statistical consultant Patrick Ball justifies the multiplier of 6.7 in terms of sampling procedure. In view of all the information gathering that fed into the CEH, it is very pessimistic to assume that the CEH received compiled testimony about fewer than one of every 6.7 killings or dis-appearances.[2] While the figure of 29,830 dead is obviously too low, the over 200,000 estimate is rather high. Yet in scholarship it is becoming the "documented" (Manz 2002, 294) death toll.

One reason the 200,000 figure is becoming canonical is that it substantiates another term that is becoming mandatory in discussions of Guatemala, the genocide (and increasingly, holocaust) of the Mayas. According to the CEH, the army "defined a concept of internal enemy that went beyond guerrilla sympathizers, combatants or militants to include civilians from specific ethnic groups" (CEH 1999). But because the army targeted villages that it suspected of supporting the guerrillas, much of the Mayan population did not experience massacres. Hence the CEH confined itself to indicting the army for genocide in four local populations between 1981 and 1983: the Ixil Mayas, the Q'anjob'al and Chuj Mayas, the K'iche' Mayas of Joyabaj, Zacualpa, and Chiché, and the Achi Mayas.

Unfortunately, the 1948 Convention on the Prevention and Punishment of Genocide excludes mass killing based on political criteria. Thus, if the army was targeting civilians for supporting a political movement, then its massacres would not be genocide. Instead, they would be crimes against humanity—a category that does not resonate the way genocide does. The CEH chose to go with a looser definition of genocide, preferred by most scholars and activists, which includes political killing (Hinton 2002). On the down side, the term racializes a history of political violence in which other dimensions were often more important. The Guatemalan civil war began in 1962 among the country's non-indigenous Ladino population. For the first sixteen years, most of the victims were Ladinos. Even at the height of the killing, from 1980 though 1983, Ladino settlements could be massacred just like indigenous ones.[3] But genocide is such a quick source of political capital that it has become the tag word for Guatemala that resonates around the world. It enables the country to be self-righteously invoked and safely pigeonholed in the same breath. As Guatemalans struggle with their past, is it really a good idea to persuade them that a class war with an ethnic component was actually a race war (cf. Nelson 2003, 123)?

In each of the above cases, what inflates scholarly discourse is more than a high number. Any of us have the right to argue that two-thirds of the Guatemalan population is indigenous and that more than 200,000 people died in the Guatemalan violence. What creates inflation is a moralistic attitude that protects high estimates from being debated by using rhetorical devices that preempt questions by discrediting the questioner. Protected from scrutiny, debatable propositions harden into political litmus tests. Political litmus tests define the boundaries of morally permissible discussion, discourage the communication of unwelcome information, and become the basis for further inflation, creating further distance between our representations and the people whom we wish to support.

The Not-Truly-Indian Paradox and the NGO House of Mirrors

Let us now turn to the moral economy behind these practices. What is being offered by whom, to whom, and in exchange for what? The crucial offering is a preferred version of events that stresses the victimhood of indigenous people but also celebrates their revolutionary agency and naturalizes their earthy persistence. It preserves the vision of Guatemala as a moral opera, where the struggle between good and evil stands out in high relief and the critical theorist gets to sing the aria. It is preferred not just by a good number of Guatemala specialists but by other constituencies who are crucial to career advancement—university press editors, senior colleagues from the 1968 generation, funders of righteous causes, and graduate students looking for gurus and scapegoats. Even though these other audiences do not have much experience with Guatemala, they rely on it as a symbol of political evil—terror, genocide, holocaust, and such—about which they can shudder knowingly and against which they can validate themselves as people of conscience.

But it isn't just wine-and-cheese liberals whom anthropologists need to impress. Anthropologists take pride in epistemological skepticism, to the point that some of us are eager to undermine our credibility as a social science. But if science is a dubious Western construct, on what do we base our professional license? For those of us who are fed up with the solipsism of high theory, support for indigenous people is a moral imperative. This is how we give ourselves a sense of direction, a moral narrative, and a place within it as moral actors. Yet our solidarity with indigenous people has to be translated into the meritocratic discourse that determines who survives and who doesn't in our field. It has to be theorized, which is to say that it has to be ritualized in the odd ways that confer merit in higher learning. If we now recur to Roy Rappaport (1999) and his thinking about how rituals confer authority, the competitive academic rituals determining who wins career advancement require ultimate, sanctified propositions, that is, propositions that are impossible, difficult, or costly to question.

What operates as an ultimate, sanctified proposition in contemporary anthropology? Certainly not our identity as social scientists—most cultural anthropologists no longer have much invested in that claim. Instead, unquestionability resides in other locations. There is the occasional political saint, such as Rigoberta Menchú, but such figures do not appear in most of our ritual productions. There is also the kind of theory that cannot be questioned because no one understands it—hence the popularity of our latest sages. Last but not least, unquestionability resides in certain terms that are loaded because, as deployed by theorists, they conflate what is with what theorists wish would occur. Thus "Maya" is an empirical referent that presumes how Guatemalans of indigenous descent should identify themselves. Genocide is one of several possible terms for mass killing that presumes that killing was racially motivated. Transnationalism refers both to exchanges that cross national boundaries and, as used by many scholars, the moral superiority of such exchanges over nationalism (Friedman 2003, 13–17).

The need for moral authority is just as evident in the realm of nongovernmental organizations. In recent decades, NGOs have proliferated as a vehicle for bypassing unresponsive governments and channeling resources to local groups. They have helped indigenous people break through institutional roadblocks and climb onto official agendas. As anthropologists look for ways to repay people who have provided us with hospitality and information, NGOs enable us to reciprocate by delivering tangible benefits. Without NGOs it is becoming harder to visualize a career in anthropology; they are increasingly the framework through which we relate to Guatemala. And yet, when NGOs substitute for the state, they produce state-like effects.

Adams and Bastos (2003) point out that the NGO moniker tends to lump together the efforts of foreign governments, international bodies, and private and religious organizations, as well as local groups that execute projects but depend heavily on foreign financing. The discourse of these networks is communitarian and localizing and often ethnic or even nationalist, but their international funding makes them inviting targets for nationalist backlashes (see Kampwirth [2003] for a Nicaraguan example). In a comparative analysis of the "transnational indigenous peoples' movement" (TIPM) in El Salvador, Virginia Tilley summarizes the bad news:

> Outside funding can have corrupting and fragmenting effects, and the TIPM's transnational consultations and conferences tend to favor and promote more literate and therefore often less representative leaderships. . . . A third hazard . . . derives from the very activity that has made the TIPM so constructive a political force for many indigenous movements: that is, the TIPM's success in codifying and promoting formal precepts about indigenous peoples' characteristic qualities and needs. In doing so, the TIPM has conveyed unprecedented political juridical and rhetorical leverage to local groups. Yet when adopted as a master frame

by sympathetic outsiders (international funders, human rights groups, even other indigenous peoples), those same precepts tend to gel and re-ify as a new definition for indigeneity that can bring considerable pressure on those indigenous peoples whose "fit" in that master frame is less than exact. (2002, 528)

In El Salvador, where visible markers of indigenous identity are scarce, TIPM criteria have deepened what Tilley (2002, 541) calls the "not-truly-Indian" stigma. So have efforts to "Mayanize" Salvadoran Indians in imitation of the more successful Mayan movement in Guatemala. Yet the Mayas of Guatemala are hardly strangers to the "not-truly-Indian" paradox because of the contrast between what they prioritize and what foreign funders do.[4]

In the view of all but the most sophisticated funders, real Mayas still consult with traditional priests and shamans. They are still *costumbristas* and Catholics but not evangelicals. They supported the guerrillas but not the army, and they consider themselves victims of the army but not of the guerrillas. They support political parties identified with the left but not the right. In contrast, the many Mayas who have joined Pentecostal churches, who submitted to conscription into the Guatemalan army's civil patrols, who distrust the guerrillas and have voted for the former dictator Ríos Montt—these Mayas are suspect. They have been hegemonized or "duped" in Diane Nelson's (2004) perceptive comparison of politically committed anthropology with carnival-style hucksterism. Once you factor in all the requirements, most Mayas do not merit support. But of course you can find Mayas who do fit your criteria, more or less, and these become the Mayas who deserve support from abroad—antagonizing others who feel excluded.[5]

NGO subsidies have helped indigenous-led organizations proliferate, but at the cost of aggravating factionalism and also at the cost of encouraging what amounts to fund-raising language in scholarship. The mighty Wurlitzers I am criticizing—the Rigoberta Menchú and Zapatista cults, premature celebration of the Mayan movement, high-end estimates of Mayan population and war deaths, the use of genocide as a political litmus test (e.g., Sanford 2003)—are rhetorical devices to simplify and enlarge a particular slice of Mesoamerica as a fundable proposition. Most donors want high-legibility, low-complexity readings of situations that guarantee a certain kind of return on their dollars, pounds, or euros. Donors seek not the profits of a capitalist enterprise, but confidence that they have invested in a righteous cause. What they receive is reassurance that they are on the side of the angels.

In each situation—the URNG collapse in Guatemala, the Zapatista deflation in Chiapas, and the disappointment hanging over the Mayan movement in Guatemala—what remains alive and well are transnational funding and scholarship. Why? Because a fundable definition of the problem has been achieved by discounting features that could upset donors. When foreign donors are lured by pleasing simplifications, they invest in situations without fully grasping that their interpretation originated as a carefully constructed projection designed to attract their money. As a result, they end up in a house of mirrors that they themselves financed. Anthropologists are not exclusively responsible for the house of mirrors, but some of us have helped build it by encouraging certain images of the Mayas to become icons or fetishes, symbols that conceal complexity in congenial wrappings.

NGOs and activists must always use language strategically because, in order to carry out a program, they must commit to one of many possible definitions of a situation. Exploration of different possibilities, the production of unsettling new evidence, the encouragement of debate—this is what we should expect from scholars and serious journalists. Yet the academic left and the NGOs that look to it for guidance have cultivated their own preferred and partial set of facts, similarly to how the religious right and other hardshell US conservatives have. A very basic issue in social science is whether it is our job simply to describe society and diagnose social pathologies, or whether we also have a duty to become committed to solutions of one kind or another. Among anthropologists working with native people, the rhetoric of solidarity has become almost mandatory, which creates powerful incentives for dismissing information that does not fit. Once we as anthropologists enshrine certain personages and causes, we turn ourselves into a branch of theology.

Ritual Inflation, Ritual Collapse, and Who Pays the Bill—Everyone but the Successful Theorist

In this chapter I have argued that selecting certain kinds of indigenous people and idealizing them has become a way of deriving moral authority. Now that many cultural anthropologists have abandoned the claim to be social scientists, we need to find moral authority elsewhere. Political solidarity with the oppressed—or at least with carefully chosen representatives of the oppressed—is a tempting place to find it. This choice is even more tempting because nongovernmental organizations have become the framework for how many anthropologists do fieldwork, and NGOs require simple, clear messages to raise funds for their causes. In view of these needs, deconstruction and re-essentialization are not just an unfortunate paradox in contemporary anthropology. Instead, they complement each other, in a two-stroke engine of career advancement called strategic essentialism.

Looking at representations in terms of moral economy requires us to compare how anthropologists generate moral authority with how the people we study do. Analyzing representations in terms of hegemony might seem a more obvious approach. Certainly, many scholars prefer it. Yet the way we use hegemony tends to situate us safely outside the exchanges we analyze, leading to the imputation of false consciousness to our misguided subjects. Hegemony also implies a uniform field of conformity enforced from the top of a power structure. Accounting for pluralism leads to contortions such as "alternative hegemony" and "counter-hegemony."

In contrast, moral economy in the pluralistic sense that I define it requires us to situate ourselves within symbolic exchanges, to specify how we establish our own sense of moral authority. In the case of Guatemala, former guerrillas and soldiers, Mayan activists, anthropologists, and NGOs engage in exchanges that invest different propositions and symbols with sanctity or unquestionability. By specifying these different moral economies, we can protect ourselves from enshrining Durkheimian projections of our own desires.

Just how different peasant moral economy can be is suggested by the characteristic expectations of folk Catholicism. In keeping with Eric Wolf's (1982, 79–88) tributary mode of production, subordinate groups render tribute, taxes, or rent to elites in exchange for predictability and security. Under the influence of the Catholic Church, God becomes the Big Patrón in the sky, as do the Catholic saints who serve as his intermediaries. Hence the many obligations of the civil-religious hierarchies or *cargo* ("burden") systems serve as a form of ritual taxation. Yet this system of subordination also moralizes the obligations that tribute-takers owe to tribute-givers. Traditional expectations can become a basis for protest. While the rich have the right to a lot, the poor have the right to what they need to survive. If subsistence is threatened, the same saint that enforces subordination can authorize rebellion—a paradox that Paul Diener (1978) found among the Ch'orti' Mayas of eastern Guatemala in the late 1960s and early 1970s.

Like any system of exchange, moral economies can inflate and they can collapse. Authority-building rituals are usually expensive, increasing their frequency is more expensive, and people would not go to the trouble unless the rituals were helping them deal with some problem. So as a rule of thumb, the more ritual that occurs, the more tension and conflict there is to defuse and the more authority is perceived to be needed. Thus, rising tension leads to more ritual and expenditures to pay for it. In the case of folk Catholic cargo systems, anthropologists have documented how cargo rituals became more and more elaborate in the nineteenth and early twentieth centuries. But if the rituals do not resolve the underlying problems, the results are disillusion, ritual deflation, and collapse. In the indigenous Mesoamerica of the twentieth century, ritual deflation often took the form of conversion to Protestantism, which meant abandoning expensive obligations to folk Catholic saints. The insurgent Guatemala of the early 1980s was a case of rapid inflation, stimulated by the countervailing power of the guerrillas, and of rapid deflation, prompted by army massacres. For survivors, the rituals of joining the rebel movement were replaced by the rituals of demonstrating allegiance to the Guatemalan army.

It is at this point, in the continuities between the guerrilla and the army agendas for militarizing village life, that the most influential political figure in Guatemala since 1982, the "born-again butcher" General Efraín Ríos Montt, poses a challenge to which anthropologists have yet to rise. Ríos Montt plucked the strings of moral economy with amazing success—the 1990, 1995, and 1999 presidential elections were all won or nearly won by his surrogate candidates with strong support from indigenous voters. Only after Ríos Montt regained power from 2000 to 2003, and only after his party cronies set new records for corruption, did his reputation as a defender of law and order deflate. Yet his last bastion of electoral support consisted of Mayan peasants in the Quiché, Huehuetenango, and Baja Verapaz Departments. If Ríosmonttismo is the unexplained vacuum in the contemporary anthropology of Guatemala, then the scholarly inflation I am critiquing is a way of downplaying the bad news.

To put this another way, scholarly inflation results from the collision between the moral economy of anthropology and the moral economy of indigenous peasants. Inflation shuts out contradictory information by building strategically essentialized defenses around a preferred bunch of Indians. The contrast between inflated expectations, unwelcome new information, and disappointing outcomes becomes the impetus for more theorizing. As disappointment and theory spiral heavenward, like the smoke from an Old Testament burnt sacrifice, what maintains the illusion of grounding in ethnographic reality is the back-and-forth of deconstruction and re-essentialization, the demonization of unwelcome information, and the sacralization of what fits. What this kind of anthropology preserves is the reputation of the academics who presided over the inflation.

That the main beneficiaries of academic theorizing are certain academics is hardly news. But it raises an important question: Do high estimates and genocide rhetoric make any difference to Guatemalans and other Mesoamericans?

Isn't exaggeration an inevitable property of political discourse? Maybe high estimates are essential to attract the attention that Mayas and other Central Americans deserve. Yes, maybe, but I think we've gone down this road far enough. Once high estimates are accepted as fact, or just as the most defensible mid-range estimate, this sets the stage for further inflation, culminating in high optimism about what can be achieved politically by appealing to Mayan solidarity. If more than two hundred thousand people were killed in the violence, a larger slice of the population wants justice for dead relatives, and presumably will rally in favor of genocide prosecutions, than if one hundred thousand were killed. If almost two-thirds of the Guatemalan population defines itself as indigenous, finding a common denominator for the indigenous vote sounds like the way for the left to win a national election. On the other hand, if indigenous identity does not carry that much weight in the population, harping on it could produce more antagonism than sympathy. Blatant displays of favoritism toward selected Mayas and prognostications of how Mayas are destined to take over a country could be a recipe for political reaction. Anthropologists have seen so much political disappointment in Guatemala that it is time to ask how we contribute to it.

Notes

1. The 42.72 percent of the population identified as indigenous in the 1994 census is probably too low, for reasons discussed by Adams and Bastos (2003, 59–80). The 1921 census identified 64.84 percent of the Guatemalan population as indigenous, and the 1950 census showed 53.45 percent as indigenous. For 1964, the demographer John Early estimates the indigenous population as 50.37 percent, and for 1973 as 47.95 percent (Adams and Bastos 2003, 64, citing Early 1982). Two phenomena could explain the decrease: (1) individuals, families, and communities deciding to backstage their connections to indigeneity, and (2) improvements in public health benefiting ladinos earlier than *indígenas* and therefore diminishing infant mortality among ladinos more rapidly than among *indígenas*. Now that public health campaigns reach the indigenous population, higher indigenous fertility could make the indigenous population grow more rapidly. But if enough parents and children stop identifying themselves as indigenous, then the indigenous proportion of the population is not growing except in the mind of optimists.

2. Here are the main steps in Ball's (1999, 237–60) approach:

1. If CEH, CIDH, and REMHI compilations of victims do not overlap each other, they list a total of 54,643 dead from 1978 to 1996 (238).
2. Since a sample of 1,412 cases from the CEH database shows an overlap of only 11.3 percent with the other two databases, the three databases contain an estimated non-

duplicated total of 47,803 dead (239, where Ball concedes that this estimate of the overlap is probably too low. for example, dead people whose names have been lost cannot be checked for duplication).

3. Through sampling procedures, Ball estimates that another 84,468 assassinations were committed between 1978 and 1996 that never were reported to the CEH, REHMI, or CIDH (245). This is a multiplier of 2.77; in view of all the reporting by the Catholic Church, the guerrillas, refugees, international human rights groups, and the press at the height of the violence, and all the investigation that occurred in the 1990s, it could be too high.

4. To his estimated total of 132,000 killings between 1978 and 1996, Ball adds generous estimates of the number who were killed from 1960 to 1977 (22,000), of the number who were "disappeared" (kidnapped) from 1960 to 1996 (40,000), and of the number killed in regions not covered by the three databases (7,500) to arrive at a total of 201,500 killed and disappeared from 1960 to 1996 ("Mandato y procedimiento de trabajo," CEH 1999, 73).

To show what Ball's approach means at the local level, consider the Ixil case. For the Ixil area between 1978 and 1996, the three databases came up with relatively congruent totals of 4,609, 4,028, and 5,423 killings. On the basis of his sampling procedure, Ball (1999, 250) estimates a total of 16,655 victims in the Ixil area between 1981 and 1983. When I analyzed census shortfalls in the Ixil area (Stoll 1993, 232–33), I came up with a missing population of 15,000. One source of confusion is the term *asesinato* and whether it includes people who died of hunger and illness while hiding from army offensives. Judging from what Ixils told me, the number who died of hunger and illness paralleled the number who died in massacres. If *asesinatos* are defined strictly as extrajudicial executions, then Ball's methodology probably overshot by a factor of two or three. But some of the difference would be made up by the deaths of refugees from malnutrition, exposure, and illness.

3. See the CEH's *Caso Ilustrativo* No. 31, "Masacre de las Dos Erres," in which the army murdered 178 defenseless and mainly Ladino villagers in December 1982. http://shr.aaas.org/guatemala/ceh/mds/spanish/anexo1/vol1/no31.html (accessed June 2, 2012).

4. For the Amazon, compare Ramos (1998) on hyperreal Indians and Jackson (2002, 119–20) on identity rent.

5. For an example of the dilemma, compare C. Taylor (1998) and Manz (2004) on Santa Maria Tzejá, an NGO hub in the Ixcán where rivalry has been aggravated by the army—guerrilla conflict, displacement to Mexico, and NGO favoritism.

3
Yucatecan Food and the Postcolonial Politics of Representation

Steffan Igor Ayora-Diaz

During the last two decades, Yucatecans, in general, and Meridans, in particular, have witnessed (and many have suffered) the growing immigration of individuals from different Mexican regions but, particularly, from the center of Mexico.[1] The relationship between Yucatan and Mexico has always been an uneasy one. Many immigrants from the central highlands are locally perceived as arrogant, triggering strong reactions against them in Yucatan as in other states, to the point that it is possible to find car stickers or graffiti with hate messages against central Mexicans, all around the country. Locally, inhabitants from regions such as Yucatan, Monterrey, and Guadalajara, for example, invoke the moral superiority of the locally born over central Mexicans.[2] In Yucatan, this feeling is sometimes extended even to individuals with Yucatecan ancestors born in central Mexico (sometimes derogatorily called *yucauaches*).[3] In this struggle to represent oneself in a positive light and to portray the foreigner as evil, different cultural resources serve as vehicles for the affirmation of local identities and local values over foreign ones. For Yucatecans, hospitality is one of the practices seen as encapsulating the virtues of Yucatecan morality. In Mérida, the capital city of Yucatan, there are negotiations of meaning whereby local people attempt to defend their positive image while seeking to contain the perceived threat to local culture that foreigners represent. Along with this process, Yucatecans revise their understanding of hospitality and, when needed, the rules that govern its practice.

The contemporary world has been often described as one of cultural globalization and, in optimistic readings of the process, as one of blurring and making obsolete cultural and political boundaries (Appadurai 1996; Clifford 1997; Kaplan 1996). An enhanced will to travel, migration flows identified as exile, diaspora, political displacement, economic migration, and mass tourism have changed the face of contemporary societies. Ours are multicultural societies. However, this coexistence of members of different cultures has seldom fostered a sense of multicultural solidarity or respect (M. Joseph 1999; Rosello 2001; Tully 2002). Cultures and nationalities in interaction are often marked by unequal positions in the international and state orders (Benhabib 2002; Juergensmeyer 2002). New forms of cultural colonialism and economic expansionism, as well as postcolonial transformations (such as the massive arrival of migrants from former colonies to the metropolises), complicate and confound social interaction at the local, regional, and translocal levels, in some cases triggering passionate defenses of the local (Bhabha 1994; Herzfeld 2002; R. Smith 2003). In this chapter I explore how in Mérida, the capital city of Yucatan, Mexico, food can work as a vehicle for local identity and for the affirmation of the superior value of the local over the "Mexican." This relationship between locals and outsiders is marked by ambivalences in the moral realm that reveal tensions between the discourses and practices pertaining to hospitality and generate in many local people the certainty that foreigners, particularly those coming from central Mexico, are undeserving of locals' trust and hospitality. The gastronomic field is transformed into one of the arenas in which the boundaries of the local are defended against outside aggression.[4] In the process of constructing a strong sense of regional identity, Yucatecans have created a gastronomic field that exemplifies a form of cultural hybridity that combines the global and the (trans)local, creating a new cultural space. This specific form of hybridity allows the affirmation of a local/regional identity against the force of Central Mexican cultural colonialism, as the Yucatecan field welcomes global and cosmopolitan influences while resisting Mexican ones. However, I argue, this very sentiment of regionalism obscures the processes of hegemony construction among the different groups and social classes within the state of Yucatan itself.

Food, Cuisine, and Identity

There is an expanding field, anthropological, sociological, and historical, that explores and describes the ties between food, cuisine, and identity. Anthelme Brillat-Savarin's aphorism, "Tell me what kind of food you eat, and I will tell you what kind of man you are" ([1826] 2004, 4), is often cited to stress the common perception that a people may be recognized, both by self and others, by their food preferences. The historical literature records, for example, cultural strategies deployed by Christians, Muslims, and Jews in Spain and by the British and French to mark their radical differences through food (Montanari 1999; Mennell 1996). In contemporary societies, cultural pluralism and flexible capitalism have fostered the expression of a group's ties to a place through food, particularly to those localities that individuals recognize as their ancestors' place of origin. Thus, Asians, Italians, French, Mexicans and other Latin Americans, and Caribbean islanders re-create in the United States, Canada, and other places the food they affirm as their own cultural and national creation (e.g., D. Bell and Valentine 1997; Gabaccia 1998).

Contrary to widespread images abroad, Mexican cuisine, far from being monolithic and homogeneous, is regionally diverse. Yucatecan cuisine today is a distinct culinary field that emerged over the twentieth century as a hybrid blend of different cultural influences, becoming firmly established during the second half of the twentieth century. Although the ties of Yucatecan food to other Caribbean cuisines can be traced, increasingly, Yucatecan food is defined as a "regional" version of a national culinary tradition (Long-Solis and Vargas 2005). In response, locally, we now witness an emphasis on the "locality" of Yucatecan cuisine while stressing its global ties.

Since the 1970s, Meridans took advantage of the expansion and fragmentation of the local foodscape, broadening their food experience. In those same years, Yucatecan food carried by Yucatecan migrants to other Mexican regions was adapted to local taste in each particular region. The 1990s Yucatecan economic boom attracted waves of immigrants, primarily into Mérida. Migrants have added to the complexity and diversity of the local foodscape. Foodstuffs and meals previously unavailable, or at least available in limited supply, are now regularly found in new restaurants and homes. At the same time, those who grew acquainted with their own local versions of Yucatecan food, after moving into the state of Yucatan, expected to find their favorite renditions of Yucatecan food in Mérida. Consequently, in present-day Mérida restaurateurs must negotiate between the rules of the gastronomic field and outsiders' food preferences: there are now restaurants specializing in other Mexican regional cuisines (and ones that organize food festivals on a regular basis, e.g., the week of Oaxaca food) and, in some touristic restaurants, some regional dishes have been adapted to fit the tastes of immigrants and tourists.

The Politics of Representation

A sector of the anthropological community has undertaken a profound reflection and carried out a rigorous critique of the discipline's representational practices (e.g., Clifford 1988; Geertz 1990; Marcus and Cushman 1982; Marcus and Fisher 1986). Undermined by postmodern philosophy (e.g., Derrida 1980; Lyotard 1984; Rorty 1982), we have seen crumble, one by one, the foundational certainties that warranted our belief in the universality, objectivity, and truth, of "our" scientific representations (e.g., J. Anderson 1995; Brown 1995; Denzin 1995). While some anthropologists may regret this lack of irrefutable foundations, others are rising to the challenge and attempting to continue in our quest for understanding our own society's and other societies' cultural practices and ways of life as rather complex forms of social articulation: beyond the local and the global, we have to consider multicentric and decentered globalities and translocalities (M. Fischer 2003; Tsing 2004).

Also, we have come to terms, in anthropology and other social sciences, with the principle that there is no single truthful account of events and actions. Although there may exist, in any society, a homo/hegemonic narration of events and history, other accounts exist that offer alternative plausible interpretations. Every group and, by extension, any society is divided into different groups with unequal access to power; some produce hegemonic stories, and others produce subaltern, alternative stories (Dube 2001; Guha 1988). In the midst of this multiplicity of voices, stories, histories, and reports of facts, anthropologists are faced with the responsibility to "represent" subjects' everyday struggles, maneuvers, strategies, and tactics of both domination and resistance.

In this effort, anthropologists always run the risk of overrepresenting one view or another. The interaction between anthropologists and local subjects weaves competing, contesting, and complementary interpretations that ultimately congeal into a single narration: the ethnographic monograph. The problem we face, in postcolonial society, is that, since we cannot hold to one single account of the truth, our accounts can be (and are) contested by other colleagues who disagree with our accounts, as well as by local people who belong to heterogeneous groups (hegemonic or subaltern); one or more of these groups are bound to perceive that they are not fairly represented in anthropological texts and other ethnographically based formats. It is precisely those who see disciplinary accounts as monolithic, universally valid, objective, and true who demand the truth, *their truth,* about themselves to be voiced. Thus, our recognition that identities (ethnic, national) are constructed relativizes political claims and destabilizes the power positions that individuals and groups hold in society at large.

Of particular concern, in this chapter, is the affirmation of a regional identity that has been constructed by regional elites. This account of a Yucatecan identity, against the hegemonic and homogenizing force of central Mexico, can favor a monolithic representation of local culture that obscures the diversity of cultural forms and voices within the Yucatecan territory. While here I concern myself with the reactions to Mexican cultural colonialism, I also recognize the different groups that have collectively generated both Yucatecan identity and the regional gastronomic field.

Finally, I should recognize the ambiguous position in which I find myself: some local colleagues have corrected my self-definition as an anthropologist. I have been told that I am a Yucatecan *who is* an anthropologist, but I am not a Yucatecan anthropologist. I grew up in Yucatan, where I studied and practiced medicine, but I studied anthropology in Canada and belong to anthropological associations in Canada and the United States. Because of this some of my colleagues have suggested that I represent the cultural, colonizing force of Anglo-Saxon anthropology in the region. More often, this accusation has come from Mexican anthropologists (or other anthropologists trained in Mexico City) working in Chiapas and Yucatan who consider Mexican anthropology under colonial aggression, while refusing to recognize that there is not a single "Mexican anthropology." Throughout the twentieth century, like food, regional anthropological traditions informed the regional interaction of local anthropologists with anthropology and anthropologists in the international arena. However, the force of central Mexican institutions that claim to be the "national" schools of the discipline often silences regional diversity. It is in this context that I face the task of describing the society in which I was born.

Yucatan is a complex society that encompasses class and ethnic differences defining one's position and gives every Yucatecan group a different view of their own participation in the regional political field. Thus, representation turns into a contentious issue: Can I represent all Yucatecan identities and cultural forms? I believe that we can aspire to show that societies are not monolithic, that multiple voices and positions exist, and thus relativize our own accounts. On the other hand, we as anthropologists always aspire to grasp the "native's point of view." While I can claim, as Yucatecan, to partake of the native point of view, I cannot profess to represent *the* Yucatecans.[5] I engage in a description of Yucatecan identity politics partly as an inquisitive outsider (an anthropologist) but also, and partly, as an interested member of the complex society I describe. I can only hope that my efforts to provide a balanced account will be fair to the complexity of the issues and will contribute to a better understanding of the conformation of a postcolonial and neocolonial structure of power between central Mexico and its regions.

State policies endorsing the Mexican imagined community have silenced regional and local cultural expressions in the public sphere and triggered local identity politics seeking to affirm the local against the homo/hegemonic "Mexican" voice. In the following section I will discuss the context that allowed Yucatan to grow and establish a gastronomic field distinct from the national, Mexican cuisine. The emergence of a local culinary tradition is charged with power inequalities that have contributed to construct a gastronomic field where different groups vie to place their own cultural expressions in a more favorable position. Politics of many types and levels inscribe insiders' and outsiders' positions in a neocolonial order. Regionalist politics are part of that larger configuration. Regional cuisine, I argue, is tied to the historical and moral construction of an identity separate and distinct from the Mexican. Immigrants from other Mexican regions often reactivate this local sense of identity when their practices and discourses challenge the integrity and legitimacy of local practices, values, and worldviews.

Yucatecan Regionalism

In the late 1990s I used to spend my holidays in Yucatan. In different trips, I found myself uneasy at the broadcast of radio and TV spots that asked those moving into Yucatan to respect the local values and integrate into the local way of life. These spots continued into the year 2000, when I moved back to Mérida to establish my residence. I felt them to be aggressive, running against the hospitality Yucatecans are always proud to affirm as a sign of superior local values. These spots triggered my interest in the historical, structural, and cultural bases of this regionalist feeling and identity. To my surprise, I was unable to find references to the independence movement that existed in Yucatan during the nineteenth century. It seemed as if the secessionist movement was taboo.

Michael Herzfeld (1997) has developed the concept of "cultural intimacy" to refer to the local responses to the revelation of actions or discourses that are known to exist, and even feel rightful, but shame the group when they are made public. As Melchor Campos García (2002) suggests, during the construction of the modern nation-state, regional movements seeking autonomy or special rights were disqualified as infantile, archaic, (politically) less developed, and chauvinistic in scope. The strong secessionist movement that existed in Yucatan through most of the nineteenth century has been largely disqualified and silenced in the academic literature but for a few sources.

Campos Garcia (2002) describes the historical process whereby Mexico and Yucatan grew separate throughout the colonial and postindependence periods. During colonial times Yucatan was in an uncertain administrative position. After independence from Spain, Yucatan joined Mexico on the condition that the region would keep its own autonomous government and the new national government would have a federalist agenda. However, Mexican governments sought to impose a centralist political and economic structure, triggering three different attempts to separate from Mexico (Campos García 2002). The end of the nineteenth century and the beginning of the twentieth was a period when local Yucatecan elites grew stronger and established preferential commercial ties with the United States, Cuba, and other Caribbean islands. Commerce with England prevailed through Belize. The henequen boom allowed the regional elites to gain power and to establish the basis for their legitimacy and the advancement of their worldview and ethos as the source of regional identity (Aliski 1980; Hansen 1980; G. Joseph 1980; Terry 1980).

Although the secessionist movement ended during the nineteenth century, Yucatecans have preserved a strong sense of regional identity that sets them apart from Mexico and other regions. Food, music, and other cultural products are often used to mark local identities as distinct from the Mexican (Ayora-Diaz and Vargas-Cetina 2005b). As has been the case in other imagined communities (B. Anderson 1983), the dominant elites of Yucatan have controlled the printed media in the region from the nineteenth century on. However, the construction of local identities may also be understood as an undesired (from the nation-state's perspective) by-product of the different ideological programs that legitimated the modern nation-states in Europe (P. Sahlins 2004), subordinating regional identities to the broader program of ideologically constructing a homogeneous nation (Weber 1979). This subordination, in turn, inspired the development of local strategies to affirm the local against the national (Gerson 2003). In this vein, postindependence Mexican governments adopted a blueprint of a nation-state that could be filled in only by the imaginary of a unified Mexico. Despite constant efforts to keep the nation together, in Yucatan there was a strong sense of difference, setting people apart from central Mexican cultural values and mores (Cortés Campos 2004; Rosado Avilés 2004; Suarez Molina 1996).

Historically, it was the Mexican army that ensured Yucatan's permanence in the Mexican Republic. However, it was not until the second half of the twentieth century that Yucatan and Mexico were joined by land, with fully operational roads built only after the 1960s. Previously, most travel to Mexico had to be done by boat through the Gulf of Mexico (G. Joseph 1980). Yucatan had developed its own industries and services and directed its market to the Caribbean, the United States (Texas and Louisiana), and Europe. A regional culture developed under the cultural influence of the latter regions, steering Yucatan away from the Mexican cultural blueprint. Against this regionalism, in Mexico, the nation, promoted by the state and enforced by the army, was inscribed in the public sphere by different means that relied on the growing power of the media. The *Mexico* invented and inscribed in nineteenth-century maps was promoted during the first half of the twentieth century in radio and cinema (Craib 2004; Dever 2003; Hayes 2000).

However, this imagined Mexico has found obstacles to keeping its hold on the nation at large. Regional groups continue affirming and defending what they understand as their own cultural values, practices, and way of life against perceived new forms of Mexican encroachment. In the different states of Mexico one can find small businesses displaced by national ones. For example, large beer corporations have taken over regional breweries and forced them to produce goods that fit their quality standards but depart from local taste. Local businesses must fulfill the corporation's goals or they are penalized. For example, in 2003 in Yucatan, the Modelo national firm closed the local brewery and moved the production of Yucatecan beer to the state of Oaxaca. Today, "Yucatecan" beer is not produced any longer in Yucatan. (Though the legendary "Yucatecan beer" has been removed, it continues to be tied to the imagination of Yucatecan culture.) Also, chain department stores are moving into medium and large cities, displacing local businesses; and, what many Yucatecans complain about, they bring along even their own floor salespeople from central Mexico, instead of giving employment to local women and men. These well-paid employees are frequently blamed for the rising real estate prices in Mérida.

It is the history of these difficult relations between the region and the nation, throughout the last two hundred years, that marks the relationship between locals and outsiders. Jacques Derrida (2000) reminds us that hospitality may encompass entangled forms of violence running against each other: On the one hand, the violence of language, for example, the imposition of a cultural code on the guest. On the other, the violence of making a hostage of the host—that is, of making the hosts accountable to a law that is not their own. Meridans and other Yucatecans often define the newcomers as "invaders" who violate the local codes and seek to impose their practices and morality and their tastes and worldview on the local people. For these Yucatecans, "Mexicans" do not fit their definition of guests (who would accommodate to the local ways and respect them) but are seen as individuals who actively and aggressively seek to impose a way of life that is alien to the local. In contrast to a "good guest," central Mexicans are the bearers of an imperial certitude: they come from the metropolis onto the province. They have the right to govern local social interaction and to impose their way on the local culture. As Yucatecans have never fully accepted Mexican colonial rule, the tensions between locals and outsiders inform the negotiations that take place in different cultural arenas. In the following section I focus on how, in this context, the culinary field and the local foodscape in the city of Mérida have been transformed into one such arena for cultural struggle.

Food, Power, and Local Identities

The Yucatecan gastronomic field gives shape to the contemporary urban foodscape. When other culinary traditions are incorporated into the urban foodscape, they may or may not inspire changes within the local culinary field; but, in the taste of local people, they remain subordinated to regional cuisine. However, changes are often implemented in the domestic sphere that seldom make it into the public domain. The market of international cuisines has allowed for the local claim to Yucatecan food as being on par with other culinary traditions. One consequence is that out of the great diversity of Yucatecan recipes, a limited number have constituted the regional gastronomic canon. Recipes common at home are denied entry, for different reasons, into both recipe books and upscale restaurants.

Nonetheless, the Yucatecan gastronomic field is, as most fields are, unstable over time. As Pierre Bourdieu suggests (1993), a field is a space where different forces face each other, attempting to improve their position in relation to the others. The structure of the Yucatecan gastronomic field lies in the relationships among different culinary traditions that make up what today is known as "traditional" Yucatecan food. These traditions are the Creole, European (mainly Spanish, French, and Italian), the Mayan, and, since the turn of the twentieth century, the Middle Eastern (Syrian and Lebanese) cuisines. At the time of independence from Spain, one of the cooking guides printed for domestic use was based mainly on the local adaptation of dishes of Spanish, Italian, and French origin (Aguirre [1832] 1980). By the end of the nineteenth century, cookbooks such as Manuela Navarrete Arce's attempted to integrate a more balanced fusion of high European cuisines and local dishes, giving an official (i.e., printed and public) recognition to a few dishes attributed to Mayan culture, to Creole inventions, and to local dishes that gave ascendancy to local cosmopolitanism and sophistication (Navarrete Arce 1889).[6] Successive waves of migrants from Lebanon and Syria, coming into Yucatan at the end of the nineteenth and beginning of the twentieth centuries, contributed to the expansion of the regional culinary field. For example, some Lebanese dishes were adapted to the availability of local ingredients and the scarcity of original ingredients, and some even took a Mayan name (e.g., *x'nipek,* "dog's nose" in Mayan, is a sauce said to be inspired in the Lebanese tabbouleh salad [see Infante Vargas and Hernández Fuentes 2000]).

The ingenuity of regional cooks in blending and amalgamating culinary traditions made possible the creation of a number of dishes that, with local ingredients, attempted to display the sophistication of European haute cuisines. In consequence, many regional dishes have adopted and adapted sauces that instead of the original ingredients use tomato or use corn flour to thicken broths. The paradigmatic dishes of Yucatecan cuisine are based on pork and poultry (turkey or chicken). For example, chicken or turkey in *escabeche* is a stew that uses the same condiments used to pickle vegetables, thus *escabeche* (pickled); although *cochinita pibil* uses some local condiments (ground *achiote* seeds), it is made with pork marinated in Seville oranges, onion, oregano, and black pepper, and wrapped in banana leaves, all products originally imported from the Old World; stuffed cheese (*queso relleno*) is made out of the shell of a Dutch edam cheese, stuffed with ground pork, ground almonds, capers, olives, and onion. To serve, the slices of cheese are covered with a white sauce, reminiscent of béchamel but based on corn flour and chicken broth, that receives the Mayan name of *k'ol*.

The regional culinary field contains a code that asserts the equal, creative necessity and importance of the participation of the indigenous, the local Creole, and the foreign cuisines for its own existence. The Yucatecan gastronomic field is a blend of different world cuisines rather than an encompassing listing of old, Mayan, and "modern," European recipes and ingredients. In general, this field reproduces the local rhetoric that silences ethnic or cultural differences and gives a high value to integration. In the Yucatecan gastronomic field, the imported and the Mayan are all subsumed into the "local." It is the local, the Yucatecan, that speaks and silences all the other voices. The Mayas, the Lebanese, the French, and the Italians must speak in a code that is not their own but that of the hegemonic classes of Yucatan. I have found, speaking to restaurant managers, that when some dishes are clearly identified as belonging to other traditions, they are excluded from Yucatecan regional restaurants and secluded in the "ethnic" or "international." For example, whether they are "truly" Mayan recipes, or whether they are a Creole invention, cooks attribute to all local tamales a Mayan lineage; and some foods, such as *mondongo* (tripe), are defined as "more indigenous" and "low class" and thus deemed as "uncouth," lesser dishes relegated to cantinas, eateries, and domestic spaces but excluded from upscale restaurants' menus.

Similarly, during the first half of the twentieth century, the Lebanese-Syrian population reached both economic prominence and numbers large enough to grant the existence of a Lebanese club, a Lebanese association, Lebanese carnivals, a Lebanese business association, and Lebanese Catholic Churches, allowing Lebanese food in recent years to become a separate local category. Although Yucatecan families have their own recipes of kibbeh, hummus, baba ghanoush, and tahini in the domestic menu, and some dishes (e.g., hummus, baba ghanoush, and *kibbeh*) have been locally adopted as *botanas* in some cantinas, they are also excluded from the gastronomic field.

The expansion of the Yucatecan foodscape in the 1970s was limited. It incorporated Italian pizzas, Chinese chop suey and chow mein, and Mexican pozole, tacos, and carnitas as part of an incipient market for exotic foods. This expansion helped Meridans who did not travel to get acquainted with the foods eaten in other parts of Mexico and the world and to assert their cosmopolitan disposition: local people were open to the outside world. This limited intrusion of the Other was not seen as a threat to local ways. Local people could see themselves in control of what went on in and outside their homes and (individual and social) bodies. The foreign bodies were few and introduced simply as something "different." Yucatecan cuisine had grown, after all, from the incorporation of the alien into the local.

However, during the 1980s, first after the Great Earthquake of Mexico City in 1985, then with the boom of the service sector, triggered by the creation of Cancun, plus the federal policies aiming at the decentralization of the Mexican government (offering prizes to those moving to the "provinces") and the regional economic boom of the 1990s, triggered by the expansion of the service sector and the impulse given to the maquiladora industry, Yucatan and Yucatecans saw how large numbers of Mexicans began to migrate into Yucatan. Now the immigrants are perceived as having turned the host into a hostage. In large numbers, central Mexicans, supported by a history of colonial domination of the "provinces," moved into Yucatan with full confidence that they could impose their own customs elsewhere. Many Meridans find that Mexicans dominate some neighborhoods and have become segregated from local people. Some of my friends complain that they are now unable to find their favorite local dishes in their neighborhoods because the street and small vendor market is now dominated by Mexican-style tamales or by dishes from other Mexican culinary traditions. Supermarkets, restaurants, and businesses of a different nature are now locally perceived as addressing mainly either locals' or foreigners' needs.

Since about 1999, celebrations have been turned into an arena for the confrontation between local and foreign foods. In an instance reminiscent of the "ugly American" [*sic*] who demanded hamburgers everywhere he went, a woman from Mexico City told me that she has a hard time finding pozole in local restaurants. She was often told that it is a September food (for the celebration of Independence Day). *Chiles en nogada,* seen as the symbol of Mexican nationalistic cuisine, is also available in Mérida at a limited number of restaurants only during that same month. The festivities for the Day of the Dead and All Saints, on November 1 and 2, have been also turned into an occasion to affirm the local. In newspapers and in everyday conversations, local people reject the transformation of a "traditional" Yucatecan chicken tamale (*mucbil pollo*) that has had its traditional stuffing replaced or supplemented with ham and cheese. Some complain that this is a "perversion" introduced by Mexicans, who add cheese onto and into everything. A female friend told me that she and other girlfriends visited a nightclub, and during the night preceding the days of the dead one of the male dancers took the microphone and bitterly complained that the Mexicans were changing local traditions, asking them to leave the state of Yucatan and go back to where they came from, to eat whatever they want at their own homes elsewhere. Similarly, Christmas, Easter week, and other celebrations are becoming occasions for the affirmation of local identities.

However, global society is growing multicultural. It is now impossible, if it ever was possible, to maintain the inviolability of national and local boundaries. If anything, globalization has contributed to relativizing the value of all cultures (Appadurai 1996). In the next section I will discuss the negotiations that must be established to guarantee coexistence and respectful interaction among different cultural groups. Nonetheless, it is important to recognize the difficulties that derive from a history of structural domination between different societies. In this sense, it may be necessary, in the future, to reshape the interactions between members of a colonial culture (even if it is internal colonialism) and members of a historically colonized group, including the local elites.

Locals and Outsiders: Communities and Their Others

Anthropologists and sociologists alike have long been attentive to the forms of interaction between local people and outsiders. If, in general terms, classical anthropologists were concerned, chiefly, with the mechanisms that ensured the reproduction of social structures and cultures *within* communities, researchers working in so-called modern(izing) settings were forced to look at the arrival of newcomers. Hence, sociologists working in modern cities and anthropologists of the Mediterranean have looked at the interaction between hosts and guests since the late 1950s (see Ayora-Diaz 2000). Although studies about hosts and guests are widespread in anthropological studies, the figure of the *stranger,* often forgotten, is important for our understanding of the different strategies deployed by local groups to neutralize the threat imposed by newcomers (e.g., Z. Bauman 2001; Elias and Scotson 1994).

Strangers, as Derrida (2000) suggests, pose "the question" on the locals.

There is, he says, an absolute hospitality whose rules of disinterested generosity prevent the host even from asking the stranger's name. The absolutism of this rule overrules the local rules and practices of hospitality. In this instance, the guest takes the host as hostage and demands a welcoming without questioning, while challenging local practices and rules regarding hospitality. Although it has been argued elsewhere (Ayora-Diaz 2000) that hospitality does not necessarily entail aggression, we must recognize that the presence of unequal structural relations of power, where they exist, re-signify the displacements of people and their integration (or lack thereof) in host societies. Mirelle Rosello (2001) has argued that, in France, *hospitality* is the term of choice to describe the reception of immigrants from the former colonies. However, she demonstrates, this practice is now conditioned, and the status of the "guests" is subject to new legal definitions and policing actions. One pressing problem is to define how to host, for long periods, guests that were not invited. This blind alley shows the limits of using "hospitality" as a trope to describe practices involving the reception into a territory of scores of migrants. The interactions between migrants and receiving societies are only metaphorically analogous to the practices described as hospitality that occur between householders and their visitors at the domestic level.

There is no absolute rule. For example, although many Lebanese arrived in Yucatan as poor, itinerant merchants and then progressively became wealthy, in general terms they are accepted as full members of Catholic, mainstream Yucatecan society. In fact, they have seldom been defined as "invaders," and they are seen as having adopted and being adopted by Yucatecans. In contrast, central Mexicans are seen to represent the power of the Mexican highlands, and they know it. Hence, instead of adapting to local conditions, Mexicans are perceived as seeking to impose their views and tastes on local people.

Also, from the political use of language in the media, Yucatecans get cues about the ways in which members of a colonial force perceive them. In 1945, José Díaz Bolio (1998) complained that the Mexican media overrepresented Yucatecans as criminals in the crime sections of the newspapers of Mexico City. He repeatedly complained about the negative influence of Mexico on the Yucatecan economy and society. During the 1950s Mexican cinema introduced some Yucatecan characters, stereotyping them as naive dopes. In TV and radio programs broadcasted from Mexico City, Mexicans often referred to Yucatan as the "sister republic"; also, the states of United States of Mexico are called provinces, disregarding the fact that, for many people in the states, to be called provinces reminds them of the colonial and imperial power of a strong central government; and, adding insult to injury, Yucatecans are often the target of Mexican jokes that represent them as dumb and simple.

In contemporary Yucatan some of these roles have been reversed; but, also, some Mexicans continue to think of Yucatecans as slow-minded. For example, local media and people in daily conversations are quick to point the finger at "Mexicans" as responsible for the rise in crime, violence against women, and the aggressive traffic on the streets. National and regional newspapers are filled with stories of frauds, rapes, and robberies in which the criminals are from central Mexico.

Taking this context into account, during 2004 I was eating with three Yucatecans aged between sixty and seventy. I told them, "You know, I find something interesting: we Yucatecans are proud of our ways and believe that hospitality is one of our highest values." They wholeheartedly approved my statement. Then I added, "But why when we look at the Chilangos we don't usually feel that hospitable?" And they said, "Of course! How can we? Since they arrived women are not safe on the streets, crime is high, and they offend people everywhere."

In sum, Mexicans are seen as strangers undeserving of Yucatecan hospitality; that is, there are local rules of interaction that Mexicans constantly break. One is that Yucatecans expect respect for local practices and values. Those who adopt and respect them are granted respect and a place in Yucatecan society; those who don't, those who want to assert their origin, are not granted hospitality. Local people are inclined to accept the affirmation of cultural practices by Germans, US citizens, French, and other foreigners who reside in Mérida; they hold cultural preferences and values worth preserving as they enrich urban life (they open German charcuteries, manufacture Belgian chocolates, open Italian restaurants, or renovate and give new life to old buildings). After all, Yucatan has an old history of commerce with the United States and Europe. But the cultural practices of Mexicans are perceived and defined as intrusive, disrespectful of local ways, and disruptive of local morality.

This difficult and tense interaction between Yucatecans and Mexicans permeates different cultural realms. Although there is a process of negotiation between representatives of both "cultures," this negotiation is already marked by structural inequalities. Thus, neither Yucatecans nor Mexicans define the results as neutral. It is in this context that Meridans appeal to the "community" of local, Yucatecan people, against the strangers who seek to impose themselves upon local society. As Zygmunt Bauman (2001) reminds us, these communities are re-created to counter the threat of the different. Communities seek to enforce homogeneity and sameness over all their members and do not allow deviation from the norm (see Ayora-Diaz 2003).

The gastronomic field is thus turned into a battlefield where the locals defend the integrity of the culinary tradition as a token for the integrity of the community. From the local point of view, strangers not only invade the social body, but also seek to introduce customs and tastes that are strange to the regional culinary field and, consequently, threaten to transform it in ways not controlled by the community. It is at times like the present when cooks, domestic and commercial, seek to preserve the authenticity and tradition of local culinary recipes. Innovators are not to be trusted as they introduce the alien, the stranger, into the local in uncontrollable ways.

Vendors of Yucatecan food may at times harden the "purity" of their recipes. For example, at a regional food restaurant, one of the waiters explained to me, when I asked whether the recipe for a dish had been changed, that outsiders (i.e., non-Yucatecans) often ask for toppings or for adjustments in the recipes that degrade the dish. In their restaurant, he said, they sell the food as it must be eaten and no longer make allowances for such requests. In other restaurants, managed by more market-oriented individuals, they are not afraid to sell dishes with the names of traditional Yucatecan dishes that hardly resemble the original recipe. Some Yucatecans like these innovations and describe these dishes as *nouvelle Yucatecan cuisine,* but others dislike them and complain that they give people the wrong message about local food.

Discussion: Food and Postcolonial Representations

During the unfolding of global processes, throughout the history of colonial relations between Mexico and Yucatan, Yucatecans have engaged in creative articulations of the local and the global. Yucatan is not a closed society, but one that has resisted the imposition of the Mexican cultural blueprint with varied degrees of success at different times in history. Through radio, cinema, newspapers, religion, and economic expansionism, Mexican culture has become the homo/hegemonic representation that veils abroad the diversity of Mexican regions. Mariachi music; the mescal-, pulque-, or tequila-drinking, chili-eating, sombrero-carrying macho *charro* (cowboy), and Guadalupano (cultist of the Virgin of Guadalupe) Mexicans of movies and novels have been turned into stereotypical icons of national culture. During the twentieth century some Yucatecan Catholics have abandoned their parish saints to devote themselves to the Virgin of Guadalupe (Fernández Repetto and Negroe Sierra 2002), others have created and joined *charro* associations, the national media corporations have sought to homogenize musical tastes, imposing *ranchero* and *grupero* music (Pedelty 2004), and national restaurant chains have homogenized regional cuisines into some generic assortment of dishes they offer to their customers. However, resistance, defiance, and sometimes rejection of the national cultural imagination counter this homogenizing tendency.

If, during the creation of the Mexican imagined community, books about Mexican cooking and the history of Mexican food privileged central Mexican cooking, silencing the regions, regional cuisine exponents are now responding with a proliferation of regional cookbooks. The gastronomic field has been turned into a contested site for the articulation of global, cosmopolitan trends and local tastes and preferences. It is local people who, thus far, control what belongs or does not in that field in Yucatan and who protect it from Mexican interference.

Mexican gastronomic practices are often perceived as rather aggressive: Yucatecan food is spicy but not spicy-hot. Mexican food, in contrast, is perceived as imposing chili pepper on everybody. This is, from the Yucatecan point of view, a transposition of the colonial disposition to other cultural realms. All must accept spicy-hot food as Mexican culture. Yucatecan gastronomy, in contrast, uses chili peppers for aroma and flavor but serves peppers as side dishes to add to one's own food according to individual preferences and taste. Although habanero pepper, reputedly one of the hottest peppers in the world, is grown in Yucatan and enjoyed by many, it is always offered as a token of Yucatecan gentility and hospitality at the table, but never imposed on the guests. In the culinary field this non-imposing practice metaphorically represents the Yucatecan value of hospitality in contrast to the imposing dominance of Mexican culture.

In Yucatan the Mexican is the perceived stranger: a menacing body whose presence threatens local values and traditions. In the postcolonial world the metropolises must confront the fact of massive migration from their former colonies and deal with the historical guilt of impoverishing their nations (Rosello 2001). Forced to migrate, the guests feel regret and nostalgia for their places of origin that, they may perceive, they were forced to abandon (M. Joseph 1999). In Mexico, in contrast, where a central cultural power has colonized the regions, the many natural disasters, criminality, insecurity, and unemployment that characterize central Mexico launch central Mexicans to the different states in search of safety and employment. These migrants, outside central Mexico, feel nostalgia for the big city and see their former lives as giving them the right to embody imperial power. Many who arrive in Yucatan are perceived as despising Yucatecan culture and Yucatecans and as seeking to impose their tastes, values, and cultural forms over the local ones. As a response to this perceived threat, some Yucatecan groups have tended to close their affective doors and refuse to be hospitable to these strangers who seek to impose their own rules in foreign ground. It is from this struggle to assert Mexican and Yucatecan rules that the hybridity of Yucatecan gastronomy often appears as closed to Mexican influences, while to local people it has been for centuries the open door to global and cosmopolitan dialogue.

Notes

1. Mérida is the capital city of the state of Yucatan. Its inhabitants (close to one million) are called Meridanos and Meridanas (male and female, respectively). To avoid a gender-biased use, I call them all Meridans. Over 50 percent of the population of the state lives in Mérida. From the 1980s to date, the population of Mérida has expanded greatly due to immigration from other Yucatecan cities, towns, and villages, from other regions of Mexico outside Yucatan, and from other countries. Throughout this chapter I sometimes use "Yucatecans" when the events, perceptions, and stories are shared by Meridans with other Yucatecans. I use "Meridans" when the description is restricted to the inhabitants of Mérida.

2. There are similar reactions elsewhere expressed in many forms; for example, the Alaskan bumper sticker asking, "If it's tourist season, why can't we shoot them?" (Canestrini 2004, 39); or the strong feeling against Swedes in Copenhagen, exemplified by slogans that ask Danes to keep the country clean and accompany Swedes to the border (Löfgren 2002a).

3. *Chilango* has a morally ambivalent meaning: while many residents of Mexico City that I know call themselves that (*soy chilango*), and even the *Ortografía de la lengua española* gives this word as the patronymic (Real Academia Española 1999, 126), some central Mexicans feel the word to be derogatory. *Huach,* in turn, is a Yucatecan word used derogatorily to refer to non-Yucatecans. However, some outsiders with Yucatecan origin have appropriated the term and use it to name themselves and their equals as *Yucahuach*.

4. Elsewhere (Ayora-Diaz 2007), I have defined my understanding of the gastronomic field as a normative, exclusivist field constituted by recipes, ingredients, techniques, technologies, cooking procedures, and the etiquette for eating that has been instituted as particular to the regional culture of Yucatan. I am also arguing that this field is constituted and instituted under the authority of restaurants and cookbooks that authorize the food preference of regional elites.

5. Derrida (1997) suggests that in belonging to a culture where one homo/hegemonic language silences the other ones, it is questionable to presume that any individual perspective can represent all others.

6. In contrast to the rigid, institutionalized gastronomic field, I call the culinary field to the collection of recipes, ingredients, techniques, and cooking technologies that characterize domestic cooking. It is what Yucatecans eat at home and it is, hence, open, inclusive, ludic, and experimental.

4
Subverting Stereotypes

The Visual Politics of Representing Indigenous Modernity

Beth A. Conklin

In the media politics of contemporary indigenous rights activism and advocacy, representations based on strategic essentialisms are both tools and traps. Positive representations have proven enormously effective to develop solidarity and rally support for indigenous causes. But idealized representations have their downside. However sympathetic their content, such representations constitute a "legislation of authenticity" (Thomas 1994, 179) that can work against native peoples' interests. Overgeneralized claims about identity create unrealistic expectations that limit indigenous communities' choices. When individuals or groups fail to live up to impossibly high standards of purity and nobility, critics seize on the gap between image and reality as evidence of inauthenticity and unworthiness. These contradictions plague native movements worldwide, wherever indigenous rights struggles depend heavily on symbolic politics framed around idealized images of indigeneity.

In response, indigenous activists have developed a variety of innovative tactics to escape this representational trap. While capitalizing on the utility of certain positive representations of indigeneity, they simultaneously criticize the limits implicit in these representations. Their evolving struggles to change public attitudes and broaden understandings of indigenous culture parallel, and add urgency to, anthropologists' struggles to articulate understandings of *culture* as dynamic, changing, and constantly in the making.

All politics makes use of essentializing representations, such as idealized images of patriotism, the unity of the nation-state, or the virtues of a dominant culture or religion. But contemporary indigenous identity politics depend especially heavily on sympathetic imagery. As Roland Niezen (2003, 186–87) notes, indigenous formulations of tradition and nationhood require some degree of public approval: "Indigenous nationalism is shaped more significantly by the demands of consumer export than are other forms of group identity. . . . Indigenous nationalism thus usually shapes itself around those core values that resonate most strongly with the nonindigenous public."

In native peoples' struggle to make themselves and their causes *visible* to dominant societies that have long ignored them, outsiders' stereotypes are realities they must deal with: native activists are forced to manage their self-representations to work around and through the cultural codes of both racism and romanticism. Marginalized groups mobilize outsiders' support by framing their causes in terms that appeal to ideas about the virtues of indigenous cultures, deploying the symbolic codes of primitivism, exoticism, and authenticity that identify native cultures with deep spirituality, ancient origins, and distinctive forms of community. Identifying indigenous cultures with principles of Western ecology and the goals of international environmentalism has been especially effective in broadening the base of public support for environmental causes (Conklin and Graham 1995).

The downside of this politics is that again and again, indigenous activists run up against the problem that idealized, unrealistic expectations limit the range of actions open to native people. Niezen describes these pressures:

> It is not enough that peoples and communities are destroyed, removed from the land, politically marginalized, unemployed in an unfamiliar formal economy, exposed to addictions, and educated in a way that convinces many individuals of their innate inferiority. To satisfy the public that can help them—the audiences most concerned with human rights and the environment—they must also be noble, strong, spiritually wise, and, above all, environmentally discreet. The reality of destroyed communities, however, is rarely consistent with the expectations placed upon them. There can be little nobility, wisdom, or environmental friendliness where addictions are rampant, economic desires are unfulfilled, and political frustration pushes regularly against the barriers preventing violence. (2003, 186)

No matter how positive, essentialist stereotypes backfire. When native groups or individuals *fail* to live up to other people's expectations, their opponents turn these failings into fodder for criticism.

However, few successful native activists deal exclusively in the simplistic symbolic currencies of exoticism and nobility. Instead, they try to revalue those currencies, working to change outsiders' ideas about who native people are and what they want and need. At the same time that activists capitalize on the utility of essentialisms, they also criticize their limitations. Ultimately, they aim to challenge and *expand* public ideas about what it means to be indigenous in the contemporary world.

One common representational tactic employed by indigenous rights activists worldwide involves foregrounding images that combine elements of tradition and modernity. Such representations aim to escape and transcend the limiting binary categories that equate indigenous authenticity with cultural purity and continuity with the past, and see modern knowledge and technology as antithetical to *real* Indianness. The popular assumption that being authentically indigenous means following ancient lifeways untouched by modernity and its discontents relegates native people to a position of passivity and victimization, outside history, disempowered and devoid of agency.

Native activists attack this stereotype in a number of ways. By demonstrating sophisticated abilities to communicate through the languages of citizenship, ecology, and human rights; by putting video, e-mail, and Internet technologies to new uses; by calling attention to native people's existence in cities, shantytowns, and other *invisible* sites; and by articulating innovative critiques of global political-economic systems and non-indigenous issues such as the North American Free Trade Association (NAFTA) and global warming, activists stake claims to new kinds of indigenous global citizenship.

This chapter explores one tactic prominently employed in many indigenous rights movements: the innovative use of visual symbols to critique and undermine pervasive assumptions about the opposition between tradition and modernity. Visual images are key resources in media politics. Dramatic images—especially distinctive costumes and body adornment—are powerful tools to claim public attention. Many non-Indians see costume and bodily appearances as prime markers of native identity. This intersects and resonates with the emphasis that many native groups place on the primacy of the body and its adornment as a locus of personhood, sociality, and morality. Visual representations are thus a prime stage for communicating, performing, and potentially transforming, new indigenous identities.

This chapter examines visual communication in three very different cases. Two examples represent the two most successful indigenous movements of the 1990s: native Amazonian activism in Brazil and the Zapatista rebellion in southern Mexico. In both cases native leaders and spokespersons used dramatic, attention-getting costumes as a focal media strategy. In both cases, these dramatic body images expressed new self-consciousness and self-confidence, a pride in being indigenous. But the costumes themselves could scarcely have been more different. In Brazil, activists capitalize on the display of exoticized (and often seminude) native bodies adorned with colorful feathers, beads, and handmade decorations. In Mexico, Zapatistas hid their faces behind black, generic, commercially manufactured ski masks or red bandanas.

Though the images differ radically, both visual strategies developed partially in reference to Western primitivist codes based on the supposed antithesis between tradition and modernity. Subverting this binary coding is the focus of the third case examined here, an exhibit created by Native American educators, artists, and activists at Santa Fe's Museum of Indian Arts and Culture. These diverse settings demonstrate the emergence of creative new ways that indigenous intellectuals and activists represent their cultures and what it means to be indigenous in the contemporary world.

Visual Codes of Authenticity in Native Brazilian Activism

Throughout the Americas, two opposing stereotypes permeate public attitudes toward native people. The *good* Indian is pure and noble, living close to nature, untouched by civilization or consumer culture. The *bad* Indian is either primitive, barbaric, and backward or, more commonly these days, degraded and hopelessly corrupted by the ills of civilization—poverty, addiction, alcoholism, loss of cultural traditions (Berkhofer 1978, 27–28; Ramos 1998, 62). In this binary logic, the authentically indigenous and the modern/corrupted/civilized are opposite and incompatible. Jonathan Warren describes such attitudes among non-Indians in northeast Brazil:

> To be an authentic Indian, one must live like a primitive in a traditional manner. One must embody the antiself of civilization, which in Brazil means living in a hut in the middle of the forest, naked, and with no contemporary technological conveniences. . . . Indians are imagined as "primitive/traditional" in the sense of being outside of and in binary opposition to "civilization/modernity." . . . If Indians participate in professions, use technology, wear clothes, and inhabit urban geographies (which denote modernity), then they are not considered Indian [regardless of their bloodlines or physical features]. Thus imagined as antithetical to the modern, Indians become locked in time as static beings of a distant, lost past. . . . The more someone deviates from this image of the past, the less Indian that individual is deemed to be. Change and adaptation are conceived of as racial contamination by non-Indians. (2001, 173, 172, 176)

For Brazil's media and most of the non-Indian public, the centrality of exotic body images in defining authentic indigenous identity is deeply entrenched. *Real* Indians should *look Indian,* which means going naked or wearing feathers, beads, and paint. Native people who live in Brazilian cities constantly confront questions about their identity, authenticity, and bodily appearance. "We spend most of our lives trying to reaffirm that we are Indians," says Eliane Potiguara (1992, 46), an urban native activist, "and then we encounter statements like, 'But you wear jeans, a watch, sneakers, and speak Portuguese!' . . . Society either understands Indians all made-up and naked inside the forest or consigns them to the border of big cities."

For native Brazilians themselves, the emphasis that outsiders place on nudity and visual exoticism as an index of authenticity often has little to do with their own sense of self-identity. Few Indians see cultural change as incompatible with being indigenous. Rather, as Warren (2001, 189) notes, they tend to see the loss of traditions and pressures to wear Western clothing more as signs of racism and repression rather than indicators of their own inauthenticity. However, in Brazil's highly charged cultural politics of race/ethnicity, to dress in Western clothing is to run the risk of being seen as not really Indian, or not the right *kind* of Indian. As Alcida Ramos (1998, 77) observes, individuals who do not look Indian are not respected for their ability to pass as whites, but are seen as corrupt and degraded, losers in both societies. To be accepted as authentic, activists must dress the part. Those whose effectiveness depends most on media politics do. Feathered headdresses and body paint have proven spectacularly effective at attracting attention and journalistic coverage that lets activists' messages be heard.

The problem—the vulnerability that can turn this tool into a trap—is that indigenous people must use body ornaments and dress selectively in different contexts. All of us do this every day. Dressing for an awards ceremony, a US president puts on a tuxedo and a Kayapó leader puts on a headdress. The next morning, both may relax at home in T-shirt and jeans. We think nothing of the president's "strategic" use of costume; on the contrary, we would lambast him if he attended the ceremony in casual dress. But the public tends to have different expectations for indigenous activists. Contextual usage of native adornment contradicts the idea that Indians' natural body decorations express deep spirituality, intimate relations with nature, and distinctive cultural roots (Conklin 1997, 725).

In Brazil, enemies of indigenous rights have repeatedly seized upon the supposed contradiction when activists use native dress in some contexts and Western dress in others. Critics cry fraud and hypocrisy, claiming that activists are staging their Indianness for a gullible foreign public (cf. Gomes and Silber 1992; and see McCallum 1995 for analysis). A series of vitriolic journalistic exposés have used photographic layouts in which pictures of exotically costumed Kayapó activists were juxtaposed against pictures of the same individuals off-stage, dressed in Western clothes and engaged in civilized, modern activities—driving a car, eating at a fancy restaurant, using high-tech equipment (Conklin 1997, 725–26). Hostile critics represent the use of indigenous costume in some contexts and not in others as hypocrisy—a canny, calculated manipulation of the media and the public's fascination with colorful exoticism.

Where this gets more interesting is in looking at how native activists simultaneously use attention-getting visual elements while deploying counter-images that send other, more complicated messages. Instead of fitting into the pure-primitive slot, activists mark their modernity, autonomy, and agency by presenting themselves as people familiar with multiple cultural systems. They mark cosmopolitanism on their bodies with wristwatches or business suits combined with indigenous ornaments or body paint, and they make a point of displaying familiarity with sophisticated technology (e.g., cell phones, iPods, laptops). The Kayapó of central Brazil are an iconic example. Since the 1980s, Kayapó have trained a number of young men as video cameramen and film editors, pioneering the use of video to record community rituals and political events and to exercise some control over how their culture is represented to the outside world. Terence Turner has pointed out that not only do Kayapó want to film their own videos, they also want their cameramen to be photographed in the act of filming (1992, 7). Their visual display of technological competency aims to subvert limiting stereotypes that equate being indigenous with being antimodern.

Zapatista Masks: Subverting the Dominating Gaze

Like Amazonian activists, the Zapatista movement in southern Mexico used dramatic costuming and symbolic juxtapositions to challenge preconceptions, gain visibility, and stake claims to political participation as people who are both indigenous and fully modern. But instead of playing up exoticism's attractions, Zapatistas purposefully removed native faces from outsiders' gaze by covering their faces with ski masks and bandanas. Generic, cheap, and commercially manufactured, these face coverings are the antithesis of Amazonian feather headdresses.

The masked face that became the identifying symbol of the Zapatista movement provided a metaphor that their spokespeople deployed brilliantly to articulate their critique of racism and oppression (cf. Ponce de Leon 2001; Rugglers and Sahukla 1996). References to faces and masks pervade the speeches and writings of the mestizo (non-Indian) leader who goes by the name of Sub-*comandante* Marcos. A former university lecturer in sociology, steeped in readings of Antonio Gramsci, Michel Foucault, and other social theorists, Marcos explained the mask as a way to remove the exoticized but anonymous indigenous face from the exploitative, commodifying gaze of more powerful others. At the same time, he and other Zapatistas have pointed out, the mask calls attention to indigenous people's position—faceless, invisible to society, ignored until they put on a threatening symbol of criminality that negates stereotypes of Indian passivity. The mask asserts agency and the demand to be taken seriously.

Another metaphorical valence of the mask is the idea that it transcends individual identity to affirm a collective, broadly humanistic solidarity. Masks negate prior personal differences, say Zapatistas, especially gender distinctions between male and female. Hiding individuality, the mask also is said to prevent the kind of cult of personality that has turned some native activists (such as Brazil's Kayapó) into media stars.

Like native Amazonians, Zapatista leaders have tried to make indigenous people and their causes visible while simultaneously using this visibility to expand public notions of what it means to be indigenous. Their work has aimed to relocate native people from the periphery to the center, asserting their full participation as citizens in national and global society.

Like the headdress-wearing Kayapó cameramen who want to be filmed in the act of filming, indigenous Zapatista leaders combined traditional clothing with defiantly non-indigenous elements. The elderly Tzotzil leader who went by the name of Ramona, for example, always appeared in public wearing an embroidered blouse and flowered skirt along with her ski mask. The weapons, cell phones, laptops, Internet communiqués, and other artifacts that Zapatistas display so prominently communicate complexity, assertiveness, empowerment. The novelty and media appeal of these images derive from the jolt of juxtaposition: the indigenous and the commercial, the handmade and the high-tech. The visual message echoed the theoretical sophistication and poetic nuances of the movement's rhetoric, not just in Marcos's speeches but in other native leaders' messages as well. In the fine art of Zapatista media politics, subverting stereotypes served as a powerful way to put the world on notice that indigenous people are active participants in the modernity.

Solidarity behind the Mask

Zapatistas did not speak only on behalf of indigenous causes; they asserted a broad critique and moral rejection of neoliberalism, with which many non-Indians identified. Masks offered a tangible device to affirm solidarity. Anyone can don a mask, said Zapatistas: the mask invites other oppressed and dissatisfied people to feel part of the struggle. A 1996 declaration from the Ejército Zapatista de Liberación Nacional (EZLN), the Zapatista Army of National Liberation, proclaimed, "Behind our masks is the face of all excluded women, of all the forgotten native people, of all the persecuted homosexuals, of all the despised youth, of all the beaten migrants, of all those imprisoned for their words and thoughts, of all the humiliated workers, of all those dead from neglect, of all the simple and ordinary men and women who don't count, who aren't seen, who are nameless, who have no tomorrow" (Rugglers and Sahukla 1996, 24–25).

Masks are a long-running theme and metaphor for Mexican national identity, most famously explored in Octavio Paz's (1962) "Mexican Masks" essay. The idea of a masked figure protecting the interests of the poor resonated with the populist politics of a cadre of masked superheroes who, adopting the masked style of *lucha-libre* professional wrestlers, have been popular figures on the streets of Mexico City since the late 1980s. Super-Barrio, Super Eco, El Chupacabras Crusader, and other masked superheroes have shown up at demonstrations and media events to confront government officials and exploitative business interests (L. Taylor 1997). The Zapatista uprising added another face to the Mexican mask identity complex. As they became symbols of dissent for a wide spectrum of the Mexican populace, black ski masks repeatedly sold out in shops all over the country.

At the international level, the Zapatista uprising was the most prominent new leftist movement of the 1990s. Black ski masks emerged as iconic international symbols of anticapitalist critiques of globalization. By 2001, ski masks had become so ubiquitous at anti–World Trade Organization demonstrations that during the Summit of the Americas in Quebec City, officials tried to ban possession of ski masks, scarves, and other face coverings (ISR 2001). In addition to their symbolic identification with the outsider positions of both Zapatistas and urban criminals, face coverings help protestors avoid being identified in police surveillance.

Any iconic costume becomes a convenient target for hostility and cynicism. As with Brazilian journalists' use of photographic juxtapositions to challenge Kayapó legitimacy, Mexican skepticism about the Zapatistas was articulated through questions about the mask. Why does Marcos wear a mask, and what is he hiding? asked critics. Che Guevara never wore a mask; even Emiliano Zapata showed his face (Feder 2001).

Zapatistas turned such questions around. "Why so much scandal about the ski-masks?" asked Marcos.

Isn't Mexican political culture a "culture of hidden faces"? I am willing to take off my mask if Mexican society takes off the foreign mask that it anxiously put on years ago. . . . [I]t has been sold an image of it-self that is fake, and the reality is more terrifying than people supposed. If we show each other our faces . . . civil society will have to wake up from the long and lazy dream that "modernity" imposes on every-thing and everybody. "Sup-Marcos" is ready to take off his ski-mask; is Mexican civil society ready to take off its mask? (quoted in Rug-glero and Sahulka 1996, 88)

Zapatistas repeatedly affirmed their hope to arrive at the day when, with Mexican society having recognized the rights of indigenous and other op-pressed peoples, they would be able to remove their threatening masks and live as ordinary people with full citizenship in a modernity reshaped and redefined by their movement.

In their very different ways, Zapatistas and native Amazonian activists made the self-conscious use of essentialist symbols of tradition and moder-nity as key tools, appropriating the symbols and their meanings but giving them a twist to claim space in the media-driven public arena and convey mes-sages that challenge, critique, expand, and redefine popular understandings of what it means to be indigenous. By displaying sophisticated complexities of thought and bicultural/multicultural competencies, these strategic mixings project the message that one can be an active agent in cosmopolitan moder-nity and still be authentically indigenous.

The Museum of Indian Arts and Culture

North American public attitudes echo the primitive-modern binary that lo-cates indigeneity in opposition to change and modern consumer goods and treats costume as an index of authenticity. Lucy Lippard observed: "Even to-day, when Zunis wear rubber boots or sneakers at Shalako [ceremonies], or when an Apache puberty ritual includes a six-pack of soda among the offer-ings, tourists and purists tend to be offended. Such 'anachronisms' destroy the time-honored distance between Them and Us, the illusion that They live in different times than We do" (1992, 26–27).

An exhibit inaugurated at the Museum of Indian Arts and Culture in Santa Fe, New Mexico, in 1997 explicitly challenged this set of assumptions. The exhibit was produced through eight years of collaboration among Na-tive Americans from Southwestern groups: Native American elders, artists, scholars, teachers, writers, and museum professionals. It continues on dis-play as a long-term, permanent exhibit from the museum's collection, with changes and modifications made over the years.

The exhibit's title, "Here, Now, and Always," stakes a claim to contemporaneity and cosmopolitanism, to identities as modern and alive as they are traditional. This theme structures the entire display and numerous strategies of presentation. Many displays are organized around categories of material culture—artifacts, architecture, art. There is, for example, a glass case with a display of devices for carrying babies: a classic papoose, cloth and skin slings, and a Graco infant car seat. Moving on to the children's toys display, one finds "traditional" balls, tops, animal figurines, a Nintendo remote controller, and a set of plastic Power Rangers. Stark, minimalistic labels identify each item: ceramic figures, 1863; Nintendo, 1992. Reconstructions of two Native American kitchens sit side by side. There is the *traditional* kitchen with hearth and stone corn-grinding implements. In the *modern* kitchen, bundles of sage drying over the window mark the household's traditionalism; a Gustav Klimt calendar and *The I Hate to Cook Book* on a Formica countertop mark its cosmopolitanism.

This is a remarkable exhibit in the pervasiveness of its commitment to destabilize popular notions about the antithesis between tradition and modernity. There is none of the quasi-apologetic exegesis one might expect (about how Native Americans live in the modern world but still honor the sacred traditions of their ancestors, etc., etc.). Instead, displays simply present elements of material life that outsiders will readily identify as traditional/authentically native or modern/Western and grant these equal status as integral elements in real native peoples' lives, as if challenging the viewer to suggest otherwise.

The Santa Fe exhibit can get by with this symbolic destabilizing—can project confidence in its defiant assertion that complexity, hybridity, and cosmopolitan sophistication are *not* antithetical to authentic indigenous lives— partly because of its privileged location in an utterly secure identity frame. This is the Museum of *Indian* Arts and Culture in Santa Fe, one of the most elite and authoritative venues for encounters with Native North American art, which is an elite, authoritative category in itself. How many non-Indian visitors will dare say aloud what they might be thinking: "But Formica countertops and Klimt calendars aren't Indian!"

A factor in establishing the exhibit's position is that it is framed at the start by powerful symbols that proffer unassailable indigenous credentials based on spirituality and language. Approaching the entrance to the exhibit when I first visited in 2005, I encountered a sign that said, "Stop!" The sign explains that some native people believe that no one should enter this exhibit. Visitors are directed to listen to two messages recorded by tribal elders, explaining their opposition to the display of cultural and religious artifacts. The spoken messages are lengthy, and they are heard first in the tribal language, which will be unintelligible to all but a handful of museum visitors (speakers of these languages). English translations follow; the visitor learns about each group's differing ideas about artifacts and relations to dead ancestors, spirituality, and tribal traditions. The visitor is put on alert not only to indigenous sensibilities and the need for respect and reverence, but also to the fact of diversity and disagreements among various Southwestern native people.

The genius of this device of stopping visitors and making them consider reasons not to go into the exhibit they have paid to see is that it creates an embodied experience that destabilizes conventions of museum-going. The patience exacted in requiring visitors to stand waiting for the English translation is, in itself, a lesson in respect and the requirement for heightened cultural sensitivity. Visitors who choose not to enter the exhibit follow an arrow directing them through a special passageway to the later sections of the exhibit, which contain fewer ancient artifacts associated with the dead. Those who do decide to enter (as most visitors do) proceed with clearer awareness of the spirit in which some native elders wish them to approach. The exhibit's opening frames thus establish vivid, direct, embodied encounters with three prime markers of indigenous cultural distinctiveness: language, spirituality, and continuity with ancestral traditions.

Conclusions

The Kayapó, Zapatistas, and Santa Fe museum use three distinct representational strategies to convey anti-essentialist messages about indigenous peoples' cultural complexity, cosmopolitan competency, diversity, and modernity. For the Mexican Tzotzil, Tzeltal, and Tojolabal speakers who are core Zapatista supporters, the Kayapó living in their classic circular villages in central Brazil's savannas, and the elders recorded in the Santa Fe exhibit, native language signals authoritative claims to unquestionably genuine indigenous identity. Within secure frames, individuals can work to undermine, subvert, and expand the constraining boundaries of stereotypes in ways that groups whose identity claims are less secure cannot.

The messages that native activists and intellectuals try to convey in these and other contexts are largely compatible with the directions in which anthropological understandings of culture have evolved. One of the biggest contributions anthropologists can make to indigenous rights struggles is to find effective ways to communicate our current understandings of culture and identity as dynamic and processual. We need to break down the authenticity trap that equates real indigeneity with traditionalism and develop popular understandings to help indigenous politics escape the "noble savage slot" trap. If we really believe our constructivist insights that strategic pre-sentations of self-identity are not just hypocrisy; that performance does not equal fraud; that learning to communicate in the language of foreign dis-courses (ecology, human rights) is smart and necessary, not inauthentic, then we need to find more persuasive ways to communicate this to the public (Conklin 2003).

This is what many indigenous activists themselves are working on. For anthropologists, our evolving understandings of culture and identity may be some of the more useful ideas we can offer. The challenge is to recover the disciplinary self-confidence to feel we have something coherent to say; find clear ways to talk about culture, tradition, and identity that get past reifying essentialisms; and use our ethnographic skills to convey and legitimize the dynamism of native peoples' efforts to carve out new political, cultural, and social spaces for being indigenous in the twenty-first century.

5

Labels, Genuine and Spurious

Anthropology and the Politics of Otherness in the United States

Vilma Santiago-Irizarry

Growing up in Puerto Rico, my sense of identity was primordially informed —bad pun intended—by the notion of simply being *puertorriqueña,* however conscious I eventually became that differentials of race, gender, and class complicated such an insidiously placid nationalistic claim. In turn, *hispano* or *hispana, latina* or *latino*—the closest Spanish-language terms for the English labels Hispanic and Latino—were generalizing markers that I was socialized into using interchangeably for designating fellow travelers from Latin American nations to distinguish them, generically, from other nationalities and, contextually, from the predominantly English-speaking denizens of the north whose history was so intertwined with ours.[1] The labels established instrumental identity boundaries, complementing and overlapping with national ones in a play of context-based relations indexing both difference and commonality. In the United States and in the English language, conversely, the labels are pragmatic markers of ethno-racial difference.

Thus, labels of national indigeneity (*puertorriqueña*) represent efforts to domesticate the intrinsic heterogeneity within nation-states. In Latin America, monolithic national identities operate as local homologues to the supranational ones that *hispano* and *latino* represent. Both kinds of labels are meant to exert a centripetal force, an "[orientation] toward unity" (Bakhtin 1981, 274), by which dominant national and transnational groups constitute nested identity arrays meant to be simultaneously inclusionary *and* exclusionary, perhaps even soothingly harmonious.

In a career and life-changing repositioning, I arrived in the United States in the mid-1980s, when an anticipated surge in Latin American immigration marked a shift in the national demographics of minoritization from African American to Hispanic/Latino ascendancy.[2] Since the 1970s, national censuses had documented significant numerical increases among the latter and projected them into the twenty-first century. This has come to pass: it is common-place to note that Latinos/Hispanics occupy the top slot in the nation's ethno-racial arrays, publicly foregrounding their long-standing struggles within ongoing US politics of identity, recognition, and representation. Within the prevailing processes of identity construction in the United States, choosing a label—among other such exercises, opting between Latino and Hispanic—acquires an urgency lacking in the Latin American context, where overlap-ping identity categories and racial continua remain the norm. What I wish to suggest is that in the United States identity categories are transformative, transmuting nationalities into marked ethno-racial identities, while race re-mains a biologized quality dichotomized into a white–black binary. Ethno-racial labels in the United States index subsidiary sociocultural categories that, as Joshua Fishman (1966) once argued, emanate from an *American ethno-nationalism* that erases indigenous peoples and presupposes a nation composed of outsiders—in a nutshell, Margaret Mead's infamous statement, "We are all third generation" (1942, 31). "American ethno-nationalism" authorizes the incorporation of immigrants through legal citizenship yet re-inscribes their sociocultural and structural markedness vis-à-vis dominant Anglo-American groups (cf. Warner and Srole 1945, 284–96). Moreover, as happens in the La-tino case, the status of racialized groups whose place in the national history began under conditions of war, conquest, enslavement, and a variety of co-lonial forms of intervention is refracted through ingrained racist ideologies, practices, and structures, thus complicating their potential for nationalist in-corporation.

I here examine politics of representation in the United States through the perspective of labeling. Elsewhere, I have remarked on the tensions inher-ent to the relationship between the two umbrella labels—Latino and His-panic—as ironic indices of a communal heterogeneity that the labels them-selves are meant to transcend—minimally, to conciliate (Santiago-Irizarry 2001, 1996, 4, 19). I focus on a particular outcome of this tension: the mutual attribution of oppositional identity constructs among the very people who are meant to coalesce under these labels. For expediency, I follow the now-generalized practice of designating the individuals and groups whose con-dition I address as *Latinos,* while acknowledging that the very label and its relation to representational processes are at issue.[3] I believe sociocultural ex-perience is primarily marked by ambiguity, fluidity, and contestation, and our anthropological task is one that historicizes and localizes sociocultural phe-nomena in order to understand them.[4] Although focused on labeling, my cri-tique is directed to foreground, however generally, what anthropology con tributes to these debates: the interrogation of commonplace political arguments developed to marshal a heterogeneous ethno-racial community in the United States under a homogenizing umbrella label.

For Latinos, their demographic surge made pressing the adoption of an essentializing umbrella label for political mobilization. Labels, particularly in the United States, remain significant constructs for organizing individual and communal entitlement within the nation's redistributive structures and processes.[5] But intrinsic differences among Latino groups—of nationality, racial and class structures, sociopolitical ideology, immigration trajectory, history of relations with the United States, and so on—complicate these processes. By the 1990s, widespread debates over each label's *adequacy* generated a variety of representations about the *nature* of different Latino groups, indexing the positional fissures among them. These debates emerged in multiple venues, but I here focus on e-mail exchanges that proliferated in electronic Latino Listservs throughout the 1990s. My selection of the most typical of these messages shows them to be pithy, yet paradigmatic, inscriptions of the oppositions in question.[6] Generally, *Hispanic* is associated with conservative values and positions, and *Latino* with a progressive stance; concomitant oppositional arrays of racial and class attributes emanate from this strategy of ideological stereotyping. Though stereotyping is consonant with strategic essentializing (Spivak 1990), the labeling debate among Latinos paradoxically stresses internal difference rather than homogeneity. *Latino* currently appears ubiquitous as *the* homogenizing term of identity, having entered common usage as, allegedly, the preferred umbrella term. Yet myriad historical and regional labels subsist among Latinos throughout the United States. The persistence of *Hispanic* and other hyphenated and compound designations, national terms of identity, even prefacing the umbrella label with "US," as in "US Latino," and ongoing debates over the meaning and consequence of any identity term, all document how labels remain contested among Latinos. Scholarly attention to the debate is equally ongoing (see Flores 2000; Laó-Montes and Dávila 2001; and, especially, Martín Alcoff 2005). The apparent primacy of *Latino,* I would suggest, responds to the hegemonic constitution of umbrella labels as necessary instruments for legitimating dominant claims that the United States is unproblematically moving toward an equalizing and empowering multiculturalism. Legitimating a label for constituting individual and group identity implies acceptance into a national imaginary that is being construed in multicultural terms, especially when it involves a label that is being represented by some members of the group as indigenously produced and chosen. These superficial signs of inclusion mask actual Latino experiences of marginalization and racialization. Notably, in my experience, these debates are most trenchant among Latino elites; I do not mean to argue that others—recent immigrants, the working class—are not affected by these debates or the issues surrounding labeling. It is simply that my exposure to these debates is shaped by my own research experiences in institutional settings and social location in academia. I cannot vouch for it, but I suspect that outside these fields the inclination to identify through national origin prevails.

Labels index perceived sociocultural differences among groups and constitute the means to police identity boundaries for managing authenticity: who can legitimately claim belonging and, consequently, tap into established structures of ethno-racial entitlement as organized through the apparatus of the nation-state. Ultimately, labels are instruments for monitoring sociocultural groups and their members, a tactic of governmentality that operates inwardly and outwardly within and across identity boundaries in complex ways (Foucault 2000, 201–22). It is thus not surprising that they become sites of contestation and for articulating what are, after all, shifting and ambiguous ideological positionings through the mobilization of identity discourses that are manifold, containing within them other (interwoven) discourses about race, gender, class, and history.

Enthroning and Dethroning

In the article whose conceit I borrow, Edward Sapir argues that we use labels, which he characterizes as "empty thrones," in a necessary attempt—for ontological and epistemological reasons—to encompass and objectify intrinsically ambiguous and contradictory concepts. Our ability to analyze, or even conduct sociocultural life, is facilitated by a willful finding of commonality among these concepts and by choosing particular labels that help us fix the meaning of concepts (Sapir 1927, 401, and 1949, 308). Sapir's metaphor of enthroning and dethroning through the contextual choice and deployment of contending labels implicates political contingency as well as a struggle over the significance, value, and consequence of particular labels. Insofar as an ethno-racial terrain is involved, labels become polysemic sites in which difference, rather than homogeneity, is made tangible, represented, and foregrounded, as well as challenged and re-construed. Micaela Di Leonardo (1984, 22–23) similarly stresses the place of labeling when she argues, within the context of the United States and the construction of Italian American ethnicity, "Ethnicity is a phenomenon of state societies . . . involving the labeling, from within or without, of particular populations as somehow different from the majority, and of their members as genealogically related to one another. The members may not necessarily *be* related to one another, nor do they necessarily behave differently from the majority; it is the labeling itself, the cultural process, that is crucial to the construction of ethnicity."

Through labeling, identity processes acquire a dubious concreteness in

collective and individual consciousness. Yet it is precisely through their objectification that these schemas gain political force. To paraphrase Sapir, one person's esteemed category of ethno-racial identity may be another's undesirable
one, and the clash between them contributes to the quality of contestation
that characterizes identity processes in the United States. To reiterate what I
have argued elsewhere (Santiago-Irizarry 1996, 4), ethnic labeling, as a classificatory subset of sociocultural identity, involves issues of specification and
homogenization and of power, dominance, and resistance, but, importantly,
also of agency.

However imbued they may be with essentializing power, though, labels in
and of themselves do not solve issues of inequality and differential power relations, even when self-consciously deployed in the strategic politics of recognition that mobilize entitlement in the United States. Labels contribute to
the production and reproduction of hierarchical relations even while osten-
sibly countering the very inequalities that the dominant structural conditions
in the United States generate. Intrinsic to labeling is precisely the differential value assigned to particular labels themselves as well as the meanings they
embody as indices of specific sociocultural attributions, histories, and subject
positionings. The debate over the appropriateness of *Latino* vis-à-vis *Hispanic*
as signifying labels too often revolves around oppositional ideological ascriptions that locate Latino groups and communities differentially, negating the
unity that the labels are, ironically, designed to effect, mark, and foster.[7]

Constructing Identity over Cyberspaces

Electronic communication has become a commonplace site for sociocultural production and reproduction, allowing for speedy, widespread networks
among otherwise unrelated people. Over the last fifteen years, I have moni-
tored the periodic eruption of debates over the labeling of Latinos in a variety of electronic media. What circulates electronically is as animated by
strategic essentializing (Spivak 1990) as are other political and institutional
processes. Although in my work I have critiqued essentializing and primordialism, I have also argued that the *essences* that are strategically deployed emanate from *native* assessments, however contested, about what being an *X* in the
United States is or should be about. Whatever scholarly critiques we may direct at strategizing, we should not, as anthropologists, allow our ambivalence
to trump *native* agency, especially in strategic self-representation and in the
articulation of political agendas.

I here focus on messages that circulated in the 1990s over the Listserv (IPR-
Forum) of the Institute for Puerto Rican Policy (IPR). IPR was founded in

1982 as a nonprofit and nonpartisan research and advocacy organization to address Puerto Rican and, despite its name, Latino political issues and behaviors. A loose coalition of Latino and Puerto Rican scholars researched and published under its sponsorship. In the 1990s, it established an electronic presence through a website (IPR Net) and a Listserv. IPR eventually merged with the Puerto Rican Legal Defense and Education Fund (PRLDEF) to continue its advocacy and research initiatives.

Working with electronic sources, one is hampered by the anonymity that characterizes these exchanges. Texts need to be taken at face value; those who produce them control their presentation of self, including their own identity. Although some contributors explicitly self-labeled, others "universalized" themselves, so to say, through circumspection. My task here is thus circumstantial, an exercise in textual analysis to which I bring to bear my own personal, professional, and research experiences. What I wish to foreground is really a situation of objectification through labeling by which difference is established within an ethno-racial community in the United States that is simultaneously subjected and self-subjected to homogenizing labeling for political purposes. Because of the nature of the organization that sponsored the Listserv, the tenor of the debates, and the very fact of electronic access, the people whose messages I examine constitute a self-selected group with the cultural capital, structural position, and knowledge to exercise agency within cyberspaces. Yet, these debates are appropriated by other media and actors, objectified and made normative, and are circulated broadly, informing how others conceptualize Latino identity in the United States.

Debating Identity

The participants in these electronic exchanges over identity generally strive, to varying degrees of consciousness, for closure and the resolution of intra-Latino differences through the adoption of a label. This is consonant with the adversarial techniques of institutional politics, authenticity discourses, and quantified models of entitlement that subsist in the United States. Yet the very fact of contestation shows the slipperiness of closure. Thus, these messages also underscore how discourses surrounding Latino identity stem from and are organized by the acknowledgment that labels and labeling are necessary evils for asserting a politically nuanced ethno-racial *character* in the United States. The messages I focus on here document how the labeling process implicates ways of thinking about ethno-racial identity that are locally produced (i.e., in the United States) rather than rooted in the cultures of *origin* even when they draw from long-standing stereotypes about one group or another through mutual or self-ascription. A typical message begins by generally stating the issue: "Do we call ourselves Latino or Hispanic? To some the answer is simple; to others the answer is as complicated as it is abstract. One would think that the question of our identity would already be clarified. Yet the debate continues in politics, educational settings, and in the media: Latino v. Hispanic" (May 5, 1996). The producer of this message goes on to stress the political need for indexing numerical strength. Not without contradiction, he deems *Latino* the most appropriate choice for those who are "conscious-minded," a virtue that goes undefined. By directly addressing his imagined audience, he bolsters the rhetorical impact of his argument on behalf of *Latino*:

> You are a Latino whether or not you speak Spanish or whether or not you choose to acknowledge it. It is how we and other conscious-minded brothers and sisters choose to identify ourselves. It is a term of choice; a choice which often seems to cause heated debate and controversy. . . .
> We should be beyond this; after all, how often does one hear a debate about whether to use African American or Negro? There are more important issues concerning our community; we simply don't have time to argue about what to call ourselves.
>
> But the debate continues . . . and we ask ourselves, what's in a name?
>
> The term "Latino" is not a cultural, but a political term. It is simply impossible to use a single term to describe a group including people as diverse as Cubans, Puerto Ricans, Dominicans, Mexicans, Salvadorians, Costa Ricans, Peruvians, etc. It is necessary, however, to have a name.
>
> Political power in a democratic society, such as the United States, is based on numbers. Agglomeration is necessary in order for us to have a voice in national politics. It is therefore crucial that we agree on a name. But any ol' name will not do. We need a name that invokes pride and awareness of our rich heritage; and most importantly a name that will address all of the facets of who we are as a people. (May 5, 1996)

This participant thus invokes a series of ideological principles and circumstances—choice, the numbers-based nature of democracy, history, and cultural heritage—that he deems are highly valued in the United States as grounds for a name. He discursively mobilizes a folk Weberian analysis by discriminating between cultural and political identities. For minoritized ethnoracial communities in the United States, the political needs to be embodied in labels. Yet, paradoxically, a name is also necessary for Latinos to invoke a common history and culture, thus reinserting culture and homogeneity into the political domain as dimensions intrinsic to identity claims, although it is Latino heterogeneity that requires the umbrella label. I found many invocations of William Shakespeare's "What's in a name?" as a recurrent cliché in these electronic exchanges. Yet Shakespeare's own question foregrounds, rather than resolves, the semiotic ambiguities of signs and essences.

History, be it of Latino national groups or of the labels themselves, was often invoked to legitimate the choice of label. The arguments usually advanced are, by now, *doxa* among many Latinos (Bourdieu 1977). *Hispanic* is a label generated by the US government and operates through ascription rather than native choice, while *Latino* is construed as a native construct emerging within an imagined community of shared colonial history, language, and ancestry, but also of difference (multicultural, multiracial):

> We are eternally linked through our common suffering and oppression under Spanish colonialism and United States imperialism, the Spanish language and our common ancestry. We are truly a multicultural and multiracial people.
>
> In the Caribbean, our African ancestry clearly dominates our music, the food we eat and the way we speak Spanish, just as in Mexico, Central and South America our indigenous ancestry rules. Our heritage is intrinsic to who we are. And the term "Hispanic" does not acknowledge or respect this.
>
> In the 1970's, the Federal Office of Management and Budget (OMB) created the term Hispanic, which they defined as "A person of Mexican, Puerto Rican, Cuban or Central American or other Spanish culture or origin, regardless of race." In the 1980 United States census, the term "Hispanic" was chosen by the government to describe people with Spanish surnames, of Latin American descent. In fact, all federal agencies have adopted the term "Hispanic." Thus, the term "Hispanic" was given to us by the U.S. government, in an attempt to define us. (e-mail message, May 6, 1996)

The historic record, though, is neither that straightforward nor monoglottic. Several scholars have documented that, in the 1960s, Latino activists, militating for enfranchisement and recognition, actually supported the adoption of the term *Hispanic* in the US census.[8] They rejected *Latino,* arguing that it underscored Latino origins in a Euro- and Hispano-centric, highly stratified, Latin America. (This argument is strategically inverted in another message, below, vis-à-vis "Hispanic.")

To make matters more ambiguous, *Latino* may also be traced to nineteenth-century French efforts to counter Anglo-American, German, and Russian hegemony over the hemisphere. By constructing an oppositional identity subsuming Romance language–speaking nations into a supranational block that could claim historical, linguistic, and sociocultural continuity with the Roman Empire and its founding "tribes," the French attempted to constitute themselves as a hemispheric force in the Americas. Michel Chevalier, French economist, politician, and promoter of the unfortunate French intervention in Mexico under Napoleon III in the 1860s, is often credited with this coinage:

> Our European civilization has a twofold source, the Roman people and the Germanic tribes. . . . These two branches, Latin and German, reappear in the New World. South America, like Southern Europe, is Catholic and Latin. North America belongs to the Protestant and Anglo-Saxon population. . . . Both occupy in Europe and in America, by land and by sea, admirable outposts and excellent positions around that imperturbable Asia into which it is their object to force their way. But during the last age [i.e., the nineteenth century], the superiority which formerly belonged to the Latin family has passed into the hands of the Teutonic race, owing partly to the energy of England in the Old World and its sons in the New, and partly to the loosening of the old moral and religious ties among the Latin nations. . . . The people of Latin stock must not, however, stand idle in the coming struggle, or the case will go against them by default. An admirable opportunity offers them the chance to regain their lost rank. (Chevalier 1961, 6–7)

While imperial, Eurocentric, and hegemonic in tone—and although *Latin* contemporaneously emerged locally—Chevalier anticipated a state of relations that is tellingly close to our own contemporary global order. More importantly, whether he actually originated *Latino* or not, his historic intervention, along with 1960s Latino activism in the following century, complicates the received history about the origin of *Latino* that these electronic exchanges perpetuate.[9] At least one other participant in these electronic exchanges challenged pro-Latino arguments by invoking a similar origin history, although attributing it to "the French King (one of the Louis' [*sic*]) [who] wanted to get his hands on Mexico" (February 13, 1997).

To cap the historical argument, the author of the message I have noted assigns sets of oppositional attributes to each label, playing into general stereotypes encompassing what he assumes are (should be?) preferred and not preferred ideological stances and values among Latino groups. IPR has a well-grounded history of progressive and radical advocacy; supporting *Latino* is consonant with this history as are the stereotypes that are invoked to support it. Progressive values become metonymically embodied in the (allegedly) natively produced Latino label:

> The term "Hispanic" is generally preferred by Cubans in Florida. It is rejected in California, where the terms Chicano and Latino are used. In New York City, both Latino and Hispanic are common. In an article printed in the *New York Times,* Earl Shorris . . . states, "Latino and Hispanic are the left and the right. . . . Democrats are generally Latinos, Republicans are Hispanic." Whites who support English Only laws and oppose bilingual education prefer Hispanic.
>
> In the *Random House Dictionary of the English Language* Unabridged Edition (1976) "Hispanic" is defined as "derived from the people, speech, or culture of Spain or Portugal; often Latin America." It is not only important for us to understand what the term really means but the political and social implications the terms suggests. . . . [It] overidentifies with Spanish colonization. . . . "Latino" refers to all people of Latin American origin and descent born in the western hemisphere irrespective of race, language, or culture. It does not refer to people of Spanish, Portuguese, Filipino, or Cape Verdean origin. Those that are in favor of the use of Hispanic, claim that Latino is the Spanish word for Latin, thus encompassing various nationalities such as the French, the Italian, and the Spanish, "whose culture and language descended from Latin." This is not an acceptable argument. The term "Latino" is a generic term derived from Latino Americano. Granted, Latino is a misnomer. It is, however, the best alternative to using a term that implies inferiority.
>
> Finally, Latino is an inclusive term which best describes our diverse national origins. The use of the term *Latino* promotes a pan-national consciousness, which enforces the unity necessary for us to liberate ourselves and our communities. It rejects white terminology and our past Spanish colonization. It invokes political consciousness and cultural awareness and pride. Now why would anyone prefer to refer to themselves as anything else? Eventually, the term *Hispanic* will be buried in our collective psyche. History tells us that positivity and progress always wins [*sic*] out. (May 5, 1996)

Time and space are thus invoked and reworked to sustain preordained representations about each label. Stereotypes about different Latino nationalities metonymically sustain each label's meaning: Florida Cubans—stereotypically white, middle class, well educated, ideologically desirable for their propaganda value in the Cold War, Republican, model minority—allegedly prefer *Hispanic.* California Chicanos—working class, brown, progressive, deprived, oppressed—opt for *Latino.* Ethno-racial spaces are geopolitically and ideologically homogenized, with the possible exception of New York City, whose acknowledged heterogeneity seemingly mystifies labeling choices.

However forcefully presented, these arguments are neither fully cohesive nor coherent. Yet individuals and groups are invested in [re]producing these stereotypes as normative and "naturalizing" strategies that will provide closure and solve powerlessness. The labeling controversy, these Listserv participants argue, needs to be resolved to reap the benefits of solid numbers, critical mass, and, thus, political primacy.

Significantly, contrary to what these representational strategies imply, the Latino National Political Survey (de la Garza et al. 1992) was then documenting that an overwhelming majority of Latinos preferred the national term of origin as the identity of choice—Puerto Rican, Colombian, Mexican, and so on. The survey also showed that more people of Mexican descent—predominant in the West and Southwest—preferred *Hispanic* than did other groups. While survey data present their own set of problems, they are, nevertheless, indicative of general trends. Most importantly, these survey findings coincide with the identity preferences that I have observed and experienced in my own life and research: most Latinos primarily identify with the national term of identity and contextually draw upon the umbrella label to comply with institutional requirements, for political coalition and mobilization, or simply for referential economy. The umbrella terms are, more often than not, acknowledged and deployed for their political and institutional potential rather than for their sociocultural or historic resonance, or even any kind of ideological weight in the oppositional terms in which they appear in these debates.

Other subsequent survey data do not necessarily bear out the author's expectations that *Latino,* as a native term, has the historic edge as the label of choice. In 2000, *Hispanic Magazine* commissioned yet another survey that documented a preference for the term *Hispanic,* but in such contested terms that the magazine's editors concluded what I myself pose here: the difficulty, even potential impossibility, of closure to the label issue.[10] Yet the labels' ideological associations and attributions persist: the magazine editors speculate that since the survey drew on voters' lists, their respondents were more likely to be assimilated, well-off, educated, and, thus, conservative. This reinserts common stereotypes concerning Latinos, but also an assumption at the core of identity constructs in the United States: that wealth, success, and education mark assimilation or acculturation and generate an ideologically conservative mindset while poverty, exclusion, privation, oppression, and alterity are radicalizing. Note the claim that Republicans and English-only gringos support *Hispanic*. Latino stereotypes thus converge with equally stereotypical national myths of inclusion and belonging, the American Dream, upward mobility, the Protestant ethic, civic participation, and the assimilationist power of material success.

A friend of mine used to claim, half facetiously, that the problem with stereotypes is that they hold a kernel of truth, a statement that informs my argument here: These strategies metonymically draw on essentialized sociocultural elements and acquire a problematic aura of apparent veracity. These characterizations further reify the labels by imbuing them with fixed, metaphoric entailments. The hegemonic assumption subsists that the numerical increase among Latinos mechanistically correlates with empowerment, not just on sheer numerical strength, but also because the United States is allegedly becoming Latinized, as the author of the following message argues (even harangues) for the benefit of an imaginary non- or anti-Latino reader.[11]

Since the 1960's persons of Latin American descent have become an increasingly important part of the country's population. In the early 21st century, Latinos will become the largest so-called minority group. . . . Whether you welcome, resist, or are indifferent to the change, Latino individuals, groups, and concerns will contribute to the shaping of our common future within your lifetime and even more within that of your children.

The integration of Latinos into the national mainstream will require a number of major adjustments—some pleasant, some difficult. One of the most immediate is simply determining what to call the large heterogeneous population and its various subgroups. One or two nationwide terms are essential for easy reference on political, economic, and other key issues. The new terms are not simply shallow labels. They represent new identities in the public and personal realm for the individuals and groups who either adopt the terms or have them applied to them. (December 17, 1996)

Latino numbers thus loom over mainstream Americans, who need to consider that Latino ascendance requires new modes of naming and of interaction. Everyone needs to adopt and use the appropriate label:

Many Americans, though, are confused about what is politically or culturally correct in the new terminology. Should they call someone a Hispanic or a Latino? Are they dealing with a Chicano or a Mexican American? What about Puerto Ricans, Haitians, Central Americans, and people from South America or even Spain? Most people have already faced the dilemma. Should I risk the embarrassment or even the ire of a friend or a stranger by using a term that he or she may judge as ignorant or racist on my part? Where to go for help? There are no easy guides in the library and no one has though[t] of setting up a hot line.

Let us take a look at the broader terms of identification. Hispanic has traditionally been used in a neutral sense by Puerto Ricans and Cubans on the East Coast to refer to themselves. The term Hispanic, however, also has political and class implications. . . . Politically, the term has become identified with the establishment. It is widely used by HUPPIES, Hispanic Upwardly Mobile Professionals, who want to integrate themselves into the mainstream and corporate cultures. Hispanic is a non-threatening term and it avoids any negative stereotyping that still might be attached to national-origin labels. Hispanics tend to be politically conservative. If they become unhappy with the status quo, they prefer to work within the system rather than rock the boat. (December 17, 1996)

Conversely (and predictably), *Latino* "is a term adopted by groups primarily in the West and Midwest who reject Hispanic as a colonial imposition by the government. . . . It too has a political charge. Self-identified Latinos are more confrontational than Hispanics and feel that the struggle for equality and opportunity in America [sic] is far from over. Latinos know that rocking the boat is the other side of the American way" (December 17, 1996). Attributing *Hispanic* to East Coast Puerto Ricans and Cubans and *Latino* to groups in the West and Midwest operates as a coded reference to historic bicoastal tensions between Mexican Americans and Puerto Ricans as the two largest—and pioneer—groups among Latinos. These tensions were particularly evident in the late 1950s and early 1960s, when assimilationist and nationalist factions within each group clashed with each other. Invoking the conservative-progressive correlation invidiously characterizes internally heterogeneous nationalities as ideologically monolithic, exemplifying how the political cohesion that adopting an umbrella label pursues is diminished by negative ascriptions through veiled historical allusion. There is subtle gendering in the confrontational and combative stance that allegedly characterizes *Latino* supporters: supporters of *Hispanic* are represented as politically complacent, silent, passive. Such stereotyping provides non-Latinos with negative ascriptions for different Latino nationalities that are legitimated because they are being produced by Latinos themselves:

> So what does a culturally and politically sensitive American [*sic*] who is not of Latin American descent do with all this information? Apply it carefully. If you are talking to someone who—more often than not— looks European and is wearing corporate stripes, he or she is probably a Hispanic of Argentinian, Spanish, or Chilean descent. They could also be of Mexican or Puerto Rican descent but of the middle class or upwardly mobile. If you are at a union rally, and most of the brothers and sisters are Brown, they probably identify as Latinos, Chicanos, and Boricuas. If you have any doubts, wait to see what they call themselves. They may prefer an identity based on the nation of origin. The term Creole, for example, is used by Haitians. If you still cannot tell what someone wants to be called, then do not be afraid to ask. They still would prefer this to being mislabeled. (December 17, 1996)

It is harder to document support for the term *Hispanic*. IPR's support for progressive ideological positions fosters the self-selection and participation of *Latino* advocates, perhaps with a chilling effect upon others' ability to express oppositional views. The exchange of electronic messages can be liberating, but these networks reach an unknown audience, and expressing minority views exposes one to strangers. The kinds of entailments that these exchanges ascribe to *Hispanic,* within this progressive electronic context, restrain dialogue. Nevertheless, several respondents agreed that

> the term Latino is not any better than Hispanic. . . . This kind of debate (unless there is a really good reason) tends to be a waste of time which could be better spent promoting the welfare of Hispanics in more concrete ways. Not to say that I am opposed to political correctness or to changing our use of language when it is politically advantageous. . . . [G]ive me a REALLY good reason for using Latino instead of Hispanic. Otherwise, I will think it is a hypersensitive reaction and a waste of time. (February 13, 1997)

For these participants, each of the umbrella labels anchors boundaries of political inclusion and exclusion. They need to be exploited for their currency as viable terms that index preferred ideological stances. As Félix Padilla (1985) argued, Latinos are a prime example of the viability of consciously claiming a multiplicity of overlapping identities. Yet, the specious distinctions established between *Latino* and *Hispanic* redraw boundaries of exclusion among certain nationalities, classes, regions, political ideologies, even genders, re-inscribing hierarchy into intra-Latino relations and perpetuating the very divisiveness that the pragmatic umbrella labels are meant to address.

Asymmetry, Pragmatism, and Identity Construction

In sum, these electronic exchanges document that, despite consensus among Latinos communities for the need (even fostered desire) for strategic essentializing by clustering under an umbrella label, each of the two potential labels is differentially defined and assigned truth value as *actual* embodiments of assumed—and irreconcilable—ideological distinctiveness. The labels acquire the constitutive aura of an authentic folk spirit that should characterize Latinos, carrying a semiotic sediment of differential value, fragmenting the group, informing movements toward collective mobilization, and perpetuating essentializing definitions of Latinidad in the United States.

As Lynn Stephen (2001, 54) argues, strategic essentializing has been critiqued and identity categories have been interrogated, seemingly rendering debates about them superfluous. Yet, as she points out, identity remains a significant concept for many grassroots social movements. Quoting Stuart Hall (1996), she supports thinking about identity as a de-totalized and deconstructed form, and the process of identification as a contingent project of construction that is never completed: "Identification is, then, a process of articulation, a suturing, an over-determination not a subsumption. . . . [I]t operates across difference, [entailing] discursive work, the binding and marking of symbolic boundaries, the production of 'frontier-effects'" (in Stephen 2001, 54).

The construction of Latino identi*ties*—as I prefer it—is not generated in a historic or sociocultural vacuum, obviously, but shaped by the dominant ideological context of the United States. As many have stressed, contact and interaction foster the production of ethno-racial identities (Barth [1969] 1998; John Comaroff 1992, 1996) as indices for sociocultural difference.[12] But the process is fraught with ambiguities and contradictions.

Ethno-racial labels are intrinsic to the work of ethnicity in the classic Barthian sense, as indices of boundary construction and maintenance among culturally differentiated groups. As Barth ([1969] 1998) classically argued, ethnic boundaries persist in spite of interethnic contact and interaction, the interdependence of ethnic groups, and flow across ethnic boundaries. Latinos in the United States have become a prime example of this phenomenon, maintaining a sense of sociocultural difference for generations that has been exacerbated by their structural exclusion from the mainstream by a dominant discourse that sets up an Anglo-American sociocultural majority as the identity standard for the nation (Horsman 1981). Labels are meant to signal an assumed identity for public recognition and legitimation within this established structural order. They signify precisely through their strategic mobilization to mark an in-group membership directed to constitute and represent a lived-in experiential reality.

Yet, as John Comaroff (1992, 1996) argued, ethno-racial identity is not produced within level playing fields but in situations of asymmetrical power relations rooted in specific historic contexts. Under historic conditions and relations of inequality, identity labels are expressions of sociocultural difference, but also markers of subordination within local hierarchies that are naturalized as intrinsic to a group's sociocultural identity, shaping its position within the local political economy and establishing the group's subject condition vis-à-vis dominant groups. To claim identity markers as core components of one's personal and collective identity amounts, in practice, to mobilizing the very same hegemonic constructs and attributions that, for many in a given society's dominant groups, mark individuals and communities as subordinate subjects. Labeling and strategic essentializing, for that matter, carry with them the potential for the unintended consequence of contributing to the reproduction of a group's status quo of inequality rather than transcending it.

For analytical productivity, the process of identity construction that is indexed through ethnic labeling needs to be localized and historicized. This is particularly important when dealing with identity processes in the United States, where an aura of exceptionalism surrounds identity construction, especially under the arguable ascendance of a multiculturalist discourse as a defining criterion of the nation that constitutes its society as historically built upon immigration yet struggles to address the very visible presence of racialized constituencies whose historical path has been marked by marginalization and whose everyday experiences are imbued with the discomforts that such marking still brings.

Conclusion

As I point out above, anthropology has the theoretical and methodological potential to address these politics of identity, recognition, and representation by documenting and analyzing what Sally Engle Merry (2003, 67) calls "the active making of culture, society, and institutions and the grounding of this action in specific places and moments." Though I have only (very) generally historicized and localized the labeling conundrum among Latinos in the United States, I have attempted to document what labels entail. Through oppositionality and differential valuing, those who debate over the terms *Hispanic* and *Latino,* to my mind, simply stratify them by rendering one better or more authentic than the other, rather than acknowledge identity as a manifold phenomenon. Ironically, both labels are ideologically and historically rooted in Occidentalist processes of identity construction and in an ongoing history of colonialism and trans-hemispheric intervention. The master narrative contained by an ideology of choice curiously de-historicizes these labels while claiming their historic rootedness, authenticity, and validity.

As Suzanne Oboler (1995) argued, debates over the labels are very much of a red herring, divisive and enervating, which articulate with subtle neo-colonial strategies of hegemonic control. Yet, the nationalist context of the United States requires—even rewards—minoritized groups that engage in typification and self-reification as means toward recognition and inclusion into the ethno-racial array that currently constitutes the *new* imagined multicultural polity. Labeling is not a corrective for sustained structural inequalities, nor are these debates really amenable to tidy closure among such a diverse, complex, and rich identity group as Latinos and, for that matter, other ethno-racial communities that diversify the United States.

Too many years ago, having coffee in New York City with a couple of Latino acquaintances, I was spouting off about one of my pet peeves: the co-optation of *America* and *American* by people from the United States as their term of identity. One of them dismissed me: "Why should *we* care? It's still the name of some dead Italian guy! Me, I'm Peruvian, and that's what I call myself. Let them keep their stupid European name!"

By Way of an Epilogue

In May 2009, President Barack Obama nominated US Appeals Court justice Sonia Sotomayor, a New York City–born Puerto Rican to the US Supreme Court. This constituted an ostensible gesture and acknowledgment of a Latino seat on the court. Yet what many would have considered a benchmark for the nation's politics of identity and of recognition also raised oppositional positions and opinions. The National Institute for Latino Policy (NILP), IPR's current reincarnation, soon enough circulated a column that the *Los Angeles Times* published June 1, 2009. Bylined by one of the newspaper's regular contributors, Gregory Rodríguez (2009), the piece, titled "The Generic Latino: What does the nomination of Sonia Sotomayor really say?," challenges the coalescing power of *Latino,* invokes the Pew Organization's 2002 survey to reassert that (still!) Latinos harken to national identity categories and not the umbrella label, and challenges the adequacy of Sotomayor's nomination as politically significant for Mexican Americans.

Claiming that praise for the nomination as a Latino achievement comes from media and political elites (which go undefined), Rodríguez draws on the arguments of another *Los Angeles Times* columnist, Frank del Olmo, to position Mexican American hegemony and exceptionalism. Based on the reiteration of the numbers argument, they agree, supporting or identifying with the Latino label simply disempowers Mexican Americans because the label allows other, less numerous Latino groups to draw on their numerical strength for political purposes. Both imply and impute deliberate opportunism to all other Latinos. In this sense, they also imply, Mexican Americans should not celebrate Sotomayor's nomination. On the contrary, "because the media and the political elites make no distinctions among Latino groups, Mexican Americans may find themselves waiting a very long time for one of their own to be nominated to the Supreme Court" (Rodríguez 2009). What obviously comes to mind is whether such an article would have been published or the argument even been made if Sotomayor had been of Mexican origin. Suffice it to say that after it circulated over NILP's Listserv, subscribers, self-identifying as members of different national Latino communities, duly reacted and responded to these arguments. But that would be the topic for another chapter.

Acknowledgments

A longer version of this chapter began a very long time ago, in 1998, as a presentation at a symposium on the invention of Latin America, organized by my colleague Jeannine Routier-Pucci, who, as Michel Chevalier's translator, brought his work to my attention and asked me to address the *Latino* versus *Hispanic* debate for its intriguing possibilities, for which I thank her. I am also grateful to the symposium participants for their comments and suggestions. I also thank my husband, Frederic W. Gleach, for his ideas and contributions, including his proposition that the appropriation of *American* could perhaps be addressed by adopting "USers" as a particularly adept national label, given the society's nativist orientations.

Notes

1. As I point out further on, the Spanish- and the English-language versions of these identity labels are sociolinguistically distinct. The labels are most commonly used in US English, especially now, to designate sociocultural components associ-

ated with an ethno-racial community, to distinguish them from what, as Urciuoli (1996) underscores, semiotically constitutes the unmarked identity standard in the United States, still defined, however mythically, as white, English-speaking, male, middle class, and heterosexual. In Spanish, these are supranational labels that complement national ones. This distinction underlies my analyses concerning processes of identity construction specific to the United States vis-à-vis generic terms that are grounded on hemispheric identity designations—for example, *Latino* and *Hispanic* used to designate a shared history and sociocultural circumstances that characterize Latin American societies. Consonant with anthropological thought, translation is at issue here, but ironically related to what I attempt in this piece. Among other issues, I examine how the English labels are differentially legitimated by drawing, to some extent, upon a reconstructed history about their emergence and use in Latin America in spite of the pragmatic, and thus semantic, gap between their English and Spanish versions.

2. After practicing law in Puerto Rico for eleven years, I left for England—at the ideological moment when Ronald Reagan began emasculating public law programs nationally—where I did a certificate in movement analysis at Goldsmiths College's Laban Centre. This led me to New York University, a master's degree in anthropology of dance and human movement, and a PhD in sociocultural anthropology.

3. Also for simplicity, I have opted to use the male form, though much ink has been spilled over the need for de-gendering it. *Latino* is amenable to gender declension by applying Spanish grammatical rules, readily implemented in English by using *Latina* for the female; using *Latino* without qualifying it re-inscribes gender hierarchies. A series of alternative forms address this gap: *Latina/o, Latino/Latina, Latino and Latina,* and *Latin@,* a relatively recent coinage. None of these is very economical for a short piece, though, and *Latin@* may be somewhat unfamiliar, even jarring, for some readers.

4. Merry (2003, 67) best articulates the notion of culture that I believe currently animates our anthropological agenda, as a "more dynamic, agentic, and historicized way of understanding culture."

5. See Nash (1989) for a case study of how redistribution contributes to other hegemonic processes in the United States as a paradoxical strategy for overcoming the inequities and vicissitudes of capital accumulation in an economic system presumably driven by the leveling effects, objectivity, and efficiency of the free market mechanism of capitalist exchange. For Nash, "the structure of redistribution gives vitality to the myths of equal opportunity, of mobility, and of justice" in modern states (1989, 23). In another context, Marable (2000) argues that to transcend race-based politics of identity and achieve true multiculturalism we need to begin by critiquing the structures of power and privilege that characterize the United States as a postindustrialist capitalist society.

6. Shorris (1992, xvi–xvii) provides an early and influential example of the debate's terms and tone. It is invoked in one of the messages I focus on further along.

7. Similar debates concerning the desirability of umbrella labels (pre)occupy

other ethno-racial communities in the United States, but except (perhaps) for the "Native American" versus "American Indian" case, I can think of no other in which the label itself has been so strongly at issue. Asian Americans debate over the desirability of homogenizing themselves and may chafe at discarding national identities, even in the hyphenated ethno-nationalist forms that emerge in the United States (see, e.g., Wu 2002). Or African Americans may debate whether this particular compound label may apply to all immigrants of the African diaspora or is exclusive to those whose ancestors were enslaved. Non-African groups critique the dominant black-white dichotomy as a technique of erasure. But it seems to me that the *Hispanic* versus *Latino* debate is relatively unique.

8. See special issues on Latino identity published by the *Latino Studies Journal* (1991) and *Latin American Perspectives* (1992) that examine and historicize the labeling debates, especially Giménez, López, and Muñoz (1992).

9. See also Gossett (1997), who examines the Teutonic principle of racial superiority so prevalent in much of nineteenth-century United States. Part of its thrust was precisely to counter the reemergence of "Latin" peoples, who could claim historic continuity with the Roman Empire, by portraying Latin imperial culture as tyrannical and less virile than Germanic cultures.

10. A Google search on the debate generates other sources documenting how it is still ongoing, though many have opted for using the two labels interchangeably or in specific contexts: for example, *Hispanic* for institutional, historic, or self-referential usage and *Latino* as general designator.

11. Darder and Torres (1998, 3), among many others, critique this assumption by underscoring that numerical mass in and of itself, without greater structural advancement and consequent sociocultural penetration, is a somewhat equivocal kind of Latinization. I strongly agree. See also the essays in Laó-Montes and Dávila (2001).

12. Sollors (1996) summarizes theories about identity processes specific to the United States from a diversity of disciplines.

II
Decentering the Ethnographic Self

6
"Gone Anthropologist"
Epistemic Slippage, Native Anthropology, and the Dilemmas of Representation
Bernard C. Perley

It all began so innocently. How did a nice self-respecting Native American man working on a career in architecture become an anthropologist?[1] Regarding innocence, don't we all say that when find ourselves mired in existential and, apropos for this chapter, epistemic dilemmas? As for my decision to become an anthropologist, I do have to plead some innocence. I was unaware of how broadly Vine Deloria Jr.'s 1969 publication of his critical essay "Anthropologists and Other Friends" struck a resonant chord in Native American communities across North America. In that essay Deloria states, "Many Indians have come to parrot the ideas of anthropologists because it appears the anthropologists know everything about Indian communities" ([1969] 1988, 82). Not only were Native Americans "parroting" anthropologists, many were "going anthropologist" while pursuing degrees and careers in anthropology. However, what it means to have "gone anthropologist" has changed over time. At first, native anthropology conformed to social, scientific conventions in the pre-Deloria period (before the 1969 essay); then discourses shifted to postcolonial critiques of the discipline during the Deloria period and shifted again to a post-Deloria period (let's call it the "indigenous turn") of global indigenous self-making.[2]

Epistemic Slippage

"Going anthropologist" represents concurrent and seemingly contradictory practices of epistemic discovery—or epistemic slippage. When anthropologists represent Others, they draw from fieldwork experiences as participant observers, which in turn extends their experiences of epistemic slippage.[3] The firsthand accounts of personal experiences become the sources for ethnographic speaking and writing. The practice of representing Others through the authoritative voice of qualified and objective disseminators of Other ways of knowing—be it as professors teaching anthropology classes or through ethnographic accounts—is a practice of slipping into Other systems of knowing. Such slippage is characteristic of the discipline's Enlightenment heritage.[4]

Immanuel Kant conceived of anthropology as a science of humankind that attempts to catalog the acquired knowledge of all the "particulars of different languages and customs" while hoping that such a catalog will be "beneficial to the human community" ([1978] 1996, 5–6). Or, as Johannes Fabian states, "The discipline's origin and motor has been—scandalizing as this may sound these days—the Enlightenment utopia of radical future-oriented modernity, taken as the challenge to understand (and demonstrate) humanity's unity" (2007, 3). The utopian vision of modernity entailed the systematic collection of all the "particulars" of "the human community." It was a "frame of mind of our predecessors who were certain that anthropology had an object which it had found rather than made: primitive (later traditional, premodern, developing) society/culture" (Fabian 2007, 11). The "catalog" took the form of fieldnotes, reports, ethnographies, ethnographic collections, exhibits, displays, and many other forms of representation. While acknowledging the changes the discipline is undergoing, Fabian cautions that the transformations

> seem to have left the agenda of traditional ethnographic subjects of inquiry . . . untouched, notwithstanding important additions such as gender, literacy, material culture, the media, and ecology. Myths and cosmologies, religion and ritual, magic and witchcraft, chieftainship and clans, kinship and alliances, gifts and exchange—all of them persist or are rediscovered as unexpected practices of modernity. Does that mean that anthropology is unreformed in maintaining a metropolitan gaze, an Enlightenment perspective? (2007, 11–12)

Furthermore, Fabian argues that anthropologists "became serious about epistemology, that is, about the specific conditions of producing anthropological knowledge based on empirical work we call, not quite appropriately, ethnography," and that the "literary turn" made us more scientific because it sharpened our awareness of the epistemological significance of presentation and representation" (13–14). Those specific conditions prompt Fabian to argue, "Anthropological practices happen in events and movements. They don't acquire their collective identity from subscribing to a single discourse but from having to face a common predicament: they must let themselves be constituted by facing a world that is non-anthropological" (15). More important for this chapter, Fabian states, "I deeply believe that a realistic view of our discipline must acknowledge that our kind of science is practiced in the presence of other kinds of knowledge production" (15). In short, disciplinary practice is grounded in epistemic slippage, the process of *knowing.*

The presumption that anthropologists are authorized to present and represent Others, or, more radically, to present and represent *as* Others, not only is an uncritical Enlightenment stance of privileging the Western scientific episteme over Other epistemes, but is itself a form of Othering.[5] In summarizing his argument presented in *Time and the Other,* Fabian states:

> Anthropology has its empirical foundation in ethnographic research, inquiries which even hard-nosed practitioners (the kind who liked to think of their field as a scientific laboratory) carry out as communicative interaction. The sharing of time that such interaction requires demands that ethnographers recognize the people whom they study as their coevals. However—and this is where the contradiction arises— when the same ethnographers represent their knowledge in teaching and writing they do this in terms of a discourse that consistently places those who are talked about in a time other than that of the one who talks. (1983, 22)

The discourse places Others not only in another time but also in another place, thereby relegating Other epistemes to secondary status. Does such Othering perpetuate a Manichaean dichotomy between primary and secondary epistemes such that primary epistemes are the at-home knowledge systems that serve as the ground for knowledge production and the secondary epistemes, as the Other epistemes, are waiting to be discovered?[6] What happens when the epistemic stance is inverted? For a native "going anthropologist," will the native episteme invert the knowledge production privilege?[7] What kinds of epistemic slippage must be negotiated when a native goes anthropologist? Does the native lapse into "reason"?[8]

Lapsing into Reason: "Going Anthropologist"

E. E. Evans-Pritchard, in *Witchcraft, Oracles, and Magic among the Azande,* famously recalls witnessing witchcraft on its path. He explains at length that he was able to slip into the native episteme by learning Azande idioms of thought and applying them appropriately. So much so that he states, "I, too, used to react to misfortunes in the idiom of witchcraft, and it was often an effort to check this lapse into unreason" (Evans-Pritchard 1976, 45). This excerpt from an extended paragraph where he claims to have been "thinking black" and "feeling black" is indicative of the epistemic slippage that Evans-Pritchard claims to have successfully negotiated. Slippage, as Evans-Pritchard illustrates, begins when anthropologists introduce themselves to Other epistemologies, and slippage increases as anthropologists engage those other epistemologies. Finally, anthropologists develop a facility to slip into and out of not only Other's way of knowing but anthropology's way as well. What is the value of such slippage? According to Evans-Pritchard, its value rests in the awareness it offers. By engaging other systems of knowing, Evans-Pritchard believes we can come to know ourselves and "our human predicament" (245). Most important, however, alterity is built into epistemic slippage. As Evans-Pritchard observed, he had to "check this lapse into unreason." Not only is alterity acknowledged by Evans-Pritchard, but it is hierarchical. For Evans-Pritchard, Western reason is the privileged system of knowing that serves as the episteme from which epistemic slippage exchange can take place. Epistemic slippage not only describes slippage between systems of knowledge, but is a process that allows anthropologists to "go native." Will that process allow for the same kinds of slippage when a native "goes anthropologist"? The following examples of natives going anthropologist describe the kinds of slippage that native anthropologists had to negotiate during the modernist pre-Deloria period and the postcolonial Deloria period.

The Deafening Modernity of Pre-Deloria Epistemic Slippage

The long history of Native American contributions to anthropology as practiced in North America is as long as the discipline itself. At first, the role of informant was the only possible role Native Americans could play as American anthropology practiced its salvage operations to save what was left of the vanishing race. Ella Deloria is an important example. She worked off and on with Franz Boas to translate George Bushotter's Lakota texts from the mid-1910s to the late 1920s, but she was relegated to the role of an informant. All the while their collaboration required Ella Deloria to learn phonetic transcription and grammatical analysis that would later result in the publication of her *Dakota Texts* ([1932] 2006). Raymond DeMallie praised the text as "the single most important publication on the oral literature of the Sioux" (2006, v). Yet, despite this contribution, Ella Deloria's most important contribution to anthropology was the role of informant. As the late Beatrice Medicine observed, "the role of informant as anthropological reporter creates qualms among Natives who contemplate becoming anthropologists, and it is not surprising that early contributions by Native Americans were primarily in texts on the Native languages and in folklore and mythology" (2001, 4–5). While there were many Native Americans who participated in anthropological research as informants, there were others who were interested in careers in anthropology.

Edward Dozier represents an important case of a native "gone anthropologist." Paul V. Kroskrity characterized Dozier's importance in the following: "In 1949, when Edward P. Dozier ascended the then narrow path up to First Mesa of the Hopi Reservation in northeastern Arizona, he began a remarkable but unappreciated episode in the history of anthropological confrontations with various forms of identity. Dozier, a Tewa Indian from Santa Clara Pueblo in New Mexico, was one of the earliest 'native' anthropologists" (2000, 329–30). As Kroskrity points out, Dozier received his training at a particular period in the discipline's history that promoted a particular ideology toward "field" languages, which thereby constrained Dozier's analysis. Without the benefit of the "experimental moment," the "linguistic turn," or the "reflexive moment" in anthropology, Dozier had to confront the fact that "the appeal of native anthropology lay in its promise of validation of anthropological authority. Native anthropologists knew the cultures they studied as insiders and also acquired the approved methodological sophistication and the endorsed technologies of scientific representation" (343–44). Kroskrity's analysis is a cautionary tale that speaks to the dilemmas in going anthropologist. Dozier had learned the idiom of anthropological practice all too well and had been "deafened" by "his uncritical use of then current ideologies of language and culture contact" (357). In short, despite being "native," he slipped too far into the anthropological episteme. However, "going anthro" presented different dilemmas from the mid-1940s to the early '60s than it did in the late '60s. The 1960s was an important decade that witnessed the dissemination of postcolonial critiques of colonial hegemonies. For natives who wanted to "go anthro," a scathing critique came from Vine Deloria Jr. in his essay "Anthropologists and Other Friends," in his collection *Custer Died for Your Sins* ([1969] 1988).

Postcolonial Ambiguities in Deloria-Period Epistemic Slippage

The late Beatrice Medicine shares her personal account of the dilemma of a native "gone anthro" in her book *Learning to Be an Anthropologist and Remaining "Native"* (2001). Medicine confronts head-on the dilemma of choosing anthropology as a professional career. She begins by stating, "I am a part of the people of my concern and research interests. Sometimes they teasingly sing Floyd Westerman's song 'Here Come the Anthros' (1969) when I attend Indian conferences. The ambiguities inherent in these two roles of being 'anthro' while at the same time remaining a 'Native' need amplification. They speak to the very heart of 'being' and 'doing' in anthropology." She also argues that the popularity of Deloria's "attack" overlooks Deloria's statement about placing his greatest hope for Indian futures "in Congress, the anthropologists, and the churches." Medicine states, "Because the churches and Congress have eroded my faith in the institutions of the dominant society, I shall focus on anthropology. It is, after all, the source of my livelihood" (2001, 3). What dilemmas and what kinds of slippage did Medicine have to negotiate during the Deloria period of Native American postcolonial anthropology?

Medicine recalls her academic training was filled with great ambivalence. She describes her childhood experiences with her aunt Ella Deloria:

> Aunt Ella's participation in a world far removed from Standing Rock Reservation where she lectured "about Lakota" presented a model I found attractive. Much later, I attended a lecture by a physical anthropologist (now deceased) who asked, "Will all the persons in the room with shovel-shaped incisors please indicate?" This experience and being used as an informant (together with a Swedish student) in a "Personality and Culture" course raised many questions in my mind about becoming an anthropologist. Would it be possible to retain dignity as a Native while operating in roles other than informant? Would anthropological training alienate me from my people? Would it affect my marriage? (Medicine 2001, 7)

Those questions were partly answered by Medicine's native experience as a Lakota:

> I am pleased that my father was sufficiently farsighted to enroll his children as full-bloods. It has made my life and acceptance on reservations and reserves easier. I was also appreciative that my father took me to tribal council meetings when I was young. It was in this context that I was remembered and asked to translate for a Lakota elder, a non-English speaker, in the Wounded Knee trials in 1974. Such was the socialization for modes of Lakota adaptation and persistence and the demanding and expected behavior of a Native (anthro—and female at that). (Medicine 2001, 7)

Medicine goes on to state, "Being Lakota was seen as the most essential aspect of living. It was from this cultural base that strong individual autonomy was fostered and an equally strong orientation to the group's welfare and interest was instilled" (2001, 7). This statement speaks to her privileging a Lakota episteme that serves as the "cultural base" from which she can slip into an anthropological episteme. Unlike Dozier, Medicine places her community's welfare and interest first. This allows her to recall Dozier's thoughts on natives "gone anthro," "The late Ed Dozier, a Pueblo anthropologist, once commented that many Native Americans 'went into anthropology as a means of helping their people' (summer 1948). This suggests strong interest in the application of anthropological knowledge and is tied to the Native idea of education, no matter in what field, as a means of alleviating the problems and providing self-help among Native groups" (Medicine 2001, 4–5).

For both Dozier and Medicine, anthropology is conceived as an application that can alleviate problems and provide self-help for native peoples. To that end, Medicine recounts her efforts to teach native students, work alongside native researchers, translate research terminology into English vernacular, and work as a teacher-counselor. This last "application" of her anthropological training is directed to promote Native American students to explore their own research agendas and work in their communities. "A number of these students, who have absorbed anthropological theories and research methods, are working on areas of concern to our people" (Medicine 2001, 12). Medicine concludes her chapter by stating, "I know I went into anthropology to try and make living more fulfilling for Indians" (14), and she has certainly accomplished that through her mentorship with young "native anthros" at American Anthropological Association meetings. She also stated that she attempted to make "anthropological application meaningful to Indians and others" (14), and she has certainly set the stage for meaningful conversations toward that goal.

Limiting Slippage

Epistemic slippage as a process of *knowing* others is a strategy used by anthropologists trying to slip into native systems of knowledge and by natives trying to slip into anthropological systems of knowledge. Significantly, and paraphrasing Fabian, all knowledge production "is practiced in the presence of other kinds of knowledge production" (Fabian 2007, 15). The key is recognizing that some systems of knowledge production are accorded greater value than others.

Evans-Pritchard clearly recognizes that some degree of "going native" is required if anthropologists are to understand the communities in which they work. Yet he is also clear that a Western social scientific episteme is an important ground to check his lapses into unreason. There is a constant danger that his "reason" will give way to naïve accounts of events as observed in daily life. His slippages into "thinking black" and "feeling black" were convenient for understanding, but slipping back into "reason" would allow him to represent native understanding (albeit naïve) for audiences back home. To convey an authoritative voice, the anthropologist must not slip too far.

For Native Americans the dangers of "going anthropologist" presented some fear of contamination. For Dozier, his perceived justification for becoming an anthropologist was his desire to find some application of anthropological knowledge that would help solve problems and provide self-help for native communities. Kroskrity argues that Dozier slipped too far into the anthropology episteme and was "deafened" by his professional training. Medicine reiterates Dozier's motivation for engaging the anthropology episteme as a means to make "anthropological application meaningful to Indians and others" (2001, 14). Medicine's mentorship of young Indian anthropologists during the Deloria period of postcolonial critique was important in providing more room for slippage into anthropology epistemes.

For both anthropologists and natives, shifting from colonial to postcolonial practices of knowledge production and subsequent politics of representation has rendered antecedent epistemic grounds much more slippery. How have the terms of slippage changed for the native going anthropologist in the new millennium, where discourses of postcoloniality and decolonization have given way to globalization and indigenous cosmopolitanisms? How have native anthropological representations responded to the new terms' slippage?

The Dilemmas of Representation in Post-Deloria Epistemic Slippage

The first decade of the twenty-first century has been a productive period of articulating new quandaries, queries, and practices for anthropologists and anthropology. Be it postulating an "emergent" anthropology (M. Fischer 2003, 2009) or working as an "outsider within" (Harrison 2008), designing an "anthropology of the contemporary" (Rabinow and Marcus 2008) or reversing the anthropology gaze (Ntarangwi 2010), these critical discourses continue a long tradition of disciplinary recalibration that has been variously described as "reinventing anthropology" (Hymes [1969] 1974), "recapturing anthropology" (Fox 1991), "experimental moments" in anthropology (Marcus and Fischer 1986), and "decolonizing anthropology" (Harrison 1991). Significantly, the start of the new millennium has also prompted critical discourses on globalization, inequalities, and commodification (M. Kirsch 2006; Abélès 2010; Comaroff and Comaroff 2009), where the once imagined, traditional, bounded, and colonial subjects have become postcolonial interlocu-tors (S. Kirsch 2006), cotemporaneous (Fabian 2007) and transnational as well as transcultural (Forte 2010) in both global and local domains.

In this post-Deloria era, some of the dilemmas of going anthropologist have changed while some continuities remain. Native Americans who chose anthropology as a career continue to benefit from a discursive and practical space from which to work as carved out by native anthropologist forebears. Continuities, such as the commitment to finding applications from the disci-pline's knowledge systems supportive of community self-determination and engaging in meaningful dialogue, continue to resonate with native anthro-pologists. The continuing dilemmas lie at the heart of representation. Aca-demic requirements compel native anthropologists to publish texts that serve the discipline's conditions of merit, but all too often those texts are too spe-cialized in terminology, research focus, and methods of dissemination to be of practical use for the communities from which those academic texts derive. From the perspective of the communities, such studies and scholarly texts are inaccessible and of limited value to the community. Such texts provide evi-dence that the native has slipped too far into the anthropology episteme. In other words, the native has "gone anthropologist." On the other hand, texts that communities understand and draw significant benefit from may not be accepted by the discipline because they lack scholarly merit. The dilemma facing native anthropologists is determining how far one can slip from one episteme into another and maintain balance, being native and anthropologist simultaneously. One strategy is to produce two sets of texts, one set for the anthropology discipline and one set for the community. Unfortunately, the two sets of texts are often separated from one another. Can there be a middle space where both epistemes may come together to promote mutual slippage toward each other's episteme? As a native anthropologist I offer a possible so-lution to this representational dilemma.

Alternative Epistemic Space

As a member of Tobique First Nation and an anthropologist, I have grappled with the dilemmas of representing the important issues and consequences of Maliseet language endangerment to both anthropological and Native American audiences. To accommodate the discipline's merit requirements, I have published peer-reviewed texts such as articles (Perley 2006), book chap-ters (Perley 2009, 2011a, 2012a, 2012b), and a monograph (Perley 2011b). To satisfy the community's need for practical solutions to prevent Maliseet lan-guage loss, I have produced illustrations for Maliseet texts; made artistic pro-ductions linking language and landscape; and designed, wrote, and produced a graphic novel reintegrating Maliseet language with Maliseet oral tradition and contemporary issues. These works will not meet academic, peer-reviewed merit requirements. These are two different sets of texts for two different audiences reflecting two different epistemes. Is it possible to bring the two epistemes together onto a common ground from which the members of the two epistemes can understand one another by slipping into a common epistemic world? My solution to this quandary was to bring the two audiences into an alternative epistemic space.

An important first step was to rethink ethnographic representation. In my dual position as a scholar working on language endangerment and language revitalization issues and as a native who has personal experience with the trauma associated with language loss and cultural alienation (Perley 2009, 2011b, 2012a), my academic texts seemed inadequate in conveying the visceral emotive experience when grappling with language and cultural oblivion. I sought to produce an alternative ethnography that graphically represented the trauma of language death, the desperation of language maintenance, and the optimism of language revitalization. The graphic ethnography (fig. 6.1) was presented to my colleagues, and they received it with appreciation. However, their perception of the work was through their experiences viewing artwork rather than viewing ethnography. Undeterred, I produced additional graphic ethnographies that reintegrated language, stories, and landscape, and some of the ethnographies created alternative ethnographic spaces (fig. 6.2). Figure 6.2 is a photograph of a 360-degree primordial landscape with twelve verses of a Maliseet prayer of "giving thanks." The space integrates an oral traditional story with a construction of a particular point on the reservation and the incorporation of the Maliseet prayer in the Maliseet language. The installation can be experienced by anthropologists as an ethnographic space, while members of the Maliseet community can experience it as a sacred space. Most important, both audiences can experience the installation as ethnographic and sacred space simultaneously. As these various pieces of my graphic ethnography were completed, it became important to assemble the graphic work into an alternative ethnographic space that integrated my textual ethnographies with my graphic ethnographies.

In the fall of 2008 I organized an exhibit of creative work that addressed issues of Maliseet language endangerment, Maliseet cosmogony, and Maliseet "texts." Included in the exhibit were illustrations (as well as text) for the Maliseet prayer of giving thanks; my visual essay on language death, language maintenance, and language revitalization (fig. 6.1); a twenty-eight-foot-diameter installation of the Maliseet thanksgiving prayer (fig. 6.2); the original artwork and text of a graphic novel; and a graphic display of an essay

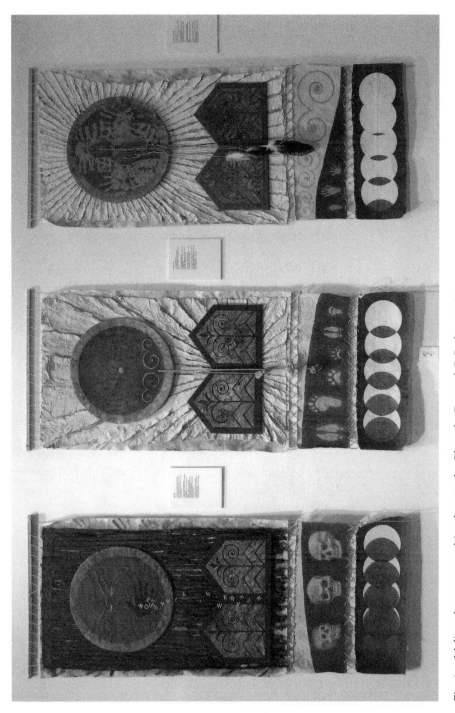

Fig. 6.1. Maliseet language graphic ethnography. Photo by Bernard C. Perley, 2008.

Fig. 6.2. Maliseet alternative ethnographic space. Photo by Bernard C. Perley, 2008.

on intertexuality in Maliseet storytelling. The collected works were gathered and displayed under the title "Journeys in Spirited Landscapes" (fig. 6.3). The collected works were presented in a university gallery space and arranged to prompt viewers (readers) to see (read) the connections between the textual and graphic ethnographies.[9] My goal was to represent my collected ethnographies of Maliseet language death, maintenance, and revitalization as one intertextual, intermediated, and interdiscursive event so that the participants approached the exhibit as a graphic, spatial, and experiential ethnography. More important, the ethnographic texts are simultaneously representations of epistemic slippage as well as invitations to engage in epistemic slippage by immersing visitors in an alternative epistemic space.

My ethnography is about two hundred pages of specialized vocabularies, theories, and analyses that will be of interest to academics and perhaps some members of the community (Perley 2011b). Along with my other publications, it will serve as a marker of "merit," indicating that this native has "gone anthropologist" enough to satisfy the requirements of the discipline. However, over two hundred pages of "pure reason" were not enough to capture the visceral impact of the tragedy of language death and subsequent cultural loss that I suffered as a child. Nor will it adequately represent the potential

Fig. 6.3. The *exhibit* as an alternative epistemic space. Photo by Bernard C. Perley, 2008.

trauma the community faces with Maliseet language and cultural loss. The text is ill suited to convey the vitality and beauty of language, oral traditions, and landscape that is interwoven into an integrated Maliseet cosmogony. My solution was to create alternative texts that conveyed the emotive force of language and cultural loss. Furthermore, the spatial and experiential ethnography created an alternative space for experiencing my representation of Maliseet epistemic space in its textual, graphic, spatial, and integrated complexity. The spatial ethnography provided the visitor an opportunity for multimodal slippage into Maliseet language, culture, and landscape. Rather than invite the viewers to "read" Maliseet ethnography, it invited the viewers to experience Maliseet ethnography by creating a space into which they could slip into a Maliseet world that I conceived, constructed, and re-presented.

Epistemic Slippage and Emergent Representations

In *Anthropological Futures,* Michael Fischer argues, "Cultural analysis has become increasingly relational, plural, and aware of its own historicity: its openness to the historical moments in which it is put to work makes it capable, like experimental systems, of creating new epistemic things" (2009, 46). Further-

more, "cultural analysis involves the work of interpretation. It requires chari-
table readings to get the 'native point of view' in a form that natives recognize as right and to elicit the context for the work of analysts, native or
otherwise" (48). Fischer's fascination with "synthetic and systems biologies
and regenerative medicine" as experimental systems for understanding "biological interactions" prompts him to suggest that "emergent cultural models
must handle similar complex relations, transcending simplistic oppositions"
(44). The opposition between native and anthropologist is never simple, as
Deloria's, Dozier's, Medicine's, and my own experiences illustrate. Nor were
such oppositions static. Going anthropologist is a mode of epistemic slippage
that has changed and continues to change according to the contingencies of
emergence (Perley 2009).[10] Epistemic slippage, then, although it may seem
to echo Fischer's characterization of culture—"as a methodological concept
or tool of inquiry, [it] might be best understood in terms of its historically
layered growth of specifications and differentiations, refined into a series of
experimental systems that . . . allow new realities to be seen and engaged as
its own parameters are changed" (Fischer 2009, 3)—focuses on agency rather
than system, on process rather than structure. To what purpose do anthropologists engage in epistemic slippage? Fischer argues that "it is a form of
knowledge, ever evolving, urgently needed today" (49). The experimental
systems approach to epistemic slippage is important as a system that produces
"epistemic things" from emergent cultural "models."

But, as Fabian argues,

> historically and theoretically, our subject matter (an object *made* at least
> as much as found) has been peoples we represented as an Other. We
> may regret and lament the fact, as I do, that this critical insight is in
> constant danger of evaporating in clouds of fashionable talk about
> "othering" . . . but this should not make us abandon a vision of agency
> that is in essence dialectical. Anthropology may be what anthropolo-
> gists do (as someone from my teachers' generation once defined the dis-
> cipline); but anthropologists do what they do by doing it with, perhaps
> sometimes onto, others. (Fabian 2007, 5)

For anthropological knowledge to grow, Fabian argues that it requires a dialectical exchange with Other knowledge systems. Anthropological agency,
then, is based on

> our claims to validity on fieldwork, on direct interaction with those
> whom we study. Ethnographic authority may be said to rest on "hav-

ing been there," that is, on our presence. But what would our presence count if it were not matched by the presence of those whom we study? Neither presence, ours or theirs, is a natural, physical fact (nor is inter-subjectivity as a condition of communicative interaction); it must be achieved and it is always precarious. (Fabian 2007, 5)

Fabian's insight that presence and intersubjectivity themselves are not natural or physical facts can be extended to experimental systems and cultural analyses. "Doing anthropology" implies agency, and that implies engagements with other agents. Fabian states, "What enables us to communicate with and represent other practices is not (only) our command of contents, which count as data or as our findings; it is our ability to converse with knowers, and that conversation includes confronting each other, arguing with each other, negotiating agreements, stating disagreements, as well as conceiving common projects" (15).

Both Fischer and Fabian are articulating possible solutions to the dilemmas of engagement and representation for anthropological practices, but they do so from the anthropologists' perspective. How do their programmatic statements address the dilemmas from a native perspective? One answer can be found in the recognition that the opposition between anthropologist and native was never simple and that there have always been anthropologists studying "exotics" at home. American anthropology has a long history of studying Native American communities. Furthermore, many anthropologists trained in anthropology programs in US universities have done and continue to do fieldwork "at home." The slippage between anthropologist and native was always precarious, but more recently the slippage has become more complicated in its directionality as well as the degrees of accepted slippage. Equally complex are the emergent representations of such slippage.

Epistemic slippage, as a process of knowing others, is the contested ground from which ethnographic representations emerge. The juxtaposition of a set of texts for anthropologists and a set of texts for the communities from which (and for whom) the texts are produced make possible the rekeying (Fischer 2009) of how we think of ethnographies. The standard model of disciplinary merit, the ethnographic text, need not limit the kinds of representation we as anthropologists can produce. Graphic ethnographies can convey other kinds of knowledge and can encourage other kinds of slippage. Assembling the various "texts" into alternative epistemic spaces can enhance slippage between worlds through multimodal slippage. The alternative ethnographic space I propose is the collected and arranged ethnographies produced by an ethnographer and based on the representations of epistemic slippage from working with (as Fabian stated) a community of knowers. It is a public invitation to anthropologists and to natives to evaluate, appreciate, contest, and know something of Other worlds. It is more than a collection of ethnographies or an "epistemic thing." The space represents ethnography as *process*. As process it is a catalyst for epistemic slippage. And, in turn, epistemic slippage provides the critical ground for our future in anthropology.

Notes

1. I use the term "Native American" instead of other terms, such as American Indian, First Nations, and aboriginal, to indicate the slipperiness of term "native" as it indexes the semantic particulars between "being native" and "going native."

2. The phrase "native anthropology" has become increasingly complex as the distinctions between natives and anthropologists become increasingly blurred. For this chapter my focus is on Native Americans who find themselves, for one reason or another, pursuing careers in anthropology. Those reasons may, by varying degrees, coincide or diverge from the reasons proffered by other natives. For example, Harrison's postcolonial feminist project (1991, 2008) does not necessarily address the same issues with the same urgency that Native Americans, be they men or women, find as compelling anthropological stances. A more recent example is the "reversed gaze" that Ntarangwi (2010) offers when he does his ethnographic study of American anthropology. Finally, when Americans trained in American institutions pursue field research "at home," should we consider them "native" anthropologists? As Fabian (2007, 5–6) notes, the changing terms of "native anthropology" create more dilemmas when "us" becomes "them."

3. Anthropological Others have a long and difficult history, both in terms of theory and practice, that cannot be adequately addressed in this chapter. "Others" and "othering" and the subsequent inequalities brought into play with such referential descriptors continue to infiltrate the profession's discourses. Johannes Fabian suggests that the concept "sneaked up on anthropology" and that "as a designation of anthropology's object, 'other' (adjective or noun, capitalized or not, singular or plural, with or without quotation marks) did not seem to require more than a common-sense understanding; the term was handy because it was so general and its very vagueness allowed us to keep talking about topics of research while avoiding expressions that had become unsavory as a result of (then) recent decolonization. Savages, primitives, tribal peoples, and the like were disguised as others" (2007, 17–18). Fabian also suggests that the discipline should move away from othering and that "alterity" has been misconceived in anthropology. He insists "that being a stranger or 'exotic' (visibly different) is not a necessary attribute of alterity" (27). Fabian ruminates that the compulsion for othering is "that we (the West, whoever wants to be included in that 'we,' or, for historical and political reasons, belongs to that 'we') seem to require alterity for sustenance in our efforts to assert or understand ourselves" (29). In short, truly, "we" are the "other."

4. I use "slippage" to indicate the changes that define how, when, and why we "know" something or anything. To know is not a static proposition. Whatever we may claim to know is always changing with additional experiences that inform that knowledge. Just as semiotic signs incur slippage from one moment to the next, from one context to the next, and from one generation to the next, so too, do our epistemic systems. It is in that sense that I use "slippage."

Immanuel Kant is the perfect spokesperson for the Enlightenment spirit of the anthropology project. In his *Anthropology from a Pragmatic Point of View,* he states,

> A pragmatic anthropology which has been systematically devised and which can be understood by the general reading public (because a reference to examples which can be checked by the reader), has the advantage of that the completeness of headings, under which observed human characteristics of practical consequence has been subsumed, offers many occasions and challenges to the reading public to study each particular characteristic in order to classify it accordingly. Any study of a certain characteristic will attract the attention of specialists in the same area and, because of the unity of the design, they will be integrated into a comprehensive whole. Thus the development of a science which is beneficial to the human community will be furthered." ([1978] 1996, 6)

5. I use "episteme" to differentiate between "knowledge" as a noun and "knowing" as a process. I draw from Foucault as he defines "episteme" in the following:

> I am not concerned, therefore, to describe the progress of knowledge toward an objectivity in which today's science can finally be recognized; what I am attempting to bring to light is the epistemological field, the *episteme* in which knowledge, envisaged apart from all criteria having reference to its rational value or to its objective forms, grounds its positivity and thereby manifests a history which is not that of its growing perfection, but rather of its conditions of possibility; in this account, what should appear are those configurations within the *space* of knowledge which have given rise to the diverse forms of empirical science. (1973, xxii)

The "conditions of possibility" is the critical ground for epistemic slippage. Furthermore, Derrida echoes Foucault with the following: "Before being its object, writing is the condition of the *epistémè*" (1974, 33).

6. Alvin I. Goldman distinguishes primary epistemology as cognitive processes particular to individual epistemology and secondary epistemologies as processes of social epistemology (1986, 4–5). While Goldman's project is focused on the dialectic between individual cognitive epistemologies and social epistemologies, I am interested in articulating the "primary" epistemic field of reference from which anthropologists evaluate the "secondary" epistemic fields of Others. As Fabian (2007) notes, social scientific training is a privileged episteme that "does onto" Other epistemes.

7. What is the native episteme? Philip Deloria suggests that there is a "trickster

ethos" perhaps better characterized as "shape-shifting." Deloria writes, "Attuned to the ethos of tricksters, Indian people shapeshifted from suits to headdresses to buckskins and back to as suited their needs" (2004, 235). This can be said of epistemic shape-shifting as well. Natives can be anthropologists at one point and go back to being natives at another. However, I problematize that position by arguing that I am both at the same time (Perley 2009, 270).

8. While many would credit the Enlightenment for the modern articulation of "reason" and the category "native," it is important to recognize that "reason" and "native" are more historically complex. I argue that the critical issue concerning "reasoned" debate about "nativeness" that has greater salience for the New World is the debate between Bartolomé de Las Casas and Juan Ginéz de Sepúlveda at Valladolid in 1550. Therefore, for this chapter, rather than blame the Enlightenment thinkers, we need to acknowledge the abuses of "reason" and the concomitant abuses of "natives" that early practitioners of anthropology have exercised in the name of their fledgling science.

9. I am aware that my exhibit will prompt comparisons to other kinds of ethnographic displays in other kinds of museum spaces. Ethnic and ethnographic museums do present ethnographic materials through intertextual and intermediated displays. Museum professionals have their own critical discourses regarding the role of museums and the politics of representation (Karp and Lavine 1991). Museums were theorized as "contact zones" (Clifford 1991, 1997; Erikson et al., 2002) where colonizers and colonized enter the same space and structural inequalities are displayed and reified. However, as Isaac rightly points out, "the methodologies behind theories of the 'middle ground,' 'hybridity,' and 'contact zones,' however, are centered largely on textual analyses. As a result they downplay the distinct dynamics of oral tradition and alternative methods for the transmission, negotiation, and control of knowledge" (2007, 16–17). The similarities between museum displays and my proposal for alternative epistemic spaces are important, but the distinction that is relevant for this chapter lies in the fact that museum displays present varieties of collected ethnographic objects in a committee-coordinated exhibit within a particularly demarcated space—a museum. My exhibit is ethnography in *process*. See the conclusion for clarification.

10. My use of "emergence" comes from many sources. With each passing year more publications use "emergence" and its variants in both titles and theoretical frames. I credit Tedlock and Mannheim's (1996) usage in helping me conceive of the coproduction of ethnographic experience and knowledge as mutually unfolding and mutually negotiated conditions of possibility.

7

Matthew the Canadian Journalist

Engagement and Representation in Highland Guatemala

Timothy J. Smith

This chapter represents an attempt to address the difficult balance between writing about the contingent nature of *truth* and participating in a local struggle, taking heed of the critiques levied at and from anthropology over the past twenty-five years with regard to ethnographic authority and the impossibility of representation (Clifford 1986a, 1988; Clifford and Marcus 1986; Dreyfus and Rabinow 1983, 106; Marcus and Fischer 1986, 23; Quigley 1997). I offer an ethnographic portrayal of a year spent doing fieldwork in Guatemala (2001–2002) working with an indigenous government in the western highlands. It involves a conflict that I was unexpectedly put into a position to write about, an exercise that has required me to question my own positionality, which both limited and made possible what I knew or could say about the event (Caton 1999, 9). In light of the goals of this volume, I will discuss how I dealt with both fieldwork and the multiple angles from which I was affected as an ethnographer-in-the-world, hoping to offer a discussion of multiple implications for negotiating the politics of representation.

Maya Landscapes and Representation(s)

In the earlier part of the twentieth century, the creation of knowledge about Mayas and their sociopolitical formations mirrored an academic construction of "the Maya" and "Mesoamerica" through ethnographies that focused upon the idea of bounded and neatly structured communities.[1] Nearly one hundred years later, ethnographers working in Guatemala make use of radically different theoretical lenses and assumptions, in part due to the postmodern critiques offered in the 1980s and the violence that scarred the country in the

1970s and '80s. Ethnographic portrayals of Guatemala Mayas after the end of thirty-six years of armed conflict in 1996 have included topics of identity formation, multiculturalism, neoliberalism, citizenship, memory, and democracy, all of which have become fashionable and have received more attention by foreign anthropologists in the past decade (T. Smith and Offit 2010).

And while these engagements were born in the shadow of ethnographies published by non-Mayan anthropologists during the conflict about Guatemalan highland communities that attempted to substantially include (if not privilege) an indigenous perspective (e.g., Carmack 1995; Falla 1994; Hendrickson 1995; Stoll 1993; K. Warren 1989; Watanabe 1992; R. Wilson 1995), these new framings and modes of representation have brought additional challenges to ethnographers both from within and outside of their traditional audiences. Regardless of their academic or political intentions, new literature and critiques by Latin American authors still offer a caveat to those social scientists working in the region—be wary of continued forms of romanticization and stereotypes draped in new covert paradigms and structural essentializations, despite political convictions or commitment to advocacy (T. Smith 2006).

In this chapter, I look at a pan-Maya-oriented political organization and how it mapped (or did not) upon a geographically located community in highland Guatemala through the rubric of indigenous governance and competing notions of democracy. In addition, I will offer my own personal experiences in struggling to capture the cartographic complexities of such a project as a foreign ethnographer who earnestly attempted to reconcile my own politics with a charge to provide a representation heavily colored by the politics of intimacy. I seek to illustrate how the politics of identity may play out in institutionalized terms and how contested vocabularies and internal conflicts can open the door for new disputes and political categories, which can rewrite our terms of engagement. Moreover, I hope to show that just as I gave multiple identities and hats to the indigenous activists and authorities with whom I worked, so was I given multiple hats and personas to fulfill their own agendas.

A Brief History of the Resurgence of an Indigenous Government

The municipality of Sololá is a county-like unit in western Guatemala that also serves as the seat of the Department of Sololá and is one of the largest market centers in the western highlands. This chapter stems from a fourteen-year study of its Indigenous Municipal Government (hereafter referred to as the Indigenous Government).[2] Although it does not receive official recognition by the Guatemalan state, it has existed in this town for nearly 450 years. It is comprised of elected community leaders whose main task is to provide a liaison between the official Sololá Municipal Government (hereafter referred to as the Official Government) and the predominantly indigenous population of Sololá (in 2001 the population was 63,973, 89 percent of which was indigenous), in many cases addressing civil disputes and providing a buffer between the judicial system and the rural hamlets.[3] In addition, it also oversees the ceremonial activities of the religious social organizations (*cofradías*).[4]

In the years between the height of the thirty-six-year armed conflict in the late 1970s and the peace process of the mid-1990s, the Indigenous Government changed dramatically due to the violence, intelligence apparatuses, and increased military presence. After continued persecution of its elected officials and death threats, the Indigenous Municipal Council (the Indigenous Government's subdivision of leaders) was largely disbanded, given the reluctance of community members to fill the positions of the cofradías, as well as those of *su'es* (bailiff) and village representatives (MIS 1998, 83–84). For periods of two to three years at a time no positions were filled and cofradías were frozen, with saints remaining in some houses for many years.

In 1994, Mayan leaders in Sololá met in order to revive the Indigenous Government; they split the traditional civil-religious hierarchy of the Indigenous Mayoral Council (executive branch) into two groups: a civil council and a religious council.[5] One of their goals was to unify the Mayan nongovernmental organizations (NGOs) of varying political stripes in town (including Campesino Unity Committee [CUC], National indigenous and Campesino Coordinator [CONIC], National Coordinating Committee of Guatemalan Widows [CONAVIGUA], Majawil Q'ij, the Comité Indígena de Sololá, and Usaqil Tinamït) during a rebuilding process that commenced before the conflict's end in 1996.[6] Mostly as a result of the political organization and mass protests directed by the civic committee, Sololatecos United for Development (SUD), and the popular organizations in Sololá from 1994 to 2000, the Indigenous Government began to receive the support of foreign embassies in postwar Guatemala (notably, Spain, Norway, Sweden, Japan, and Canada), MINUGUA (United Nations Verification Mission to Guatemala), the Guatemalan state, and other local NGOs.[7] These organizations began to work closely with the Indigenous Government following the signing of Peace Accords in 1996. Between the years 1996 and 1999, additional support was provided by many ex-guerillas from the URNG (Guatemalan National Revolutionary Unity)—mostly from the EGP (Guerilla Army of the Poor) and ORPA (Revolutionary Organization of the People in Arms)—

who worked closely with the SUD civic committee during the formative years of the Indigenous Government's resurgence.

The newly reconstituted Indigenous Government focused on land issues, agricultural innovations, higher education, and professional occupations for Mayas.[8] It sponsored civil protests (against the national government, tax increases, and the privatization of phone, water, and electricity companies) and helped to rescind school uniform requirements for Mayan children, whose families generally preferred their own ethnic clothing (*traje*). The most important achievement for the Mayan activists was the election of the first indigenous citizen as the municipality-wide mayor of the Official Government in Sololá. The election of Pedro Iboy Chiroy in 1995, a schoolteacher with a long-standing history with the ALMG (Guatemalan Mayan Language Academy), marked the end of the Ladino-dominated Christian Democrats' control of the Official Government between 1986 and 1995.[9] Iboy had run as the candidate for the SUD civic committee, comprised of both underground URNG supporters and members from the Sololá Indigenous Committee (who were responsible for revitalizing the Indigenous Government), which billed itself as an *anti-party,* free from the favoritism and corruption of the national political parties and more reflective of local concerns.

Once in office, Iboy's agenda focused upon education, indigenous rights, cultural events, the formation of a strong working relation between both municipal governments (Official and Indigenous), and a campaign for an end to the armed conflict. Following the signing of the Peace Accords in 1996, many ex-guerillas and the newly formed SUD civic committee worked together to improve the situation of Mayas in a town that historically had been dominated politically by Ladinos, although 89 percent of the town identified as indigenous. Many of the projects that Iboy's administration supported were oriented toward cultural issues, informed by a larger network of indigenous intellectuals whose work has become part of Movimiento Maya. Receiving particular attention from foreign anthropologists, who dubbed it "the pan-Maya Movement" (e.g., E. Fischer 1999, 2001; Fischer and Brown 1996; Hale 2006; Hendrickson 1995; Nelson 1999; C. Smith 1991; K. Warren 1998a; cf. Montejo 2005), its foundations date back decades but gained strength in the ashes of a thirty-six-year armed conflict in Guatemala.[10]

In addition to championing a culturist-oriented agenda supporting the above initiatives both within and outside of the municipality, leaders from both municipal governments during Iboy's term in office were also instrumental in introducing new fertilizers and farming cooperatives, as well as organizing protests to pressure the national government to close down a local military base located just north of the town center, which had been the site of state repression, torture, and troop deployment during the war. The conversion of the military base to a university stands as a particularly proud moment in Sololateco history, for both URNG and SUD civic committee members alike, signaling a partial fulfillment of the Peace Accords, which called for a downsizing of the military and its reorientation toward community development. After three years of debate surrounding the issues of whether a university or military institute would control the campus, the curriculum, and scholarships for indigenous students, the new Universidad del Valle-Altiplano campus opened in June of 2000.[11]

This was a bittersweet victory for many of the individuals involved. While both URNG and SUD civic committee members had worked together toward the establishment of an affordable university for Mayan students, 1999 was marked as a year of both unity and rupture in which both groups from the united municipal governments parted ways shortly after the *consulta popular*—a national referendum on constitutional reforms and, in particular, indigenous rights—was voted down.[12] Shortly thereafter, the alliance started to fracture as the members of the URNG left due to their organization receiving official party status in 1998 and becoming more interested in pursuing projects focused on infrastructure and the economy. In a surprising event for the SUD civic committee members, who had worked alongside many of the URNG followers for years, Pedro Saloj Poz, the URNG candidate for official mayor, won the 1999 election. For many, it was a fluke caused by a misreading of the ballot, similar to the "butterfly ballot" dispute in Palm Beach, Florida, during the 2000 US presidential election. In the end, Saloj was declared the winner and the conflict between both groups began, with the URNG controlling the Official Government and the SUD civic committee controlling the Indigenous Government (see T. Smith 2003, 2009). I will now turn to an ethnographic (re)presentation in which I insert myself as the observer, the anthropologist who struggled to capture not only the events of this conflict on the ground but the messy process of representing them.[13]

Lost in Translation: An Anthropological Offering

On Monday, August 9, 1999, I visited Sololá, overlooking beautiful Lake Atitlán, the magnificent body of water surrounded by mountain ridges and three volcanoes. In the center of the municipality, nearly ten thousand residents bustle to and fro on a daily basis, a population that can nearly double on market days. This doubling, however, pales in comparison to the festival activities of the week surrounding August 15, the annual feast of the Virgin of the Assumption, the town's patron saint. For many visitors, both national and international, Sololá is a must-see town on the pilgrimage of Guatemalan photography, beckoning would-be disciples of Edward Curtis to the main market days of Tuesday and Friday.

Like most others who lined the town square, I edged my way to the street, hoping to catch a glimpse of the religious processions of the town's local cofradías. After taking my own much-needed, much-desired photographs of the day's activities, I walked over to the Indigenous Government, which I erroneously believed to be the municipal government of Sololá. Set at the northwestern corner of the central park, the Indigenous Government is housed in a wooden-columned building that was inaugurated on January 13, 1978, built with donations by the Canadian Embassy and Plenty International to replace the previous building, which had been destroyed by an earthquake in 1976.[14]

I entered the building, hoping to meet with some of the leaders and see if I could practice a bit of my then-rudimentary Kaqchikel Mayan.[15] Sitting upstairs in one of the meeting rooms was Ma Bartolo, speaking with four members of the Indigenous Civil Council.[16] Dressed in tight blue jeans, button-down shirt, and cowboy hat, he introduced himself as the second indigenous civil mayor of the Indigenous Government.[17] To my right, dressed in full Sololateco indigenous traje, was Ma Ruben, the first indigenous civil mayor. I introduced myself to all, nervously shaking their hands. Almost immediately, Bartolo told me that the "official" municipal government was across the street, that perhaps I was lost. I asked why there were two governments. "Because that's what the [national] government wants," he said, "but the people give more respect to Ruben." After this short exchange, Bartolo laughed at my broken Kaqchikel, telling me that I sounded more like a gringo from Tecpán (another Kaqchikel-speaking town located to the east) than anyone from around the lake, and he asked other questions about who I was, apparently to hear me mutilate the language for humor's sake.[18]

To add salt to my wound, one of the men greeted me and asked, "How is your meat?"[19] This rather than what I was expecting from my Kaqchikel classes, "How are you?"[20] Again, he asked me, "How is your meat?" I honestly didn't know how to answer out of sheer confusion brought on by the nature of the question itself. Lacking a familiarity with the Sololateco dialect of Kaqchikel, I failed to realize that he was asking me, "What do you say?"[21] That certainly got them rolling; and, after the laughter died down, I switched to Spanish and told them that I was an anthropologist from the United States and that Sololá was familiar to me from working for two years on a research team that translated the *Annals of the Kaqchikels,* which told the history of the town and of the Kaqchikel Nation before the arrival of the Spanish.[22] I told them that most of the annals documented the sixteenth and seventeenth centuries and that I learned quite a bit about the origins of the Indigenous Government and the history of Sololá. In addition, I said that I would make sure that they received a copy of the new translation once it was published.

Bartolo showed me a thin book that had been published in the previous year with support from the Norwegian Embassy (a publication that I had been looking for). It was short and written in Spanish, giving a brief sketch of the history and positions of the organization (MIS 1998). Unfortunately, much had been left out and some items were incorrect, he said. Bartolo then asked what I could do for them. I suggested that when I returned next year, we could form a research team and expand the book while writing a bilingual version for use in the local schools. They all agreed that this would be an interesting project and certainly worthwhile. I told them that I could also take pictures of them for free and bring back large prints to hang in the offices upon my return. They liked the idea and we agreed that I would return on Friday at noon.

I showed up on time and was ready to take pictures for the different groups. Bartolo asked if I would like to meet the Indigenous Religious Council, whose members he suggested have their pictures taken first. I followed him into the adjoining room, which was an intimidating experience. Six men, dressed in ceremonial dress, sat on benches and chairs staring at me as I entered their space with Bartolo. Immortalized on postcards (and caricatured in paintings) from Guatemala, they were the same individuals whom I had seen earlier in the day in front of the main cathedral in town. Each had a large bluish-gray wool jacket, cut short at the waist, with crisscrossing stripes near the arms and thick black stripes running vertically, and black over-trousers split at the thigh, exposing the elaborate red, black, and white design of their pants, indicative of Sololateco textiles. Hanging over their heads on the wall were long blackish-brown scarves with white checkers, each covered on top by a large hat, reminiscent of those worn by bullfighting's *picadores,* only colored black with shoe polish. The most salient markers were the large head coverings, worn like those of Egyptian pharaohs, wrapped around their heads and of the same distinctive textile pattern as the pants, but with shining silver- and gold-embroidered eagles, plants, dogs, and stars.

Three of the men sat on benches against the wall and the other three sat behind a rickety old wooden table, covered with a gaudy vinyl tablecloth with a fruit basket print. Laid in front of them were three staffs of office (*varas*), each three feet in length, tipped on one end with metal and the other covered with a metal cap on which were attached black tassels with miniature pom-poms. Heaped next to them were thirteen other short wooden staffs, with multicolored tassels and pom-poms. One candle sat next to the staffs, flickering within its glass mug.

Bartolo explained to me that the three men sitting on the street side of the room were the three councilmen, and that to their right were the three indigenous religious mayors (ranked like their civil counterparts: first, second, and third).[23] He went into a long speech, saying that I was interested in returning to live in Sololá to write a book about the town's history and the organization. The first indigenous religious mayor slowly rose and spoke in a hushed voice, high-pitched and barely discernible. I assumed it was positive (given his smile and hand gestures back and forth between Bartolo and me). I learned later that he was very pleased that I wanted to return and believed that a thorough investigation of the history and structure of the Indigenous Government was important. Seeing the camera around my neck, he then asked if I would take a picture of them and present it upon my return. They had no pictures of their council hanging in their space and wanted one to hang on the wall. I was excited at this opportunity and took pictures of the group. After a nightmare of camera angles, lighting, group shots, personal portraits, and buddy shots, I thanked them and said that I looked forward to returning. Bartolo left me to attend other matters. I was not sure that he wanted me to follow him, so I stayed put, frozen with excitement and fear. Within a matter of minutes, Bartolo came back into the room and told me to come with him. I thanked the men in the room, bowing and kissing their hands as Bartolo had done. Over a couple of laughs as I further stumbled into an abyss of a standardized Kaqchikel Mayan not spoken in this town, I excused myself out of the room.

I left Sololá the next week and returned home to the United States. Between the political questions that I had and the comedic foreignness that I had only felt once before while traveling to New York City as a child, I decided that I would make every effort to go back. It turns out that I did, nearly thirty times over the next fourteen years, and my studies (and adventures) in Sololá shaped my misguided understandings of Guatemala, pan-Mayanism, and indigenous politics in a way that would lead to this chapter.

The Canadian Journalist Arrives: Strategic Misrepresentations and Tweaked Identities

Upon my return in January 2001, Bartolo introduced me to other members of the Indigenous Civil Council as Matthew, a journalist from Canada, who was going to collect information about their organization for a new study and that I was here to inform them of my plans. I was the one, he said, who had taken the large photos of the various committees hanging in the offices.[24] He could vouch for my project and said that I needed to find three other workers. He quickly turned to me and gestured for me to speak. In nervous, but significantly improved, Kaqchikel, I pitched my research project idea to them, saying that I was also writing a dissertation in the United States. I was hoping to work with local Mayan intellectuals to give something back to Guatemalans, in exchange for the information I would collect, so I explained that it would be a collaborative project between myself and three Mayan students and that I wanted to form a research team as soon as possible. Then Bartolo spoke. He said that there would be some problems with the study. For example, not all of the thirteen cofradías still existed as separate entities, many having been disbanded due to violence during the armed conflict. He then said that since I had learned Kaqchikel in Chimaltenango (a neighboring department), it would be necessary for him to re-explain my project in Sololateco Kaqchikel to the council members, to make sure they understood the nature of the project. Soon after, the grilling began. "Are you really working with the US Embassy or with another group?" asked one of the men. I nodded yes and said that I was a Fulbright scholar. Another man asked if I would be introduced to the village representatives, because if I was not and showed up in the villages and hamlets, I might be attacked or lynched. Bartolo told them that I would be introduced next week to the representatives. Another inquired as to how long it would take for the book based on the study to come out. I responded that it would probably take two years, one year for the study and one year to write up the results. I told them that I wanted to print one thousand copies of a bilingual book that could be sold, with proceeds funding new projects for the Indigenous Government (MIS and Smith 2012).[25] The Indigenous Civil Council members remarked that we needed to find three men for the positions. I interrupted and said that I was firm on appointing two women and one man in order to balance the team. After all, I thought to myself, wasn't harmony and balance a big issue for pan-Mayanists? Dominga, the only woman on the council, smiled as the men frowned and shrugged their shoulders.

I finished by telling them that I wanted to interview every elected official in the Indigenous Government, "The village representatives, Indigenous Civil Council, Indigenous Religious Council, COMS [a consortium of Mayan NGOs in Sololá]," at which point they started to shake their heads. "No," Bartolo said, "You cannot speak with COMS. They are a separate organization and apart from the Indigenous Government. Plus, they might be upset that you are writing a book about the [Indigenous] Government. This project is sponsored by the Indigenous Government, not COMS." Surprised at this, I inquired about the Indigenous Religious Council, which provided guidance to the town's cofradías. They said that would not be a problem, along with the village representatives, and the Indigenous Civil Council. We needed to convene every Friday and present reports to them. I agreed and they told me to come back next week with the formed research team. Thanking them, I walked out of the room and toward the stairs, shaking from the formality, nerves, and the intimidation that I felt.

Out in the corridor, Bartolo reviewed with me what the meeting had accomplished and what was to be expected. Confused, I asked him why he had referred to me as Matthew, a Canadian journalist, if my name was Tim (Timoteo) and I was an anthropologist. Switching to Spanish, he said, "Oh, well you aren't small, so I called you Matt.[26] It also sounds better if you are from Canada. Many of our people here don't think highly of the United States, because of what the CIA did here in 1954."[27] After acknowledging the logic in that, I explained to him again that I was an anthropologist, not a journalist. "What?" he asked. "Journalist is easy for me to understand and it will be for others as well." In the end, I helped to organize a research team that would be sponsored by the Indigenous Government. We worked closely together, shaping the research project and planning our strategies on a weekly basis. However, apart from my work with them and with the civil side of the Indigenous Government, I also participated in the activities and collected personal narratives of those working on the religious side.

In was certainly an interesting year in the field. Was I respected walking down the street in full traje, speaking Kaqchikel as I passed people? No, the majority laughed and pointed fingers, jokingly addressed me as "our father" and "sir." And there was the constant questioning of where I came from, why I was there, where Osama bin Laden was hiding, what the exact dimensions of a Patriot missile were, and why Bush was "warring" with Afghanistan. It was a very difficult and dreaded task traversing the municipality to a particular meeting place, and it always seemed that couldn't have been farther from my house.

Serendipity and Conflict

At the annual meeting of the American Anthropological Association in Washington, D.C., at the end of November 2001, I gave a paper to present my findings on the history of the Indigenous Government and how the pan-Mayan SUD civic committee had been responsible for its renaissance. I concluded by telling the audience that I would be flying back to Guatemala right in time for the December 12 election for the new Indigenous Civil Council. I was optimistic and hoped that the new administration would forge a different type of relationship with the Official Government, with whose members they had been quarrelling since the disputed official mayoral election of 1999. I didn't know that, while I was speaking, Sololá was already electing the new council, ten days in advance.

On December 12, I was back in Sololá and walked over to the Indigenous Government to witness the election. It was sure to be an exciting event, capping off one full year of studying this organization and the various offices. As I walked up to the building, I noticed that the main door was locked. Wondering why that should be, or if the election had been moved elsewhere, I entered the first-floor pharmacy and asked the manager, himself a SUD civic committee supporter. He told me that the election had taken place on December 2. As I clutched my hair, completely upset with myself for missing it and selfishly worried about how it might affect my research, he told me who had been elected. He said that some of the village representatives were upset and that I should find the first indigenous civil mayor, Bartolo.

I was upset. I couldn't believe that after all I had witnessed and every event in which I had participated, I missed this one major event. One of the Official Government police officers saw me and asked me how the north was, about the war in Afghanistan, and about anthrax. I told him that things were tough but that the people were getting by. I then said that it was a shame that I missed the elections and that I must have mixed up the dates. He said that I hadn't, that the dates were changed at the last minute by Bartolo and the SUD civic committee leadership, as well as the location of the election. Furthermore, he said that not all of the villages had been represented because of the changes. Because of that, there was a growing dispute. He told me that a large number of the village representatives were very angry about not being able to participate or to inform their residents about the election and that they were going to have their own election, to take place in four days on December 16. I thanked him and ran over to Bartolo's house to find out what happened.

He was not at home and his father greeted me at the gate. He said that things were bad and that certain members of the URNG and the Official Government were out to get Bartolo and hijack the Indigenous Government. Suggesting that I come back later, he told me that I was going to have to speak with Bartolo for more information. I thanked him and left for my house. On the way back, I saw Abel, one of the members of the Indigenous Religious Council. He was smiling as always and asked me how Osama bin Laden was doing. "Very funny," I told him. I asked him if he meant Adolfo Perez (who had been nicknamed Osama in the village of San Jorge, according to residents). At that, Abel became very serious and asked me if I knew about how the SUD civic committee and Bartolo had stolen the election. I told him that I was ignorant of everything that had occurred in the past week because I had been in the United States. He started to criticize Bartolo, describing him as a liar and a cheater. Bartolo only cares about money and power, he said. Abel believed that Bartolo wanted to run for official municipal mayor in the next election. He then invited me to the second election and told me that I would see democracy and hear the true voice of the people of Sololá. Jumping on his ten-speed, he zipped down the hill to his carpentry job.

On Friday, I went to the Indigenous Government as usual, only to find the main hall full of angry men, shouting and yelling. Nearly all of the village representatives were there, as well as all of the elected and appointed officials of the Indigenous Government and representatives from the Mayan NGOs (COMS). Many of the men were yelling at Bartolo, who stood in the middle of the room trying to calm them down. "Kixuxlan jub'a' . . . kixuxlan jub'a' (Just calm down; just calm down)," he kept saying. The representatives said that they were not given fair representation because not all of the village representatives had shown up. Many others were calling Bartolo a liar and complaining about the change of the dates. Finally, the majority of the village representatives stormed off, telling Bartolo that they intended to hold their own election on Sunday. As they filed past me, many of them shook my hand, smiling, and exclaimed, "Mateo! How are you?" Uneasily, I shook most of their hands as they squeezed past me, under the fixed eye of Bartolo. He walked into his office and shut the door.

I met with my research team members, Pedro, Alejandra, and María, in order to talk about our last month together and what I thought we should try to accomplish. This election, however, might interfere with that. I asked them what happened, and Pedro said it was a problem with political parties. Both Alejandra and Pedro told me that they heard rumors that certain members of the Desarrollo Integral Auténtico of the Unidad Revolucionaria Nacional Guatemalteca (DIA-URNG) coalition from the Official Government wanted to put their people in office in the Indigenous Government so that they could finally control both. These unnamed individuals were also reportedly rallying the village representatives to stand up to Bartolo and demand a new election. In exchange, they would receive financial promises and favoritism when it came time for community project funding from the Official Government. The other big problem for them was that the two men who had been elected on December 2, Domingo Choy and Jorge Samines, were both SUD civic committee members.

According to the village representatives, only five of them had been present for the first election on December 2. The majority of them told me that it wasn't democratic and many of them had been deceived and not informed about the change. Explaining his side to me later, Bartolo said that November 25 was a bad date because not as many people would have had the opportunity to attend. It was moved to the Universidad del Valle's campus because there it was free, whereas the gymnasium charged a hefty fee, in addition to setup and cleanup fees. During the first election, a group of village representatives showed up at Universidad del Valle's campus in anger and refused to participate, according to his story. Another fifty people, whom he identified as URNG disciples, showed up to *fuck with* the elections.

The United Nations Observer Arrives: Reluctant Legitimization

In the middle of December, a major protest in the form of a second election took place, which would mark the end of the SUD control of the Indigenous Government and put into question the future of how pan-Maya activism played out in this town. After the majority of the village representatives disputed the first election, held on December 2 (and which was declared fraudulent by URNG-sympathetic leaders), a group of about two thousand voters showed up to hold a second vote.[28] I showed up on that Sunday for the election at 8:00 in the morning, where the communities were starting to gather. Set up against one of the concrete walls of the soccer field was one of the tables from the Indigenous Government and, to its side, one black loudspeaker. A stack of ballots sat next to the speaker box, each with a logo for one of the thirteen candidates. Nobody's name was on the ballot, only logos for a candidate's affiliation. People will usually vote for their hamlet or village and only rarely for a candidate outside of their immediate community. On the wall behind the table were taped thirteen large white pieces of paper with each of these symbols drawn on them.

Marimba music was playing on the speakers and two men with baskets walked around shouting over each other, "Ice cream! Cold ice cream! Carrots! Carrots!" Almost immediately, Miguel (a URNG affiliate) saw me and called me up to the main stage, where ballots were laid with the pile of varas brought by the village representatives. Without telling me first, he announced to the crowd of nearly two thousand over the loudspeaker, "The observer from MINUGUA [United Nations] is here! The human rights election observer is here!" as hundreds of people turned to the stage and clapped. Well, I thought sarcastically to myself, I was a Canadian journalist, why not an observer from the United Nations? Rather than following my gut and telling him that I was not an election observer, I looked out across the field and saw that I was the only foreigner there. I remembered the countless blank stares given to me when I told people that I was an anthropologist. I also considered the fact that I had over and over again corrected people, telling them that I was not from the United Nations or Canada or the CIA.

This would be a major decision for me and I want this to be clear to the reader. Risking criticism, I am going to be honest here and provide an account of what happened. On one hand, many of the people gathered on that field were there to express their right to vote and to participate in an electoral process that has been and, in many places, continues to be viewed as corrupt and far removed from their influence. My presence was symbolic of larger international organizations, something larger than one tall white gringo. As Miguel later explained, I was the international community and my being there would legitimate their election and give the winner his or her mandate to lead. On the other hand, if I took on this role, rather than a strange anthropologist dashing in and out of crowds, talking with people (which I was going to do anyway, regardless of my role in their eyes), I feared that I would be jeopardizing my relationship with the Indigenous Government leadership: Bartolo, the SUD civic committee members, and essentially everything that I had been studying for the past year.

I was caught in a moment of depression, confusion, guilt, and anger. After speaking with people for the past four days and now seeing two thousand people on this field (not a few dozen disgruntled village representatives and URNG supporters), I started to feel betrayed and asked myself: What was Bartolo thinking? Why did they change the election? Maybe they forgot to get the word out. Maybe, just maybe, they just slipped up. Still, if I participated today, even symbolically, I might be in danger of being perceived as having crossed over to *the other side* (to the Official Government and the URNG).

In my newfound role of UN observer, I made my way around to different groups of people, speaking with the village representatives and their constituent voters who had accompanied them. Francisco, representative from the village of Triunfo, told me that only seven of the thirty-four village representatives had been present for the December 2 election. That wasn't enough votes, he argued. Today, however, they were expecting nearly two thousand votes. He said, "Today we are all united, the *tinamït* (town, people), Evangelicals, Protestants, Catholics, URNG, SUD."

The mounting crisis that followed came in the form of a dispute over the election and the outright rejection of the first indigenous civil mayor's authority by the village representatives who were the leaders and voices of their communities. This mutiny put into question the legitimacy of the Indigenous Civil Council in the eyes of the satellite communities. The election became a point of contention that, if carried out properly, had the potential of not only securing the legitimacy of the winning faction, but also testifying to the dependable tenure of the Indigenous Government's decentralized mode of governance and representation. Nobody was removed from office. Neither the military nor the police were called in to establish order. The idea of the relatively new civil wing of the Indigenous Government was not scrapped.[29] Moreover, the "covert antagonisms" (V. Turner 1982, 70) that became visible were the passions and contempt put into play when the URNG won control of the Official Government in 1999. The crisis of 2001 was the boiling point, at which all of these feelings came to the surface between the two groups. Once formed publicly, this crisis made transparent the animosities between the two governments. Then again, it is plausible that this is what the URNG leaders were waiting for—the chance to, in their eyes, both expose the SUD civic committee for coveting personal aspirations and to do so by morally and legally mandated means.

It was this exposé of fraud and manipulation, I will argue, that the SUD civic committee leadership was most anxious to suppress. They did have valid reasons for changing the date and the place of the election, but they did not sufficiently announce those changes to the voters. Rather than explaining this publicly—compounded with the fact that they refused to have another election, even when presented with the voter turnout—they chose to appeal to the URNG leadership at the Official Government with arbitration. During the failed meeting, the representatives shook their heads at Bartolo and the SUD civic committee, asking why they should meet with them about the election when they had nothing to do with it in the first place. The SUD civic committee leadership carried through with every possible form of redress (filing a complaint; pursuing legal channels; writing letters to embassies, NGOs, MINUGUA, the Spanish Embassy representatives in town, CALDH; using arbitration, finally meeting with the renegade village representatives, etc.). They even resorted to naming their own scapegoats for the problem: the village representatives, who (in the SUD committee's eyes) were bribed and manipulated by the URNG leaders in the Official Government. Bartolo consistently painted the representatives as innocent but greedy individuals who rebelled against his authority in exchange for payoffs. Whether this was true or not, he never directly blamed them (he believed the official municipal mayor was pulling the strings), but he did scold their weak character and leadership. However, the damage had been done and by the early part of 2002, SUD relinquished control of the Indigenous Government to the opposition.

Little Narratives, Local Philosophies: Challenging Representations

The challenge that continues to present itself to the practice of ethnography involves how to effectively balance our desire to show the contingent nature of these truths (which may undercut our co-subjects' agendas) while at the same time remaining engaged with the individuals with whom we live and interact in the field. We may be asked to abandon our credentials and research agendas—effectively checking our pens in at the front door and suspending our anthropological belief(s)—in favor of providing the means and support by which local communities and individuals may advance their locally authored visions. In these moments the politics of representation come to bear on the ethnographer, the representation of anthropology, and the ethnographer-in-the-world.

How could I offer what I believe is a correct interpretation of the events without appearing to either (1) potentially represent one of the arguably greater success stories of pan-Mayan activism in post-conflict Guatemala as one of personal interests, politics, and manipulation; or (2) reveal my own frustrations with the people with whom I had worked for nearly one year (not withstanding some feelings of betrayal). By focusing on local processes and outcomes, I wanted to complicate urbancentric stereotypes of rural politics and illustrate the salience of multiple political identities and differing ideas on what democracy and *participation* meant for the indigenous actors of Sololá. The outcome, however, was a complex yet tainted view of indigenous leaders and Mayan activists, whom I had erroneously (perhaps unconsciously) believed to be innocent of any wrongdoing, given their just cause. How was I to balance and negotiate these concerns?

I was most especially concerned that my writing would indirectly portray a vulnerable underbelly of Mayan activism and indigenous politics, a dark side of political infighting, lying, and fraud, which could be used by anyone choosing to undermine the work of Mayan leaders in Guatemala, who are working to shape new communities of belonging and markers of identity. In the end, I believe that I did have a responsibility to show these conflicts in order to highlight that Mayan politics and indigenous activism are just as complex, viable, and functional as any other political system one would find elsewhere in the world. In fact, if democracy involves dissent and challenges, I think that by showing these events it becomes obvious that Mayan voters and political leaders have indeed succeeded, which makes one wonder why the US Embassy and the United Nations would have thought otherwise given the events surrounding the disputed election (T. Smith 2009).

Along the way, I would argue, we may discover that it would be more prudent—and positively less clear (read: less fixed)—to resist choosing between building our theoretical models around our political engagements and positions or vice versa. It would be too simplistic and disingenuous to privilege one over the other. Just as our politics are formulated and shaped by our experiences, so too do we choose our projects and banners, which provide the grounds from which we make our decisions. In other words, while I think it would be wrong to ignore what would otherwise be considered fallacies, inconsistencies, and shortcomings on behalf of those with whom we work in solidarity, I think it would be equally unwise (and patronizing) to not call attention to those problems in our representations. If we are to treat our consultants as equals both in and out of the field, to be given the opportunity and guaranteed the right to openly criticize our portrayal of their work, then let us treat them with equal standards, characterizations, and measures—not to undermine or undercut their agendas (of course, extreme examples would require a careful consideration of potential harm), but to show their complex gifts for deliberation, compromise, contradiction, struggle, error, apology, adaptation, and success, just as we would expect ourselves and our work to be characterized.

Positions, Serendipity, and Othering the Ethnographer

In striving toward a more accurate rendering of both our position and that of those with whom we work (and about whom we write), the production of knowledge will continue to be shaped by power differentials and claims to authority unless we might perhaps envision *us* and *them* as co-subjects (Greenwood 2008, 324). For just as ethnographers have been and continue to be critiqued for *othering,* so too are we *othered.* Our actions and words provide but lagniappe for how we are viewed, positioned, and represented in turn by former subjects of ethnography (Fabian 2007, 2008). This dynamic requires more than a search to eliminate the dichotomy between us and them and the rejection of claims to truth (cf. Eagleton 2003). Some scholars have suggested that the inability to blur the lines between us and them will remain elusive regardless of changing political climates, given the foundations of our own subjectivity, that anthropology is and will remain a descendent of modernist thinking (Bowman 1997, 34–35; cf. Fabian 2007). Glenn Bowman, writing in response to *Writing Culture* (Clifford and Marcus 1986) fourteen years later, suggests that the solution to the crisis of representation lies in a pursuit beyond the stalemated rejection of "the 'other' is not like 'us' mentality in favor of one that comes to recognize that the 'other' is exactly like 'us' in that their subjectivities are grounded through interaction with social facts," to *identify with* rather than *identify ethnographic subjects* (1997, 45).

As for challenging the anthropologist/Canadian journalist/United Nations observer roles: given a constant revamping of the methods and ethics involved in ethnographic fieldwork, we continue to struggle in our writing and fieldwork with attempts at political engagement, false detachment, objectivity, situated knowledge(s), and building solidarity with the communities in which we work. These arguments have played out in the academy through literature, panels, and public forums. Despite the countless panels at professional meetings, articles, specialized graduate courses, and books aimed at these issues, most anthropologists would agree that the difficult act of balancing academically sound research with an honest attempt to portray and understand those communities we write about remains a cornerstone task of our profession, if not an imperative. One of our responsibilities continues to be the avoidance of capturing histories and regions within yet another intellectual net that is unkind to alternative interpretations even if those interpretations counter current trends and political correctness. How we effectively represent cultures while avoiding the creation of more intellectual baggage might very well remain a double-edged sword, but we must strive toward the creation and casting of a new net, one that truly weds the political with the contingent and attempts to understand communities from their perspective, notwithstanding the herculean task of not claiming to speak for them (as well as deciding whether or not to speak on behalf of them, if asked). In other words, only once we have accepted that our intended audience(s) may drive our initial questions, and that we therefore have multiple responsibilities that call for multiple goals and multiple selves at the onset of research, can we be best prepared for both rigorous documentation and ethical representations.

Thus, the need of understanding multiple epistemologies in the field is always already contingent upon the flexibility of the researcher, which is precariously (un)structured. Anthropology can only continue to see itself as sanctioned to understand and represent cultural logics if we accept the multiplicity of the researcher's non-unitary self. In this chapter, I was interested in examining some of the methodological and theoretical discussions of multiplicity by opening some of the behind-the-scenes interactions of my own fieldwork. I attempted to fulfill my responsibilities to the Indigenous Government and to my research team throughout the course of the year, although at points this proved futile. I included the above tale of my awkward introductions and (at times) ambiguous persona to emphasize that I could not escape a special status as the intrusive observer, no matter my own participation, ethical priorities, or obligations. On the other hand, I was an outsider with a camera and pen, shooting and recording and collecting information. This did open doors for me and gave me access to certain events that my Indigenous Government identification card did not. Because of this, I am inclined to argue that many of the conflicting stances and agendas that I had in the field stemmed from a necessary and inescapable split personality that I myself created. And I am often reminded that I was being objectified and strategically used as a foreigner (given multiple identities) whose affiliation for either side in the above conflict was deemed advantageous. As Dorinne Kondo points out, however, we should be interested in asking how selves in the plural are constructed in different contexts and should resist thinking of a singular bounded self (1990, 43, 310). I might even embrace an argument that it is better for the ethnographer to have multiple personalities rather than one that is dysfunctional and to perhaps intentionally "scramble all the codes" which we create ourselves—as well as those projected upon us in the field— by "quickly shifting from one to another" (Deleuze and Guattari 1983, 15). In my attempt to find pan-Mayanism on the ground in Guatemala, I wonder if there were multiple Mateos, Timoteos, and Tims that surfaced at different times and under difficult circumstances in Sololá. Was I an anthropologist? Was I a Canadian journalist? Was I a United Nations observer? The answer to all of these is yes.

Notes

1. For a more comprehensive overview of the history of Mayan community studies see Carmack 1973; B. Tedlock 1993; Watanabe 2000. Even the very use of *Maya/Mayan* is problematic. Following American anthropological expeditions in the early part of the twentieth century, much of what we had come to consider Mayan came from the writings of archaeologists, foreigner travelers, and their commercial associations. The term *Maya* was used generically by archaeologists to describe populations throughout an enormous region that covers southern Mexico, Belize, Guatemala, Honduras, and El Salvador (Castañeda 1996), although the use of the term by Guatemalan Mayas themselves has only been gaining since the early 1990s, a time when it was being used by mainly culturist-oriented groups (Nelson 1999, 21).

2. Sololá has both an official municipal government and an indigenous municipal government. Both institutions can be traced back to the colonial period (Maxwell and Hill 2006; T. Smith 2002, 2003). For more on indigenous municipal governments in Guatemala, see Barrios 1996, 1998a, 1998b; Carmack 1995; Hill 1992.

3. XI Censo Nacional de Población y IV de Habitación, Instituto Nacional de Estadística de la República de Guatemala (INE) 2002, Guatemala.

4. It is beyond the scope of this chapter to provide an in-depth analysis of each

position or to reconstruct the civil-religious hierarchy from the colonial period up until the present. For a more complete description of the offices and history of this institution, see T. Smith 2003. Four brief studies should also be consulted: Mayén de Castellanos (1986); Barrios (1998a, 1998b); MIS (1998); and MIS and Smith (2012).

5. This was not a dispute. It was a strategic move by the Mayan revitalizationists. In different highland communities the splitting of municipal governments occurred for different reasons.

6. CUC (Campesino Unity Committee, works for rural affairs), CONIC (National indigenous and Campesino Coordinator, focuses on land issues), CONAVIGUA (National Coordinating Committee of Guatemalan Widows, grassroots organization of widows of the war), Majawil Q'ij (New Dawn) Comité Indígena de Sololá (Sololá indigenous committee, responsible for revitalizing indigenous political resurgence), Usaqil Tinamït (People's Dawn, Mayan legal defense team).

7. Civic committees are community-based alternatives to traditional political parties and are gaining considerable support in Guatemala. The SUD had originally been created by Mayas as an anti-party; disgusted with the continual corruption of national politics, the marginalization of the indigenous voice in all levels of government, and puppet rulers who answered to concerns outside of the municipality, they had created a civic committee that would provide an alternative solution to political parties.

MINUGUA was established in Guatemala after the signing of the Peace Accords in 1996. Its goals included overseeing the implementation of the accords, assisting in disarmament, investigating human rights abuses, and strengthening of civil society.

8. Most salient was the return of communal lands to the *aldea* of San Jorge, located below the municipal center, toward Lake Atitlán (see T. Smith 2003, 92–102).

9. *Ladino* is a complex term in Guatemala and, problematically, is often used in reference to one who is not indigenous (see Nelson 1999; Grandin 2000). The term comes from the Sephardic Ladinos.

10. Many Mayan intellectuals publicly use *conflicto armado,* also known as *la violencia* (violence) in the countryside, while some North American anthropologists prefer "counter-insurgency war," and those working at the US Embassy use "civil war." Each of these phrases may reflect a particular subjectivity, but their connotations for receivers involve a political semantics when used in the dissemination of information.

11. The Guatemalan military proposed to open the campus of the elite military academy Adolfo. V. Hall, while many Sololatecos pushed for either the Universidad de San Carlos or the Universidad del Valle.

12. For more on the 1999 referendum, see K. Warren 2002; and Carey 2004.

13. With the exception of Iboy and Saloj, both of whom are identifiable as elected officials, the rest of the names used in this chapter are pseudonyms.

14. A spin-off NGO of The Farm community in Summertown, Tennessee, Plenty International came to Guatemala after the devastating 1976 earthquake. The old building for the indigenous municipal government was destroyed and Plenty volunteers helped to rebuild it. Having to leave Guatemala in 1980 due to the increase in vio-

lence of a growing counterinsurgency war, they have returned and continue to help in community development projects. See http://www.plenty.org for more information.

15. Third largest of the Guatemalan Mayan languages with a speaking population of nearly 500,000.

16. *Ma* is the honorific for men in Kaqchikel.

17. There are three mayors: first mayor, second mayor, and third mayor (or *síndico*).

18. See Hendrickson 1995 and E. Fischer 2001 for detailed ethnographies of this town.

19. ¿Atüx ati'ij?

20. ¿La ütz awäch?

21. ¿Atüx na'ij? /b/ is deleted inter-vocalically (V_V) in the Sololá dialect.

22. Kaqchikel Chronicles Translation Project, funded by NEH, under the direction of Judith Maxwell and Robert Hill.

23. There were only three councilmen in 1999. The optimum number is ten.

24. I made it a point to take pictures of the successive governments each year and present them with large, framed photos for their offices.

25. Municipalidad Indígena de Sololá and Timothy J. Smith (2011). The book was written in Spanish and Kaqchikel and published in 2011 by Editorial Junajpu', an indigenous-owned and indigenous-operated publishing house in Antigua, Guatemala.

26. /ti/ is a diminutive that precedes nominatives. In other words, rather than calling me Timoteo (Timothy), he was calling me *ti* (little) plus Mateo (Matthew) but dropping the "little" (hence the comment about my size, because I am 5 feet 11 inches). Throughout my time spent in Guatemala, when I said Timoteo people often heard *ti* Mateo (little Matthew), dropped the diminutive, and called me Matthew (Mateo).

27. It has long been suspected and documented that the CIA, after its success in Iran, was responsible for underwriting the coup that ousted the progressive Arbenz administration, which marked the end of Guatemala's ten years of spring. For ethnographic representations of the events leading up to and resulting from the coup, see Smith and Adams 2011.

28. For a detailed description of this conflict and analysis of the two elections, see T. Smith 2003, 2009.

29. I have thought it similar to Louis Menand's observation of how remarkable it was that the United States had "fought a civil war without undergoing a change in its form of government. The Constitution was not abandoned during the American Civil War; elections were not suspended; there was no coup d'état" (2001, ix). While their very different temporal and cultural contexts are obvious, it is nonetheless an interesting comparison between both conflicts if one considers the "influential power to motivate" (Menand 2001) afforded to those Sololatecos who best wielded concepts like democracy, civil society, and decentralization during a time of increased pressures by foreign aid donors and their demand for democratic change.

8

Performing Music, Silence, Noise, and Anthropology in Yucatan, Mexico

Gabriela Vargas-Cetina

Representation, including self-representation, is a necessary tool for everyday communication. It is important to keep in mind that all categories, including representational ones, are contingent and subject to contextual change. *Indigenous, white, black,* or *Yucatecan* can only be understood historically and contextually; anthropology has to map these referential categories and also, especially, the contexts and processes that make them intelligible. *Anthropologist* is also a category of self-representation, and when combined with *local,* as when anthropologists do fieldwork in their own societies, it needs to be constantly redrawn. This is the general field to which this chapter is seeking to contribute. This account is based on my fieldwork among *trova* musicians in Merida, Mexico, since December 2001. (Trova is a type of music consisting mainly of romantic songs and written mostly during the twentieth century.) Here I explore the way in which ethnographic representation touches specifically on performance, including performance in the field and in the anthropological milieu. Through notions of music, noise, and silence, I delve into my own ethnographic and representational practices to explore these politics and their implications in anthropology as a whole.

Ethnography as Performance

The systematic description of cultural practices we call ethnography is one of the main components of anthropology. The anthropologist's manner of collecting information leading to ethnographic texts is highly idiosyncratic, considering the methods of other disciplines: we take part of everyday life in our chosen research site and become familiar with others' information sources, including texts and other results of memory inscription, to then transform the whole into yet new texts that package and convey this information to others. It is because of this double movement of apprehension (which mostly takes place during fieldwork) and inscription (which mostly takes place during write-up) that Johannes Fabian (1988) speaks of ethnography as performance, since it all happens having a *public* in mind. Each of these types of performance, in turn, is subject to different forms of evaluation.

First, we are judged by locals in the places where we conduct fieldwork as having—or not—successfully understood and embodied local conventions and codes. Participant observation is the process of acquiring experience, knowledge, and understanding in and pertinent to local life. It requires complex interpersonal negotiations whereby anthropologists and locals become acquainted. Research, especially when anthropologists engage directly in expressive culture productions, involves cultural performance subject to local norms and standards. Most anthropologists have to find their place in the localities where they carry out field research, but this is particularly exacting for those of us doing fieldwork as musicians, dancers, and theater performers; we must achieve acceptable dexterity so as to become part of local bands, troupes, and productions and thus must measure the success of our fieldwork performance by the appreciative judgment of local performers and their public.

The negotiations leading to ethnographic writing are arguably more complicated when the anthropologist is established in the locality where he or she is conducting fieldwork. Whereas some might think that access to information is facilitated by one's prior relationships on site, this is not necessarily the case, since any locality will have a wide variety of networks and groups. Also, once the anthropologist negotiates access to the group or groups of his or her interest, the fact that he or she is there to stay can complicate the situation because of one's particular loyalties and viewpoint.

Second, anthropology has its own codes and conventions, and a successful anthropological career has to conform to the expectations of our peers. Ethnography has to meet established disciplinary standards, both in content and in the manner of arranging and discussing what we gather in the field. Most anthropology research leads to textual production in the form of conference papers, academic articles, and theoretically informed ethnographies and other types of books. Also, teaching feeds off fieldwork and theoretical ideas spurred and supported by it, while taking place within parameters established by the larger academic context of the university and research centers. In the case of practicing anthropologists, their reports and presentations also have to meet standards set out by the funding and research agencies and firms for whom the anthropologists work.

All of this sounds like seamless process, but, in fact, every step is the result of complex negotiations and forms of textual construction. How do we speak about the Others we encounter in the field? Lived experience can only be imperfectly rendered post-factum, and ethnographies generally are the result of friendships and alliances we make in the field, which also translate into commitments and ethical imperatives. At least in my experience, most field research involves good and bad feelings, along with fears of spying, revealing, and betraying on the part of both the anthropologists and the locals with whom we work. We must adapt to local understandings of what a regular person is expected to be and behave like in any given setting and to what personal relationships demand in the way of mutual recognition, exchange, and shared cultural intimacy (Herzfeld 1997). Second, we have to find ways to report and theorize that are respectful of the people we meet during fieldwork and are intelligible to our audience. To do this, we take into account prior ethnographies and theories while trying to say something new of our own. So, we share our ideas and writings with our colleagues, ask for feedback, and react to their criticism and suggestions. In short, during both moments of anthropological performance, we rely on interpersonal relations to acquire and to report information sources and results; both during fieldwork and during textual production we come to rely on the answers and opinions of many people, some of who become our friends.

Issues of research and representation ethics necessarily stem from the fact that we always find ourselves in others and create personal bonds. Since our subject matter refers to people, our textual products are open to contesting interpretations from both our colleagues and those on whose lives our descriptions are based. Ethnography is necessarily a partial representation of local life, and it has the potential to leave both parties (researcher and locals) unhappy or at least unsatisfied with the resulting textual outcomes and their possible implications.

But how would all this relate to music research and theorizing since music is such an enjoyable part of culture and seems to be so far away from most mundane and material considerations? Music, in fact, is a very charged field in most societies (Giovannetti 2001; Kramer 1995; Wade 2000). Trova music, which I have chosen to focus on since 2001, is no exception to this. Representing what goes on in any music scene is a political exercise that necessarily takes us back to the question of whether or not, through analytical description, we are acknowledging the full complexity of our own field performance and adequately honoring the people who made it possible, including those who became our friends.

Music, Noise, and Silence

Many music theory books define music as the harmonic organization of sound and silence. Noise is often understood as the opposite of music. Music books describe music as pleasing and noise as displeasing to the ear. Whereas music is often thought of as predictable because of its relative regularity, noise is considered random, chaotic, and incoherent. Noise, however, is a necessary raw material from which music is created. Silence is the other main raw material necessary for musical creation and performance (Attali 1985; Kahn 2001; Pedelty 2004). Here I extrapolate notions of music, noise, and silence to guide me in the ethnography of trova in Yucatan. Music here means the harmonic effect in musical production and performance as recognized by Yucatecans; noise is what Yucatecans see to be other than harmonic within and around the music; silence refers to the way noise is kept out of the music in Yucatan.

Trova is a genre of music played in Yucatan, one of the three Mexican states into which the Yucatan peninsula is divided. Contemporary trova in Yucatan is the result of a historical mixture of European, African, and indigenous Amerindian musical influences. Trova encompasses various distinct rhythms, including *bullerias,* bolero, *bambuco, guaracha,* Peruvian waltz, waltz, Yucatecan *clave, jarana,* habanera, mazurka, schottische, *danzón,* rumba, *cumbia, son,* jazz, cha-cha, and *beguin* (Dueñas Herrera 1993; Manuel 1988; Vargas-Cetina, fieldnotes 2001–2006). Today in Yucatan most trova is performed in duets, trios, and ensembles featuring two main types of guitar: the *guitarra sexta* for rhythm and the *requinto* for lead guitar. The guitarra sexta is a classical-like guitar, also tuned like a classical guitar, and the requinto is a smaller guitar, tuned like a sexta but in a higher register. The singing in trova usually uses two main voices: one called *primera* sings the melody and another called *segunda* makes a harmonic counterpoint, at times described as a "shadow" melody (see World Music Network 2002). Sometimes, there is another voice called *tercera* that maintains a bass tone and weaves its way around and sometimes in between the other two. Except for bolero, beguin, and jazz rhythms, all trova songs mostly make use of full major and minor chords. Here it is important to note that bolero in the rest of Mexico and Latin America refers to romantic music in general, whereas, in the Yucatan Peninsula, bolero is a specific rhythm with a strong bass line and modified chords.

Trova is only one genre of music in the contemporary soundscape of the Yucatan. However, it is regularly described as the quintessential Yucatecan music, often said to portray the "true soul" of Yucatecans as gentle and romantic people. Its lyrics are reminiscent of medieval chivalry and courtship. Yucatecan men are represented in trova as romantics continually trying to court women whose love they feel they do not deserve. Yucatecan women are represented as beautiful, faithful when they fall in love, and as objects on a pedestal to be adored and wooed for eternity if the love is unrequited. Merida and Yucatan are almost always described in trova as a primordial garden for romantic love. I have found that trova musicians, fans, and sponsors often believe it to be the most beautiful music in the world because of what they see as the intrinsic *harmonic* quality of the music and the *romantic* nature of the lyrics. Furthermore, even Yucatecans who do not like trova say that this music reflects the Yucatecan character truthfully because they are gentle people who sing mostly contemplative and melancholy songs, in contrast with the more violent lyrics of many *corridos* and other song genres of central and northern Mexico. This self-representation is also validated outside of the Yucatan since Yucatecans are frequently portrayed in the popular media distributed from central Mexico as mellow and provincial.

The popularity of bolero music in the rest of Mexico and Latin America has gone in hand with its historic association with Cuba and the Yucatan Peninsula as the joint birthplace of the genre (Dueñas Herrera 1993; Pedelty 2004). The bolero revival of the 1990s rekindled the interest in Yucatan as an important repository of the cultural roots of contemporary Latin American romantic music. In Merida and in the rest of the state there are many organizations supporting trova music, including municipalities, the Yucatan state government, the research center Centro Regional de Investigación Musical de Yucatán, and many civic associations, such as Friends of Trova (Amigos de la Trova A.C.), the Museum of the Yucatecan Song (Museo de la Canción Yucateca A.C.), and Friends of Trova in Valladolid (Asociación de Amigos de la Trova de Valladolid, in the city of Valladolid). In addition, many groups of friends, known in Merida as groups of bohemians (*grupos bohemios*), meet regularly to sing trova and other romantic music.

As sweet as trova might appear to Yucatecans and outsiders, its production and preservation are predicated on social inequality and power struggles. There are at least three interrelated sources of disruption, and thus of noise, in the context in which trova is created and performed: class, gender, and politics. In addition to these, a relatively recent source of noise is the flow of immigration from other regions of Mexico and from non-Caribbean countries.

Since trova is considered to be at the crossroads of popular music and high art, classically trained composers and laureate poets engage regularly in making trova songs. There are two main categories of musicians within the trova community, and these are related to class differences in Yucatecan society. Classically trained composers and performers come from well-off, socially established Yucatecan families. When they engage in trova production and performance, they regularly achieve the status of trova *artists.* Troubadours (*trovadores*), instead, tend to have no classical education; their trova skills are handed down by their families and friends and learned by rote trial and practice.

In the state of Yucatan there is a hierarchy of those seen as the intellectual designers at the top and the manual workers who implement the design-ers' plans at the bottom. For example, it is an architect, engineer, or contrac-tor who has to direct master carpenters, who in turn direct other carpenters to build anything with wood, including shelves, doors, and furniture. In the same guise, a jewelry designer would create a setting for a piece of jewelry, then the master goldsmith would be in charge of actually creating the piece of jewelry, either by himself or herself or with assistance. There is great dis-crepancy between the earnings of those at the top of the social pyramid, who tend to lack many manual skills, and those at the bottom of the pyramid, where these skills are absolutely necessary.

This same hierarchy exists in the world of music. Those who are in charge of directing musical ensembles of any kind usually have formal music school-ing and are expected to compose or, at least, make original arrangements. Music workers, instead, are expected to follow directions with great skill and precision but without necessarily having an input in the composition or ar-rangement of the pieces. This class difference crossing the trova world also is expressed along gender lines. Most female trova musicians and composers come from the middle and upper social classes and often direct official mu-sical organizations. Most male trovadores come from relatively poor sectors of Yucatecan society. Also, while male trovadores usually have to support their families, female troubadours (trovadoras) and artists tend to be involved in trova as a hobby. This is one of the reasons why, although there are fewer female guitarists than male ones in Yucatan, women are very visible as musi-cians and performers of trova music.

Trova music production is also crossed by political tension between the two main political parties that receive Yucatecan's votes during local, state, and national elections: Partido Revolucionario Institucional (PRI) and Par-tido Accion Nacional (PAN). Here, while members and voters for PRI come from all social classes, most PAN card-carrying members come from the middle and upper classes. When PRI candidates are elected to office they tend to support a wider variety of music and a wider range of expression within trova itself. When PAN is in power trova is reduced to those rhythms and po-etic forms that can be considered closer to high art. For instance, in 2003, after PAN won both state and city elections in Yucatan, the annual trova compe-tition only contemplated songs performed in the rhythms of jarana, bambuco, bolero, and clave. In previous years when the contest was sponsored by a PRI state government, the rhythms accepted in the competition were not even specified in the call for submissions. Those songs that won the competition and were recorded on the official CDs included the four already mentioned plus guaracha, cumbia, jazz, Cuban son, balada, and habanera. Also, the instrumentation of songs that can be sponsored as trova by the city of Merida and the Yucatan state government changes with political swings. While officers associated with PRI would allow trova to be practically any kind of *romantic* music, whether or not performed with guitars, PAN officers define trova more narrowly as music either played on guitars or played by full concert orchestras with a major guitar section, and within a limited number of identifiable rhythms.

Another source of noise in trova music is its use as a symbol of regional identity that differentiates so-called real Yucatecans from newcomers arriving from other parts of Mexico. These are often seen as invaders who are affecting the culture of Yucatan, including long-established local traditions (see the chapter by Steffan Igor Ayora-Diaz in this volume). Even when these people sometimes become trova fans, they bring their own musical tastes with them, so they are having a major impact on the city's soundscapes. *Música ranchera, música grupera,* and regional types of music from all around Mexico are now regularly heard in the streets, homes, and public spaces. In the 1980s and 1990s the state of Yucatan received strong waves of migration from other Mexican regions and particularly from Mexico City and its surroundings. The Mexico City earthquake of 1985, first, and then the economic boom Yucatan experienced in the 1990s made the city of Merida a very attractive place for thousands of Mexicans who have since chosen to reside in this city. There is a feeling, which was probably stronger at the end of the 1990s but still lingers today, that within Yucatan the central Mexicans and their culture are displacing and excluding local culture. This dislike resurges periodically, especially around the dates of celebration of Mexican independence and when violent crimes are found to have been committed locally by people who came from outside Yucatan. Yucatecans who do not like trova are often called *malinchistas* by trova fans, a *malinchista* being somebody in Mexico who loves the foreign. Foreign rhythms and melodies, however, have always been incorporated into local music, and it is unclear exactly where the line between local and foreign could be drawn. The political climate strongly influences the way trova may change in any given period of time.

Social and political tensions are never spoken of within the trova world unless something really outstanding happens. For example, in 2003 and 2004 the Yucatan state government made it mandatory that those trovadores being sponsored through its programs learn to read musical notation in transposable mode. Many trovadores who never had a reason before to read music scores now had to attend extensive courses in musical notation, theory, and harmony, sometimes having to pay for the courses out of their own pockets. In the past, musical notation taught in the Yucatan was related to absolute *Do,* which was the central *C* note of the pianoforte. As of 2002 the Yucatan state government has been promoting the *ABC* notation system where *Do* can be located and sung anywhere along the musical scale. In order to accomplish this shift, the Yucatecan Institute of Culture officers fired many Yucatecan musicians from state-sponsored orchestras, replacing them with professional musicians mainly from European and South American conservatories.

A particularly shocking event was the disbanding of the Banda Sinfonica de Yucatán (the state's symphonic band) in March 2002, after 125 years of uninterrupted service and many musical awards. This caused an outrage among Yucatecan musicians in the guitar group in which I play and throughout the city. The news made the pages of all Merida newspapers, including those that regularly support the decisions and activities of PAN, the party then in the state government. Musicians, both within and outside the organizations in which the foreigners were placed, discussed this situation among themselves, and the musicians who had been fired met with the Yucatecan state's cultural authorities. They asked to be compensated for their years of service during this meeting, clearly manifesting their outrage verbally. However, the musicians, who did ultimately receive their requested compensation, never discussed this issue or lobbied their position outside of their internal networks and organizations. Although these and other local musicians were certain that the foreigners would never understand the spirit of the music of the Yucatan, which is something they said you must be born into, there was no violent rebellion. Those few who publicly complained soon found themselves marginalized or even removed from their former positions in the state government's cultural institutes. As usual, the patrons funding trova wavered with the changing politics and continued to support whatever Yucatecan cultural authorities chose to recognize as trova at that time.

Trova patrons, however, were quietly active during the mandate of the 2001–2007 PAN state government, renegotiating a place of recognition for trova within the musical activities sponsored and funded by the cultural authorities of the state and city. The PAN government favored European classical, *high art* music (*musica clásica*), as opposed to *folk* music (*musica popular*), which they often called *backward* music. Trova patrons maneuvered to replace the idea of backwardness in its negative overtones when it came to trova, with a positive idea of a tradition that had to be preserved and made part of high art music (*música culta*). For example, the state government wanted to disband the Orquesta Tipica Yucalpetén. This is an orchestra specializing in the vernacular music of the Yucatan, founded in 1943 by Daniel Ayala, probably Yucatan's most famous academic music composer to date. Trova patrons, however, managed to convince the state cultural authorities that Típica musicians should be retrained in the *new* notation systems and that the same music could be performed by that and other state orchestras under the direction of classically trained arrangers and directors. Thus, the patrons managed to reframe the authorities' understanding of trova as *backward* into trova as *tradition* and their understanding of trova as *folk music* into trova as equivalent to *high art*. The PRI state government of 2007–2012 has validated this changed status of trova.

We can see from these examples that within the trova world conflicts are resolved in relatively *quiet* ways that do not actually disrupt existing social and political positions. The noise surrounding the production and performance of trova and other types of music is silenced within the actual music, although participants may whisper around and between its harmonies. In the end, this silence is probably not broken because of two factors. First, trovadores are socially and economically disadvantaged, as already described. Many receive a supplementary income or other support and recognition from activities related to trova. It is not in their interest to create havoc and lose income in the process. In fact, they find it worthwhile to engage in nonpaying musical activities that will help them to increase their visibility in the trova circles where they prefer to be hired. The group in which I perform, for example, does not pay us in money, but it is associated with one of the most important trova organizations in the city. This association is very hierarchical along social class lines, but it brings our group's members closer to being recognized as *artists* and increases their prestige and the demand for their music outside of our group, such as on the streets of Merida in the evening. Making apparent the noise (power struggles) within this network could seriously damage one's viability as a trova musician in the city.

A second factor maintaining the silence is that trova is a passion for the musicians who perform it. They often say it is a way to bring beauty and joy into their lives and to help oneself and one's friends and family during times of pain and trauma. Two illustrative stories come to mind. A woman in her early forties told me that when she was growing up in Mexico City her mother told her that she should never marry a Yucatecan. Yucatecans, from the mother's point of view, were men who, instead of working, prefer to play guitar and sing romantic songs. However, she met a Yucatecan musician who during the day worked repairing typewriters and computer keyboards and at night and during weekends found employment as a musician. She fell in love with him and followed him to Yucatan. When her mother asked her how she thought he would support her, she answered that she was training to be a certified nurse, and she was willing to support him and their children so that he would continue singing to her all the beautiful songs. They have now been married for almost twenty years and she says that she has never regretted her decision.

Another story concerns a retired literacy worker, part of our trova choir, whose son had an automobile accident in 2004. The young man fell into a coma and the father decided that as long as his son was in the hospital he would not miss any of our rehearsals. He explained to us that playing and singing helped him to feel better and be able to withstand the pain of seeing his son close to death. He only missed one of our rehearsals during the weekend his son died. Later he returned and told us that he needed the music to help him, and he believed that if he felt better he could also help his wife and family.

As we can see both noise and silence are necessary for the continued production and preservation of trova music, at least under current social, economic, and political conditions in Yucatan. Income, class, and gender disparity are all reflected in trova performance, but the perception of this music as *beautiful* and as historically tied to Yucatan itself makes it possible for it to survive and thrive as a marker of Yucatecan identity, *its soul,* even under difficult circumstances.

Performing the Anthropologist

Michael Herzfeld has coined the concept "cultural intimacy" to refer to those elements that people find shameful about their own culture and society but that nevertheless provide them with a sense of common recognition, which is not always positive since these elements emerge from power relations and positions (1997, 3–4). He suggests that anthropologists have to find a way to deal with issues of disclosure about those things considered culturally intimate each time they write about such things (Herzfeld 1997, 156–59 and 167–73).

First to become a trova performer and then to continue being part of trova circles, I have had to negotiate with my fellow musicians the way in which I perceive and can describe this music, even during regular music practice. For example, the trova world is characterized by an absence of direct reference to sex and class, but it is easy to find sexual and class tensions behind trova lyrics. I studied folk guitar for a year, learning mostly trova songs. Our class consisted of a professional musician who taught us the chords, the rhythms, and the songs, four women in their twenties, a retired man who seemed to have hearing problems, and myself. Sometimes they would ask me, "Gaby, what do you want our class to play today?" and I would answer things like, "Let's play that song about the old man who is in love with the teenager" or "Let's play the song of the man who is so angry at the woman he loves because she does not love him back that he wants to kill her." Each time they looked at me quizzically and with great suspicion. They continuously remarked that I was a dangerous person with a dirty mind who could not catch the romantic essence of Yucatecan music. They said that the problem with anthropologists is that they think too much and see things that do not exist.

One of the women in our class loved a schottische written most likely before the 1930s, and I always had to refrain myself from explaining what I thought it said. The song's lyrics are about two men talking about a young girl, wondering where she is from. I asked them what they thought the song meant. The woman who loved it said that it is about a girl who likes to go around the city always carrying the veil with which she wants to get married, and she thought that was very funny. I kept thinking to myself that this song is about two men not daring to ask the young woman to sleep with them because she was from a Meridan family, whether from the working-class neighborhood of Santiago or from the rich neighborhood of Itzimná; but she was rather unreachable ("of no light footing," which in Spanish generally means women who do not sleep around with men), so they did not stand a chance because she would only have sex with the man she married.

Another song, written at the end of the nineteenth century or beginning of the twentieth in Yucatec Maya, says, "Come and sit by my side, dark woman. Yours is my heart. Tell me why you want to leave. Is it only because you cannot stop yourself from attending the annual festival in your village?" Here, obviously, a rich white man is singing to a rural dark woman who is probably employed in his house as part of the domestic service. He makes fun of her because, instead of wanting to stay by him, she wants to go to her village's festival. That the song is in Yucatec Maya only reflects the situation described by Robert Redfield (1941) when he did fieldwork in Yucatan, where the language of everyday life was Mayan and not Spanish, even among the rich sectors of Yucatecan society.

Clearly, my views on trova and my representational strategies of this music are related not only to the music itself but also to my belonging and personal position in Yucatecan society. As a member of the upper middle class and as an anthropologist, I can understand the trova community and its activities from multiple perspectives. When the local musicians were fired and then replaced by foreigners, for example, I could empathize with those who found their musical knowledge suddenly considered obsolete and had to relearn how to describe and write the same music they had been playing their whole lives. But I could also understand the reasons behind this drastic move, an important one being that learning the *ABC* notation system could facilitate the communication between young Yucatecan musicians and their international peers. Although there had been efforts toward implementing this international notation system, their success had been limited. In the weeks after the disbanding of the Yucatan state music band and the public declarations of the cultural authorities to the effect that everyone had to read music if they wanted to be sponsored, in both the group in which I perform and the folk music class I was taking, we were told that we should forget the names of the chords according to what in the Yucatan is known as the *circle system* (a system of chord progressions used for transposing) as well as the *note system* that makes use of the syllables Do, Re, Mi, Fa, Sol, La, Si, and where *Do* is always middle C on the piano, in favor of the *cipher* or *ABC system*.

One of the major interpersonal challenges faced by anthropologists is writing about those people who during fieldwork become close acquaintances and friends. Through my fieldwork I have become recognized as a true Yucatecan *trovadora;* I am now invited to sing and play with professionals who a few years ago considered me a bad musician because I could not understand or play trova songs. I have been since invited into fellow musicians' homes, and they have befriended me despite claims that I am the *spy* of trova. Writing about the noise within trova could be construed as a betrayal of these friendships because my writing might ruffle cultural intimacies. The fact that I'm Yucatecan only complicates this situation. I grew up in a small city of Yucatan. People in my family and many of my friends believe that trova represents the essence of Yucatecans. The silencing of the noise is for them as important as it is for many trova musicians and their patrons. Also, a major source of constant ambivalence and difficulty in representing one's findings relates to ethnographers' lack of control over how our texts will be interpreted and perhaps used, now and in the future. For example, had I pointed out before that many trovadores cannot read any kind of musical notation, PAN authorities could have used my writings as a good excuse to stop supporting them; they thought that only those musicians with formal musical education belonged in the musicscape of Merida. Also, the description of the noise (of the *tensions*) around trova could be seen as a betrayal of musicians' trust, despite my anthropological, ethical practice of informed consent.

The ethical issues surrounding the representation of musical worlds have often led to a dual solution: when it comes to studying vernacular music and dance, many anthropologists and musicologists write ethnographies based on internal cultural dynamics and the performative aspects of the genres, so the music and the social relations around it appear as self-contained (Bennet and Dawe 2001; Delgado and Muñoz 1997; Jardow Pedersen 1999; Kaptain 1992; Miller Chernoff 1981; Reynolds 1999; Seeger 2004; P. Williams 2000). When it comes to classical or commercial music, music anthropologists and musicologists can be more critical aesthetically in terms of social analysis (García de León Griego 2002; Giovannetti 2001; Kramer 1995; López de Jesús Lara 2003; Pedelty 2004; Peterson 1997; Schade-Poulsen 1999; Stokes

1997; Wade 2000). This is because these are seen as nonendangered forms of music, unlike vernacular or folk forms. This situation has been changing in the last twenty years (Goertzen 1997; Mendoza 2000, 2008), but locals and the general academic environment still expect this binary way of looking at music. Likely, the separate approach emerged with folklore studies in the nineteenth century, when popular traditions were seen as endangered and in need of careful descriptions of their musical elements. It was thought that pure folk music had to be collected and recorded so as to leave for future generations a careful description of musical worlds past (Bartók 1979 [1948], Densmore 1992 [1916]).

I believe that this academic binary should be finally shaken up, given that musicians themselves regularly question its limits and boundaries through their musical praxis. For example, Béla Bartók ([1948] 1979) based much of his academic music on folk melodies he collected in the Balkans; Franz Liszt based his *Hungarian Rapsodies* on Gipsy music (see P. Williams 2000); and Aaron Copeland and the Mexican Nationalist School of classical music drew on Mexican folk music as a major source of inspiration (García Bonilla 2001). In Yucatan, from the beginning, trova music has always been at the crossroads of folk and academic music (Baqueiro Foster 1970). Anthropologists can and should question this binary construction. After all, many anthropologists writing about music and dance are performers in our own right, and we often find ourselves, as part of the groups and ensembles in which we perform, dealing with issues similar to those we face in academia and other realms of our societies, such as class, gender, and power differences. My own work, addressing trova critically, instead of from a purely descriptive point of view, attempts to do some of that shaking, so that trova can be understood within the larger sociopolitical context of the contemporary Yucatan.

Fortunately, Yucatecans have a long legacy of publishing about trova (Baquiero Foster 1970; Heredia and De Pau 2000; Pérez Sabido 2003; Pérez Sabido, Hadad, and De Pau 2000; see Vargas-Cetina 2010). These publications provide a general textual context to my own writings; they can be placed and read alongside each other and my own writing so that my perspective becomes only one among many. Practically anything I might say could be argued for or against by locals, especially intellectuals, if they so choose. Furthermore, I see my own writing about trova as a way to give something of value back to the musicians, who are always expressing interest in what I can see in this rather self-contained world of trova. Maybe the ways in which I might be breaking the silence by talking about our cultural intimacies will steer new discussions in Yucatan about the place of music and musicians in our society.

Conclusion: Ethnographic Performance
and the Politics of Representation

Anthropology as a discipline is both performative and informative. It is based on participant observation, a form of cultural performance as a research tool; on the creation of cultural artifacts we call ethnographies; and on the existence of communities of peers, teachers, and students among whom anthropological knowledge is shared, reconstructed, and debated (Fabian 1988). Field research occupies a central place in all these endeavors, whether during its performance, its results in ethnographies, or its constant referencing during public presentations and teaching. Ethnographies, in turn, are expected to have an information component based on the experiences and knowledge that the anthropologists acquire in the field; anthropologists have to find ways to make sense of these collective self-representations in ways at least other anthropologists can understand. Anthropologists, therefore, have to perform both in academia and at their chosen field sites, behaving in ways that are comprehensible to their interlocutors in each distinct environment. In order to arrive at ethnographic description, which is a form of representation, anthropologists become familiar with local self-representations, gathered through constant interaction with local groups and individuals. During fieldwork, many of these personal interactions transform into bonds of friendship. However, in the translation from lived experience to academese, the local alliances the anthropologist has made, along with their intense emotional component, usually disappear from sight.

It is clear that during fieldwork anthropologists often form relationships that they and local people recognize as friendships, implying the shortening of interpersonal distance. Friendships allow ethnographers to acquire detailed information that will be later presented in textual forms to audiences beyond the groups with whom the ethnographer worked. Most people I have encountered during fieldwork everywhere, including trova musicians in Yucatan, understand this role of the anthropologist as an information specialist. They are aware of the fact that through their friendship I am arriving at (negotiated) non-textual information that will ultimately be rendered in textual form. This is why my fellow trova musicians sometimes refer to me as a *spy of the trova*.

The figure of the spy has a double meaning: one who knows and one who tells. Merida musicians have seen me develop musical skills and become a regular member of a trova group. They also know that I write about trova, and they believe I will be publishing a book. Most of the musicians with whom I play are comfortable with the fact that the book will be about them, although they do not know in what terms it will be written. The figure of the spy, however, also has the negative connotation of betrayal. The spy is usually associated with situations of conflict and with the revealing of secrets to some other side. As I have been explaining, there are many tensions within the trova world, and revealing them could be construed as working for the other side. In this sense they think that I will be *telling on them*. One spies on someone else to then reveal secrets (often obtained through friendship) and to cause harm if necessary. By calling me a spy, the musicians are also expressing their concern that I may reveal information they consider sensitive for my own, possibly exploitative, purposes; I may harm them by betraying their confidence. Their lives, like mine, are marked by the constant shifts in power relations at many levels. Families, friends, jobs, political parties, trade unions, and the competition for city, state government, and federal resources affect us all on an everyday basis.

Ethnographers, in fact, could very well be spies if ethnography is written or information is presented without regard for local sensitivity or for the local sense of secrets, since in such cases it could be construed as the exploitation of friendship and, thus, a form of betrayal. Very often the best way to balance all our different acts is by keeping private those aspects of our lives that contrast or even conflict with what is expected of us in other circles. As Herzfeld (1997) points out, after all, cultural intimacy refers not only to the way in which we deal with outsiders but also, and primordially, to the way in which we understand ourselves as part of larger society and as subjects of national states.

Ethnography is, to some extent, a way of making public figures (at least among anthropologists interested in the region where the ethnography took place) out of private individuals. We see today that many people would like to become public figures overnight, as in TV reality shows, where the entertainment value is said to come from the fact that the participants are regular folk and not professional actors. However, most people I know like to retain some degree of privacy, and as my fieldwork progresses I generally gain a sense of what degree of privacy I would like to retain, were I in their place, if an anthropologist was talking to me. I believe that because we owe it to our friends not to betray them by telling their secrets, we must abide by local rules of boundary respect, if those boundaries are fundamental for cultural continuity; however, there is never full consensus anywhere, and to paint only one side of each argument may not be just to all parties involved. And, to complicate matters, each anthropologist has a personal view of the world based on his or her own beliefs and convictions.

Research ethics protocols, now required by many universities, are not a good answer to the dilemmas anthropologists face when writing ethnography. These protocols are based on the model of the biological and medical sciences, which hardly apply to a discipline like ours, specializing in interpersonal, subjective interaction and its textualized representations. Often, to ask people to record their consent before we can ask them any questions only makes them more suspicious, especially if, as in the case of trova musicians, some of them are lawyers, like one of the women in our guitar choir: Does recording consent mean that the researcher can do anything with the information collected? Informed consent, in the form of signed papers or voice recording, may have the effect, she explained, of practically freeing the researcher from accountability. She told musicians not to sign the forms another researcher brought with her when she tried to interview people in our choir. I came to see, following her reasoning, that through informed consent the sense of mutual obligation that friendship creates is superseded by a quasi-legal document, where the answers the *informant* gave become the property of the anthropologist, first, and, later, of the publishing house holding the copyright to his or her published work.

Human interaction is always negotiated interaction. The reproduction of informed-consent documents, on paper or on tape, takes place in a context different from that where the consent was obtained. It is very difficult to say that yesterday's consent would have been today's consent to the same thing. During my research I discuss my own ideas with trova musicians, and sometimes they disagree with me profoundly. At other times they think I am finally beginning to see things the way I should. In all cases, they appreciate that I take the time to tell them what I am thinking, since I am always asking them for their thoughts. I find this to be the most ethical way in which I can conduct fieldwork. Were I to engage in political activism in favor of the trova world, perhaps I would have to hide some "secrets" related to the noise and silence surrounding this type of music and the groups of performers and fans that cultivate it. At the same time, the fact that I am part of Yucatecan society myself would compromise my future research and publications since the power structures that are the context of trova also apply to me. My work on trova, in all cases, will be only one form of representation among many others, some of which will be locally seen as more truthful or more interesting than mine. I have chosen a different type of activism: to engage with the musicians and the trova fans as people who have to be represented in their human, coeval dimension—that is, no better and no worse than others and belonging in the same time as me and my other groups of reference (anthropologists, Yucatecans, Mexicans, academics, musicians, my family). This applies to the music too. Trova is a genre of music and is not the only music that is important in Yucatan; some songs are better than others, and while some trova musicians are extremely skilful, others are not as good as their peers within the Yucatan or elsewhere. I know that this position makes me not only a scribe of noise and silence, but also part of both noise and silence; at the same time, it also makes me part of the music.

After many years of fieldwork with people who are outside national mainstream culture (like many trova musicians), I have come to the conclusion that anthropological representation necessarily has to rely on a radical politics of friendship: we have to represent those with whom we work and engage in the field the way we would represent ourselves, our colleague anthropologists, and our other friends.

Acknowledgments

The fieldwork behind this chapter took place with funding from the Autonomous University of Yucatan (UADY) and the Programa para el Mejoramiento del Profesorado (PROMEP) of the Secretary of Education of Mexico (SEP). I thank the many trovadoras and trovadores who have allowed me to participate in Merida's trova universe. Sarah Evans, Fred Gleach, Stacy Lathrop, Micol Seigel, Nora Vaissman, and Magnus Fiskesjö gave detailed comments on successive versions of this piece. The fabulous libraries at Cornell University supplied me with access to materials difficult to find in Yucatan. My colleague and husband, Steffan Igor Ayora-Diaz, read all different versions and gave me careful feedback, besides his constant support. I dedicate this chapter to my late father, Eduardo Vargas Vargas, who loved trova music and instilled in me the love for the guitar.

9
Ethnography and the Cultural Politics of Environmentalism

Tracey Heatherington

During my first months of ethnographic research on the island of Sardinia, Italy, I found myself one afternoon in a restaurant in a town near the eastern coast as the guest of six men who had befriended another anthropologist the year before. The men were workers in their thirties and forties whose economic strategies included flexible combinations of informal and formal construction jobs, herding, bartending, and entrepreneurial tourism. None of these men possessed the university degrees and political connections that would allow them to contend for steady, salaried, government positions. Over a communal dish of *fave con lardo,* a traditional bean and pork recipe often enjoyed at festive gatherings, they brought up the subject of my fieldwork interests in environmental management with some suspicion.

One of them asked me with a sideways look, and perhaps a little aggressively, "Sei contenta che stiamo tagliando la legna?" (Are you happy that we are cutting wood?). Aware that the town had witnessed episodes of marked contestation with the Forest Ranger Corps the previous year over access to winter fuelwood quotas from the woodlands under communal management, I shrugged and said, "Si, perchè non?" (Yes, why not?).

He did not answer but continued to interrogate, "Cosa vuol dire WWF?" (What does WWF stand for?).

Grumbles resounded at the table as I stumbled tentatively over the words, "World Wildlife Fund."

Immediately my inquisitor demanded to know, "Sei d'accordo con il parco del Gennargentu?" (Are you in favor of the Gennargentu Park?).

Before I could respond, a passionate debate flared up about a plan to establish a national park. The men shouted their positions to one another in Sardinian and to me in Italian. Confused and energetic discussion continued. Nobody seemed to agree with anyone else about exactly how the town should approach environment and development. What emerged, nonetheless, was a tacit consensus that the proposed national park would be bad for local residents because it would prevent the free continuation of hunting, wood-cutting, tourism development, and pastoral herding on the commons. All these uses of the local territory were recognized as essential to their aspirations for the future.

The point in demanding to know whether I agreed with their exercise of rights to take wood from their communal territory was essentially the same, for them, as asking if I agreed with the creation of a national park. These men wanted me to clarify whether or not I supported their rights to use and benefit from the local commons. If I was for these rights, for the *usi civici* (rights of communal usufruct), then I could be considered to be on their side. Only on these terms, I suspected, were they prepared to accept me into their social world, whether as an ethnographer, an advocate, or a friend. By contrast, if I were seen to support the WWF or the Gennargentu National Park, then I would be persona non grata working against their interests. I had already met certain forest rangers, stationed in the town from other parts of Sardinia, who were pointedly denied some customary local hospitality precisely because they were taken to be associated with both environmentalists and the state.

"Non puoi fare l'antropologa e l'ambientalista alla stessa volta!" (You cannot be an anthropologist and an environmentalist at the same time!), one of them insisted emphatically.

I remember asking quite timidly, "Ma perchè?" (But why not?). This reductive dualism continued to haunt me, expressing what seemed to be a classic conflict between anthropocentric and biocentric values and perspectives.[1] In retrospect, I see that this brusque warning against divided loyalties was both more astute and more intriguing than I realized at the time. Even in Western Europe, the paradoxes of advocacy in environmental anthropology have turned out to be dramatic.

Anthropological work on traditional environmental knowledge in tribal and peasant societies has made significant contributions to cultural recognition in many contexts.[2] Yet it remains problematic for local groups to lay claim to cultural authority over landscapes and biodiversity resources without essentializing culture. For example, the guidelines of the Convention on Biological Diversity (CBD) leave government elites to arbitrate which local communities truly embody "traditional lifestyles relevant for the conservation and sustainable use of biological diversity" (UNCED 1992). As we move toward more nuanced assessments of political ecology in a changing world, the representation of *authentic* or *traditional* orientations to environmental management has become more fraught. It is problematic for many minority groups to be recognized for their cultural knowledge traditions as a result of their growing participation in a global economy, resulting in patterns of change in contemporary natural resource use and a symbolic failure of authenticity. As anthropology comes home to Western contexts, the boundaries between cultural advocacy and cultural critique become harder to gauge. I faced these quandaries in my work on Sardinia.

Neoracisms and Environmental Justice

The rise of global environmentalism, with the recent synthesis of efforts toward protecting biological and cultural diversity, constitutes one aspect of what Michael Herzfeld has described as "a global hierarchy of value." According to Herzfeld, the "increasingly homogeneous language of culture and ethics" (2003, 2) practiced across transnational spheres of government, interest groups, and business constitutes the rhetoric of universal morality. This indicates one of the subtler, but most nefarious, forms of globalization. The global hierarchy of value is "a logic that has seeped in everywhere but is everywhere disguised as difference, heritage, local tradition" (2). This effect can be noted in moral discourses of environmental governmentality that treat local culture as a black box that should fit within highly conventionalized categories of *tradition*. In the conventional narratives of international, environmental nongovernmental organizations (NGOs), representations of rainforest tribes as historically and culturally diverse as the Penan and the Kayapo are made to fit the mold of *noble ecological Indians*.[3] This is a strategy that belies the real roots of their sophisticated ecological practices. Further, by expecting indigenous peoples to live up to the stereotype of the ecological Indian, we assert the privilege of Western cultural paradigms associated with environmentalism and conservation, which are equally problematic.

Looking at a case in Southeast Asia, Tania Li notes that notions of indigenousness are somewhat mobile; but, within a given regional array of state and activist discourses, "if they are to fit the preconfigured slot of indigenous people, [rural people] must be ready and able to articulate their identity in terms of a set of characteristics recognized by their allies and by the media that presents their case to the public" (2000, 157). Beth Conklin's (2002) account from Amazonia suggests that the cultural essentialism inherent in environmentalist models of the noble, ecological Indian has provoked some groups to reappropriate visions of indigenousness and invent more fluid paradigms for ecological authenticity. The Sardinian case both complements and complicates the study of such cultural engagements in postcolonial and aboriginal contexts by developing a European perspective. The heirs of rural peasant/herding cultures fit into postmodern visions of landscape and bio-diversity management only with awkwardness. My concern is that, in a period when huge and prosperous environmental NGOs have begun to mediate environmental politics and governance internationally (Chapin 2004), anthropological advocacy has become too vulnerable to the clamorous expectations of a generic brand of global environmentalism. When strategic representations of culture are undermined by embedded cultural prejudices, they may poorly support environmental justice.[4]

Faye Harrison (1995, 2002), for example, argues that the kinds of cultural essentialisms at play in today's ethnic identity politics are often de facto forms of racism. In Italy, cultural differences between the industrial north and agricultural south have been essentialized through the interpretation of post-war economic statistics, demographic patterns, and evidence of sociopolitical organization.[5] The island of Sardinia is considered part of the troublesome southern Mezzogiorno region and has a peculiar history in Italian discourses of governance. Perceptions of innate cultural difference in central Sardinia are deeply biologized. Nineteenth-century physical anthropologists made explicit connections between race, culture, and criminality in the shepherd towns of highland Sardinia. Central Sardinia has long been viewed as a *criminal zone* (cf. Niceforo [1897] 1977; Corda 1985) and continues to garner notoriety for its association with famous kidnappings and political intimidations. Frequent media reports about homicides and other criminal phenomena are referred to as Sardinia's "black chronicle," an image grounded in the work of criminologists and economists who had envisioned central Sardinian towns as repositories of ignorance and violence, apt to inflict damage upon the environment.[6] Equally damaging is that central Sardinia is represented as a landscape of vehement resistance to government and external authority. The defense of pastoral traditions and village commons has been an important focus for grassroots action since the early nineteenth century, at the time of the enclosure movement associated with the so-called Sardegna Sabauda.[7]

This perceived cultural-economic backwardness and ongoing criminality of central Sardinian shepherds by urban elites and policymakers was one of the factors legitimating the first concerted initiative to create a national park in highland Sardinia. The initiative coincided with an Italian parliamentary inquest into banditry in the central region called the Barbagia in the late 1960s. Policy studies linked the culture of mobile herders with practices such as kidnapping, poaching, and forest arson.[8] The original park plan was designed to emulate the American model for national parks, entailing the exclusion of human inhabitants and a ban on virtually all resource extraction within the largest part of the protected area (Bodemann 1979). Because shepherds, goatherds, pig herders, and cowherds would have no more access to communally owned pasturelands, herding mobility would be reduced and modern tourism would be encouraged at the expense of pastoral activities. National legislation to create the Gennargentu National Park in 1969 provoked so much protest in the herding-dependent towns of central Sardinia that it was later rescinded.

During the 1980s, the Region of Sardinia acquired authority over environmental governance. The plan to create a national park in Sardinia was redesigned and set in motion, promoted by organizations such as Legambiente and WWF-Italia and supported by government authorities from the provincial level up. Recent models for parks and protected areas worldwide have taken a *participatory* approach to local residents since environmental conservation has become linked to issues of human rights, international development, and social justice in the aftermath of the Brundtland Report (World Commission on Environment and Development 1987). In Italy, environmental governance was increasingly associated with structural investments and regional development was associated with the emerging European Union. Socioeconomic development projects were announced in connection with the park, to be managed at the provincial level. Yet the centralization of authority over parklands belonging to thirteen different towns in Italy created potential problems with the equity of structural development, job creation, and compensation. The alienation of communal lands was also an inflammatory issue within communities because it threatened to jeopardize herding practices and heighten inequities in the distribution of resources and opportunities across socioeconomic classes.

Residents of rural, east-central Sardinia, with whom I spoke between 1990 and 1991, tended to distrust environmentalism, as a whole, and the park plan, in particular, because they understood them as linked to the erosion of the usi civici in all its forms and tacit possibilities. Although a few might have benefited overall from the creation of a protected area, collaboration to resist the undermining of the usi civici furthered the interests of most, whether they wished to continue to practice herding, lobby for a share of socioeconomic funding initiatives, gain greater freedom to pursue entrepreneurial initiatives predicated on construction and infrastructural development, or maintain control over future development decisions. Although the national law (*legge* 16 *giugno* 1927, n. 1766) protecting the usi civici, in fact, referred only to the use of wood resources, pastures and agricultural plots, and the gathering of acorns for animal feed, in some towns of rural Sardinia the usi civici were often taken to establish more profound natural historical rights to local control over resources. People who might otherwise find themselves at logger-heads over the path of local development were instead unified to protect a degree of autonomy in land-use decisions, working together to contest inva-sive conservation initiatives *callato dall'alto* (imposed from the top down).

In late March of 1998, while I was in the field again, the final act of leg-islation associated with law 394, confirming the borders of a new national park in Sardinia, was approved by Italian parliament in collaboration with the Region of Sardinia. Local mayors in the towns that stood to lose control over large areas of communal territory immediately objected. In the cen-tral Sardinian herding town I had chosen for research, there were grassroots protests, political intimidations, and acts of environmental vandalism that erupted to discourage the government from enacting the legislation. People there felt angry and politically marginalized; social tensions ran high. Some joked about their own resemblance to the historical Indians of America about to be removed from their homelands, and a few elaborated sophisticated po-litical narratives about the ties between environmentalism and neocolonial-ism in modern Italy.

A growing body of literature calls attention to protected areas as loci of contention and disempowerment, as well as opportunity, from the perspec-tives of resident peoples.[9] The politics of cultural representation are vital to how forest rangers, resource management bureaucrats, environmental NGO advocates, and other environmental experts interpret the guidelines for valu-ing local knowledge and local participation in environmental management in places like central Sardinia. Anthropology has a role to play here in mak-ing visible how current systems of environmental governance are negotiated through discourses of power/knowledge and what effects they ultimately produce.[10]

The Ambivalent Ethnographer

With my research, I had hoped to challenge the legacies of earlier scholar-ship about banditry and backwardness in Sardinia. At first, I imagined that my role would be to interpret local feelings for the landscape across linguis-tic and cultural divides, affirm local ecological knowledge, and contribute to a critique of top-down environmental management. My sense of anthro-pological advocacy verged on the romantic. The difficulty with this became apparent during my very first trip to Sardinia in 1990, when I visited a town near my field site on the coast. Invited by a friend into the privacy of one relatively poor herder's home, I was offered a roasted meat dish that I later learned was made from one of Sardinia's most famous endangered species, the wild sheep of Sardinia, or mouflon (*ovis musimon*). These animals were the *poster children* for environmentalist campaigns in Sardinia and had not been legally in season to hunt since before protection was legislated in the 1970s. The family had followed a different logic and morality in choosing to cull an older animal from the herd.

"Meglio mangiare e non dire niente" (Better to eat [it] and say nothing), I was quietly admonished by my hostess, with a challenging wink. Her warning was redoubled with a keen look when an unsuspecting forest ranger arrived on a personal errand as we sat at lunch.

Forced to confront the limits of my own cultural relativism, I wondered what I should write. For me as an ethnographer, the ironies and ambiguities of Sardinian cultural ecology represented a series of ethical quandaries. In my earliest ethnographic writing I instinctively accepted many of the boundaries marked by Sardinian demonstrations of "cultural intimacy" (Herzfeld 1997). I wished to avoid talking about poaching, for example, because it might only highlight negative images of criminality and backwardness in highland Sardinia. While I knew many Sardinians to be openly critical of local politics and practices when it came to environment and development, I could not imagine how to support their critiques without undermining the efforts of other Sardinians to assert their cultural identity and sustain authority over landscape.

I shared with my Sardinian interlocutors a critical standpoint on the kinds of global discourses articulated by wilderness movements at the time, including the WWF. Yet, along with a quiet minority of residents in central Sardinia, I was also critical of the changing land management practices that might seriously compromise local ecologies over the long term. I believed that it was important to address the inequalities associated with emerging differences in structural access to various kinds of resources, including land, funding, and "symbolic capital" (Bourdieu 1984, 1991), and to seek out environmental partnerships that might provide alternatives to the highly centralized national park model. The bipolar discursive formations that have dominated the Sardinian politics of environmentalism tend to preclude such options. Both strategic essentialisms adopted by Sardinians and negative stereotypes circulated in the Italian media and bureaucratic discourses tend to heighten and reify this bipolarity.

So-called traditional and modern, local and extralocal knowledges and institutions have become intrinsically engaged with one another on the Sardinian landscape, while the gaps and incongruities of each contribute to environmental problems today. The Sardinian case was particularly fraught for me as a young ethnographer because I wished to both support grassroots initiatives to resist new embodiments of environmental racism and retain a degree of integrity in my own visions of appropriate social and ecological models. The difficulty involved in supporting and respecting local knowledges on their own terms while engaging in productive critical discourses represented a deep paradox. I was not prepared for the ambivalence I felt as I came to recognize how events of homicide, vandalism, violent threats to politicians, forest fires, and public tensions undermined the vision of community by which my hosts struggled to live.

What to write? If I ignored the ways my field sites failed to sustain the positive stereotypes of tradition that Sardinian residents themselves presented to outsiders in support of their claims to authority over the landscape, then my own cultural representations would reify the secondary status of local knowledge vis-à-vis science by promoting static, homogenized, and standardized visions of *local* cultural practice. Minority initiatives to revitalize cultural knowledge and manage important community resources could be undermined by my own effort to support representations of cultural authenticity. There was also the danger of reinforcing insidious cultural racisms now transposed to the plane of discourses about environmental governance. How could I take into account processes of structural marginalization without condoning kidnapping and arson or negating the existence of creative political subjectivities?

When Conklin (2003) invoked the responsibility of anthropologists to "speak truth to power," she called upon us to find ways of communicating contemporary models of dynamic cultural process to the wider world and acknowledge the complexity of social and ecological critiques internal to indigenous communities. In highland Sardinia, such auto-critiques were intrinsically part of wider community efforts to define environmental justice. People were critical not only of the policies, governments, and broader economic structures they perceived to shape their lives, but also of their own actions and decisions as a community. Often veiled by "cultural intimacy" (Herzfeld 1997), for fear that the self-recognition of faults, tensions, and problems in central Sardinia might reinforce the negative cultural essentialisms ever present in media representations and policy discourses, the voices of internal cultural critique are nevertheless powerful instruments of social change and ecological improvement.

Fire and Ice

They have covered the mountains of my town with fire. They have reduced the whole place to charcoal and in the winter the ice has destroyed it all.

Tonino Cau, "Su Ballu De Su Fogu"

This excerpt comes from a popular folk-style song written in Sardinian for a neo-traditional *canto a tenores* quartet. The writer, Tonino Cau, was influenced by the thriving folk traditions in the Sardinian Barbagia and inspired by the poetry of Peppino Marotto, a well-known Sardinian balladeer from Orgosolo. Cau was impassioned to speak out against the terrible forest fires caused by arsonists that devastated areas of the territory. As a result of summer droughts, forests throughout highland Sardinia are highly at risk of fires from June through September. Devastation of Sardinian landscapes and biodiversity by anthropogenic forest fires peaked in the early 1980s, and the region responded by increasing its investment in firefighting technology and manpower. Thousands of hectares are still affected by fire in Sardinia each year, and a significant number of these fires are thought to be set deliberately, either with the purpose of clearing and regenerating pastures, creating new jobs in the forestry service, intimidating political representatives, or as a tacit form of resistance against unpopular policy shifts.[11] The threat of new fires hung over the landscape whenever tensions over environmental governance and the use of the territory flared. During the 1990s, Cau's traditional *tenores* quartet produced two music videos related to landscape and environment in Sardinia. As examples of cultural authenticity, Sardinian tenor singers and folklore troupes became popular tourist attractions during the 1970s and continue to tour abroad. As a critical genre, however, Sardinian poetry has particular resonance and popularity on the island itself, and especially throughout central Sardinia. The medium of a culturally and linguistically *authentic* music tradition created a somewhat intimate space for the tenor singers to engage other Sardinians in their concerns about abuses to the landscape undertaken in the name of political and economic resistance.

This illustrates a thread of cultural auto-critique that mobilizes social sanctions against those who practice forest arson to protect or avenge their own perceived interests. In the central Sardinian town where I undertook further ethnography during the late 1990s, informal social mechanisms helped to protect the commons against fire. During this period, I met a number of young men, working-class herders, construction laborers, forestry personnel, and others who outspokenly denounced arsonists and threatened angry repercussions if they found out who was responsible for certain attempts. Others worked calmly behind the scenes to dissuade fiery tempers, so to speak. Pyromaniacs were typically disdained by other rural Sardinians as deviant and ignorant—the real examples of criminality, immorality, and backwardness who tainted their own living cultural heritage. The town's forest fire problem had diminished markedly during the 1990s. On those isolated occasions when fires were discovered, many volunteers from the community arrived to assist forest rangers and professional firemen in putting out the flames.

It was Carlo, a quiet forest ranger, who brought my attention to "The Ballad of the Fire" in 1991. Like many of his colleagues, Carlo had strong family ties to the pastoral community in central Sardinia. He had studied agriculture at a university and gone on to join the Sardinian forest ranger corps when it expanded in the late 1980s. As a ranger, he helped to monitor for signs of fire throughout the dangerous summer season around the territory of the town where he was posted then. He loved the long walks in the countryside that were associated with his jobs on patrol. Carlo took seriously the project of learning about local ecology and displayed a consciousness of environmental issues that was crafted from both historical experience and global discourses. Carlo's personal career choices reflected not only economic and political transformations in Sardinia, but also a new way of articulating local knowledge and cultural attachments to traditional Sardinian landscapes with the formal, expert knowledge of forestry and environmental science.

During my time in Sardinia, I listened to a number of friends like Carlo as they struggled to reflect upon current events. I witnessed some of them launch new social and economic initiatives with the possibility to transform the invidious and arbitrary symbolic boundaries that distinguished *modernity* and *tradition* as polar opposites. Now, I try to guide my own efforts at cultural representation by their initiatives to engage in critical debates and public dialogues. By highlighting complexity and contradiction in my writing about culture and environment, I hope to help to open more legitimate space for autochthonous critical voices in Sardinia.

Auto-Criticism in Action

When I arrived in Sardinia in 1996 prepared for research work in a central Sardinian field site, I was sent to Dr. M., a local intellectual, retired teacher, and former mayor, with an old-fashioned letter of introduction from a gracious and well-regarded lawyer from the Ogliastra. By the time I heard the chronicle transcribed below, of his time in public office between 1975–1980, I was already aware that the town had undergone tremendous socioeconomic transformations during the late 1960s and the 1970s. Dr. M.'s communist-led administration was the first coalition of the Left to be elected at the local level. At the same time, both demographics and cultural ecology were changing across Sardinia as patterns of outward labor migration became established. Gradually, cereal cultivation was abandoned and herding practices were transformed to use more land, fewer men, and more inputs, with larger herds (Meloni 1984). Eventually, motor vehicles were introduced, although many herders in the town continued to milk by hand and produce their own cheeses. Traditional grazing areas on the commons remained important.

Of the total territory associated with the town today, about one-third remained under town management, subject to the exercise of rights of usi civici, permitting access to firewood, fodder, and pastures. This land cannot be alienated, although it can be leased out for particular extraction and improvement activities. Historically, a balance of agricultural and pastoral activities were rotated on this area of the commons, and a fallow period of two months was mandated annually during the spring transhumance, when herders would move their animals out to privately contracted pastures. This excerpt from our interview documents a decline of fallows regulation, *su vardau,* in the town. Dr. M. gave me the following account:

> After seventeen years, I express an [overall] positive judgment of [our] experience [in office]. . . . That which leaves a bitter taste in my mouth, which leaves me unsatisfied, is the question relative to the management of the communal patrimony. . . . Up until my administration the communal resource-use norms were generally observed by everyone and particularly by the herders. . . . *Su vardau* was the best part of the communal territory [each year], where the grass was allowed to grow. . . . [G]enerally, from March twentieth until May nineteenth to twentieth, pasturing was not allowed. Every year, in particular to allow the shepherds to be able to leave their late autumn/winter pastures, pastures that were often outside [the town's] territory, private pastures, expensive pastures [for which] very often the shepherd [was obliged to pay] a great part of the product—milk, lambs, and wool—therefore in the pastoral economy, the return to protected communal pastures that had been rested for two months represented a relief, a lightening of the burden. Naturally this was all relative because not everything depended on [simply] protecting the territory [from grazing], it also depended on the year, the climate, the rain, and so all these [factors were taken into account each year] in the communal resource use norms. During my administration what happened?
>
> A small group of herders did not want to obey this rule, a rule respected for perhaps 100, 150 years. These herders said that they could not transfer their herds from the prohibited areas because there was *ferrula* in the area where pasture was allowed. [But] we have always had *ferrula* . . . for 20 years previous . . . and the herders made sure their animals stayed away from lethal plants or removed the pernicious weeds

from the area of pasture, but this required more labor. It was a pretext, a means of saying that they didn't care about the rule. It was perhaps [only] ten herders, and naturally the other herders said that the administration must intervene, and [so it did]. It intervened in several ways, warning these herders, threatening that we would apply sanctions and provisions. But they pretended not to hear, and if they heard, they did not obey. We had two or three guards, and they couldn't very well capture two hundred sheep at a time [for] there was no place to put them. The others complained; we turned to the state police, but what could they do, poor things; they captured the sheep and then the animals wandered here and there. In the end, we applied the administrative sanctions and won the court case, but the damage was done, the rule was disrespected, the pasture degraded.

And so, the other herders, the herders obedient to the rules, [nevertheless] did nothing to help us. They did not lift a finger; they only came to protest against the administration that it did nothing against the disobedient herders. However, they just stood there looking on and complaining about the administration. . . . The [economic] interests of everyone were concentrated on the communal territory, but in 1975 the animals and the numbers of herders were fewer than before and [so] the interest in regulating the territory was diminished. . . . It was a loss for everybody, for the town, for the herders themselves. However, it must be said that since that time, the communal territory has not been regulated.

Dr. M.'s administration made several attempts to find new ways to stem the degradation of the commons. Efforts to achieve better use of the land by dividing areas of the commons between pigs, cows, and sheep, for example, failed from a similar lack of community support. The town had fencing built, only to find it systematically vandalized, dismantled, and carried off. On a larger scale, efforts to eradicate the African swine pest across Sardinia during the same period failed because a number of local herders hid their pigs rather than accepting the indemnities.

Although it suggests a number of ways that local ecological knowledge and institutions for regulation of the commons have declined, this story witnesses critical internal engagement with such problems. Dr. M. searched for the roots of declining sustainability in changing occupational patterns and socioeconomic strategies. His administration improvised a series of measures in the face of changing times. Although these measures failed at the time, they nevertheless nourished discourses of communal self-reflection about the problem of the commons. By the 1990s, the decline of the fallows was widely recognized by local residents as symbolic of cultural transformations gone wrong. Although the question of the commons in the town remains complex and contentious, local efforts at understanding and solving the problem have multiplied.

The town's elected officials since the 1970s have played important roles in finding effective ways to support positive transformations in cultural ecology. Dr. M.'s government supported the formation of an agricultural cooperative that was highly innovative in rehabilitating and improving areas of the communal territory, managing wood extraction, and seeking out international partnerships for the development of clean energy solutions. Public works have been carried out to promote aesthetic uses of the landscape and assist tourism operators. A second forestry camp was leased to the State Forestry Service. Finally, local officials have sought to establish a positive but critical working relationship with higher government in order to redefine efforts at conservation.

Revitalizing Local Ecological Knowledge

Luigino, an active, middle-aged herder who kept cattle on the commons in central Sardinia, was concerned about the effects of occupational fragmentation over recent decades. He had seen that the divergence of economic and political interests within the town had provoked misunderstandings and antagonisms between members of different occupational groups. Herders had been blamed for both public discord on and environmental deterioration of the commons, although the entire community was at fault. Ultimately, he suggested, the herders were the only ones who paid the municipality for their use of the land, but the commons was there for everyone to benefit from, to use and enjoy. "There's room for everyone," he said, "herders, forestry workers, tourist guides, everyone."

When I asked if the herders envisioned any kind of environmental improvements he said, "Yes! Instead of reforesting, we want to clear, plow, and plant [return to agricultural rotations to improve the pastures]."

Older and retired herders were sometimes very critical of the way herding practices had changed over the years. While they themselves remembered vividly the hardships of remaining with their animals away from town for months at a time, young herders all had vehicles and simply visited their flocks once or twice a day to carry out necessary tasks. Strategies of dividing flocks and monitoring pastures carefully had been simplified to minimize labor inputs. Cereal agriculture on the high plains had also been abandoned across highland Sardinia by the 1970s.

Luigino had left school as a boy to take on duties as a herder. Like others of his age and older, Luigino appreciated the positive efforts of some younger shepherds to care for their flocks conscientiously and utilize elements of traditional ecological knowledge. He respected that some young herders had also developed tourist guide businesses and "lunch with the shepherds" excursions to supplement their incomes, and he assisted with two of these. He hoped to see better collaboration between herders, forestry laborers, and eco-development entrepreneurs in caring for the commons. His vision of revitalizing local knowledge pertaining to mixed herding and agriculture emphasized the centrality of traditional pastoralism to a potentially better local economy and ecology.

Luigino's commitment to the commons was also political. He became one of the local organizers of a grassroots base committee of the Regional Movement for the Defense of Rights to the [Communal] Territories. This was a loose-knit group of people collaborating from across several highland Sardinian towns to mobilize opposition to the ratification of Law 394, pertaining to parks and protected areas in Sardinia and, particularly, the creation of the Gennargentu National Park. The group claimed nonpartisan, grassroots status and maintained a critical stance toward municipal governments, which were run by the educated, salaried class of Sardinians employed in the public sector. I knew many women and men from the families of herders and forestry laborers who, like Luigino, participated in hosting a demonstration organized by this network. Paradoxically, opposing a national park was also considered a means of protecting the forest itself from the corruption deemed to be rampant in modern Italian bureaucracies. The park, they reasoned, might prove to be yet another form of overcentralized development that was harmful to the environment as well as the community.

Luigino's vision of a return to pastoral heritage incorporated hybrid elements of forestry and ecotourism. It privileged self-critical discourses operating within the networks of local shepherds, mobilizing a commitment to pursue positive ecological relationships. Above all, it envisioned the revitalization of community, entailing the reinstatement of relations of trust, collaboration, mutual respect, and reciprocity across different occupational groups in the town.

Voicing Common Concerns

One of my favorite photographs hanging in my office depicts a *priorissa* (a member of a prestigious Catholic organization of women) at a grassroots political demonstration hosted by the town in April of 1998. In front of her old-fashioned dark blouse and skirt, she holds up a modern-looking T-shirt that says, "NO TO THE PARK!" in Sardinian. She sits among a few older men and some mature women while a handful of children move around them. We are all in the countryside, on the town commons, and over half the town's population seems to be there. Guests are still arriving from other towns. Later, newspapers would estimate an attendance of well over five thousand. Despite concerns that social tensions may erupt over controversial issues, there is a festive atmosphere to the gathering and a sense of determined optimism. Sardinian music plays over the loudspeaker. People are smiling and talking with excitement among themselves, mostly in Nuorese dialects of Sardinian, as they wait for a series of speeches by grassroots organizers and small-town mayors to begin.

To some Italian technocrats and international advocates of nature conservation, this picture might symbolize the backwardness of Sardinian environmental psychology as an example of ingrained resistance to the state and clinging to an apparently outdated agro-pastoral system of communal land use. After a decade of conversations with Sardinians, I see it quite differently. Sardinian women have taken me to their gardens and spoken to me of their agricultural work in earlier times of poverty. Others have urged me to join them in Catholic processions to pilgrimage sites in the countryside. For them, the loss of the commons implied truncating ties to a pastoral heritage with deep roots in history, land, religion, family, and language. To me, the picture in my office captures a moment of poetic and sincere attachment to the land and the community, as well as the nuances of sophisticated cultural auto-critique.

One element of this was that the organizers and participants hoped to prevent violent reactions that they thought might be undertaken by unruly men in their own towns as forms of resistance to a park that seemed created deliberately to strip them of their sole economic security and birthright. The tacit fear that this dispossession might inspire forest arson and eco-vandalism was widespread. Although people avoided talking about these apprehensions in public, one elderly matriarch and shepherd's wife articulated her concern openly to me when I joined in the work of drawing up posters with the women from the grassroots campaign against the creation of the Gennargentu National Park. "The old people don't want the park because we want the territory [to be] green, not black," she said frankly. She had seen the destruction caused by earlier forest fires on the commons.

The demonstration of April 1998 was accomplished peacefully despite grave social tensions across the town. This was due in part to the social subtlety of grassroots organizers, men and women, who were able to negotiate a contingent consensus among residents to organize a peaceful demonstration against the park. This event indicated the vitality of an initiative that, in fact, entailed strong currents of auto-critique, acknowledging an ongoing local problem of a violent minority that could target people, institutions, and landscapes. There emerged important Sardinian dialogues across the increasingly heterogeneous occupational groups, such as herders, construction workers, forestry workers, agricultural workers, salaried officials, teachers, shop owners, unemployed, and tourism entrepreneurs. What most compromised these efforts were the indications of their own political marginality that emerged over the course of planning and presenting the event. In particular, legitimate political action was undermined by the decision of national government officials to ignore the authority of local mayors who attempted to represent the interests and voices of townspeople, a clear majority of whom stood against the park plan.

Marginality in a Global Hierarchy of Value

Strategic auto-essentialisms in rural highland Sardinia are informed by a global hierarchy of value that compromises claims of authenticity from the outset. When they presented themselves to outsiders such as tourists or journalists, most of my Sardinian acquaintances essentialized culture and community in an uncomplicated, positive manner. They sought to show how life in central Sardinia was more wholesome and egalitarian than in the cities, where drugs, prostitution, poverty, and homelessness were thought to characterize modern lifestyles. They demonstrated the generous hospitality of traditional herding towns, the piety of local Catholic rituals, the continuity of Sardinian language practice, and the healthful, flavorful qualities of authentic local foods. They also claimed a special guardianship over the landscape based on their deep history of cultural inhabitation. Though by no means unfounded, this vision of tradition is ultimately too narrow and categorical to endure the fray of contemporary Sardinian reality.

Representations of ecological tradition in Sardinia will probably continue to fall prey to brutish deconstructions unless communities effectively reestablish enduring, visible commitments to ecological self-regulation. The question of the commons is genuinely important to rural people themselves. In support, I owe my friends and hosts in Sardinia, as well as my colleagues and other activists, the honor of another honest critical voice. I have come to believe that my anthropological interventions should celebrate not an essential cultural unity or authentic *tradition* in towns like my two field sites, but rather the intelligent attempts of many rural Sardinians to transcend social differences, curb violence, and pursue collective organization. Clearly, it remains crucial to recognize larger economic and cultural processes that impinge upon these efforts. Cultural racisms, for example, can contribute to the processes of political and structural marginalization, allowing some isolated members of the community to feel justified in the recourse to violence that only brings tragedy and undermines further the political position of local residents. The ongoing effect of cultural racisms embedded in the institutions and the politics of Sardinian conservation is part and parcel of the global hierarchy of value that has taken root in international discourses about environment and development. As anthropologists, we must challenge biologized or essentialized cultural categories at the source of environmental racisms and champion the creative possibilities of cultural hybridity and heterogeneity.

The Sardinian voices in this chapter reflected explicitly upon the complex and fluid class formations in which they themselves were embedded, from rather different subject positions in the forestry administration, local government, herding and tourism enterprises, and grassroots activism. What I have begun to appreciate in the course of trying to write about Carlo's love of landscape, Dr. M.'s disillusionment, Luigino's hopes for ecological revitalization, and an elderly woman's fear of forest fires is that their individual sentiments, their critical contributions, and their distinctive cultural visions hold real productive value for a transformative political ecology. Despite the appearance of fractiousness, the efforts of some residents to revitalize local knowledge and explore the larger implications of institutional transformations—expected to affect them all in different ways—were deeply meaningful. Their initiatives to reflect critically on questions of contemporary land use, to recognize failures of environmental governance at the community level, and to seek out a positive means to resist marginalization in political debates must all be recognized as worthy cultural resources in a context of dynamic change.

Acknowledgments

I am grateful to Gabriela Vargas-Cetina, Stacy Lathrop, and Beth Conklin for initiating an important conversation in the *Anthropology News,* which inspired this discussion. I also thank my husband and colleague, Bernard Perley, for his many insights into the complexities of indigeneity.

This chapter is adapted from materials in my book *Wild Sardinia: Indigeneity and the Global Dreamtimes of Environmentalism* (University of Washington Press, 2010). Fieldwork in Sardinia since the 1990s has been generously supported by Fonds FCAR, the Mellon Foundation, the Krupp Foundation, the Wenner-Gren Foundation, the Weatherford Center for International Studies at Harvard, the University of Western Ontario, and the University of Wisconsin, Milwaukee.

Notes

1. Environmentalist critiques of Western culture have often focused upon the conflict of interest between human needs and aspirations to exploit natural resources for livelihoods, personal benefits, and economic growth versus the need to constrain resource use within the parameters of sustainability. This is epitomized by processes such as ongoing urban sprawl, deforestation, and the development of industry in fragile ecological zones.

2. Posey's work (1999, 2004) is particularly salient, given his championship of indigenous ecological knowledge and sovereignty over resources. Indigenous groups have apparently attained a degree of respect and value in global environmental discourses, reflected, for example, in the Convention on Biological Diversity (CBD) and subsequent United Nations Development Programme (UNDP) programming. Nevertheless, easy alliances between environmental groups and indigenous peoples can no longer be assumed (Brosius 1997; Conklin 2006).

3. See, for example, Vargas-Cetina (2001), as well as Braun (2002) and Slater (2002). Note, however, that attempts to deconstruct stereotypes that naturalize a link between "primitive" cultures and sustainable cultural ecologies are often problematic. Krech's (1999) claim to debunk myths of the "ecological Indian," for example, failed to interrogate the complex postcolonial contexts with which Native American and indigenous self-representation and economic strategies are necessarily engaged. See Doxtater (2004) and Ranco (2005, 2006) for critical discussion. Karlsson's (2006) critique of Ellen (1986) and Ingold (2000) provides a similar perspective, drawing on a case study from India.

4. The concept of environmental justice has been applied to study how power differentials associated with race, class, and gender converge with environmental issues and is now recognized by the US Environmental Protection Agency. A grassroots, community-based environmental justice movement has grown in North America since the 1980s. In the European context, racisms and cultural racisms are somewhat differently configured, but the concept of environmental justice can be applied to study differential access to natural resources, including green space, as well as the impacts of industrial development on different socioeconomic groups, particularly minorities.

5. Kertzer (1996), J. Cole (1997), Schneider (1998), and Bull (2000) have reflected on various aspects of this.

6. See Bodemann (1979) and Ayora-Diaz (1993) for discussion.

7. This coincides with the period 1831–1861, when the *legge delle chiudende* were introduced under the House of Savoy, just prior to Italian unification. The expulsion of herds from traditional common lands inspired unrest in Nuoro and, particularly, the uprisings of *su connotu* in 1867.

8. In Tanzania, comparatively, indigenous pastoral peoples have been vilified as poachers and encroachers at the same time they are marginalized as cultural, racial, and linguistic minorities. Neumann (1998), Brockington (2002), Igoe (2004), and Walley (2004) have all documented the racist legacies of colonialism in Tanzanian protected areas. In all of these cases, the moral rhetoric of conservation priorities largely overwrites evidence that the apparently *natural* beauty of African landscapes has actually been supported by traditional cultural ecologies. Tanzanian tribal groups are made to appear at once primitive and backward, dangerous and uneducated, basically unsuited to play active positive roles in ecological management.

9. See, for example, discussions on parks and people in Brechin et al. (2003); Dove (2006); Haenn (2005); West (2006); West, Igoe, and Brockington (2006).

10. Escobar (1995, 1998), Gupta (1998), Li (2007), and Agrawal (2005), among others, have suggested ways in which the critical vision of Michel Foucault ([1978] 1990, 1980) can be adapted to the study of environmental governance. Efforts to analyze environmental science and sustainable development discourses as forms of power/knowledge suffuse much of the literature on political ecology (for example, Raffles 2002; Lowe 2006).

11. For detailed statistics and analysis of the ongoing problem of forest fires, see Regione Autonoma della Sardegna (2004). A historical perspective on Sardinia's forest landscapes and the incidence of forest fires is available in Beccu (2000). Current data on forest fires from remote sensing is available at http://www.incendi.sardegna.it/ (accessed April 16, 2012).

10

Notes on the Use and Abuse of Cultural Knowledge

Frederic W. Gleach

When I started working as an archaeologist in Virginia in the early 1980s, we used to joke that if you wore a sign saying "I'm an archaeologist" you wouldn't be able to walk down the street for all the people stopping you to ask questions.[1] I have since found similar levels of interest in other forms of anthropological inquiry, from language to cultural practices to evolutionary biology to material culture. The introductory hook is often curiosity about differences—a version of the fetishization of the exotic that one finds still even in some professional anthropologies—but it often doesn't take much to get people beyond that level to considerations of cultural-historical systems, relationships, and processes. Despite the strength of ethnocentrism in human cultures, people have strong and genuine interests in the ways and lives of others.

In *Ulysses Sail* (1988) Mary Helms presents a case for a generalized category of *culture specialists*: people who go out from their own society to bring back knowledge of the outside world in its human dimensions and who deal with outsiders when they enter one's own society. A subset of this group would be *cultural mediators,* people who take an active role in intercultural interactions—translators and diplomats, if you will (see, e.g., Karttunen 1994; Kidwell 1992). Shamans may also be understood in some cases as culture specialists, mediating between a human society and what A. Irving Hallowell called, in the Ojibwe context, "other than human 'persons'" (1976, 361). The specific processes and situations in which these people work may vary widely, as may their status and other qualities, but the general pattern is both globally widespread and temporally persistent.

Anthropologists also can be viewed as members of this class. We spend years learning our craft, developing arcane skills in such areas as language and specialized knowledge of particular cultures, times, places, and things. Most of us work to develop an ability to step outside ourselves in order to overcome as much as possible the dangers of ethnocentrism, of simply carrying our own cultural understandings to a new setting and imposing them on other, distinctive cultures.[2] Others carry with them theoretical frameworks that are intended to overcome their cultural blinders, or they seek an imagined, unbiased objectivity.[3] We usually, eventually, return to our normal places in our home communities, where we produce the scholarly works that mark our occupation.

It is these products and their consequences that I want to consider here. In most societies, culture specialists must provide some service to the community in return for the resources they consume and the products they could otherwise produce. They may provide access to luxury goods or other exotic materials, they may provide knowledge, they may help to control processes and interactions with the outside, but in some way their practice is productive for society. In the context of scholarship, anthropologists have also constructed different kinds of products, generally based in knowledge and packaged variously as courses, publications, ethnographic films, museum exhibits, and such. In exchange for these products we get salaries and status. For some practicing or applied anthropologists this may be a direct exchange of payment for codified knowledge; one contracts to undertake a study and provide the resulting information. For most academic anthropologists the exchange is less direct, obscured as a contract for service to an institution. The payment is for a range of services rather than a specific product—but the qualification for obtaining such a contract is the production of the same sorts of products: the reports, articles, books, and other things that derive from experience as a culture specialist (research).

In our research as anthropologists we participate with others. We select from the individuals we meet and the experiences in which we participate—and from which we are excluded—those which seem productive. We learn from them; we take knowledge. We also generally give something through this participation. It may be as unsubtle as payment for information or gifts of goods, or it may be something far less tangible. In many settings today, anthropologists must contract as clearly with the people we study as with our home communities (in the form of the institutions in which we are embedded and employed).

As scholars we also have a responsibility to knowledge itself, to information, to *truth*—whether one espouses a scientific or humanistic perspective.[4] Most anthropologists would freely agree that our findings are interpretive, to at least some degree, and that those things we think of as *facts* are generally shaped by cultural perceptions. There may be more or less interest and willingness to pursue semiotic interpretations or games of deconstruction, but we generally recognize the socially and culturally constructed nature of human reality. Nevertheless, we do not generally absolve ourselves and our interpretations from the need to be truthful, to reflect that reality to the best of our abilities.[5]

If we have these responsibilities to the knowledge and the people we study, we also have responsibilities to our audiences. What do they want or need from us? First and foremost, clearly, we have a responsibility to communicate with our audiences in ways that they can understand and that are appropriate to the contexts. Beyond that, we must balance their needs and desires against our commitments to the knowledge and its origins. The American Anthropological Association (AAA) Code of Ethics, to take but one example, specifies that "anthropological researchers have primary ethical obligations to the people, species, and materials they study and to the people with whom they work"; "responsibility to scholarship and science" and "responsibility to the public" are secondary concerns (AAA 1998). This obligation, combined with the recognition of anthropological evidence as interpretive, has led some to question the truth-value of anthropological knowledge—particularly in court cases such as the Mashpee recognition case (Campisi 1991, 31–56; see also Clifford 1988, 317–25) and the *Delgamuukw v. the Queen* case, discussed below. The priorities of the AAA Code of Ethics have thus at times worked against the very people the code was intended to protect.

This position of having obligations in three directions can produce serious complications when it comes to producing our product. For whom can we speak? As outsiders, with limited experience, restricted interpersonal networks, and little real political stake, we lack the authority to speak for the whole society—and yet in some ways that is what we have contracted to do, even if explicitly only offering one window onto the scene. To whom can we speak? We may speak directly to other scholars or to a general but discreet audience, such as a class or auditorium of people, or we may broadcast in print, film, television, or radio. Information, knowledge, is appropriate to certain specific groups; some things might be told to an audience in our home institutions that could not be discussed in the field, while other things openly talked about in the field should never be mentioned to outsiders. I always tell students that there are some things you can write about, where anyone might read them; there are things you can talk about with anyone, but that should never be recorded; there are things you would only talk about with people whom you know to understand the implications, through shared or equivalent experience, and who won't go repeating them; and there are some things that you just can't repeat at all.

The situation of culture specialists and their/our knowledge is not simple—but neither is it impossibly complex, nor remarkably unusual. In my opinion it is not easily codified in guidelines or formulae, but must come out of specific situations and can only really be evaluated through the lens of experience. For the sake of enriching and augmenting individual experience, we turn to examples from others.

The Utility of Anthropological Knowledge

In *Blessing for a Long Time* (1997), Robin Ridington and Dennis Hastings recount the story of "Umon'hon'ti, The Venerable Man," the sacred pole of the Omaha Indians, traditionally reckoned a living being and an active member of the community. When the Omahas were forced to abandon buffalo hunting in the 1870s and pressured to give up their traditions in favor of Western laws and customs and Christianity, the care of Umon'hon'ti became complicated; and in 1888 he was given to the young Omaha ethnographer/ translator Francis La Flesche to be carried to dwell in the *great brick house*: the Peabody Museum at Harvard (Fletcher and La Flesche 1911, 248–49; Ridington and Hastings 1997, xviii–xix, 75–89). La Flesche had grown up with Umon'hon'ti, indeed, had personal experience with him, but had become also a translator and ethnographer and employee of the Bureau of American Ethnography (Ridington and Hastings 1997, 75; see also Bailey 1999). He recorded the only eyewitness account of the renewal ceremony for Umon'hon'ti and collected the associated ritual songs on gramophone recordings (Ridington and Hastings 1997, 76–84). His conflicted position cannot have been easy: he knew and respected the traditions, including restrictions on access and codes of respectful behavior to be accorded Umon'hon'ti, and yet he took the paradoxical position of violating tradition in order to preserve it. He remembered later telling the guardian of Umon'hon'ti, Yellow Smoke, "I greatly desired the preservation of this ancient and unique relic" (Ridington and Hastings 1997, 87–88).

Umon'hon'ti remained in the Peabody Museum in Massachusetts for a century. Anthropologist Robin Ridington encountered him there while a student in the 1960s and in the 1980s took an active role in his return to the Omahas (Ridington and Hastings 1997, 19–39). In 1988 Ridington was party to a visit by an Omaha delegation to the Peabody, where the groundwork was laid for repatriation (an earlier Omaha delegation had visited in the 1970s, resulting in the removal of Umon'hon'ti from public display). On July 12, 1989, Umon'hon'ti returned on an airplane to Omaha, where he was met by a tribal delegation and television crews (1997, 171–81). Ridington and Hastings wrote,

> The return of Umon'hon'ti to his home on the Omaha reservation brought forth powerful emotions. People of all ages came forward to

greet him and touch him with reverence. Many were unsure of how to make contact but others kissed him gently as they would a sacred relic. People bore witness to his return by placing their living hands upon his ancient body. They did so in a spirit of respect and welcome. Young and old alike came to him. Although the ancient ceremonies and keepers have passed on, Umon'hon'ti and his people remain. The people touched him in recognition of their common survival. They touched him as a respected elder. (1997, 181)

There was also some fear and apprehension associated with his return, based on concern that he was too powerful, that his presence might cause harm (1997, 189–93). In large part this grew from an internal conflict, an ambivalence toward tradition that was created by attempts in the late nineteenth and twentieth centuries to eradicate Indianness, to "civilize" the Indians through schooling and religion: "The experience of being told that Indian culture is bad is as much a part of Omaha history as are the music and dance of powwow" (1997, 198).

The appropriation of Umon'hon'ti in the nineteenth century can be seen as part of the movement generally referred to today as *salvage anthropology* (typically in a critical or dismissive tone), a movement aptly characterized by Curtis Hinsley as "a unique blend of scientific interest, wistfulness, and guilt" (1981, 23). Such salvage could indeed be exploitative or even rapacious and helped create the situation today with countless sacred objects having to be repatriated, having spent years locked away from their communities. But those efforts to eradicate Indianness were real, and countless other objects, stories, and songs not "captured" (as so aptly put and described by Douglas Cole [1985]) were lost or forgotten in the process. The appropriation of the "Venerable Man" did at least ensure his survival through that century, and now there is hope that, as Ridington and Hastings wrote,

> In time, he will assume a comfortable place in the tribal circle, and will return to an honored place at the center of Omaha conversation. In time, he will certainly fulfill the spirit of Eddie Cline's prayer:
>
> This tree has been living, standing.
> Whatever his thoughts, make them possible.
> Make his good thoughts possible. (1997, 198)

The case of Umon'hon'ti is far from an isolated one. Over a half century ago Alice Marriott reported a case of anthropological writings being used by Kiowa Indians to check their facts. She chose Kiowa as her graduate thesis assignment on a chance decision (Marriott 1953, 52–53) and set out.

> I started the motor, and while I waited for it to warm the heater, I remembered the Colt, lodged now in the glove compartment of the car. Here I was, about to approach my first Indian family entirely on my own. I could not—I would not—let them know that I came armed. That would be a dreadful thing. After all, I was plundering them of the knowledge of their generations. I could not do it at the point of a gun.
>
> In my suitcase, behind the car seat, there was a box of cotton pads, intended for the removal of make-up. I knelt on the seat, leaned over its back, and took the box from my bag. I put it on the seat beside me, and opened the glove compartment, from which I removed the Colt. Having broken it [open] and made sure that my memory of its unloaded condition was correct, I stuffed the barrel of the gun with cotton, thrusting the pads in as tightly as I could force them with a pencil. I then restored the gun to the glove compartment, and got started. (1953, 61)

She arrived at the house she was seeking and introduced herself to the head of the family, Mr. Camp, as a student from the university.

> "What you want?" he asked. He was not rude, just interested.
> "I want to write a book about the Indians," I informed him.
> "That good," he said, to my surprise. "What you want write?"
> "Everything," I replied comprehensively, pulling my feet back to the edge of the oven door. "How they live, what they think, how they make things—"
> He laughed, a warm, belly-shaking laugh. "You come to right place. You got lots time, too; this storm goin' to last three days maybe. Maybeso last a week. You ask us, we tell you. When we get tired talking you watch what my ole woman an' the girls do. You got pencil-paper?"
> . . . I sat and stared at him, and he saw my astonishment and answered it. "Long time now I been thinkin' somebody ought to write down ole Kiowa ways so these little young ones can know. I try, no good. I don' know English good enough. My daughter, she been to college, but she too busy social workin' for Indian Service; never got time to write for her ole dad. Now you come. We got plenty time, like in ole days, when was storm, people sit by fire and tell history stories from far-back times. We do that now."

"All right," I said, "where shall we begin?"

"You wait here," he ordered abruptly. "I got to get the record, make sure we go right when we talk." Again he departed into the other room.

While I waited for his return, I tried to decide what "record" he could mean. . . . Nobody seemed surprised by what was going on; nobody seemed surprised when Mr. Camp re-entered the room with an outsize volume, bound in shabby green cloth and stamped with dulled gold, in his arms.

"There," he announced, laying the volume on the table, "that's Mr. Mooney. He wrote about us Indians long time ago. Now when we don' know for sure what happen' we look him up in Mr. Mooney."

For a moment I wanted to protest, but I was still numb with cold and surprise, and the split second when I might have gained control of the situation passed me by. Meekly, I opened the tablet, and, guided by Messers Camp and Mooney, went to work. (1953, 64–66)

From the perspective of a salvage ethnographer seeking primary experience and knowledge of Kiowa tradition, this situation is obviously problematic, although from a broader perspective it is ethnographically quite rich. Clearly, these Kiowas, at least, saw value in having an anthropologist record their ways—demonstrated both in the enthusiasm for Marriott's project and the reverence for Mooney's publication. Other instances of people having great appreciation for the ethnographic products of anthropologists abound, from around the world.

I do not raise the idea of salvage as an ideal situation, but rather to demonstrate that even in problematic cases there may be some benefits. Despite its flaws, salvage anthropology did record and preserve information and objects that might otherwise have been lost during periods of cultural upheaval and stress, and these cultural materials are often now of great interest to many of those we study.

Specialized Utility: Treaties and Recognition

Anthropological knowledge has long had a special utility in the legal realm, where *expert testimony* has aided Native nations in obtaining and protecting their rights under treaty and has also been applied in a variety of other contexts (V. Ray 1955; Steward 1955; Rosen 1977; Kandel 1992). Anthropologists have testified in cases for recognition of a group's existence, in cases over rights to access and harvest resources, and in cases to protect other legal rights.[6] Although there are earlier examples, there was a significant increase in anthropological testimony of this sort following the institution in 1946 of the

Indian Claims Commission to hear cases involving treaty rights.[7] By 1954, when the American Ethnological Society sponsored a planning meeting and special symposium at the annual meeting of the American Anthropological Association, Indian Claims work by anthropologists was considered "already one of the most important professional issues of the day" (V. Ray 1955, 288).

Much of the legal work of anthropologists remains out of sight, available only in the transcripts of cases and other legal writings, and thus is comparatively poorly known and rarely cited in the mainstreams of scholarship. Some testimony is even sealed, prohibited from publication. But this work nevertheless has made significant contributions to the status and well-being of Native peoples.

An important example involves archaeological material from the Ozette site, in Washington. In early 1970 the coast there began eroding, exposing a series of houses that had been buried by mudslides in the fifteenth century. Makah tribal council member Ed Claplanhoo contacted Washington State University archaeologist Richard Daugherty, who had made small sample excavations on the site and who had a good working relationship with the Makah Indians on whose land it lay—and whose past it represented. Daugherty led excavations that lasted eleven years and recovered over fifty-five thousand artifacts, particularly in wood and fiber (see, e.g., Kirk and Daugherty 1974; Samuels 1991; Cutler 1994). The project was relatively unusual at the time for its close collaboration of academic archaeologists and Native people, many of whom felt the excavation was appropriate because the material was being offered up by the earth and sea.

At the same time, and like many other Native groups, the Makah Indians were involved in challenges to their treaty rights instigated by the commercial fishing industry and sport fishermen. These conflicts had been long running in many parts of North America, but many came to a head in the 1960s and 1970s. In a landmark case, *United States v. State of Washington,* the Ozette site played a crucial role.[8] The 1855 Treaty of Neah Bay, which established the Makah reservation, reserved for them the rights to fishing, whaling, and sealing. But in the 1960s this treaty, like others, was increasingly interpreted as allowing only "traditional" methods; and nets, particularly gill nets, were presumed by many non-Natives to have been introduced by white fishermen. The Makah elders could provide oral testimony of their traditional use, but that had not been sufficient to halt harassment, arrest, and the destruction of nets. The well-preserved fiber materials from the waterlogged Ozette site included nets, however, and once samples were introduced into evidence there could be no further question of their historical depth. This archaeological evidence formed a part of what became known as the Boldt Decision, which established a strong precedent to preserve treaty rights.[9]

But anthropological testimony in legal cases continues to be challenged as a variety of groups seek to prevent Native peoples from keeping or regaining their treaty rights. Perhaps the best-known example comes from the case of *Delgamuukw v. the Queen* in British Columbia.[10] In this case a position was taken by many of the consulting anthropologists for the plaintiffs, the Gitksan and Wet'suwet'en Indians, that articulates well with contemporary anthropological practice and rhetoric but proved less than effective in the court: the plaintiffs themselves were to provide the primary testimony, with the anthropologists to serve more as "cultural translators whose job it was to assist the court to understand the view of the plaintiffs" (Mills 1994, 11; see also Mills 1996).[11]

This position is defensible, indeed desirable, for several reasons. It properly places the emphasis and responsibility with the tribal nation rather than with non-Native *experts*. It demands for Native voices a place in the courts. It depends on an assertion that Native cultures are valid and that there should be some process of negotiating the differences between nations in treaty disputes.

What this position ignores is that federal courts, whether in Canada, the United States, or elsewhere, have their own hegemonic practices and that these courts exist for the positivist purpose of creating or validating a legal reality. There is little or no room for relativistic positions or for recognition of alternate cultural realities. As Robert Paine notes, following Douglas Elias, in a court case involving Native (aboriginal) rights there are "three 'truths' jostling each other in a courtroom: the Aboriginal, the legal, and the anthropological. This signals an imperative: the parties to these different truths must 'take steps to establish ways for thoughts and ideas to flow among them'" (P. Elias 1993, 226). "At present . . . 'each of these actors knows very little about what constitutes the roles played by others'" (Paine 1996, 63). What seems needed is a rethinking of anthropologists' role as experts—a call that has gone out repeatedly for decades.[12]

The original 1991 *Delgamuukw* decision prompted waves of "doom and gloom" (Thom 1999, 1) responses among those involved in First Nations rights in Canada and among anthropologists elsewhere concerned with legal testimony. Judge Allan McEachern dismissed native testimony as a matter of belief rather than fact (Paine 1996, 60–61) and wrote in his ruling that "the anthropologists add little to the important questions that must be decided" (quoted in Waldram, Berringer, and Warry 1992, 310), essentially arguing that they were unscientific and thus nonobjective and biased. They seemed to him to simply support the positions of the native testimony without properly and scientifically evaluating it.

The 1997 appeals decision clarified some of the issues from McEachern's 1991 ruling but refused to overturn his dismissal of anthropological testimony. The latter ruling did, however, clarify possibilities for more productive testimony, which others have elaborated on (e.g., Culhane 1998; Thom 2001a, 2001b). Although this ruling was specific to the Canadian jurisdiction, the issues are more generalized. In the face of literalist challenges and the textual basis of historians' evidence, anthropologists need to explicate carefully for the court their criteria for accepting evidence as factual. Established professional credentials and a record of research in the relevant area beyond the immediate context of the case may be quite helpful. And materialist positions may prove much more effective than more abstract, theory-driven formulations that emphasize the constructedness of sociocultural realities. As Paine wrote, "as anthropology re-constructs 'culture' itself as a constructionist entity, the distance between the anthropological notion of 'truth' and that held by either the judge or the plaintiff becomes all the greater" (1996, 64).

The Betrayal of Privileged Knowledge

There is a critique of anthropology popular in some circles that paints the entire discipline as a handmaiden to imperialism and colonialism.[13] There is, of course, validity to the charge, at least in some cases, but it is not the whole truth; anthropology and anthropologists have long critiqued and challenged hegemonic regimes (although the effectiveness of these efforts is often questionable). Although there is no question that in some cases anthropologists have behaved very, very badly, it is likely that arrogance is more often at fault than complicity with colonialism or imperialism (cf. Napier 2004).

Perhaps one of the most disrespectful cases was that of Elsie Clews Parsons's writings on Puebloan Indians (see Zumwalt 1992, 229–79). In some ways Parsons was an exemplary fieldworker; she advocated establishing and maintaining true relationships with people and adopting a stance of ignorance from which to learn (Zumwalt 1992, 230). But she carried with her an arrogance that caused major problems. She wrote her husband from Sichumovi, a Hopi community, in 1920: "My own family here are particularly pleasant folks.[14] 'My sister' has just washed my hair for me in yucca suds. After the ungraciousness of the Laguna & San Felipe people, it is a treat to be appreciated.... Doing well in every way, altho' 'my father' wouldn't take me into see his ceremony, the private part of it, because, he said, I was a woman. But George, my host & interpreter, thinks he was merely putting me off, as a white" (quoted in Zumwalt 1992, 234). Her arrogance begins to be seen here, in imputing "ungraciousness" as if she innately deserved to be "appreciated." But it was her drive to know and document secret ceremonies that reveals it in its fullest. At Taos in 1922 a resident explained to her the need for secrecy: "People want to find out about this pueblo; but they can't. *Our ways would lose their power if they were known,* just as Zuñi ways and the ways of other places have lost their power" (Parsons 1936, 14, quoted in Zumwalt 1992, 240; emphasis in the original). Taos was a particularly suspicious community, but Parsons took this situation as a challenge, seeming to take pride in her ability to obtain secret knowledge (see Zumwalt 1992, 240–47).

Parsons was fully aware of the tension between her desire to collect and publish secret knowledge and the wishes of the Puebloan peoples to keep it secret. She believed that by publishing the material in academic sources of limited circulation it would never get back to the communities. In the case of *Taos Pueblo* (1936), for example, Parsons stipulated that the book not be sold to people in New Mexico and had a note from the publisher added to each copy, asking readers to follow suit (Zumwalt 1992, 247–48). Inevitably, the restriction failed, and there was outrage in the communities that Parsons had learned and divulged religious secrets that had been protected for centuries. She maintained the elitist perspective that the information was recorded only "for a very few white people, all of whom are friends of the Indians" (quoted in Zumwalt 1992, 249), as well as for the generations to come, preserving customs that would otherwise be forgotten.

As noted above, such preservation is sometimes appreciated, at the time or later. But even in the face of condemnation and hostility from many Puebloan people over her publication of secrets, Parsons continued to allow their publication and distribution, with requests to keep them from the Indians (Zumwalt 1992, 248). Individuals suffered humiliation, dishonor, and threats of violence for being implicated in her research, particularly at Jemez and Taos (248–56).

When Theory Is a Bad Thing

Parsons's determination to learn the secrets of Pueblo religion and her insistence on publishing them in professional works stemmed from her understanding of *science* as demanding the fullest, most detailed possible record for analysis, present and future, and her prioritizing those interests ahead of the lives and concerns of individuals (see Zumwalt 1992, 256–57). She was not alone in this position, and this is far from the only instance in which a scholar's theoretical positions or interests caused an injustice to the people being studied. Julian Steward's application of cultural ecology and Oscar Lewis's *culture of poverty* model, for example, have been critiqued on these grounds.[15]

I am seeing a similar pattern in some of the responses to a project in which I am currently engaged (e.g., Gleach 2005), looking at the career of Diosa Costello, a prominent and important Puerto Rican singer and dancer of the mid-twentieth century who is today largely forgotten. My work chronicles her life and career; I attempt to represent her experience so that it resonates with the experiences of others and with the general cultural-historical issues, using the specifics of her life history to elucidate cultural patterns of performance and represented identity, then and now.[16] Such analytical frameworks underlie the constructed narrative but are not themselves the focus—a style that is sometimes denigrated as *atheoretical*. Some viewers have responded to this work by saying that my focus should instead be on the processes of stereotyping and the hegemony of Anglo-America—analyses that are well represented in the literature on Latino performers and grounded in critical and literary theory (see, e.g., Noriega 1992, Ramírez Berg 2002) and, in fact, are embedded in my narratives. My position is that prioritizing such arguments ultimately shifts the focus away from the performers and their struggles to move forward in that context, shifts it back to Anglo-American promoters and audiences and the frameworks of power they maintained. That approach also grants *theory* the spotlight—along with the presumably brilliant scholar who takes responsibility for it—while the people themselves are reduced to mere illustrations. This may appeal in contemporary academic circles as it allows the scholar to shine in ways that are useful in the marketplace of ideas and jobs. But in subordinating the subject to the author and his or her theoretical constructs, that supposedly more sophisticated position robs Latino performers of their agency and ultimately contributes to their ongoing erasure and marginalization by moving them into the inescapable category of victim.

Conclusion

Although these examples are far from exhaustive, they should provide a foundation for thinking about issues of voice and responsibility. It is unfortunate that the structures and demands of professional careers force us to publish work targeted primarily to our professional peers rather than the broader audience of human peers. We build our careers on the people we study; I consider it an ethical minimum that we provide something in return for our lives of relative privilege (see Grindal 2004 for a similar position). I do not suggest that all professional writing must be more general, or that all specialized or theoretical writing is bad and all generalized writing good, or any other simple framework. I do, however, want to question the exclusive place of privilege accorded in academia to *abstract, theoretical* work and the parallel, automatic denigration of both advocacy and more artistic or humanistic expression and to suggest that an integration of theory, practice, and life may provide a productive framework (see Gleach 2003 and the works reviewed there). I also want to suggest that humility and selflessness in the face of the world are far more appropriate to the anthropological enterprise than arrogance and promotion of the importance of one's contributions, theories, and self.

We all must grapple with these issues, seeking a balance we can live with. But we should remember the public interest in what we do and give something back—to our home communities and to the people we study—when possible. Who knows? The public might even give us more respect and support if the return were more than a few celebrated careers and piles of books that will never be read.

Acknowledgments

I gratefully acknowledge the formative influence of L. Daniel Mouer, the director of the Archaeological Research Center of Virginia Commonwealth University. My thinking on these issues has been shaped by conversations and work with many people over the years, all of whom I thank. From this large group I must single out as particularly significant Steffan Igor Ayora-Diaz, Margaret Bender, Errett Callahan, Regna Darnell, Patricia Erickson, Ray Fogelson, Davydd Greenwood, "Lefty" Gregory, Regina Harrison, Doug McLearen, Larry Nesper, Andie Palmer, Lisa Valentine, and, as always, my wife, Vilma Santiago-Irizarry. A special thanks goes to Gabriela Vargas-Cetina and Stacy Lathrop for inviting me to join the original group from which this volume is derived and to my fellow participants here for their provocative collaborations. Finally, I would be remiss to not refer readers to Miles Richardson's passionate article, "Anthropologist—The Myth Teller" (1975), which deals with many of these issues from the perspective of a scientific-humanist poet-anthropologist reacting to the sociopolitical scene of America in the 1960s and 1970s.

Notes

1. This initial experience involved work with the Archaeological Research Center of Virginia Commonwealth University.

2. In this way anthropologists may be seen as distinct from tourists, who are generally understood as lacking both the training and the desire to get outside of themselves in order to enter a new world. The distinction can be easily overdrawn, how-

ever, and exceptions can be found on both sides. See, e.g., Errington and Gewertz 2004; Harkin 1995.

3. This dimension of ethnographic research is seen as fundamental to the field and is typically covered in introductory texts in discussions of cultural relativism and the efforts to avoid ethnocentrism. See, e.g., Barrett 1984, 7–8; Scholte 1972. For an example of how a theoretical position may blind one to other perspectives—in this case that of the Native *informant* himself—see Claude Lévi-Strauss's interaction with Nuu-Chah-Nulth (Nootka) carver Ron Hamilton (Ki-ke-in) in the film *Behind the Masks* (Shandel 1973). Levi-Strauss pointedly ignores, contradicts, and challenges Hamilton whenever Hamilton's statements fail to fit his frameworks, while Hamilton patiently listens and answers. My point is not that Lévi-Strauss is wrong in his analyses, but that his mode of analysis seems here to have blinded him to other ways of seeing.

4. The disciplinary schism between scientific anthropologists and others may not be as real as it sometimes seems, depending on one's willingness to accept alternate modes of understanding as equally valid—and equally constructed. I would not disparage those who consider themselves scientific anthropologists but emphasize the position that science itself, as a mode of knowledge, is a sociocultural construct—which is not to say there are no facts in science. The science studies literature is vast and often contentious; see, e.g., Collins and Pinch 1993; Gross and Levitt 1994; Latour 1987, 1999; Seidman 1997.

5. An exchange between Omer Stewart and Lawrence Rosen in the *American Anthropologist* in 1979, prompted by Rosen's 1977 article, offers a window onto the debates concerning *truth* in legal testimony by anthropologists. Stewart wrote, "The honesty of an expert witness is of the same order as that of any scholar—scientist, artist, historian, etc. The safeguards for promoting honesty in scholarship might be improved, but that improvement should be general, not aimed at scholars who might be considered useful in various legal proceedings" (1979, 109).

Rosen counters by emphasizing the different context of the courtroom, where "[scholars'] concepts may take on significance far beyond the limits or intentions of their original inquiry, and the implications of their testimony may go far beyond anything they had foreseen. It is this that poses the ethical issue for the expert witness, and it is this possibility—however individual scholars may feel they have coped with it—that raises broader questions of legal procedure and anthropological knowledge" (1979, 111). One's work may take on such significances and implications outside the court of law as well, but the potential consequences for people's lives (or even for entire communities) that may derive from courtroom testimony are far greater than for much academic research and dramatically heighten the concerns of all parties.

6. See, e.g., Campisi 1991 on recognition; Cohen 1986 on fishing rights; Wright 1992 on capital punishment cases; Rosen 1977 (557–62) on racial discrimination. See also Washburn 1989 for a critique of anthropological advocacy, in this case in the Hopi-Navajo land dispute.

7. Previously, these had to be authorized by an individual act of Congress to go before the federal Court of Claims; see Barney 1955.

8. There was also a resurgence of anti-Indian, anti-treaty rights conflict in the 1980s and 1990s, much of it again revolving around fishing rights (see, e.g., Nesper 2002). At present the sovereignty of Native American nations in the United States is under general challenge, with much of the conflict driven by tax issues and casino gambling; the issue is prominent enough to be featured as the cover story of *Time* magazine, December 16, 2002. *United States v. State of Washington* (Civ. No. 9213).

9. The Ozette project also contributed to the strengthening of Makah language and culture and to the establishment of the Makah Cultural and Resource Center, which houses the Ozette artifacts and hosts both Native and non-Native researchers. This reinforcement or revitalization also led to the resumption of whaling in the late 1990s, although that has been a controversial development. See, e.g., Cutler 1994; Erikson 1999, 2005; Erikson, Ward, and Wachendorf 2002.

10. The Supreme Court of Canada case, *Delgamuukw v. the Queen* (1977) 3 S.C.R. 1010. The original trial proceeded from 1987 to 1990, with an initial decision handed down in March 1991. The appeal decision came from the Supreme Court of Canada in December 1997. The fallout from the *Delgamuukw* case is still very much an active topic; I have heard it discussed at every meeting of the Canadian Anthropological Society I have attended since the early 1990s and also at meetings of the American Anthropological Association, the American Society for Ethnohistory, and the Algonquian Conference. The literature on the case is copious; see, particularly, Cassidy 1992; Cove 1996; Mills 1994, 1996; Paine 1996; Roth 2002; and Thom 2001a, 2001b.

11. The Gitksan and Wet'suwet'en Indians are two distinct groups but are lumped together by the Department of Indian Affairs as an administrative unit.

12. See, e.g., Rosen 1977; Dobyns 1978; Henriksen 1985; La Rusic 1985; P. Elias 1993; Cove 1996; Ramos 2000; and several of the papers in Kandel 1992, notably, Kandel's own introduction and the piece by Rigby and Sevareid.

13. A touchstone for this argument was the publication of *Anthropology and the Colonial Encounter* (Asad 1973), although it did not begin there. See also Pels and Salemink 1999 for further discussion.

14. She had been ceremonially adopted at the request of her host family there to minimize criticism for their housing a stranger in the community.

15. Asch and Pinkoski (2004) offer a critique of Steward's legal testimony as derived from his model of cultural ecology. Antonio Lauria-Perricelli's (unpublished) 1989 doctoral thesis focuses particularly on Steward's collaborative and multi-authored *The People of Puerto Rico* project. Sixteen scholars contributed to the 1973 volume, *The Culture of Poverty: A Critique* (Leacock 1973), challenging the model and its easy acceptance by mainstream America.

16. It warrants noting that most of the literature on Latino performers, particularly in film, is highly Chicano-centric and virtually ignores the contributions of Latinos of most other national origins, particularly Puerto Ricans. One of the purposes of my project is to counter this with an example from the vast, forgotten—or erased—history of these other performers.

III
Anthropology in Crucial Places

Rooted or Extinct?

Post-Soviet Anthropology and the Construction of Indigenousness

Sergey Sokolovskiy

Post-Soviet anthropology has undergone drastic changes during the last twenty years in terms of both its theoretical orientations and the construction of its subject. However, the liberation from the ethnographic essentialism of the Marxist brand occurred at a time when regional ethno-nationalism was on the rise. This has resulted in a split within the Russian academy and a re-inforcement of the position of the so-called neo-primordialists versus the constructivists. Another split occurred among proponents and opponents of "partisan anthropology," scholars who embraced the idea of supporting na-tional movement and those who were cautious of elitist manipulation of grassroot concerns and anxieties. The recent developments in Russian an-thropology that are relevant to the issue of identity research and politics of representation will be covered in the first part of the chapter. As I took part in the preparation of the census instruments for the first post-Soviet Rus-sian census of 2002 and witnessed a score of political clashes over alternative representations of ethnic composition of regional populations, a part of the chapter will deal with ethnic categorization and the construction of indige-nousness within the framework of the census.

The final part of the chapter is devoted to the description of the insti-tutional setup of ethnicity and indigenousness in contemporary Russia and the factors that determine the politics of identity of individuals and groups in response to the nationalities policy of the state. The contemporary legal framework that supports a special status of indigenous peoples in Russia and its historical development is outlined.

Post-Soviet Developments in Russian Anthropology and Shifts in Identity Politics Research

Thirty years ago Ernest Gellner, comparing the Soviet and British traditions in anthropology, observed:

Someone trained in the British traditions of social anthropology who enters the world of Soviet anthropology undergoes a drastic and no doubt salutary culture shock. What precisely is the message that reverberates through one's being as one suddenly immerses oneself, say for six weeks, in the atmosphere and assumptions of Soviet anthropologists? They constitute a different world, and in many ways an impressive one, a world which stands in sharp contrast to at least British, if not to all Western anthropology. Briefly and crudely, it is the contrast between the Evolutionist-historical and the Functionalist-static visions of man and society. Less crudely, it is the contrast between two traditions, each struggling with the inadequacies of its own ideas. (1975, 595)

Just fifteen years later this contrast has dramatically decreased and become substantially different: Western anthropology has been transformed by various post-structural, interpretive, and constructivist approaches, whereas the anthropology of post-Soviet Russia entered the battleground of politics and legislation with an array of mutually conflicting structuralist and constructivist ideas, partly indigenous and partly borrowed from the West.

The naturalizing paradigm in the treatment of ethnicity remains a feature of the intellectual landscape in all post-Soviet states and in many Eastern and Central European academic communities. As it is known, the basic approaches to interpreting ethnic phenomena are usually grouped into three main approaches, which are most often designated as primordialist (objectivist, positivist, or naturalistic), instrumentalist, and constructivist (subjectivist or relativistic). The first of these scholarly traditions is usually traced to ideas of nineteenth-century German romanticism and to the positivistic attempts of some social scientists to emulate the natural sciences' objectivism. Its adherents view ethnicity as an objective given, a sort of primordial characteristic of humanity. For primordialists there exist objective entities with inherent characteristics such as territory, language, recognizable membership, and a common mentality. In its extreme form, this approach views ethnicity as a "comprehensive form of natural selection and kinship connections" (van den Berghe 1981, 35), as a primordial, instinctive impulse.[1] Some primordialists even claim that recognition of a group affiliation is genetically encoded and that this code is the product of early human evolution, when the ability to recognize the members of one's family group was essential for survival.

Contemporary political discourse on ethnicity and nationalism in Russia conceptually belongs to this primordialist thinking and is influenced to a substantial degree by anthropological theories, which have been prevalent in the history of Russian ethnology and anthropology since its formation up to the late 1980s. Explicit primordialism had been entertained in prerevolutionary Russian and Soviet anthropology. Taking its origin in Johann Gottfried Herder's neo-romantic concept of *Volk* as a unity of blood and soil, it had been worked into a positivist program for ethnographic research in the work of Sergei Shirokogoroff, who had defined an "ethnos" as "a group of people, speaking one and the same language and admitting common origin, characterized by a set of customs and a life style, preserved and sanctified by tradition, which distinguishes it from others of the same kind" (1923, 122). This approach was later developed in the works of Yulian V. Bromley (1981), a former director of the Institute of Ethnography, who has given a very similar definition of ethnos.[2] Bromley and most Soviet social scientists adhered to a historical version of primordialist treatment of ethnicity, where "ethnos" had been viewed as an "ethno-social organism," an objective language-cultural entity, and a basic category of ethnological research (Bromley 1981, 1983).

The naturalistic explanations of ethnicity and nationalism in Russia are still deeply entrenched and institutionalized in state policy, scholarly thought, education, and, most importantly, in public opinion and the administrative-political structure of the federation. This is true also for all post-Soviet countries within the Commonwealth of Independent States (CIS) and Baltic states. The reasons for this institutionalization are various; among the most important are the disciplinary tradition of Russian ethnography/ethnology, close political control, censure of academic research during the Soviet period, popularization of the academic discourse through the education system and media, and, to a certain extent, "fusion" of political and academic elites in post-Soviet times. One more important reason, which needs to be mentioned in this context, is the basic similarity and convergence between popular views on ethnic phenomena and naturalistic treatments of ethnic reality, which are sometimes so striking that one can not only speak of mutual reinforcement of lay and scholarly opinions in this respect, but also claim that the context of naturalistic theories formation was formed under a strong influence of nationalistic ideas. Here the German romantic treatment of ethnic reality should be mentioned once again, as Russian ethnology and anthropology inherited from it many of its ideological biases, and even the interdisciplinary boundaries and understanding of the discipline's subject have been modeled similar to the divide between *Volkskunde* and *Völkerkunde* of the German academic tradition.[3]

Political liberalization since the late 1980s and the rise of ethnic nationalism and conflicts have brought radical changes for Russian anthropology. Already at the end of the 1970s there emerged several other approaches, which could be viewed as divergent forms of instrumentalism. Some authors, influenced by theories of systems and information, were trying to use the concept of information in ethnic phenomena analysis, combining primordialist views on ethnos as objective entity (ethno-social organism) with instrumentalist perspectives on intergenerational transfer of ethnic culture (Arutyunov and Cheboksarov 1972; Arutyunov 1989); others were experimenting with informational patterns or models of particular "ethnoses" or suggesting that ethnic differentiation could be adequately described as an information process, as a reduction of behavioral expectations in a multicultural environment to a set of typologically neat ethnic stereotypes (Pimenov 1977; Susokolov 1990). Though instrumentalist approaches to ethnicity were considered novel and exerted a certain influence, they were a sort of sideshow in Soviet anthropology at the time they appeared and were not considered much deviant from the predominant naturalistic treatments, as their authors were using the same terminology and shared many of the presuppositions of the "naturalistic school."

While the instrumentalist treatment of ethnic phenomena was formed by the end of the 1970s, the constructivist approach remained alien to the Russian social science and was never seriously tested until the start of the 1990s. With post-Soviet ethnic revival and the growth of ethnic separatism, Russian anthropologists started to pay more attention to ethnicity construction. As a result, ethnicity started to be seen as a part of the repertoire that is "chosen" consciously by an individual or a group to achieve certain interests and goals, or as a representation, actively constructed by ethnic entrepreneurs. Though social practice of the postcommunist world contains a plethora of examples of constructed and mobilized ethnicity, the instrumentalist and constructivist treatments of the ethnic phenomena are familiar only within academia, and even here they are met with skepticism and opposition; they have not achieved any popularity due to their inherent complexity and deviance from popularized versions of ethnic reality representations. For obvious reasons nationalist leaders oppose them as well and support primordialist views on the ethnic reality. During the last ten to fifteen years the primordialist view on ethnicity has come under a sustained attack and revision within the Russian anthropological community.[4] The result is that a substantive part of this community has either modified the Soviet essentialist views on cultural differences and identity to accommodate to more fluid and circumstantial portrayals of ethnic identity or switched to constructivist paradigm.[5]

Along with these developments, wherein the main object of critique and defense was the essentialist Soviet theory of ethnos as a historical-cultural entity constituting "ethnic reality," another associated line of thought was developing around the issues of ethnic identity. Unlike the previous discussion, conducted mostly by anthropologists with scarce input from neighboring disciplines, ethnic identity has been from the start a focus of interdisciplinary attention and, hence, an interdisciplinary endeavor involving, besides anthropologists and ethnologists, sociologists, psychologists, historians, and philosophers. Initially, prior to the 1970s, the notion was construed in Soviet social sciences discourse as a characteristic of the ethnos, or, in the parlance of the days, "national self-consciousness." Though national self-consciousness has been considered as an inherent characteristic of ethnos, reflecting the existence of a collective body, it has been viewed as subjected to a number of economic, political, and cultural factors, thus not perpetually fixed, but characterized by a certain degree of fluidity.[6] By the end of the 1960s or mid-1970s, "ethnic self-consciousness," treated as a group property expressed as a sense of separateness and uniqueness in respect to other similar groups, had already been established as an important indicator of an ethnic group.[7] In the 1980s, when ethno-sociologists conducted extensive surveys, ethnic identity came to be depicted as an aspect of overall identity, having both individual and group dimensions and involving complex interactions with other identity aspects (social, gender, professional, etc.). In the 1990s, due to the ethnosociological and ethno-psychological research of ethnic identity, a breakthrough was made to depict identity as a complex and fluid process having various dimensions, public and private, official and personal, institutionalized and circumstantial. Discursive, cognitive, emotional, and regulatory components of identity were integrated within a general theory of social agency, so the predominant approach turned out to be both interactionist and processual.[8] The simplistic view of a stable, fixed, inheritable identity, prevalent in primordialist speculations on the nature of ethnos, has now been abandoned, with the result that census ethnic categories are viewed as constructed, and the responses of people taken during a census survey are seen as situational. Still, the divide between adherents of primordialism and constructivism, both in academic circles and among various decision-makers at the federal and regional levels, runs so deep that it permeates every endeavor in the field of nationalities policy and makes it difficult to find consensual solutions. Ethnic identities, in Russia and in other ex-Soviet states, remain so thoroughly institutionalized in state practices and so deeply entrenched in mass consciousness that even proponents of radical constructivist views tend to take into account primordialist statements and modify their own statements accordingly.

The debate over census categories in the Russian census of 2002 is just another demonstration of this observation, as there was a tendency on the side of some scholars to view the constructed census identity categories as names of "real" social entities. There was also a problem of sharing complex constructivist views on ethnic identity both with the State Statistical Committee (Goskomstat) officials, who were in charge of the census survey, and with national and political leaders, who were in favor of certain expected results of the census and tried to disclaim those that ran counter to their immediate interests.

Ethnic Categorization and the Construction of Indigenousness in the Russian Population Census of 2002

In summer 2000, the former Russian State Statistical Committee (now the Federal Statistical Service) announced an open competition for preparation of the dictionaries of nationalities and languages for the future census. As a result of the competition, the Institute of Ethnology and Anthropology of the Russian Academy of Sciences (IEA RAS) signed a state contract in August 2000 to prepare four dictionaries (a list of nationalities, alphabetic lists of ethnic self-designations and languages, and a systematic dictionary of nationalities with explanatory notes) that would be used in coding of the completed questionnaires for the census count. The Academic Council of the institute appointed four members to its census commission.[9]

The commission was to review the state of the art in ethnic groups research among over two hundred ethnic groups and almost as many linguistic communities within a year, providing details on existing official and alternative *ethnonyms* (ethnic self-designations) and their geographical distribution (in terms of regions and districts where they were expected to be used, the information that was later used in the process of verification of the census counts) in order to say in advance what people would answer on the questions of ethnic and linguistic affiliation in various parts of the country. This guesswork was necessitated by the census-taking technology as the census questionnaires filled in by census-takers were to be subjected afterward to coding, and the computer-readable codes were then scanned and counted.

The census of 2002 was the first post-Soviet census, which was to be conducted in the diminished and reconfigured territory of the new country. The categorization of the country's population was expected to accommodate the new circumstances and changes in population composition. Thus, many small-numbered categories of the other post-Soviet countries were removed from the list as their numbers within the territory of the Russian Federation were expected to be insignificant.[10] There was additional reasoning to exclude such ethnonyms since members of the relevant minority groups, when far from their homeland, tend to identify themselves in official situations with larger categories (e.g., Shugnoni name themselves Tadjik, and Talysh tend to name themselves as Azeri). The information on geographic distribution of various ethnic groups also had to be substantially revised: not only had recent migratory flows changed the spatial distribution of many groups, but official designations of many administrative units and, in some cases, their boundaries were altered as well. The lists of nationalities in previous censuses contained information of geographic distribution of various ethnic categories in terms of large administrative regions (*oblast, krai,* autonomous region, etc.) that needed an update as well. There was an ethnic revival at the end of the 1980s. In the early 1990s many ethnic groups previously recognized only by ethnographers and linguists were officially recognized by the state. As most of these groups claimed separate identities, the census coding lists introduced them to the census ethnic categorization. These were the main considerations for the construction of the new lists of nationalities and languages for the coming census. As a result of a year's work, the IAE RAS census commission constructed a list of almost nine hundred ethnic self-designations and grouped them, in the systematic dictionary of official ethnic names, into almost two hundred census categories or nationalities. The grouping of various self-designations into subsets with official names, under which most of the census results were published, was needed because, in providing answers to the question on ethnic identity, people used a number of alternative names referring to the same group (i.e., a name in local dialect or language versus the name of the same category in Russian, local phonetic variant of an ethnonym).[11] A small number of alternative self-designations belonged to so-called historical ethnonyms, which were infrequently employed either by senior people or by some diasporic groups residing outside the traditional area of settlement. There was also a class of ethnic self-designations that I, for the lack of a better name, call subcategories. Subcategories, that is, local groups that were treated as constituents of larger entities (nationalities, peoples, or ethnic groups)—unlike the registration of phonetic variants of self-designations (which, together with historical ethnonyms, translations, and plural forms, were but *alternative names* of the same local and regional identities since a number of synonyms might identify a single reality)—usually reflected the existence of something more than just another alternative designation. Here the long Soviet tradition of ethnicity reification was in conflict with the portrayal of shifting, fluid, and politically charged identities.

The resultant ethnic categorization of the country's population, used in the coding of census questionnaires, was to some degree a compromise of conflicting conceptualizations of ethnic groups. Views on what constitutes a separate ethnic group differed not only among statisticians, politicians, and ethnic activists, but also within academia and even among the members of the census commission, who were charged with the task of preparing the list of nationalities. Since many groups that constitute what officially has been designated as "peoples" are characterized by marked internal differences in language and culture and the members of such subgroups often claim separate identity, a provision was made to code such groups separately, though in most cases their population counts were also added to larger entities in the publication of census results. The subcategories were singled out in those cases where there was a history of claims to separate identity or institutionalized acknowledgment of these claims (as reflected in prior publications of census results, ethnographic literature, or official recognition by the state in state laws, etc.). Such recognition usually implied more- or less-pronounced differences in language and culture or religion.[12] Another inconsistency that required attention was the divergence between academic and ethnic (or folk) classifications. A good example of such a disagreement would be the case of Mari and Mordvinic languages. Both Mari and Mordva use two different and mutually incomprehensible idioms (Mokshan and Erzian, in the case of Mordva, and Meadow and Mountain Mari, in the case of Mari), which are treated by linguists and taught at schools as separate languages, whereas the people themselves, though quite aware of the differences, tend to say, in response to the question what language they use, just Mari or Mordvinic without further qualification.

In the final list of ethnic self-designations that was prepared for coding, there was also a residual classificatory category of "Others" (*prochie natsional'nosti*), the construction of which turned out to be linked with the construction of indigeneity. It concealed the strategies of "owning" and "othering," which, being unscrutinized and intrinsic to classification procedures, had contributed to the creation of a peculiar optics of classificatory gaze that shielded the hidden stock of ethnic terms relegated to this residual category. In previous Soviet census classifications there was an official subdivision of ethnic categories into those more or less indigenous, such as "nationalities of the USSR," "nationalities residing predominantly outside of the borders of the USSR," and titular peoples of Soviet and autonomous republics (based on the assumption that all other groups are un-titular and, hence, settlers, minorities, or migrants), as well as "small peoples of the North," with their ethnic homelands delineated by the administrative borders of autonomous *okrugs,* and so on. The census categories in the dictionaries of the 1989 and previous censuses were listed not alphabetically, but in groups (titular groups of Soviet republics, then of autonomous republics, *okrugs,* etc.). This mode of nested hierarchy reflected the administrative division of the country with its territorialization of ethnicity, where every ethnic category of substantial size had its own ethnic homeland. In the Russian census of 2002 this elaborate structure was abandoned in favor of alphabetic enumeration. However, the ethnic territorialization principle was covertly and unintentionally operative throughout the compilation of the lists of ethnonyms. Its operation has been linked to the unscrutinized category of "the peoples of Russia." Since many foreigners and smaller ethnic groups from the CIS countries, especially those that have no common borders with Russia (such as Tajikistan, Armenia, and Turkmenistan), were not considered as belonging to this category, their self-designations were not listed, and all persons from these categories received the same census code of "other nationalities." The construction of the country's population in terms of belonging to the population of Russia can be post hoc analytically categorized into several classes:[13]

1. The group can be categorized as belonging to the "peoples of Russia" category if it is considered to have a homeland in the territory of Russia. This is, of course, a remnant of primordialist thinking, the evident case of the so-called territorialized ethnicity, based on the presumptive linkage of an ethnic group to the region of its "ethnogenesis," the link that nationalists of every making are so fond of in securing their territorial power base.
2. The group belongs to this category if it has a homeland in one of the former Soviet Union states and if it is expected to have a significant number of its members in the territory of Russia.
3. The group belongs to this category if it is expected to have a significant number of its members in the territory of Russia, meaning that its number in the Russian Soviet Federative Socialist Republic (RSFSR), as reflected in the last Soviet the census of 1989, was fairly large and there was no significant emigration. As a result of this dubious procedure, more than thirty groups were excluded as "foreign" (read "atypical" for the population of Russia) and relegated to the residual category of "others" by the head of the census commission.

The smaller ethnic groups constituting "titular nations" of the new CIS countries in many cases were also omitted from the list. A good example of progressive myopia in detailing the ethnic composition of the "indigenous" ("belonging to the peoples of Russia") and "less and lesser indigenous" categories is the comparison of approaches to the reflection of the ethnic subdivisions within Altai, Kazakh, and Turkmen in the census. Every tribal group within the category of the Altai was given a separate code, and many of the so-called tribes were further decomposed into clans with clan self-designations registered in the alphabetical dictionary of the nationalities because the Altai people were treated as undisputable members of the un-acknowledged category of "the peoples of Russia." In contrast, in the case of Kazakhs, only those tribal groups whose members live along the border of Kazakhstan and Russia were included in the list.[14] None of the tribal groups of Turkmen were included in the lists, as Turkmenistan has no borders with Russia. The rationalization for the principle of sorting and inclusion or ex-clusion was the expectation that people in their homelands or residing close to them would be more prone to give their local self-designations (including tribal and clan) than those whose places of origin are not located within the territory of Russia or on its borders.[15]

So we might conclude that within the framework of the census an implicit classification into *us* and *others* that bears a direct relevance to the topic of in-digeneity construction had been operative. This is an illustration of the pe-culiar aspect of the Russian construction of indigeneity, as here it not only is a qualitative characteristic of a particular category of ethnic communi-ties and individual persons, but also is thought of as possessing a quantita-tive property and, thus, gradations in intensity and multiple levels. Due to this peculiarity the question of who is the most indigenous among various inhabitants of a certain region has its relevance and political salience and of-ten serves as a battleground for competing claimants. Internationally known examples from the former Soviet Union include Karabakh (contested by Armenians and Azeris), Southern Ossetia (contested by Georgians and Os-setians), the Galskiy district in Abkhasia (contested by Georgians and Abkha-zians), the Prigorodnyi district in Northern Ossetia (contested by Ossetians and Ingush), and literally hundreds other less familiar cases from the Cauca-sus, Central Asia, and Volga-Urals to southern Siberia and the Far East. On the surface it seems that there are mutual territorial claims on the side of eth-nic groups, but if one takes a closer look at the discourse that supports such claims, one will trace the discourse of indigeneity, the discussion of who was the first there and who came later.[16] Russia belongs to the Old World coun-tries, which share a set of specific traits in the construction of indigeneity that are rooted in colonial discourse and are different from those of the New World countries. According to this Old World conception, many groups may legitimately claim that they are indigenous to the continents they still inhabit. Most Europeans, Asians, and Africans might successfully go through the test of verification of such a claim, though it is less obvious in the cases of both

Americas and Australia and positively false in the case of the Antarctic. This haphazard classification of continents implies that the Old World cases of indigeneity construction are mostly more complex and more often contested, whereas the relevant New World cases seem to be more clear-cut and are challenged less often. They are also contested on different grounds, which have to do mostly with blood, or genealogy, but not with soil, or historically constructed homelands. This situation reflects the presupposition that in the Old World countries most of their ethnic groups are more or less indigenous and that there is no clear-cut difference between colonists and original inhabitants of various regions within these countries. It seems that the smaller the region, the less historically sustainable becomes a claim to genealogical indigeneity, unless we want to restrict the concept to several last generations or substantiate it by always biased sources of written history.[17]

Now, Russia is still a very large country, and most of its inhabitants are understood as *indigenous* in the technical sense of the term, that is, they and their ancestors were born within the boundaries of this vast landmass. Such a technical sense of indigeneity, however, becomes problematic if one takes into consideration other qualifications of indigenous groups, such as being marginalized, powerless, and endangered. Powerlessness and marginality have their own scales and their own spectrum of relativity and are as well relational: some groups and categories within groups are less integrated into the lifestyle of the dominant society than others. Does it make relatively more integrated groups less indigenous? If we try to compare the contemporary rates of integration of various indigenous groups into the mainstream society lifestyle and values in Russia, we shall soon find out that the levels of such an integration decrease from the south to the north and from the west to the east. This southwest-northeast axis seems to reflect the centuries-old expansion of market economy and associated values from the centers of ancient civilizations to the vast steppe, taiga, and tundra spaces of northern Eurasia and the historically more recent spread of the Russian state. As for the comparison of genealogical indigeneity with the marginality scale, it seems that both of these parameters vary independently, at least in the Russian case, so being more endemic to the region than other claimants does not automatically entail being more marginalized or endangered, and in practice there are a number of reverse cases.[18]

The Institutional Setup of Ethnicity and Indigeneity in Contemporary Russia

The contemporary research of ethnicity and nationalism in Russia by historians and anthropologists demonstrates that the Russian state not only has used cultural and linguistic differences for its own purposes, but in certain periods of its history has actively imposed ethnicity and endorsed nationalism among its various regional populations.[19] The early Soviet nationalities policy could be taken as a particularly salient case in point. Among state institutes that promoted and supported ethnolinguistic diversity, there was the politics of *korenizatia* (indigenization) of the 1920 and 1930s, during which time locally trained personnel replaced the Russian administration in regions with a predominantly non-Russian population. Other institutes pursued preferential treatment of indigenous minorities in high school enrollment; alphabetization of a number of languages that were without their own system of writing; establishment of minority schools where local languages were used as a means of instruction; passport registration of ethnic identity; a body of legal provisions supporting non-Russian languages and cultures; and, most important, various forms of self-determination, including territorial autonomies and Soviet and autonomous republics and the creation of ethnically based political elites. One of the target groups of the government's affirmative action that had preserved its privileged status throughout various stages of the Soviet and post-Soviet nationalities policy was composed of various hunters, herders, and gatherers of the Russian sub-Arctic and the Far East. Among groups claiming to be indigenous to the regions they consider their homelands, this was a category that was viewed as indisputably autochthonous, thus forming the core of the indigeneity concept in Russian discourse. The reasons for this undisputable preferential treatment are both historical and ideological, as the Marxists treated natives within the framework of their social evolution theory and their views on the economic stages as "primordial communists." Their relative smallness in numerical size, the harsh environments they inhabit, and the social diseases brought by settlers often put such groups on the brink of extinction. All these circumstances contributed to the prevalent view of these populations as dying out (*vymeraiuschie*) or almost extinct. The threat of extinction, along with the communist view of noble savages, seeing their prevalent economic behavior as unselfconscious, unselfish, and naïve, was the main rationale for government's targeting this category for preferential treatment. The logic of historical construction of the legal category of the peoples of the North in the case of Russia has been explored many times, and I will not go further into it here for it belongs more to the province of history than to the construction of indigeneity within the framework of contemporary Russian state legislation.[20]

During the last years of the Soviet Union, the group that came to be called the "small-numbered indigenous peoples of the North, Siberia, and the Far East" consisted of twenty-six different peoples. Since 1993 it has been gradually growing as more and more ethnic categories (and, one might add, less and less indigenous in terms of their lifestyle and integration into the mainstream) have been added to the official lists of peoples and territories identified for preferential treatment. For methodological reasons this strategy of linking peoples to territories and, via territories, to special rights is worth noting as an effective strategy of emplacement, or as what Arjun Appadurai (1988, 37) termed "incarceration" of indigenous people to territories they inhabit. The explicit linkage of peoples and territories is found in the law "On the State Guarantees and Compensations for the Persons Employed and Residing in the Far North and Equivalent Regions" of February 19, 1993.[21] The law does not enumerate ethnic categories or territories of residence, stipulating in Articles 26 and 27 the general norm, according to which preferences in retirement benefits are given to "citizens, belonging to the small-numbered peoples of the North," and "reindeer herders, fishermen, and hunters, permanently resident in the districts of the Far North and equivalent areas." It was the official regulation of the Ministry of Social Service on retirement allowances for the persons residing in the districts of the Far North of August 4, 1994, that provided the enumeration of the peoples who were included in the special treatment within the scope of the mentioned law.[22] This official commentary mentions for the first time three new members of this group, Shors, Teleut, and Kumanda, who were added to the previous standard Soviet list of twenty-six peoples. All three new groups are highly urbanized (at a level of 50 to 70 percent), so, in terms of integration into the mainstream urban culture, they are less indigenous than the rest of the group, excluding Oroks (Uilta) of Sakhalin and Nanai of the Far East, who by this time have similar profiles of urbanization. In March 2000 governmental decree number 255, "On the Uniform Register of the Indigenous Small-Numbered Peoples of the Russian Federation," added several new ethnic categories to the list, and the number of officially recognized "small-numbered indigenous peoples of Russia" reached forty-five.[23] Most of added groups do not practice hunting, herding, or fishing as subsistence economic activities, and their special cultural and linguistic interests could have been similarly protected under minority rights provisions in Russian legislation. The 1993 list of territories—for a set of circumscribed homelands always accompanies a set of circumscribed communities of membership) (government decree number 22 of January 1993)—was supplemented by the addition of the territories of Shors, Kumanda, Nagaibak, and several other peoples.

The linkage of peoples to territories is supported along with indigeneity discourse by a complementary discourse on diaspora. In the Russian academy and in enlightened journalism, every group that migrates beyond the (often imagined) boundaries of a homeland becomes a diaspora and is subjected to the protection of the law on national-cultural autonomy of June 1996. As the boundaries of homelands are more often imagined and mental, in real situations it is often not clear whether a certain indigenous person becomes a member of a diaspora by changing her or his residence.[24] To solve the problem of the allocation of resources aimed specifically for the protection of small-numbered indigenous peoples (the underlying rationale was that more numerous people do not need such protection as they are not threatened by extinction and are protected by the governments in their own titular republics), the Russian government adopted a special law with a specific demographical threshold.[25] According to the most-cited definition of this law, "the indigenous small-numbered peoples of the North are the peoples who inhabit the traditional territories of their ancestors, preserve their original life style, count less than fifty thousand persons in Russia, and recognize themselves as separate ethnic communities."[26]

According to this and other laws on small-numbered indigenous peoples, they are exempted from military service and land-use taxes and have priority rights to wildlife resources, a right to compensation if the state uses their territory for mineral extraction, a quota in higher education facilities, an earlier retirement age, and so on if they reside in designated territories of the North or in areas with equivalent harsh climatic conditions and practice hunting, fishing, or reindeer herding for subsistence. These provisions have boosted the numbers of many small-numbered indigenous groups because people born in ethnically mixed families started to switch to indigenous identity. Some persons from numerically larger indigenous groups, such as Komi and Northern Yakut, have also changed their identity, using the neighboring small-numbered indigenous ethnic self-designations (such as Nenets, Khant, or Dolgan) for growth dynamics.

Thus the Russian population census has demonstrated the fluid nature of ethnic identity for those Russian anthropologists who are still supporting essentialist treatment of ethnicity. The new Russian legislation of the turn of the century contributed to the identity change of many people with mixed ancestry. New splinter groups that were previously treated as parts of larger ethnic categories claimed official recognition as indigenous, basing their demands on the broadly viewed concept of indigeneity and numerical threshold. The census categorization provided new and interesting data for those scholars who advocate the social constructivist approach in the study of identity politics. The construction of the unofficial group of peoples of Russia, operative in the inclusion and exclusion of certain ethnic names in the census list of ethnic self-designations described above, revealed, on the one hand, the force of collective representations in Russian ethnicity research (ethnicity was inadvertently territorialized as ethnic groups were linked to particular homelands) and demonstrated, on the other hand, the ongoing process of institutionalization of the new census categorizations and category sets (such as "peoples of Russia" and "indigenous peoples").

It is characteristic of essentialist treatment of ethnicity (still predominant in the case of Russian anthropology) that the processes of an ethnic group and ethnicity formation are viewed as anchored to a particular administrative-political space and hence are seen as *belonging* to some particular country. Only within this paradigm does it become possible to speak of ethnic homelands and—by locating these homelands within the territory of a particular state—of aboriginal or autochthonous peoples with their historic homelands *within* the territory of the country. According to one estimate, in 1989 there were "more than 90 distinct ethnic groups with their historic homelands within the Soviet Union" (Anderson and Silver 1989, 610). This view clearly demonstrates the political mechanisms of the concept of indigeneity construction. This broad category of indigenous or autochthonous populations is further subdivided by political categorization, at least in the case of Russia, into those politically viable or protected and those politically vulnerable or endangered. The first category comprises all ethnic groups with political autonomy (republics within the contemporary Russian Federation), the second includes those with or without administrative autonomy (autonomous *okrug* [districts] and national *raions* and settlements), enumerated in special legislation defining the territories of small-numbered indigenous peoples. Though the conceptual construction of the second smaller category of indigenous peoples is supported by internal and international legal norms, it derives part of its political legitimacy and logic from the first conceptually broader category of autochtonous ethnic groups. Only this latter logic made it possible for Russian legislators to list some peoples from the Caucasus and southern Siberia within the law on indigenous small-numbered peoples of the Russian Federation.

The interplay of meanings between the concepts of "autochthonous" and "indigenous," both of which could be translated into Russian by the same term, *korennoi,* blurs, at least in the case of the Russian terminological system, the dividing line between the international legal category of indigenous peoples and all the other autochthonous groups comprehended as native to the country. However, they are different in meaning. *Autochthonous* is broader or more inclusive in terms of population groups (groups with homelands within the state borders), and *indigenous* is a narrower legal concept (autochthonous groups who practice subsistence economy).[27] This by no means is an exception, as many other contemporary countries in the Old World demonstrate a similar predicament in their attempts to draw the dividing line between the autochthonous population of the cultural mainstream and marginalized indigenous cultures and peoples.[28]

Notes

1. See, for example, Van den Berghe (1981).

2. Since September 1990, it is called the Institute of Ethnology and Anthropology, Russian Academy of Sciences. The members of the institute have been involved in ethnic and languages registers for Soviet census instruments since the 1950s.

3. *Etnografia* (ethnography) and *folkloristika* (folklore studies) in the Russian case, respectively.

4. For an early discussion of the issues see Basilov (1992); Kozlov (1992); Kriukov (1988); Pimenov (1988); Sokolovskiy (1993a, 1993b); Tishkov (1989a, 1989b, 1992, 1993a, 1993b); Cheshko (1988).

5. Among the opponents of constructivism who published their critiques from 1993 to 2000 are the following: Arutyunov (1995); Semionov (1993, 1996a, 1996b, 2000), Kozlov (1995). A number of researchers tried to reconcile the constructivist and primordialist theories of ethnicity: Cheshko (1994, 1995); Kolpakov (1995); Rybakov (1998, 2000); Viner (1998); Zarinov (1997, 2000). The proponents of constructivism in Russian anthropology who took part in the discussion included Sokolovskiy (1993a, 1993b, 1994, 1995a, 1995b); Tishkov (1997); Sokolovskiy and Tishkov (1995).

6. For early treatment of the subject see Kushner (1949).

7. See Kozlov (1967, 1974); Bromley (1983); Drobizheva (1985).

8. See, for example, the works by Drobizheva (1994); Soldatova (1998); Lebedeva (1993).

9. The commission included a specialist on ethnic demography and cartography who took part in similar projects for the Soviet censuses of 1959, 1979, and 1989 (Prof. Pavel Puchkov); a specialist on Siberian and northern peoples who was also an expert of the State Duma and had been involved in the preparation of several laws on the peoples of the North, Siberia, and the Far East (Prof. Zoya Sokolova); and the author of this chapter, who had been involved in a critical assessment of the previous census of 1989. The commission was headed by the IAS RAS director Valery Tishkov, who took part in revising and editing the final lists of nationalities and languages.

10. Such as, for example, most of the mountainous peoples of Pamir and Tajikistan or some groups speaking Iranian and Caucasus languages of Azerbaijan.

11. By "most of the census results," I mean that in tables with the regional ethnic composition for the eighty-eight provinces (*oblast'*, *krai*, autonomous districts) the list of two hundred groups was used; however, the counts for more than 550 other self-designations (alternative to official names) are also available.

12. The most obvious example here is Mordva-Moksha and Mordva-Erzia, speaking two different and mutually incomprehensible though closely related Finno-Ugric Mordvinic languages and, at the same time, stressing the idea of the unity of the Mordva, irrespective of linguistic adherence. Other examples include Ossetians (with Iron and Dighor, speaking different languages and professing, respectively, Islam and Christianity), Armenians (with a special group of Cherkessogai, speaking Circassian language), Greeks (with Urums, speaking their own vernacular of a Turkic linguistic group), Georgians (with five groups characterized either by ethnocultural and confessional differences or by pronounced linguistic differences at a level of a separate language: Adjar, Ingiloi, Laz, Megrel or Mingrelians, and Svan). The traditional division of Mari into "east meadow" and "mountain," speaking their own languages, has been preserved. As Mennonites often claimed a separate origin and some of them still adhere to the idea that they form a separate people (neither Dutch nor German), they were listed in the comprehensive dictionary after Germans as a subgroup of the latter. Karagash were listed after Nogai, as they speak a vernacular very close to the Nogai language (they were previously counted among the so-called Astrakhan Tatars and were added to Tatars). The Tatars have subgroups of Mishar and Astrakhan Tatars, who speak different Turkic vernaculars from the Volga Tatars; some of them were classified by linguists as separate Turkic languages. A mountaineer subgroup of Tuvinian origin, Todja, is listed after Tuvinians (they are included in the federal law on "numerically small peoples"). Similar subgroups with special cultural characteristics were registered among Turkmen (Trukhmen of the Stavropol region), Finns (Inkeri, or Ingermanland Finns), Chechens (Akkins), and Estonians (Setu). These twenty-four subgroups, most of which had not been mentioned in Soviet censuses after 1926, thus formed a substantial increment to the previous 1989 census list.

13. The principles were not formulated during the work of the census commission and in many cases were not reflected but simply brought forward as substantive arguments for making a particular decision.

14. For example, nomadic tribal self-designations include Aday, Argyn, Bersh, Zhanpas, Zhagaybayly, Kerey, Kypchak, Nayman, Nogai, Tabyn, Tama, Torkara, Wak, and Shekty. There is practically no mention of the tribes from the Ulu Zhuz (the Great Horde), including such numerous and politically prominent tribes as Dulat and Jalair. The list enumerates mostly the tribes of the Orta Zhuz (the Middle Horde) from northern Kazakhstan along the border with Russia and some of the tribes of the Kishi Zhuz (the Lesser Horde) from western Kazakhstan, as well as the Turatinsk Kazakhs from the Ust'-Kan district of the Altay Republic.

15. Thus, a Turkmen was expected to give as the answer to the question on ethnic identity "Turkmen," but not Tekin, Goklen, Iomud, Salor, or any other tribal designation.

16. A number of such competing claims in the case of the Caucasus are analyzed in Shnirelman 2001.

17. Other ways of documenting the presence of a particular group in the territory, such as by usage of bio-anthropological, linguistic, and archeological data, though of an undeniable value in the construction of the factual account of regional popula-

tion succession and genealogy, have the innate drawback of being unable to conclusively document the fluid nature of identity of past generations.

18. In post-Soviet Russia the reverse relation between marginality and territorial indigeneity is characteristic of several republics in which national eponymous elites (or, as they are called in Russia, "titular nations" [*titul'nye natsii*]) established ethnocratic regimes, which have split the republican populations into minorities and titular groups (among such are the Bashkortostan, Tatarstan, Tuva, and Sakha republics). By ethnocracy I mean here a system of social promotion that is based on ethnic affiliation, leading to effective control of political power.

19. For extensive treatment of historical policies toward indigenous peoples, see Slezkine 1994; the historical changes of policy on minorities and titular peoples in the early Soviet period are covered in Martin 2004.

20. See Slezkine (1994) and Forsyth (1992). My own elaboration of the topic has been undertaken in Sokolovskiy (2001; 2000, 91–113).

21. Articles 26 and 27 of the law lost legal force in 2004.

22. It stipulated that "the designated peoples include Nenets, Evenk, Khant, Even, Chukchi, Nanai, Koryak, Mansi, Dolgan, Nivkh, Sel'qup, Ulcha, Itelmen, Udege, Saami, Eskimo, Chuvan, Nganasan, Yukagir, Ket, Oroch, Tofa, Aleut, Neghidal, Enets, Orok, Shor, Teleut, Kumanda." On Retirement Benefits for Persons Employed and Residing in the Far North, registered at the Ministry of Justice on August 4, 1994 (#651, Article 4).

23. This includes adding such well-integrated groups into the mainstream economy as Bessermian from the Udmurt Republic and Kirov region, Nagaibak from the Cheliabinsk region, Shapsug and Abaza from the North Caucasus, and Veps and Izhora from the Northwest (Leningrad and Vologda oblasts and Karelian Republic).

24. I have a postgraduate student who chose as a subject of her PhD thesis the Buriat diaspora in Moscow. I have asked her whether Buriats would constitute a diaspora in Irkutsk (a city in eastern Siberia, where most of Buriats live). She said, "No, in Irkuts they are local Buriats (*mestnye buriaty*)." Then I asked, "What about Tomsk (a city in western Siberia)?" She hesitated, then told me that probably one should not speak of a Buriat diaspora in Siberia, only in the European part of Russia. This anecdotal evidence illustrates well the force of the territorial component in the construction of indigeneity in Russia.

25. Part of the institutional setup that forms the backbone of nationalities policy is the so-called ethno-territorial federalism: along with territorially defined regions, Russia has regions singled out for preferential treatment, those whose territory is viewed as home of some ethnic group. Out of eighty-eight regions, more than one-third are defined on ethnic criteria. Thus, along with the *krai* and *oblast* with predominant Russian population, there are twenty-one republics, nine autonomous districts (*okrug*), and one autonomous region that are defined according to ethnic criteria. This arrangement contributes to reification of ethnicity and ethnic boundaries.

26. Article 1 of the law "Basic Principles of Legal Status of Indigenous Small-Numbered Peoples of Russia," adopted on June 19, 1996; the definition is repeated in

Article 1 of the federal law "On the Guarantees of the Rights of the Small-Numbered Indigenous Peoples of the Russian Federation," which was finally adopted on April 30, 1999, and in Article 1 of the federal law "On the General Principles of Small-Numbered Indigenous Peoples of the North, Siberia, and the Far East Communities Organization," adopted in July 2000.

27. The Russian census of 2002 implicitly and explicitly preserved this conceptual vagueness as demonstrated by the sorting of ethnic groups, which occurred at the final stage of the nationalities list construction, into those belonging to the unofficial category of the "peoples of Russia" (autochthonous groups) and migrant or minority groups. At a later stage, the narrower "indigenous proper" category was singled out for publication in a separate volume, *Korennye malochislennye narody Rossiiskoi Federatsii* (Indigenous small-numbered peoples of the Russian Federation, vol. 14 of the census results, Moscow 2005).

28. Notable examples are India and China: the governments of both countries reject the applicability of the international legal category of indigenous peoples to their population groups and at the same time single out such groups for special treatment, using their own terminology (scheduled tribes or *adivasi* in the case of India and minority nationalities in the case of China). For details, see Bates 1995; Tapp 1995.

12

Anthropology on Trial

Australian Anthropology and Native Title Litigation

Katie Glaskin

In a keynote address delivered to the Australian Anthropological Society's annual conference in 2002, Annette Hamilton considered where anthropology is heading in the twenty-first century, arguing that in Australia the discipline was in something of a crisis. One basis for her argument was the diminishing enrollments in the discipline and the attrition in the number of academic positions Australia-wide (cf. Geertz 2001, 10). Hamilton thus argued that anthropologists had to make a better case for how and why their knowledge is relevant today: "Above all, anthropology should demystify itself and its practices. . . . People quite rightly want to know: where is your data? What is your methodology?" (2003, 169). Anthropologists involved in native title cases litigated in the Federal Court of Australia are required to provide such accounts of their practice and knowledge and to do so within an adversarial context: to explain anthropological techniques and methodologies, to account for anthropological processes of analysis based on particular data, and to defend their objectivity. Regardless of the reservations many Australian anthropologists have about aspects of native title, it is evident that anthropology has an important contribution to make to native title claims. More broadly, it is also apparent that an analysis of such anthropological engagement might contribute to methodological and theoretical questions in anthropology.[1]

Native Title and the Politics of Representation

Central to issues of representation today is the question of power imbalance between anthropologists and those they describe in their anthropological discourse. The politics of who speaks for whom, from what locations, to what ends, and with what consequences are usually analyzed in relation to the continued domination of the structurally powerful over those whose labor, land, or resources they appropriate or exploit (e.g., Marcus and Fisher 1986). Understanding the complexity of the contexts and sites in which textual and discursive representations are embedded has thus become a necessity in addressing questions of power imbalances. In the context of litigation aimed at legally establishing Indigenous rights case-by-case, such representations are embedded in a complex legal terrain.[2]

My discussion of the politics of representation is situated within the relatively recent recognition of native title in Australia, the subsequent evolution of native title law, and anthropological work undertaken on behalf of Indigenous groups in litigated native title cases. In 1992, the High Court of Australia handed down its historic decision in the *Mabo and Ors v. Queensland* case, establishing for the first time that native title, a sui generis or unique form of aboriginal title, existed in, and could be recognized by, the common law of Australia.[3] In response, the Australian parliament passed the Commonwealth Native Title Act 1993. The legislation provided for Indigenous Australians to bring claims to rights in land before the Australian courts on the basis of original occupancy prior to the acquisition of sovereignty by the Crown. Since the advent of the Native Title Act, anthropologists have been engaged to research the ethnographic basis of Indigenous claims to ancestral lands and to provide expert opinion for respondent parties opposing native title claims.

In 1998, the Native Title Act was amended in response to the High Court's *Wik Peoples v. Queensland* decision.[4] In the years since, other High Court decisions, most particularly those of *Western Australia v. Ward* and *Members of the Yorta Yorta Aboriginal Community v. State of Victoria,* have shaped the character of native title law in Australia.[5] Many would argue that the amendments and these High Court decisions have seriously diminished the original character and intent of the *Mabo* decision, making it increasingly difficult for Indigenous Australians to gain even a limited recognition of native title (e.g., Pearson 2003). Today, some commentators would go so far as to suggest that native title promises at best "minimal possibilities" (Wootten 2003, 36) for most Indigenous Australians; others have argued that it is not always certain whether the conditions of these possibilities outweigh their benefits (Glaskin 2002, 2003). Indigenous Australians confront numerous issues, legal and otherwise, in their pursuit of native title recognition. For anthropologists who choose to become engaged, the forensic issues and challenges to anthropology in this context are also manifold.

In the courts, anthropological knowledge has been referred to as *specialized knowledge,* deriving from the particular function the anthropologist is required to perform and "for which he or she is trained and in relation to which study has been undertaken and expertise gained."[6] Anthropologists appearing in litigated native title cases will give evidence in chief and be cross-examined by respondent parties concerning what constitutes specialized anthropological knowledge and expertise and whether they can be considered credible witnesses in these terms. Many native title cases are negotiated through consent determinations (agreed native title outcomes) ratified by the Federal Court. Anthropologists working in native title, whether for applicant (Indigenous) or respondent parties (who oppose or seek to limit native title recognition), may, therefore, not necessarily find themselves in the courts. However, any native title claim can be referred to the Federal Court for litigation should negotiation and mediation fail. Given this, and the particular pressures litigation places on Indigenous groups and those who work for them, my focus in this chapter is primarily on anthropologists engaged by Indigenous groups in the litigated native title context. In court, anthropologists are required to defend the basis of their research to judges and lawyers testing the viability of the applicants' case and, to differing extents, the legitimacy of anthropology itself.

Among the numerous issues related to working in the native title realm are the politics of who works for whom (Bagshaw 2001); legal constraints on anthropological report writing, such as the distinctions between opinion, fact, and hearsay (Trigger 2004); the use of theoretical models in Indigenous claims (Sutton 2003); and issues concerning the ownership and control of fieldnotes and reports. Issues such as these—which are related to the kinds of issues that occur in anthropology more broadly, such as those of epistemology, representation, ownership, and ethics—are likely to fall on complicated political and legal terrain once in the native title environment; and simply positioning oneself as working only for Indigenous concerns does not necessarily ameliorate these. I nevertheless maintain that it is important for anthropologists to remain involved in this field, both with respect to the kinds of outcomes Indigenous Australians may gain through native title and in relation to the discipline of anthropology itself, given that native title is one of the most significant and visible areas of anthropological practice in Australia today.

The Place of Native Title Anthropology

Australian native title law requires Indigenous claimants to demonstrate continuity between the laws and customs (that give rise to rights and interests in land) that they currently acknowledge and observe and the laws and customs exercised by their forebears when the British declared sovereignty over their land. Thus, one of the requirements of the native title legislation is to show the continuity of a system of human-land relationships over time. Anthropology conducted in these cases therefore requires a focus on property relations, genealogies, kinship, and principles of land tenure, descent, and inheritance.

There are at least two aspects to property within the native title context: the property relations existing among Indigenous groups who are making claims to land and how these are "translated" and recognized within the Australian legal system. Anthropologists working in native title are required to bring their skills to bear on the former, while legal personnel—lawyers and judges—carry out the latter. The anthropological analysis of property relations inevitably involves a degree of translation from the individual renditions of such relations that an anthropologist gains through fieldwork and into an overarching account of the way Indigenous laws and customs distribute rights in land (in much the same way as any anthropological account involves a synthesis of information). Thus, Howard Morphy (2006, 137) says that "the structure and content" of anthropological reports presented in native title cases "are likely to have an analytical or interpretive dimension that comes out of, and is supported by, the factual evidence." The legal recognition of Indigenous property rights involves an additional and more consequential translation between the Indigenous laws and customs, which give rise to rights in country, and the Western legal system, which will only recognize some aspects of these via the legal application of its own conceptions of property.

Anthropological research, whether applied or academic, involves obtaining and synthesizing information. Along with written records (previous ethnography, unpublished fieldnotes, and archaeological, historical, and linguistic information), anthropologists elicit information concerning Indigenous property relations and their reproduction over time—underlying rules that may not have been explicitly formulated or recorded before. (An example of this might concern the kinds of rights matrifiliates or spouses have in an Indigenous society where patrifiliation is the primary basis of reckoning rights on land or sea). Like persons in any society, members of Indigenous claimant groups often have multiple conflicting views and perspectives, from which anthropologists will seek "to identify the sets of principles that operate" (Morphy 2006, 140). So, for example, detailed genealogical information, cross-referenced with written records where these exist, especially where there are previous anthropological records, can demonstrate the systematic nature of person-to-land relationships over time in a way that Indigenous claimants may not be able to provide on the basis of their oral accounts alone.

Once in a forensic setting, the law's positivism and requirements for determinacy tend to transform principles of land tenure and affiliations to land into reified *rules*. These are unlikely to adequately reflect "dynamic systems of laws and customs which determine how such rights are realized and which emerge from the material conditions in which they are embedded" (T. Bauman 2001, 216). All anthropological representation is locked in a descriptive moment—the *ethnographic present*—and could be criticized for being unable to capture the indeterminacies of everyday social life and for reifying aspects of culture in a given moment of time. Native title anthropology is not exempt from this, nor does it stand alone. What makes it more consequential is its involvement in processes where people's legal and property rights are being determined. Notwithstanding this, it is evident that the legal processes involved with native title and its recognition contribute more to the codification of indigenous property relations than does anthropology per se.

Judges and lawyers have consistently said that the evidence of Indigenous applicants is the most significant in determining native title claims. In litigation, Indigenous Australians are called on to speak for and about themselves, and it is they who carry the burden of proof in establishing their claim, albeit in the "language of the jurisprudence and property-rights regime of those responsible for their plight in the first place" (Dirlik 2001, 181). The forensic environment in which Indigenous applicants are called to give evidence is laden with relations of power and privilege that disadvantage them communicatively and otherwise in the giving of that evidence. Courts hearing native title cases have made some innovations in order to deal with Indigenous evidence: hearing applicant evidence on country, allowing Aboriginal witnesses to sit together when giving evidence, and making provision for gender-restricted evidence. Notwithstanding this, communicative issues—language itself, the meaning of cultural concepts, and the power relations inherent in these contexts—remain, and anthropologists may provide assistance to the court in its task of comprehending Indigenous evidence.

While judges place the most weight on Indigenous evidence—which, as Peter Sutton says, is "only proper" (1995, 87–88)—anthropologists typically do face the most prolonged and extensive cross-examination at trials, which is indicative of their role in these cases. The extensive cross-examinations are due to the adversarial nature of the proceedings and the anthropologists' status as expert witnesses and because the anthropologists are providing their understanding of the nature of the Indigenous group's connection to land and their opinion on the facts that are before the court. Such evidence is consequential because, as Morphy (2006, 142) has said, "the way those facts are interpreted by the Court may make a crucial difference to how a case is determined." In their determinations of native title in litigated cases, judges have usually commented on the assistance anthropological evidence provides. When a case achieves a negotiated consent determination outside of litigation, the anthropologist's "connection report" may be the main source of information upon which the claimant's case is assessed.[7]

Fieldwork and Cross-Examination

Anthropologists obtain the primary information for the reports they produce for the court by conducting fieldwork. At trial, they will be cross-examined about the accuracy of the anthropological representations they have made in their reports; a critical issue in such cross-examination, therefore, concerns the fieldwork on which these reports are based.

Although much academic anthropology is oriented toward particular problems, applied anthropology is an intensified version of this methodologically. Its research has practical, "applied" ends and is usually constrained by them. In native title anthropology, the "problems" are largely framed by the legal requirements of proving claims to native title. In applied anthropology, time and money limit the amount of anthropological work that can be performed to address research questions (Sutton 1995, 85); these limits can manifest as "unrealistically short timeframes being imposed by commissioning organizations" (Burke 2001, 6). Other constraints include the practice directions issued by "the relevant tribunal or court" and the employing bodies' contractual instructions (Sutton 1995, 85).

Native title claim research will normally be performed within prescribed fieldwork periods. These are of much shorter duration than the participant-observation fieldwork usually carried out for a doctoral dissertation (current provisions in Australia generally allow for one year of fieldwork). In applied research for native title cases, anthropologists are engaged for contracts of varying length. It is hard to quantify this since, for example, an initial contract of forty days may well be followed up by further contracts in relation to the same matter, with the amount of time on a particular case adding up during the number of years over which a native title case runs. It is still generally the case, though, that because of contractual periods and obligations, time constraints in applied work result in a greater emphasis on directed elicitation than on participation. The time anthropologists spend in the field can have considerable consequences for the Indigenous people concerned and, additionally, has significance in relation to the testing of the anthropologists' conclusions in the courts.

In litigation, an objective of lawyers is to undermine the credibility of the expert witnesses who appear for parties with whom they are in contention, and they are often assisted by their own anthropologist, who gives them advice on matters during the course of the trial. Lawyers draw on this advice and their growing knowledge of the discipline to cross-examine anthropological witnesses concerning how many people they consulted, how many notes they took, what kinds of questions they asked, how much fieldwork they have done, how "empirical" and "objective" their investigation was, and so on. Respondent parties frequently seek to undermine anthropological evidence on the basis of how much time has been spent in the field. In many cases, anthropologists are sought out to do native title research with groups on the basis that they have already worked with the group or in that region over a significant period of time. While their previous research may not have specifically focused on matters germane to native title, such as land tenure, anthropologists in this position do have the advantage of entering into the research context with a considerable amount of ethnographic background and established relationships. Empirically, this allows anthropologists to contextualize their current research with its particular focus (native title and its requirements) against the knowledge they have already gained over time; and methodologically, Indigenous Australians will often be more inclined to speak freely with anthropologists with whom they have long-standing relationships, in contrast to those whom they have just met.

Nevertheless, in adversarial proceedings, cross-examination will seek to discredit the basis of the anthropologists' work, regardless of how much or how little fieldwork they have done. If anthropologists have conducted long-term fieldwork, it will be argued that they have become too close to the Indigenous group, too involved with them to form objective opinions. While a long-term involvement with a group of people would, in usual anthropological terms, suggest a greater capacity for ethnographic veracity, in the court such involvement can and will be used against anthropologists to question their objectivity and the empiricism of their research, that is, the credibility of their anthropological representations before the court.

Advocacy and Objectivity in Anthropology

The issues of *objectivity* as a social science researcher versus those of *closeness* and advocacy are important issues confronting anthropologists, especially in litigation. Australian Federal Court guidelines specify that the expert witnesses' first duty is to the Federal Court of Australia and that they are not, in any sense, to be advocates for those represented by the party that contracts them. When a judge concludes that an anthropologist has advocated, rather than performed the role with impartiality and objectivity, the judge will correspondingly give that evidence less weight. In the *Neowarra v. State of Western Australia* case, despite the submissions of the respondent parties that the anthropologists called to give evidence on behalf of the applicant group were "unreliable" and "displayed a complete lack of objectivity," Justice Ross Sundberg found otherwise.[8] His finding—an important one for anthropologists in these cases—was that "their closeness to members of the claimant group has not affected their professional judgement or resulted in their becoming advocates for the claimants."[9] The judge arrived at this view on the basis that their "evidence and opinions were at all times entirely professional" and that the anthropologists' closeness to the Indigenous claimants—on which the challenge to their evidence was based—endowed their evidence with "particular value."[10]

The discipline of anthropology has consistently encountered this issue of objectivity, which has been closely related to questions concerning its scientific empiricism (Keen 1999, 29). By the late 1970s, according to some historians today, the "interpretive challenge" to scientism in anthropology failed to depict anything other than "a hazy, poorly focused picture of how wide-ranging fieldnotes are utilized in the writing of ethnography" (Sanjek 1990, 238). In 1986, George Marcus and Michael Fischer (1986) identified a related crisis of moral legitimacy emerging in anthropology, associated with hermeneutic and epistemological considerations concerning discursive and textual production, questions concerning power relations and anthropological discourse, and the emergence of oppositional discourses, often expressed in essentialist terms. Ron Brunton, who has been an outspoken critic of anthropologists involved in native title and Indigenous heritage claims (but has acted in them himself), identifies one of the factors leading to the "lack of candour and objectivity" in anthropology as these "tendencies within the discipline itself" (1992, 4, 5; cf. Keen 1992, 8).

The criticism that their research is not objective, that their anthropological integrity is compromised by working for Indigenous interests, and that their work is necessarily partisan is particularly directed at those who work on behalf of Indigenous groups in the applied anthropological field (Bagshaw 2001). Yet, where anthropologists who work with Aborigines do not get involved in issues that are of significance to them (such as native title), many will be criticized by Indigenous Australians for not engaging in their political struggles and instead using their knowledge solely to advance their academic reputations (T. Bauman 2001, 210). Although there are complex philosophical questions surrounding the ideas of objectivity and relativity, as

Geoffrey Bagshaw (2001, 3) has argued, "objective research does not—and should not—require an ethical disengagement from the world. What it does require is the fearless and impartial application of intellectual rigor." One example of how objectivity might be employed in the pursuit of empirical data is through consulting widely with many people in the group, checking and verifying the information gained from individuals against what others have to say, and considering what people say compared with what they do, to the extent possible within the contractual time available. In contrast, it is evident that some earlier ethnography did not necessarily attempt to cross-reference and cross-check in all cases. So, for instance, Adolphus Elkin's genealogies concerning the part of the Kimberley region in which I have worked, resulting from his 1928 fieldwork, record differing views of genealogical connections but make no attempt to either reconcile or account for the differences between such views.

One of anthropology's strengths, methodologically, is that it seeks to "understand the society as much as possible in its own terms, freed from the categories of the anthropologist's own society"; and it is this that informs "the heart of anthropological method . . . participant observation" (Morphy 2006, 139). While anthropology in the native title sphere is unlikely to have the luxury of pursuing less-directed, longer-term fieldwork, this principle—of understanding the people with whom we work in their own terms—continues to inform research conducted in the applied anthropological arena. In collecting genealogies for native title claims, anthropologists with experience working with Indigenous Australians will be careful to avoid mentioning the names of the recently deceased (Glaskin 2006) and will take heed of the prohibitions for the persons concerned on speaking the names of others where avoidance relationships preclude such naming. This is also an example of how anthropologists take on the "restrictions imposed by the sensibilities and conventions" (Myers 1986, 140) of those with whom they work. Such conventions include the nondisclosure of gender-restricted (usually ritual and cosmological) information to members of the opposite gender and have usually been adhered to by lawyers and judges in native title litigation as well.

When it comes to writing reports for the Federal Court and giving expert evidence, anthropologists need to be able to substantiate their opinions on the basis of the evidence, and demonstrable methodological rigor is crucial to how their objectivity will be evaluated and their evidence received. In this regard, one of the primary tools that anthropologists use when conducting their research will also be interrogated once in a forensic setting: their fieldnotes.

Fieldnotes

Anthropologists' fieldnotes constitute a record of information gathered in the course of their fieldwork: things they have been told, things they have observed, notes on photographs they may have taken, places they have visited, questions to follow up, and so forth. These written records are used to remember, collate, and analyze data: they are not usually intended for any audience other than the anthropologist who authors them. Roger Sanjek's edited volume *Fieldnotes* (1990) aptly subtitles the volume *The Makings of Anthropology,* indicating the primary significance of fieldnotes in generating anthropological knowledge. For her contribution to the volume, Jean Jackson (1990, 3, 8–10, 20) interviewed seventy anthropologists about their fieldnotes: many of her interviewees spoke about the private, unshared world of fieldnotes.

In contrast, in litigation, fieldnotes will usually be legally *discovered* either through subpoena or agreement. The stated rationale behind this is that the fieldnotes provide the indices to objectively test that the opinions of the anthropologist are based on empirical (recorded) evidence; respondent parties will cite the need for transparency in relation to this matter. Given the clear aims of respondent parties, though, it is evident that fieldnotes are also desirable artifacts those parties use to seek to undermine the credibility of the anthropologist (and, by extension, the claimants' case). Thus, an anthropologist's reluctance to hand over his or her fieldnotes is normally construed negatively by respondent parties. The anthropologist is said to be hiding something; if the reports are clearly grounded on the recorded information in the fieldnotes, there is no reason these should not be made public. Resistance is considered obstructionist and evasive, at odds with the role of an expert witness whose first duty is to the court.

While most anthropologists involved in litigated cases now anticipate that their fieldnotes will be used in their own cross-examination, the use of their fieldnotes to cross-examine Indigenous witnesses (as sometimes occurs) heightens their existing concerns about breaching informant confidentiality and anthropological codes of ethics.[11] Concerns about confidentiality are further exacerbated when notes contain gender-restricted or *secret-sacred* information. While judges have usually issued court orders to the effect that only counsel of the relevant gender can access those portions of the notes, this may not necessarily prevent such information from being accessed by others, given the difficulty of restricting fieldnotes according to only some data. It could be argued that such scenarios could be avoided if the information had not been recorded in the first place. Yet, that same information may be vital to understanding important aspects of Indigenous land tenure, such as its cosmological basis. Further, given the value placed on written documentation by the legal profession, if information is not recorded, it is likely to reduce the legal weight the judge may give to the anthropologist's opinion in relation to these matters.

Another concern about the implications of fieldnote discovery includes the potential for this to affect the kinds of information that may be recorded by anthropologists during fieldwork. This is also connected with the important question of what may be considered harmful to a case (and by whom). From an anthropological perspective, conflict is an important aspect of social process that reveals much about how society operates. Yet, as one anthropologist told me, lawyers he had worked with reacted with dismay to his having recorded aspects of a conflict occurring at a native title meeting, asking him why he had recorded the information which they felt would be exploited by respondent parties once in the court.[12] The tendency to self-censor in the taking of notes will undoubtedly be heightened where it is perceived that some information could be hurtful to individuals once it becomes public.[13] A common situation is for couples to marry the "wrong way" according to their own society's rules. This would certainly be known by members of their own society, but the public mention of this is still likely to cause a person strong feelings of shame (a strong emotion in Indigenous Australian societies operating as a behavioral sanction). Yet the same wrong marriage may have produced offspring whose kinship classifications have been amended accordingly—itself evidence of the society's rules in action and its ability to impose order and stability even where rules are broken. This would be an important aspect of the laws and customs of that society for the anthropologist to have understood in the native title context, and this might have implications for how rights in land are allocated in such cases. Yet if, under cross-examination, a claimant is cross-examined about this on the basis that it appears in the anthropologist's fieldnotes, the public shame likely to be engendered for the person involved is something that most anthropologists would clearly have reservations about.

Alongside these concerns is the issue of what fieldnotes actually represent. As Michael Robinson (2001, 5–6) has argued, fieldnotes are (only) "a pathway towards synthesis and the construction of anthropological models of the social world," rather than "an independent record of the truth." As many other anthropologists would attest (Sanjek 1990, 93), anthropologists rely on more than written fieldnotes in forming anthropological analyses and conclusions. Simon Ottenberg came up with the term "headnotes" to describe the information that anthropologists carry in their heads (quoted in Sanjek

1990, 93). Apropos of the discussion above, many anthropologists will carry sensitive information that is not critical to the distribution of rights in land as headnotes. Thus, fieldnotes are aide-mémoire that stand in a dialectical relationship with our experience (Bond 1990, 274). This is the dialogic, dialectic aspect of fieldwork. In this sense, not all the information anthropologists draw upon is ever contained solely in written form. This mnemonic headnote aspect of fieldwork cannot be tested in the courts against some written form.

Fieldnotes are not necessarily interpretable by laypersons, or even other anthropologists, giving rise to the possibility that one's fieldnotes will be misunderstood (Jackson 1990, 30; Sanjek 1990, 92). Yet in a forensic setting, respondent parties, keen to trap the anthropologist with any anomaly evident in the data, often construe isolated fieldnote entries as stand-alone facts. But fieldnotes are contextual, both in terms of what is recorded prior to a particular entry and after it and in terms of all the experience and interactions that lie between and beyond. They do not exist independently of the person and the interactions that created them, even though they are often treated as such. Anthropologists' elicitations can impact upon the ways that Indigenous claimants come to articulate facets of their social world; and, equally, anthropologists' participation in these interactions are, like other human experience, also constitutive of our own understandings of that social world. A literal treatment of fieldnotes in an adversarial, litigated context does not incorporate the contextual understanding of how anthropological knowledge grows through every successive interaction as information is corroborated and expanded among different persons. Nor can a literal interpretation of fieldnotes account for much of the background information anthropologists bring to their own interpretation of them, such as a particular theoretical framework or the effect of community politics on an individual's response to a line of questioning.

Morphy (2006, 146) refers to what he calls " 'facts'; 'systematic compilations of facts' that are likely to be, at least in part, the product of analysis; and 'anthropological models or syntheses.'" Morphy (2006, 146)describes most of what anthropologists present in their reports as being of a "factual nature . . . events they have recorded, a person being refused permission to enter a place, a ceremony held on a particular day." These are not the kinds of fieldnote entries for which the question of interpretation and contextualization might be so great. Rather, drawing on my own experience here, it is those entries where someone has been recorded as saying something to which a too literal and linguistically doubtful interpretation is applied out of context by a lawyer who is drawing on it for his or her own purposes. This is particularly compounded where such entries record Indigenous language terms or expressions in Aboriginal English or when a person has an idiosyncratic speech style or even just a particular way of expressing him- or herself. So, to take an example of the latter, one of the persons I worked with over the years would sometimes use the expression "I got him, but I can't get him." This would seem fairly opaque on the basis of a fieldnote entry alone, without any knowledge of this person, what may have prompted this response, and why it was written down. But, in fact, what this person is saying is that they know something, they know that they know it, but they just can't remember it. It is likely to have been written down because that person may remember the information when next asked. The fieldnote entry is unlikely to say all of that because, as the person who recorded this, I would know what this person means when he says this. This is true of most anthropological fieldnotes— we do not tend to habitually record what appears to us to be self-evident. In the forensic context though, it is increasingly the case that anthropologists will be required to do so or run the risk of not having their own interpretation of their own fieldnotes being accepted as the correct one in the court— of being told that they are making "argumentative inferences," for example, when they stand by their own interpretations of their notes in contrast to the interpretation put to them by an adversarial legal counsel.[14]

Ethically Applying Knowledge

The anthropologist who appeared in the original *Mabo* case, Jeremy Beckett, has suggested that anthropologists would "do well" to "begin working out a future for themselves beyond working for native title" (2002, 137). Earlier in the same piece Beckett also suggested that he had "some misgivings" about anthropological involvement in matters broadly related to aspects of Indigenous policy that had an advocacy element, "in particular . . . about a discipline that is focussed on native title research" (2002, 135). He went on to elaborate on these misgivings: "We are in a general sense complicit in what I would call a post-colonial situation" (135).

The difficulties facing anthropologists working in native title practice are considerable, and Beckett's comment underscores many anthropologists' concerns about the way native title is evolving. But against such concerns, other significant questions remain: Should anthropologists decline to be involved in Indigenous Australians' political and legal struggles? Should we not be involved in Indigenous attempts to have land ownership recognized and resile because we don't want to be complicit or because it is too difficult or too complicated and the outcomes are uncertain? What of those claims, success-fully determined, that bring legal recognition to those groups?

Indigenous groups will continue to pursue claims to land. At present, na-tive title represents the only means by which some groups can secure some rights over land for which they hold customary attachment and responsibility. While I think it is fair to say that most anthropologists who have consistently engaged in native title processes, like Beckett, have misgivings about them, the problem is that the legislation, and even our complicity in it, does not lend itself so easily to evaluation in dichotomous terms, beneficial or detri-mental. In general terms, my own view is that the question of what native title requires of Indigenous Australians, as against its possibilities, is one that can only be meaningfully addressed on a case-by-case basis. One of the criti-cal issues influencing this assessment is the requirement in the Native Title Act for Indigenous groups to demonstrate that they have a cultural conti-nuity with the traditional laws and customs their ancestors exercised at sov-ereignty. This poses particular difficulties for people in those parts of the country where the effects of settlement have been the most intensive, such as cities and towns; but this is also true in many rural and remote areas where Indigenous Australians have been displaced or forcibly removed from their land. Such groups face considerable hurdles in demonstrating native title and, if successful, may end up with a very limited form of recognition. In rela-tion to this, Francesca Merlan has advocated a perspective with which I con-cur: "Much might be gained by approaching restorative measures in ways not so thoroughly invested in the distinctness of Aborigines' culture and social situation, and more explicitly informed by understandings of accommoda-tion and relationship, historically and presently, with people and institutions of settler and post-settler Australia" (2006, 101). Native title is a preexist-ing land title recognized within the common law of Australia. In the origi-nal *Mabo* case that resulted in the native title legislation, the High Court said that this title continued to exist unless extinguished. For many Indigenous Australians, the native title legislation that was enacted shortly after this de-cision has provided them with their first opportunity to gain some legal rec-ognition of their customary attachments to land. The process is flawed and the outcomes are uncertain. Some groups will gain relatively strong determi-nations of native title; others will not. Engagement with native title legisla-tion will create conflict for many and will require Indigenous Australians to make numerous adjustments to participate in its legal and bureaucratic pro-cesses (Glaskin 2002). For some, native title has also provided the opportu-nity to be heard and to be recognized and for their version of history to be

told, and it has led to research around Australia which might not have occurred otherwise.

Applied Anthropology and Academic Scholarship

Martha Macintyre says that anthropologists working in the applied or consultancy fields occupy the "liminal zone much of the time—with bureaucrats
apparently resentful of them as trespassers and fellow academics suspicious
that they are debasing the currency" (2005, 132). In Australia, one strand of
academic critique of applied work has focused on the contribution that an
involvement in native title claims, or land claims, can make to the academic
discipline of anthropology (Maddock 1990, 171; Austin-Broos 2004, 215).

The dialectic of what anthropology has to offer to Indigenous Australians
in the service of their land claims, and what anthropological involvement
in these claims has contributed to anthropology, began with statutory land
rights cases in the 1970s. Commenting on the changes that followed, Fred
Myers noted that Indigenous Australians increasingly required anthropologists to work *for* them in this legal environment, in what he referred to as "a
narrowing of the gap between them and us . . . [in which] Aboriginal people
see anthropologists less as privileged Others than as human actors accessible
and responsible to Aboriginal expectations" (1986, 138). Indigenous Australians had more control over research; anthropologists correspondingly became more accountable to those with whom they worked. Thus, land claims
research impacted on "our understanding of indigenous political processes"
(138), "producing something of an epistemological revolution," in which
emergent anthropological accounts were taking "their strength from a sense
of intimacy with Aboriginal people and the privilege of their friendship"
(139). Myers thus argued that a conceptual transformation was occurring in
which there was a "growing ethnographic emphasis on the immediate, concrete processes of daily life with a distinction between long term structures
and individual action" (139).

Native title has precipitated enormous amounts of research around Australia, to a degree not previously undertaken and in areas where no research
has previously been undertaken. The issues of continuity and change have
posed particular challenges in the native title sphere, largely because of the
terms in which the Native Act is framed, in combination with its Australia-
wide application. And it is perhaps precisely at this juncture that native title
anthropology is grappling with theoretical concerns that are more broadly
consequential to the discipline. As Marshall Sahlins (2005, 508, 514) says,
for anthropology, "one of the surprises of late capitalism" is that indige-

nous peoples have not changed as much as earlier anthropologists expected they might, undoing "the received Western opposition of tradition versus change." Patrick McConvell, Laurent Dousset, and Fiona Powell's collection is one among a number of recent Australian publications that have sought to address the issues of continuity and change, their particular focus being on "how to account for changes in the kinship and marriage systems that until recently have provided a basis for social action and belief" (2002, 142). Native title has spawned an increasing number of academic works arising directly from an anthropological engagement with native title, either in terms of the practice of anthropology (e.g., see Sutton 2003; Morphy 2006) or in terms of broader theoretical issues that such an engagement provokes (e.g., see Macdonald 2001; Weiner and Glaskin 2006, 2007; Merlan 2006; B. Smith and Morphy 2007). Such works evidence a robust contribution to ongoing analytical issues and contribute directly to our understandings of contemporary Indigenous social transformation.

Anthropologists' Obligations to Those with Whom They Work

In the context of development in Papua New Guinea, Macintyre has highlighted the ways in which applied anthropological involvement may require us to squarely confront the ethical and other limitations of intellectual positions such as "moral relativism" (2005, 137). Being "on the ground," she says, can "change the ways that one engages with academic anthropological research" (137).

In the absence of other means to gain legal recognition of their proprietary interests in land, Indigenous Australians will continue to pursue native title claims. Where they instigate and pursue such claims, where their representatives hire anthropologists, where judges accord the evidence of Indigenous Australians themselves the most weight, where lawyers write submissions and argue cases, where judges make decisions but are bound by precedent and by legislation—the issue of who speaks for whom, from what locations, to what ends, let alone the question of with what consequences, is enormously complex. Despite the fraught nature of the process and the uncertain nature of its outcomes, I have argued that anthropologists should be involved in native title cases.

Indigenous groups who have chosen to claim native title will have their rights determined and codified whether anthropologists are involved or not. They will sometimes be successful, in other cases not, and the benefits and costs to them of making such claims will only be able to be evaluated, ultimately, with reference to particular cases. Where the anthropological research is conducted as assiduously as possible, where anthropologists have been careful to render complex social phenomena as accurately as they can and have crafted their reports as carefully as possible, it is my view that Indigenous Australians will be better aided in their quest to gain native title determinations that reflect their connections to land through having anthropological assistance than they would be without it. In the *Rubibi Community (No. 5) v. State of Western Australia* native title case, Justice Ron Merkel described the anthropological evidence in that case as being "important in three respects." The foremost of these, that it "provided a conceptual framework within which the indigenous evidence of traditional laws and customs was to be considered," goes some way toward identifying the importance of sound anthropological work in native title cases.[15]

Myers (1986, 152) says that anthropological understanding "requires a different sort of double vision that is promoted, actually, by the complex moral relationship we have with Aboriginal communities." This "complex moral relationship" has a particular manifestation in the native title context. It feeds into, as Myers says, "the traditional anthropological role as defender of the people we studied to an outside audience" (1986, 139). Indigenous Australians increasingly expect anthropologists to work *for* them, and many anthropologists want to give something back to those people with whom they have worked. How this relationship is negotiated will vary between researchers and Indigenous communities: not all anthropologists working with Indigenous people will engage in native title, and neither would I suggest that they should. Different anthropologists have different expertise to bring to such matters; they may have different views concerning what their reciprocal obligations with those among whom they work entail; they may have different ways of fulfilling them. Given the complexity of native title, the kinds of pressures and scrutiny involved in working in this field, and the (often) disappointing outcomes for claimants, many anthropologists decline to work in this area. As I have argued here, though, it is important that others do: it is evident that anthropological knowledge does have something to contribute to these cases, both in terms of their preparation and in terms of academic engagement with the issues arising from this conjunctural field.

Acknowledgments

I am most grateful to James F. Weiner, Geoffrey Bagshaw, David Trigger, Mike Robinson, Richard Davis, Gabriela Vargas-Cetina, and Stacy Lathrop for their comments on earlier drafts of this chapter.

Notes

1. A modified version of this chapter has previously been published in Australia (Glaskin 2010).

2. While anthropologists may also play an important role in the development of government policy in relation to native title, the focus of this chapter is on the role anthropologists play in litigated native title cases brought under native title legislation as enacted by the Parliament of Australia. Both areas might be considered to constitute the legal terrain of native title.

3. Mabo and Ors v. Queensland (No. 2), (1992) 175 CLR 1.

4. Wik Peoples v. Queensland, (1996) 187 CLR 1.

5. Western Australia v. Ward, (2002) HCA 28; Members of the Yorta Yorta Aboriginal Community v. State of Victoria, (2002) HCA 58.

6. Daniel v. Western Australia, (2000) FCA 858, paragraph 24.

7. "Connection reports" are prepared with a view to mediated, rather than litigated, native title outcomes. Other materials that may be submitted with anthropological reports include historical, linguistic, and archaeological reports.

8. Neowarra v. State of Western Australia, (2003) FCA 1402, paragraph 117.

9. Ibid., paragraph 20, point 5.

10. Ibid., paragraphs 113 and 116.

11. In Australia, this is primarily the Australian Anthropological Society's (AAS) Code of Ethics. Section 3.2 of this states, "An anthropologist should not reveal personal identities or confidential information except by agreement with those whose identities or knowledge have been recorded by the anthropologist," though section 3.3 addresses the fact that anthropologists cannot guarantee that their fieldnotes will be immune from legal disclosure. The AAS Code of Ethics can be downloaded from http://www.aas.asn.au/aas_organisation.php (accessed April 23, 2012).

12. Mike Robinson, University of Western Australia, personal communication, July 2004.

13. For example, you are told that Z's father (deceased) is not the man Z says he is. Z traces his primary rights to land through his father, and it is partly on this basis— given the politics of land tenure—that others contest his paternity. But the question of Z's father's identity is also a "public [Aboriginal] secret" (Taussig 1993, 85) that others do not publicly speak of or openly contest. If you write this down in your fieldnotes, you, Z, and others are likely to be examined about what may be a highly sensitive, personal, and inherently political issue.

14. Sampi v. State of Western Australia, (2005) FCA 777, paragraph 803; and see Edwards, Anderson, and McKeering (2006, 160).

15. Rubibi Community (No. 5) v. State of Western Australia, (2005) FCA 1025, paragraph 253.

13
The Politics of Europeanization, Representation, and Anthropology in Northern Ireland

Thomas M. Wilson

Various governmental and nongovernmental (NGO) organizations have been reinventing and representing Belfast, Northern Ireland, in significant ways since the paramilitary cease-fires and peace agreements of the 1990s. As part of this reinvention of Belfast as a location for investment and tourism, as a historical site of heritage and pride, and as a symbol of peace and progress for Europe and beyond, there have been many recent and public attempts to change Belfast's image and identity within Ireland, within the United Kingdom, and within Europe, in particular, within the Europe of the European Union (EU). Policy-makers, as well as community, business, educational, and voluntary organization leaders, have increasingly seen the need to change Belfast's image because of their interests in changing the political, economic, and social relationships that the people and institutions of the city have with their counterparts elsewhere in the British Isles, the continent, and more globally.

The causes of this shift in ideological focus—from what might be seen as an inward-looking city and region, famous worldwide for its internal ethnonational conflict, to an outward-looking province that is keen to be perceived as a site where new businesses and new visitors will thrive—are also the products of recent global and more local changes. In the United Kingdom the Tony Blair governments successfully pushed regional devolution as part of the changing dynamics of Britain at home and abroad. A long peace process led to the 1998 Belfast Good Friday Agreement, which itself had roots in the national consensuses at the heart of EU compromises. A key factor in many of these political, economic, and social changes has been the overall effects of European integration in Ireland and the United Kingdom, which have helped to transform agricultural production, consumer society, attitudes toward and practices of human and civil rights, the duties and privileges of citizenship, and fundamental notions of local, regional, and national identity.

These forces for change not only have led to efforts to change Belfast's face to outsiders, but also have made it imperative to political and economic elites in Belfast to transform its image of itself among the people of Belfast. In fact, judging from new governmental policies, media accounts, NGO efforts, and educational and business initiatives, after years of violence the majority of decision-makers in Northern Ireland have seen the need for the province overall to reinvent itself, to re-present itself to the world as something new and worthy of notice and support.

This chapter focuses on Europeanization, one of the causes of change in Belfast, the capital of Northern Ireland. It does so through the examination of one recent major policy initiative in Belfast, the bid to become the European Capital of Culture in 2008. The upshot of this failed bid—the processes of adapting to European guidelines, images, and funding possibilities, all of which were filtered through the UK central government—led to many, sometimes competing, representations of Belfast peoples and institutions. The chapter explores how notions of culture and identity intersect with local perceptions of Europeanization, widely received as a process of transnationalism and cultural diversity, which the leaders of the bid to be nominated the European Capital of Culture seemed to accept and adopt. But they did so through a process of re-essentialism, wherein national and sectarian cultures and identities, at least in terms of their local manifestations, were privileged and projected to the bid's assessors. Ironically, this was meant in part to demonstrate the vitality of local culture and the validity to locals' claims that they were open to new ideas, precisely because they were willing to open up their "national" cultures to outsiders, even though many were aware of their image as sectarian. In short, governmental and other groups sought to show that local Belfast cultures were as European as any others and receptive to the influx of ideas, people, and capital that would flow into the city if it were chosen to represent the United Kingdom in 2008.

As part of this bid, many scholars and other community representatives were called upon to participate. This chapter examines not only some of the representations that served the bid itself, but also some of the representations used in attempts to incorporate me, a local university lecturer, and my students into the overall effort to conceptualize various cultures within the potential presentation of Belfast as a European capital of culture. Thus, this chapter is also about a second arena within which failure occurred, the construction of the bid itself and, in particular, in the discussions over whether an anthropologist and his students might usefully contribute to the efforts of the private company responsible for getting the award for the city from the British governmental committee assigned to that task.

This attempt to bring local university people into the bid did not work. In fact, it was resisted by almost everyone except the enthusiastic and innovative chief executive of the company at the heart of the city's bid. For example, my students at the university felt that the organizers were unrealistic in that they did not consider the depth of sectarianism and locally felt emotions that revolved around neighborhood boundaries. The consultant also thought the chief executive of the bid was unrealistic: academics and their students were at that stage a burden for the bid, no matter how you defined their role in terms of culture.

Thus, this chapter is also about the failure of local university people to participate in the bid in ways that at its onset looked to at least a few key people to be both valuable and feasible. This was then a failed effort in the politics of representation on the part of some of the bid's designers, who boldly asserted things about culture and community and about crossing borders, in particular, which forced an order on the localities of Belfast that just did not work. In my view this represented a level of political cooperation and intimacy on the part of national and ethnic Belfast that was a false image, one that required people to act a part that suggested that they no longer feared the boundaries that separated them. This "politics of timidity" was a façade that also failed to convince and, in the end, was not sustainable.

Anthropology and Representation in Northern Ireland

For some time the anthropology and ethnography of Northern Ireland have been dominated by a variety of approaches to social order, conflict, and social change in local communities in what Thomas Wilson and Hastings Donnan (2006) have labeled the "tribal conflict and accommodation" model in Irish anthropology (which, along with the "peasant society in decline" model, is one of the two major motifs in anthropological writing on Ireland in the twentieth century). As a result of these emphases and in comparison with other areas of the globe, there has been relatively little written by anthropologists about the politics of representation in Northern Ireland, whether it be literally about political representation in local government or at national levels or about the politics of relations that are engendered in the rendering and reception of cultural representations of all sorts. Over the last fifteen years this situation has changed, however, and there has rapidly grown a substantial body of anthropological writing on the representations of personal and group bodies (see, for example, Aretxaga 1997; Bryan 2000; Feldman 1991; Jarman 1997; Sluka 1989). Much of this work has sought to explicate the symbolism, rhetoric, propaganda, and political platforms of organized paramilitary groups, fraternal and religious organizations, and political parties, but some anthropological studies have also been of people whose aspirations have been largely ignored in the course of the more wide-sweeping "Troubles" (as the conflict which began in Northern Ireland in 1969 is locally known).

As part of this new turn in the anthropology of representation in Northern Ireland, there has been increasing interest in developing new critical approaches to the theorizing of culture and identity so that we anthropologists can understand and keep pace with people in Northern Ireland who themselves seek to transcend the limits of the Troubles and of other constraints that have more traditionally ordered local society. For many people in Northern Ireland who have largely been invisible in the anthropology of that place, this also means escaping the political logic of being seen to be on one side or the other in the ethno-national conflict that so characterizes the six counties of Northern Ireland, where people are presumed to be nationalist or republicans, on the one hand, or unionists or loyalists on the other. Begoña Aretxaga's account (1997) of alternative nationalist and republican voices among the women of West Belfast is perhaps the most widely read example of this pathbreaking work in the politics of representation in Northern Ireland, and it has been followed by many innovative approaches to the difficult politics of alternative and subversive culture in Northern Ireland that have been put forward by new scholars such as Kathryn Bell (2003), Thomas Carter (2003a, 2003b), and Robin Whitaker (2008).

This turn to the politics of negotiating identities in Northern Ireland still has a great deal to do with the old politics of sectarianism and nationalism, but recent anthropological writing is more sophisticated in its approaches to the roles that culture plays in the politics of division there, as has been persuasively argued by Joseph Ruane and Jennifer Todd (1996). It has concentrated on the ways in which history, memory, place, and territoriality enable local populations and communities to alter their representations of self in response to changing national and external forces (see Anthony Buckley and Mary Kenney [1995] and William Kelleher [2003] for analyses of these politics in urban and rural Northern Ireland). In fact, anthropological examinations of the politics of culture and identity in post-conflict Northern Ireland (i.e., post-1998 and the signing of the Belfast Good Friday Agreement, which marked a halt to widespread and major violent conflict but not an end to organized paramilitary violence) mirror the anthropologies of ethnic and nationalist conflict elsewhere in the world. They are evidence of a more receptive approach to political identity, which sees identities as multiple, responsive, and changing.

Recent ethnographic studies have investigated varieties of Irishness and Britishness rather than studying Irish and British cultures in Northern Ireland (cf. Wilson and Donnan 2006). Ethnic minorities (Carter 2003a; Donnan and O'Brien 1998), racism (McVeigh 1996), and the politics of gender (Whitaker 2008) and environmentalism (Milton 1993) have become key themes in the new anthropology of politics and power in Northern Ireland. And much of this anthropology relates these new forms of politics to changing notions of policy (Donnan and McFarlane 1997). This continuing interest in problematizing the changing politics of identity in Northern Ireland is also the result of anthropology's overall engagement with the forces of globalization. In Northern Ireland it is clear that there are many important external social and political movements for change that emanate from Ireland, from the rest of the United Kingdom, and from centers of power more distant. One of these is the European Union, through its role in European integration and Europeanization.

Europeanization

Anthropologists have examined the European Union as a major site and a major source of sociocultural change, as well as one of the many hegemonic structures that are changing the cognitive maps of Europeans today (for an overview of these perspectives, see Iréne Bellier and Thomas Wilson [2000]). But the majority of anthropological ethnographers have done research within EU institutions themselves, and not on the impact of EU policy and practice in local communities or on strategic moves on the part of local, regional, and national actors to change their material conditions within the redefining political and cultural space that is the European Union.

There have been gains made, however. Anthropologists and sociologists have been at the forefront of attempts to examine Europeanization and identification with Europe as processes that are much broader than political and economic adaptations to EU institutions and policies (see, for example, Abélès 1993; Giordano 1987; Hedetoft 1994; Kohli 2000; O'Dowd 2002; C. Ray 2001; Tarrow 1994). In fact, the most useful treatment of Europeanization outside of the disciplines of political science and international relations has been that of John Borneman and Nick Fowler, who describe Europeanization as a process that is "redefining forms of identification with territory and people" (1997, 489), which they seek to disentangle from more essentializing notions of modernization, development, and European integration within the European Union. They suggest that it would be more fruitful to consider Europeanization "as a spirit, a vision, and a process" (511) and to see Europeanization "as a strategy of self-representation and a device of power," which is "fundamentally reorganizing territoriality and peoplehood, the two principles of group identification that have shaped the modern European order" (487). As such, Europeanization is most certainly a process of making things and people *more European,* not least in those aspects of everyday life and culture that Borneman and Fowler identify: language, tourism, sex, sport, and money.

But Europeanization is also a process of directed political and economic change and not just directed from the halls of government in Brussels and national capitals. Europeanization is an attempt at strategic political and economic change on the part of political, civic, business, and transnational groups and institutions that are motivated by the programs and ideas of the European Union and that are impelled by the need to adapt to the initiatives of others in what is commonly known as a game of winners and losers.

If in anthropological perspective Europeanization is about the reordering of territory and people, then anthropology must focus on the issues of culture and identity, both in terms of culture as an EU project (Shore 1993) and in terms of the ways in which EU policy has an impact on and interacts with local forms of political and cultural identification throughout the member states (T. Wilson 2000). The studies of this type of Europeanization, which perhaps have had the widest impact across disciplinary boundaries, have been of the redefinition and negotiation of identities within EU institutions, among the architects of the integration project itself (see, for example, Abélès 1993; Bellier 1997; McDonald 1996). For a range of research perspectives in the anthropology of the European Union, see Bellier and Wilson (2000).

Europeanization also points us toward the strategic use of culture and identity in order for territorial and other political entities to have an edge in what is often perceived as a zero-sum game of funding and power brokerage. This game is played within both the umbrella institutions of the European Union and the evolving political and social system of the European Union and its member states. Culture and identity are now important terms in "Euro-speak"; culture figures in all types of Europeanization, such as in institutional adaptation, the transformation of citizenship and identity, and the integration of transnational communities and social movements across national borders. This is especially apparent when urban policy-makers perceive culture and identity to be key means to effect social change in order to better Europeanize and better compete for scarce resources at regional and national levels. This is what has been happening in Belfast.

Belfast and Old and New Identities

Belfast has undergone major changes in response to many forces external to the province, Ireland, and the United Kingdom. Belfast has been swept along on the tide of deindustrialization, market readjustments, the weakening of the welfare state, the transformation of borders in the European Union and elsewhere, the end of the Cold War and the rise of new and the return of old nationalisms, peace processes in former hotspots of the Cold War, and enforced peace in new areas of hot war. The cultural shifts that have accompanied new technologies, not the least those involving the transfer of information, the flow of new migrants, the return of tourists, and the overall transformation of global relations of culture and identity, have also become part of Belfast's quotidian existence.

The numbers of tourists and foreign students are rising each year, especially since the end of major hostilities in 1996. Service and information-technology national and multinational firms are relocating to Northern Ireland while sites of industrial production close or are retooled. New sporting ventures like the Belfast Giants, an ice hockey team, capture the imagination of both sides of the divided community in new purpose-built but generally adaptable arenas. Funds are pumped in from a variety of sources to support cross-community partnerships, as well as community heritage, culture, and identity.

The contradictory air of Belfast after the Belfast Good Friday Agreement of 1998, which paved the way for power sharing in a new Northern Ireland Assembly, is a heady mix of free market capitalism, welfare state socialism, globalism, transnationalism, and internationalism among pro- and anti-Europeans and among Irish and British peoples who want a return to some version of an unshared past, but who also see that they must shape their future together in an Ireland or Britain that is changing around them. In fact, the people of Northern Ireland have brought about a great deal of social and political change themselves, including a peace process that, with many fits and starts, has seen the success of the Northern Ireland Assembly, the destruction of major Irish Republic Army (IRA) arms dumps, the cease-fires of most major terrorist/paramilitary organizations, and a return to normalcy after thirty years of war. Because of these changed circumstances, cities like Belfast—that is, cities of past wealth and power with relatively small populations, a weak economic base, and diminished influence in their national systems—must reposition themselves within new national and global networks and fields of power. They must resituate themselves in a changed international division of labor, necessitating new forms of urban planning in new global networks of services and consumption.

This is what motivated many of the city leaders who planned Belfast's bid to be the United Kingdom's selection as a European Capital of Culture in 2008, one of fourteen such bids. Planning for this bid was engineered by a private company, funded by local government, with the participation of local businesses and community and arts groups. This company decided that an effort had to be made to both foster a spirit of new Belfast identity and portray the most important and recognizable political and religious identities in Belfast in new light, which, while acknowledging the sectarian dimensions of the past, might use the past as a basis upon which to build a new sense of purpose. It was in this latter sense that many of the people I interviewed on the organizing committee suggested that they were "being," "acting," and "supporting what it means to be European" in that they saw the antinationalist stance of European integration as a model for their future.

Belfast leaders have also been influenced by the transformations achieved through the European Cities of Culture program, most notably in Glasgow and Barcelona (see Charles Landry [1999] for a review of the ways cities in Europe have used culture to remake themselves). Culture has been recognized by many of the architects of these Belfast plans as a successful strategy in the revitalization and expansion of other European cities. Before its transformation as a Capital of Culture, Barcelona was clearly seen from the perspective of Belfast to be a true European capital: as a city that has an identity, as a city of the arts, as a capital city of its own European region, as a city that has shown how to redefine itself to attract investment. Glasgow, on the other hand, was widely held to be a dreary and dangerous Scottish city, suffering from some of the same ailments as Belfast: the decline of shipbuilding and other local industries, sectarianism, and peripherality. However, in the 1980s it reinvented itself, a process culminating in it being named the European City of Culture in 1990 (the Cities of Culture program was started in 1985, with Athens selected as the first; for a review of the history of the concept and its implementation across Europe, see Peter Sjøholt [1999]). Since then Glasgow has become a major British and international tourist site, renowned for its artistic and environmental beauty, as well as for the variety of its tourist services. Belfast leaders definitely seek to emulate this success.

Belfast, European Capital of Culture?

These various types of Europeanization have all led to the initiative—headed in the first instance by an independent, limited company, known as Imagine

Belfast 2008, but mainly financed and supported by the Belfast City Council—to make Belfast a European Capital of Culture in 2008. The leader of the board of directors of Imagine 2008 was an employee of Queen's University of Belfast, the largest university in Belfast and the most influential institution of higher learning in Northern Ireland. He is a Catholic who in the past has been the editor of two of Belfast's daily newspapers, one a unionist paper and the other a nationalist one. A woman who had wide experience in the creative and arts fields in Belfast and beyond was the manager of the company and its operational leader for the day-to-day operations of the Imagine 2008 activities. Under her leadership, the company set out to design a holistic presentation of what Belfast could do as a European Capital of Culture. From its inception, however, the bid was more about the city's reimagining and restructuring of itself as a center of culture, and about this reconstruction and economic development than it was about demonstrating past achievements in local, national, and European culture. The details of the construction of the bid are beyond of the scope of this chapter. But the important waypoints and the ways that the bid was articulated by various groups are at the heart of the debates that still rage in Belfast over representations of national and regional culture and identity.

The Belfast bid to be European Capital of Culture 2008 had to be submitted to the Department of Culture, Media, and Sport in London on March 28, 2002. The short-listing took place in October and the final decision was announced in March 2003. The others cities bidding were: Newcastle and Gateshead, Liverpool, Birmingham, Bristol and Bath, Brighton and Hove, Oxford, Canterbury and East Kent, Norwich, Milton Keynes, Bradford, Inverness and The Highlands, East London, and Cardiff. In 2003 the Belfast bid failed, in that Belfast was not picked to be the UK Capital of Culture and was not even selected as part of the short list of cities from which the capital would be selected as the British government's nomination to the European Union as part of the rotating Capital of Cultures initiative (2005 in Ireland, 2006 in Greece, 2007 in Luxembourg, then the United Kingdom). In March 2004 Liverpool was selected.

What Went Wrong?

As the overall leader of the bid lamented in an interview with me on August 16, 2003, in answer to this question, "There was a *big* what went wrong and a small what went wrong." The designation of the big and small matters was not an easy thing, however, and depended on your perspective. To some, the big failure was not getting to the short list, in that they never expected to win the title but wanted to use the effort to bring economic and other attention to the city and use the occasion to mend past hurts and agree on common cultures at the heart of development policies. Others, however, saw the big failure as not winning the title, full stop. To them, the title might be an opportunity to truly reconstruct Belfast, literally, in terms of infrastructural development and investment, but also in the minds of its people and in the images of the world. Yet either set of goals, or either failure, must be placed within the context of what needed to be done and what obstacles were ahead.

The politics of culture were the bid's strengths and weaknesses. The local committee had to work with the politics of culture in Belfast today, which are about the politics of local national identity, of being Irish or being British. These politics pervade all civil and political society, all local government, and policy-making.

The enormity of convincing other people in the United Kingdom that Belfast was suited and ready to be the urban representative of the country, as a European Capital of Culture, can only be judged when the obstacles to a successful bid are examined. Consider these problems that needed to be addressed, if not solved:

1. The political organization that needed to get this bid through had to successfully navigate the political organization of Northern Ireland, where government and politics were in a state of flux due to the upheavals of the Belfast Good Friday Agreement arrangements, as well as the various political organizations, many of which have diametrically opposed political philosophies (and, in some cases, different political strategies, tactics, and agendas).

2. The three political agencies that supported the bid, the Belfast City Council, the Arts Council, and the Department of Culture, Arts, and Leisure, had their own needs, agendas, and bureaucracies.

3. Imagine 2008 and its parent bodies had a funding deficit. A successful bid was estimated to cost £150 million in a city with a limited budget, in a province that had been a drain on the British exchequer since 1969! And money was certainly a strategic factor, as was later made clear. At the point when the bid was submitted, on March 31, 2002, Belfast had spent £750,000, while Liverpool had spent £4 million; Belfast had a full-time staff of six, Liverpool had forty.

4. Imagine Belfast 2008, the private company set up to lead the bid, was given the task of raising its own financial support, basically by courting/lobbying public bodies (the Belfast City Council eventually adopted the bid as its own, but did so in ways that some suggested altered the direction

of the bid, at least in terms of strategies). The company's chief officer and assistant were appointed in April 2001, which meant they had exactly one year to find money, staff, and consensus, then design and produce the bid by March 31, 2002.

5. The Imagine Belfast 2008 directors had to be drawn from across the political and cultural spectrum, and while these people played mostly an advisory role, their goodwill and community networks were vital. As a result, both decision making and decision reporting were slow processes and always had to consider how decisions would play in West Belfast and East Belfast, strongholds of Irish republicanism and British loyalism, respectively.

6. From the very beginning of the bid, there was a question of ownership: whose notions of culture would be at the core of the exercise?

These constraints were all about the core of Belfast culture, or cultures, and whether it/they could provide coherence to the assertion that the city deserved the Capital of Culture title. This meant that the questions about what was essential to Belfast culture, to the selecting committee in London, and to local supporters and government agencies had to be answered.

The Politics of the Essential

If Belfast was to win a competition to be the British nominee as Capital of Culture, then it had to be convincing on a number of grounds:

- Could it project a persuasive image of being and fostering culture that was not just reflective of the region but also of a wider Britain and Britishness?
- Could it define and articulate culture in ways that would transcend the divisions in the city and wider Northern Ireland?
- Could it act as a showplace, including the provision of necessary infrastructure and security, in order to cater to the many types of visitors who would be attracted?
- Would Belfast's role serve economic and cultural development in the city, region, and beyond?

Within Belfast, other questions quickly emerged:

- What is culture?
- What sorts of culture are specifically included in the European vision of the EU program?

- What sorts of culture can or might be included (folk culture, for instance, or minority cultures)?
- What types of culture need to be financially supported and developed in a future Belfast?
- How would the bid match up with local public and private initiatives to develop the city economically, socially, and culturally (the political being always embedded in these other perspectives)?

The debate centered quickly around provocative statements made by a former head of the European Commission offices in Belfast, who in Northern Irish and Irish newspapers accused the planning bodies and Imagine Belfast of engaging in identity politics at the expense of the truth. In his view, Belfast could not possibly succeed in its bid because it has no major philharmonic, opera company, ballet company, art museum, or even one internationally known art gallery. In effect, he saw that Belfast's clear Irish and British roots, which had resulted in only shallow European roots over the centuries (he used the lack of European architecture styles as one example of this), made it a regional British capital with little European culture to recommend it!

The minor but important media and political furor that resulted from this public challenge by a leading citizen in the European movement in Belfast led some to debate what was meant by *culture* in both the European and British framing documents. Others focused on the notions of cultural identity, which in their view were at the core of the dispute. To many of these community leaders, Belfast had an opportunity to show that its old and, to some, sacred and traditional cultures and identities could and should be seen to be European in character, or at the least shown to be part of the same new processes of change at work in the wider United Kingdom and in Europe.

This was not cosmetic Europeanization. It was not an attempt to fool people in London and Brussels. On the contrary, this bid to be the Capital of Culture was seen in Belfast by many people I interviewed, and not only those directly involved in crafting and implementing the bid, to be a very real process of approximating European values, practices, and cultures. This was in keeping with the new politics of Europeanization that had been developing in Northern Ireland since 1973, when as part of the United Kingdom it joined the then European Community. For decades this membership had led to remarkable politics of funding, where many groups, not the least of them the farmers, had adapted to European rules and guidelines, in large part to get the added funding that was available through many local, regional, and national sources. But the politics of Europeanization in Northern Ireland are not simply economic and instrumental, even if at times that seems the main purpose of many, for example, among community groups and development specialists in the border regions (see T. Wilson 2000).

During the 1990s many other aspects of local social and political life had altered due to the new order that membership in the European Union had brought Northern Ireland, and there was a growing notion, as expressed in the university, the media, and in political circles, that Europe's role was gaining in importance and that some of the processes of Europeanization were picking up speed. A number of new elements in local politics, for instance, had their roots in the politics of the European Union, such as *partnership* and *parity of esteem.* These are widely seen in Northern Ireland to be facets of formal local politics and administration borrowed directly from the structures of the European Union, as principles of compromise, accommodation, and political efficacy.

Partnership is a principle that at its core demands that groups that have little trust in each other and often see the other as a foe must work together, in roughly equal numbers, to achieve an agreed end. This partnership principle has been made a requirement of many EU funding schemes and has taken root in political society as a result too, it must be said, of the efforts of local and national leaders. This effort has succeeded to such a degree that almost all community development projects, in rural and urban areas, seek to have this principle honored, ensuring that Catholics and Protestants are on management and implementation teams responsible for getting and spending development funds. Parity of esteem, as an aspect of politics in the European Union, also seeks to have equal participation in decision-making in government. It was a core principle of the Belfast Good Friday Agreement in 1998, a document and a process that many politicians and political critics see as very European in design and focus. When these principles are added to other features of European political and social values—such as that of subsidiarity, which calls for decisions to be made at the most appropriate level of polity and society and in the level closest, politically if not geographically, to the people most affected by the decision—then it is easy to see the impact that the forces of EU-directed change are having in Northern Ireland, where new forms of governance are being established. Overall, Europeanization in Northern Ireland followed quite closely Borneman and Fowler's (1997) notion that Europeanization is a vision and a spirit. The majority of people I interviewed who worked on the bid, and those who had reason to watch the development of the bid closely, clearly saw that this vision and spirit were good for them and for Belfast. However, this is not to say that there are not many and some major opponents to these principles and to the political actions that they imply.

All of these forces of support and subversion developed apace with Belfast's attempt to get the title of Capital of Culture. The reasons behind the selection committee's decision are not known as their deliberations were held in secret and their specific conclusions were not made public to any applicant city. However, a few of the important events and local decisions about how Belfast and its people wanted to represent themselves, as Northern Ireland men and women and as people worthy of being recognized for their culture if not exactly for their *European* culture, may serve as key illustrations of the politics of representation and identity within the shifting appreciations of Europeanization. Perhaps the best illustration to offer is that of the site visit by the London-based national advisory committee, which planned to spend one day in each city to receive its local presentation of what the city is and why it would be a good choice as the United Kingdom's representative.

In August 2002, the Independent Advisory Panel visited Belfast to witness firsthand how Belfast sees itself as part of this attempt to be the United Kingdom's European Capital of Culture. According to one of my informants, one of the panel members (all of whom were seen to be the judges of each city's presentation) set the tone of the visit the night before: "We want to see the city as if we were visitors from Europe." And the local Belfast committee was happy to oblige.

Their tour started at the Odyssey Centre, the new sports arena that is home to the local ice hockey team (but, as critics later lamented, it was not a concert hall or some other similar cultural venue). Then they visited the dry dock where the *Titanic* was built. As one nationalist community representative described it to me later, this was supposed to be an example of Belfast industry and show the spirit of its working classes, but it also represented the unionist and loyalist dimensions of Belfast in that the shipbuilding yards of the early twentieth century were almost exclusively Protestant (where Catholics were barred), and it was a place where one of the most famous, doomed ships of all time was crafted. In his view, this too was a symbolic blunder since the significance of these sectarian associations was not lost on the visitors. He and many others also wondered about the symbolism of the unsinkable that sunk!

Next stop was an arts gallery in East Belfast on the Newtownards Road, a loyalist area, where the panel met the charismatic David Ervine, a former paramilitary and one of the new voices of integration and peace among working-class Protestants. While he and others discussed partnership, the visitors were able to view the famous Loyalist murals in the area that depicted in no uncertain terms the sectarian and essentialist natures of loyalism with their particular symbolism of war and resistance to Irish and British forces of change.

After a visit to a cross-community sports center, the tour went to the Shankill Orange Hall, where they were greeted by a representation of King Billy in full regalia, in the guise of an Orangeman in costume on white steed.[1] The music was provided by traditional musicians on traditional Orange musical instruments; there were lambeg drums, a fife band, and an accordion band. Also there to greet the visitors were representatives from the Royal Black Perceptory, another Protestant sectarian institution with links to the Loyal Orange Lodge that hosted the event. But to supporters and critics alike, what seemed to stand out among the presentations to the dignitaries, where traditional Belfast culture and identity were to be privileged, were the festivities after the tea and cakes and the review of the Orange museum. A demonstration of Scottish dancing was followed by a performance by the Shankill American line dancers, who did a routine to the accompaniment of American country and western music!

The visitors were then given a tour of Protestant West Belfast. West Belfast and North Belfast have been the hardest hit areas in the cities since the beginning of the recent Troubles in 1969. It was intended to show the assessors that they were not being treated to a sanitized and saccharine tour of the city; they were to see the real city, sectarian and violent warts and all! So the boundary between the territories of the Ulster Defense Association (UDA) and Ulster Volunteer Force (UVF) Protestant paramilitary groups was visited, as was a line along the Springfield Road, a fortified wall built to separate sectarian working-class areas in order to ensure their security from terrorist and sectarian attacks.

This visit also highlighted the difficulties that Belfast faced in this bid: while one of the themes of the Belfast bid was *living without walls,* peace lines (more properly seen as *peace walls*), some would argue, were the only way that these sectarian working-class communities could live in reasonable security during the Troubles. And even though the cease-fires of the paramilitaries are in effect, Belfast has had consistent and almost continual sectarian violence—including the throwing of pipe bombs, rocks, and nails—across such walls.

The tour then went to republican and nationalist West Belfast for the beginning of the second half of the tour, which was to be dedicated to Irish nationalist sites and communities (and as a unionist critic put it to me, "To see the *parity of esteem* in full flower"). At the site of the West Belfast Arts Festival there was a poetry reading, during which local Sinn Fein representatives hosted the committee. The visitors were then shown the film *Made in Belfast,* by the actor and film-maker Adrian Dunbar. A formal lunch was had with invited local leaders and dignitaries. But this, too, was cause for criticism by some. As one of my interviewees put it, these people were "the great and the good": business people and politicians, but no arts people! Happily for the Belfast hosts, the judges said later that they were impressed that unionists and nationalists sat down to eat and converse with each other! Then there was a visit to the Ormeau Baths Arts Gallery, where there was a late afternoon reception for people in the arts and a comedy skit satirizing *Imagine Belfast*. But as the visitors left the Baths Gallery, passing demonstrators threw eggs at civil servants, scoring some hits.

The leader of Belfast's bid, despite these embarrassing last moments—one wit quickly labeled them "seggtarian" attacks—later said to me in an interview, "I thought we had got it [a successful bid] that day; it went so well!" But this was not to be. However, that verdict was a while yet in the coming, and in the meantime Belfast and all of the other applicant cities prepared a presentation to give to the government in London months later to show their progress and spirit. But, symbolically speaking, that visit by the Belfast representatives was also doomed. On the same day, David Trimble, first minister of the Northern Ireland Assembly, informed Tony Blair, the British prime minister, that he and his party could no longer remain in the Northern Ireland Assembly, while his minister for culture (of Northern Ireland), Martin McGimpsey, was heading up the presentation from Belfast at the Department of Culture, Media, and Sport. In one day, in two locations of British government, representatives of the Ulster Unionist Party were delivering messages that, symbolically, contradicted each other. One message was to trust Belfast to represent the United Kingdom as a prospective European Capital of Culture, to foster the goals of devolution and of European integration. The other message, delivered cross-town, was that the mutual trust needed to continue in government with nationalists in the new Northern Ireland Assembly could not be found, and local, devolved government should be suspended in Northern Ireland.

The Politics of Intimacy and Timidity

Now let me turn to the politics of representation of the bid's designers in Imagine Belfast 2008 and their and my failed attempts to use researchers, drawn from the local university, to represent the new forms of understanding and cooperation that the bid wished to privilege as occurring at the peace lines in Belfast. This failure was in essence an attempt by the leaders of the bid to impose an order on those streets that, in fact, did not exist.

Imagine 2008 had intended to use the peace lines, and specifically the walls that made up these peace lines, as symbolic, interactive meeting points where the people from both sides of the line could come and record their memories and impressions on digital equipment established at some of the most notable and incendiary peace lines. As the Belfast bid itself suggests,

The culture of barriers will end . . .
We will reconnect our populations.
We will cement conciliation.
We will replace the peace lines with peace.
We will bring down the walls of Belfast.
We will embed our peace in the fabric of the city and in the conscience of
    Europe. (Imagine Belfast 2008 2002, 12)

The architects of the bid were not fanciful dreamers: they realized that this peace-line initiative was going to be difficult. But, as the head of the company saw it (as expressed by her in an interview with me), there was the will and it was the right time because of the peace and because of the drive that the promise of funds and prestige would bring to the city, and this would impel disputing parties to cooperate.

As part of this effort, I entered into discussions to have my master's degree students participate in the peace-line component of the project. In a sense, these discussions were initiated by me in that I contacted Imagine 2008 to see if the company could use interns from Queens University, master's students in European integration, who in return for their help would use their experiences to write research papers on the intersections of policy and local public practice. After a few initial meetings, the chief executive of the company thought that we would best serve her company's efforts if we pitched in on local cultural efforts, especially since most of my students were from Belfast and Derry (Northern Ireland's second city) and represented both sides of the working-class sectarian divide. She reckoned that, with my background in the anthropology of borders and boundaries and my students' expertise in the day-to-day realities of communities divided by peace lines, our overall intimacy with the people and the subject would help win the day, at least among the residents of the neighborhoods affected.

However, the politics of intimacy that were needed to make this arrangement work were not there in two ways. In the first instance, my students and I, asked to help in this effort, were not prepared to re-present this image of the streets and the peace lines to the people of Belfast, at least not in ways that the bid leaders could accept. In this sense it was clear that the organizers of the bid wanted to project an image of Belfast people that implied, if did not outright assert, that Belfast people were willing to cross the social, cultural, sectarian, and national boundaries between their neighborhoods in the new spirit of integration that demanded that they look forward to the new world of EU integration and not back to the past of nationalist conflict. To the bid designers, this represented a new beginning to Belfast. In effect, though, this projection of a lack of timidity, of a preparedness built up over years of conflict to reach out to the others across the peace lines, was false. The more concrete "politics of timidity" made this aspect of the bid hollow in that there was still a great deal of evidence that many forms of communication in which people still participated across peace lines was sectarian.

In the second instance, there was a failure to manage our own politics of intimacy within the coordination of company and university. This was in large part due to the decisions reached in a planning meeting when I joined the chief executive and the consultant brought in to bring external expertise in preparing a successful bid for European city recognition. The chief executive thought that we would be a good match since we all wanted the same things.

The three of us met over coffee in what was then one of the new Starbuck's–styled coffee houses in Belfast, and the chief executive conveyed her intentions to the consultant: she wanted to use the postgraduate students in European integration from Queens University as interns on the project of peace-line displays and to use me as a consultant/aid based on my experience of the anthropology of borders. Before we went any further, however, and after a modest fleshing out of these intentions, the consultant reminded the chief executive that he was being called in to advise on such matters. Then, this Real Consultant, who had played an important role in the successful bids of both Glasgow and Barcelona, which had transformed those cities and their images in Europe, asked, but more properly declared, the following: What did Imagine 2008 need with academics, who, after all, gained a great deal but offered little (an assertion that on the surface made a great deal of sense to me). And he suggested that if you bring in these postgraduate students, the one certain thing is that in a year or two the chief executive and the Real Consultant will get requests to read and comment on students' master's theses. Moreover, he advised that the chief executive of the bid did not have the time to encourage these ancillary cultural ties and projects; they only had six months at that stage to get the real project under way. And even if the peace-lines initiative needed local expertise, this aid was not needed now, at the point of planning, but rather later, at the point of delivery. It would be then that the decision to use academics and students should be made.

The chief executive, embarrassed a bit by all of this, with me sitting there with my cappuccino, seemed to be confused too. While we never discussed this exchange later, I assumed on the day that to her these ancillary projects

were the project: to build new ways to see and encourage culture and cooperation in Belfast, particularly by employing representatives of one of the pre-
eminent institutions of education and culture in Belfast, Queens University.
As the Real Consultant concluded that day, once you get the money and are
"the capital," you can then bring in the academics and cooperate with them
on how to appreciate what is going on. But it was clear to him that anthropologists and other academics could not help to win the capital title, at least
not within the available timeframe and with the resources on hand, and as
such should retire from the scene. I did, with the agreed notion that I would
be brought back after the bid succeeded.

What may be surprising to some, but was not to me then or now, is that I
was in full agreement about the decision not to employ anthropologists in this
endeavor. Anthropologists have never played important and continuing roles
in policy making and implementation in Northern Ireland. While our ethnographic practices depend on the creation and maintenance of various relations of intimacy, these relations of trust, of common experience, and of the
abiding interest in quotidian life are not seen by policy- and decision-makers
throughout the public and private sectors to be of pressing or vital concern.
Anthropologists in Northern Ireland have avoided for some time the examination of policy and politics, but in so doing they have largely selected themselves out of public cultural debate. I could have, perhaps should have, argued
that the peace-line plans needed to be made with a clear notion of what the
people who live along the lines have been saying and doing, and much of this
cannot be gleaned from governmental reports and the rhetoric of political
parties. However, I did not, in part because anthropology and ethnography
are not widely perceived as policy-relevant disciplines. But I also knew that,
at least according to my students, the peace-line plan was daft anyway.

Conclusion: The Politics of Europe, Representation, and Intimacy

There were many reasons why the bid failed. Some of these were to do with
the planning and construction of the bid, some with the representation of the
peoples and cultures of Belfast. But the problems of the latter, of the contests
over representation, are, in fact, the recurring problems of the Troubles themselves. There was not enough political commitment to see the bid through, in
part because unionist and nationalist politicians were wary of funding cultural activities of the other side of the house. In essence, there were too many
political agendas (of local government, of the British government, of nationalists and unionists; of the European Union) working behind the scenes.
Overall in Belfast there is still precious little culture of trust and little trust re-

garding culture as a way forward, even given the European Union's emphasis on it as a solution to some past European nationalist conflicts.

But another equally fundamental cause of the bid's failure was the divergence in representation, in the assertions of what culture is and which cultures mattered, in both the presentation to the visiting panel and in how the people of Belfast were to be represented. We may never know why the selection committee did not place Belfast on their short list. But it is worth considering what they witnessed on the day of their site visit and what some may have concluded was being represented. Sport and business investment were the first images they encountered, and throughout the day of their visit there was little of high culture on view. Pride in a job well done was a clear message in the shipyards where the *Titanic* was launched, but pride in the notoriety of grand failure, disaster even, was also offered for reflection. Community development, especially through the arts, was to be expected, but I daresay the history and rituals of sectarianism, as presented at the Orange lodge, despite their importance to local British identities, are a set of images and discourses that might need to be confronted and better understood, but perhaps not in such a celebratory way. The privileging of folk and popular Scottish and American culture might also give a visitor cause to pause, to speculate as to what *cultures* would this Capital of Culture be about? Overall, in fact, the high arts, which are so intertwined with European culture, largely were ignored in favor of the low, the folk, the popular, and the national, including the sectarian, in a day where the visitors were shown line dancing but not the Belfast Opera House.

The cooperation among politicians witnessed by the committee must have been a positive force, but peace lines are also war lines, testament to the history, the memories, and the volatility of sectarian and nationalist conflict. European integration is a force against the evils of nationalism, and as such the committee should have been looking for ways forward, out of ethnic and nationalist conflict. But the Culture of Capital program does not have this as a principal concern, and when a symbolic egg attack punctuated the end of the day's activities, the committee might be forgiven if they assessed that Belfast and Northern Ireland still have a long way to go to remove the underlying causes of violence and the reasons to mistrust.

One thing was clear, though, in this bid to be the Capital of Culture. Belfast leaders saw that culture is a way to cooperate with their local and historical *others,* a way to increase economic and social development, and a way to participate in the Europeanization that has been so important to political and social change in Northern Ireland. Leaders in Belfast, like those of cities in other European locales, are mobilizing various interests and institutions in order to develop collective strategies to compete with other cities, states, and the European Union itself. As Patrick LeGalès (1999, 299) suggests, "This is probably why culture has also become so important in many cities, not only to compete, but also to be used in local mobilization; to articulate and facilitate negotiation between different social groups which are now recognized in their relative specificities."

The visions of Belfast that Imagine 2008 provided are evidence that culture is increasingly being used as a strategy for the redefinition of development politics in Northern Ireland, in the United Kingdom, and in the European Union. Culture itself is utilized as a policy strategy, as a policy program, and as a policy goal or result. It is also clear that there are many perspectives on culture in Belfast. There are those that can be found in the arts, in the traditions of Gaelic, Ulster-Scots, and English, and in the Irish and British experiences. But there are also evolving perspectives on these and other forms of culture, emanating from more distant, transnational, and global centers of change, including those in Brussels and in the wider European Union. The bid to be European Capital of Culture was an example of changing political structures and identities in Northern Ireland, concrete results of European integration. But it was also an example of attempts to participate in, if not redirect, the processes of Europeanization.

The politics of representation in this case failed, at least in terms of not achieving the stated goal. But these politics of representation were also a failure in terms of the social relations of intimacy, in the first instance among the Imagine 2008 team, who saw so much potential in Belfast and its people but whose idealism could not be matched by the actions of many of Belfast's people. But this was also a failure compounded in a very unimportant way, perhaps, by the bid organizers, but in a manner that may have more to say to anthropologists, by the inability of the Imagine 2008 team to see the potential in having a university researcher and local postgraduate students get involved early in the project to build relations of trust and to narrate the images in ways that went beyond the rhetoric that was applied to the peace lines. The politics of intimacy to which I referred earlier, which everywhere in anthropological domains are dependent on relations of trust built up by a researcher or a teacher with the people with whom one lives and teaches, made both me and my students willingly retreat from the project; and in so doing we gave support to the assertions of the consultant who suggested that we would be more work than was warranted.

This may be a surprising turn of events to some anthropologists because anthropologists, at least in our own sense of our disciplinary history, have been the academic specialists in the study of culture. But that is our view and may be an almost complete contradiction to the continuing view, still common in Ireland and elsewhere, that anthropologists study the exotic, the indigenous peoples of the world, *out there*. In Northern Ireland anthropologists have played only minor roles in public culture, especially in policy arenas. This is a failure on the part of anthropologists to build the same sort of relations of trust and intimacy among power holders in the government, media, and NGOs as we often do among other people we study. The case study just reviewed touches on many aspects of failed politics, but it also is a window on the failure in the politics of the representation of anthropology in Northern Ireland.

Notes

This chapter is based on interviews with people in the public and private sectors who were both directly and indirectly related to the Imagine 2008/City of Culture bid. This research is ongoing and is part of a wider project of mine on the Europeanization of Northern Ireland. The rural component of this project was funded in 2000 and 2001 by the Leverhulme Trust and the British Academy.

1. Protestant King William defeated Catholic King James in the Battle of the Boyne in 1690, ushering in a period of Protestant ascendancy in Ireland. King William is the principal icon of Northern Ireland loyalism, and the Battle of the Boyne is the principal historical memory of loyalism.

Epilogue

Identities and the Politics of Representation
June C. Nash

Despite my protests that I had little to add to the problematic of representation in anthropology, Gabriela Vargas-Cetina provoked me to respond with her question as to what it was like to have persisted in the ethnographic quest after two major paradigm changes.

As a student of anthropology in the 1950s I was introduced to the discipline by the generation preceding mine, which had led the critique of nineteenth-century theories and methods. Sir George James Frazer's book, *The Golden Bough: a Study in Magic and Religion* (1922), based on the perusal of travelers' and missionaries' memoirs—derisively called "armchair anthropology"—and first published in 1890, was gathering dust in the library stacks. Franz Boas had long displaced Lewis Henry Morgan's ahistorical speculations based on nineteenth-century evolutionary thought. We were assigned the works of Alfred Radcliffe-Brown and Bronislaw Malinowski, the giants who shaped ethnography based on long-term participatory fieldwork in the early decades of the twentieth century. We could not anticipate that they, too, were soon to become the targets for the advancing phalanx of students in my cohort, who were encouraged to sharpen their teeth gnawing on bones of the far more popular works of Ruth Benedict (1934) and Margaret Mead (1935).

As students in the Department of Anthropology at the University of Chicago, we were even challenged to critique the work of our professors. Sol Tax (1937) set an example by criticizing the ideal, typical, "folk" community model that his professor, Robert Redfield, claimed to have found in Tepoztlan (Redfield 1930; see also Redfield 1941) for his failure to note the highly commercial behavior of peasants that he had discovered in Panajachel. Fred Eggan (1954) challenged the comparative basis of whole cultures that was popularized in the work of Benedict (1934) and Mead (1935), pointing out the importance of contextualizing comparisons of particular cultures within the wider context in which they occur. He demonstrated that intensive wet-rice cultivation was not, as some had asserted, a sign of advanced civilization but, rather, an indication of the availability of labor in relation to land and the wider environmental context in the Philippines. Sherwood Washburn introduced brilliant insights into evolutionary theory by bridging genetic and behavioral studies in his physical anthropology seminar that launched a whole field of primate studies.

These paradigm changes might have led us to reject past scholarship had we not read E. R. Leach's (1961) lecture given in 1959 at the London School of Economics. Criticizing "the arrogant assumption that social anthropology has embodied a well-defined set of ideas and objectives which derive directly from the teaching of Malinowski and Radcliffe-Brown," Leach went on to say, "One of the things we need to recognize is the strength of the empirical bias which Malinowski introduced into social anthropology and which has stayed with us ever since" (1961, 1).

So even while we were encouraged to engage in an ongoing critique of method and theory, we learned to appreciate that the strength of our discipline lay in sustained and often humbling fieldwork. Before we received our doctoral degrees, we burlesqued this lesson in a skit presented to faculty and students as "The Concept Destroyers." It was the saga of a sorry graduate student who went from one to another of his professors asking for advice on going to the field only to learn that, after having read all that the library contained on the area, he had to keep his ears open. And as Norman McQuown often insisted, keep a tape recorder handy to make sure you heard it right.

As some of us acquired positions in US universities in the early 1960s, a radical reappraisal of the culture concept intimated by our professors was beginning to enter the undergraduate texts and classrooms. Culture was no longer conceived as an integrated whole shared by all members, but rather the way in which differentially situated individuals, in distinct structural segments of a society differentiated by lineages or age groups, embodied these principles in behavior. Margaret Mead's (1935) book comparing six New Guinea cultures, *Sex and Temperament in Primitive Societies,* was assigned to incoming freshman classes almost like raw meat thrown to tiger cubs as they were encouraged to criticize the flaws in comparisons based on cultural wholes. On the West Coast of the United States, structuralists were being hired in departments of anthropology to replace Kroberian culturologists. The rhetoric of department heads dedicated to *clearing out the deadwood* evoked imagery of a logging operation more than an academic discipline when we went to the University of Washington in Seattle, where my husband got his first tenure-track job.

Such rethinking of the field that we had experienced as students recurred frequently as the field expanded and embraced new cohorts of students. Distinctions based on gender perspectives—either within the societies studied or by the anthropologists—were still ignored, and class differences and conflict based on it were still not incorporated as intrinsic to the field study. Just as Redfield (1930) did not mention that his ethnographic work in Tepoztlan was interrupted by the violence occurring in the Mexican Revolution during the 1920s, so did Manning Nash (1956) fail to include the 1954 coup in Guatemala as part of the ethnographic frame. We were denounced by the weaving master for our support of the union and nearly expelled from our field site in Cantel, Guatemala, when the military dictator Castillo Armas took power; certainly, this was outside the structural frame of ethnology (J. Nash 2006). Yet as these tempests set off by social movements began to shake static, functionalist, structural models, the methodology based on long-term participatory fieldwork prevailed. A central focus on substantive knowledge about distinct societies gained facets as new cohorts of students, including ever-increasing numbers of women and ethnic and racial minorities, introduced distinct perspectives and strategies into ethnology.

This may have set the stage for the backlash in the mid-1960s as anthropologists from the new nations of Asia and Africa, along with those from revolutionary movements of Latin America, questioned the authority of outside observers who had served colonial states or supported imperialist rule.[1] The critique generated by Marxist and feminist inquiries challenged the field increasingly in the 1970s as researchers from former colonial areas and women who up until then had occupied marginal roles in academia broadened the perspectives in a field that had been dominated by European and male perspectives.

In the course of these paradigm changes we can discern how the subliminal understandings we gained in graduate school were now brought to bear on the discipline itself. Anthropologists trained in British universities unmasked the apolitical pretensions of scientific models underlying anthropological studies of subordinated groups (Asad 1973; Gluckman 1958). In the 1970s American anthropologists began to reinvent a discipline that was professedly apolitical and oriented to museum collections. Contributors to Dell Hymes anthology ([1969] 1974) took issue with this approach, urging anthropologists to attend to issues of class and colonialism at a time when the Vietnam War exposed the subversion of democracy in US imperialist drives.

Mexican anthropologists questioned the functionalist paradigm that underwrote a discipline devoted to development projects that, they asserted, only fortified the given structures of power.[2]

The cultural critique, introduced by James Clifford and George Marcus (1986), that came in the wake of these currents was, for someone like me who had experienced these earlier upheavals, a rediscovery of what had been critically examined in preceding decades. Their anthropological theorizing featured the writing of texts produced by anthropologists. They analyzed these texts in light of the insights revealed by informants or observed in the discovery process of substantive ethnography and once again echoed past challenges to the discipline. Clifford Geertz (1973) had already opened the door to interpretive analyses, but as Vincent Crapanzano noted in a seminar at the Graduate Center of the City University of New York, he did not walk through it. Many who did walk over the threshold tended to turn their attention inward to self-absorbed reflection or to literary allusions such as heart of darkness. The editors of *Writing Culture* appropriated the earlier critique of representation in the discipline launched by Talal Asad (1973) and ignored that of feminists (Rosaldo and Lamphere 1974; Nash and Safa 1976; Etienne and Leacock 1980). For some, the paradigm called *cultural critique* turned the anthropological gaze inward to models of representation rather than promoting inquiry into the operation of structures of power influencing that production. On the positive side, some responded to the critique by consciously avoiding magisterial paradigms whether of Marxist, liberal, or neoliberal leaning. For still others, the shift to reflexive awareness provoked inquiries into the search for truth and shared human values (Rosaldo 1989).

The contributors to the present volume reflect the shift by bringing their expertise in the study of marginalized societies into focus on the crises caused by global integration that has become ever more threatening to the survival of subsistence producers in many of our field sites. Major issues raised by social movements for civil and human rights to overcome ethnic, racial, and gender inequality in preceding decades are now in the forefront of anthropological studies of violence, militarization, drug wars, and social disorganization. These countercurrents inform the method and theory developed by anthropologists in this volume. They have gained the self-criticism that allows them to include a wide range of post-structural responses to the cultural critique while retaining a firm hold on the importance of empirical data as a basis for analysis. In their ontological position within the ethnographic frame, they often share their own understandings with the populations they study without imposing solutions. Most of all they reveal respect for the knowledge and understandings of informants, simultaneously taking notes on how they are seen as well as what they see. This balance is also maintained when they take on an activist role, as Les W. Field does in his research of Native American land claims or as Sergey Sokolovskiy succeeds in doing in his organization of the 2002 census of Russian ethnic groups. Avoiding the binary opposition of primordialist versus structuralist categories of ethnic groups, they devise a constructivist approach that historicizes the context in which these categories serve. Beth A. Conklin succeeds in rescuing anthropologists who espouse an essentializing ethnicity from the charge of romanticizing ethnicity by calling it a "strategic" essentializing.

I shall mention here only a few other contributors in the book who illustrate the balance maintained by the editor in critical self-assessment and substantive contribution to knowledge of the changing world. Vilma Santiago-Irizary demonstrates the complexity of identity formation as she reveals how she came to perceive her place in the Newyorqueño racial ethnic range. Sergey Sokolovskiy indicates the range and power of ethnic labels in the reformulation of post-Soviet census categories. Gabriela Vargas-Cetina and Steffan Igor Ayora-Diaz remind us that the expression of ethnicity, whether in music or in culinary arts, contains the significance of belonging in everyday behaviors that are the ultimate repository of identification and possibly the most appreciated by the outsider. All of them demonstrate the abiding interest of social anthropology in the infinite variety of human representations and the most truthful ways in which we try to capture these and the people's own interpretations. I am especially mindful here of Renato Rosaldo's (1989) seething reminder of how our own experiences of loss make it possible for us to assimilate the knowledge our informants impart.

The contributors' concern with issues of representation goes beyond the literary tropes advanced by the earlier cultural critique. They succeed in addressing the core interests of anthropology in human variation and the social institutions in which it is embedded while responding to the resurgence of ethnic identity among the populations they study. I have argued (J. Nash 2005, 2008) that anthropological paradigms are more explicitly shaped by the social movements they encounter in field sites because these struggles—whether for autonomy and dignity or for land rights and resources—are an accepted part of the field study. As the people who have been uprooted and dispossessed become protagonists of history, anthropologists have learned to listen to and benefit from their stories. The ethnographic relationship now includes a collaborative exploration along with participant observation, as anthropologists give recognition to the contribution they make to the discipline as well as the data gathering in the field.

I urge readers to engage with the emerging paradigm of politics of representation in the chapters presented in this volume, beginning with the theoretical guide provided by Gabriela Vargas-Cetina in her introduction and pursuing the many leads to methodological and theoretical advances provided by contributors. The collection advances our self-awareness of the processes of power affecting our discipline and the resistance mobilized by the subjects of our study to the new invasions of their territories and resources.

Notes

1. I summarized the fallout from the upheaval caused by feminist and Third World critique of "mainstream" anthropology in an article for *Annual Reviews of Anthropology* (J. Nash 1981).

2. Warman and colleagues (1970) summarized their objections to a field dominated by "functionalists" who, they noted, reinforced hierarchies of control in the development programs in which they were employed. Cynthia Hewitt de Alcantara (1984) summarizes this critique and the debate between substantivists and formalists that preceded it. The substantivist approach was spearheaded by Roger Bartra (1969), who defended the communalist model of subsistence producers against Marxists who saw the *ejido* small-plot cultivation as an atavism.

References

Abélès, Marc. 1993. "Political Anthropology of a Transnational Institution: The European Parliament." *French Politics and Society* 11 (1): 1–19.

———. 2010. *The Politics of Survival.* Durham: Duke University Press.

Adams, Richard, and Santiago Bastos. 2003. *Las relaciones étnicas en Guatemala, 1944–2000.* Antigua, Guatemala: Centro de Investigaciones Regionales de Mesoamérica (CIRMA).

Agrawal, Arun. 2005. *Environmentality: Technologies of Government and the Making of Subjects.* Durham: Duke University Press.

Aguirre, María Ignacia. (1832) 1980. *Prontuario de cocina para un diario regular. Por Doña María Ignacia Aguirre, bien conocida por lo primorosa en el arte.* Mérida: FONAPAS-Yucatan.

Aliski, Marvin. 1980. "The Relations of the State of Yucatan and the Federal Government of Mexico, 1823–1978." In *Yucatan: A World Apart,* edited by Edward H. Moseley and Edward D. Terry, 245–63. Tuscaloosa: The University of Alabama Press.

American Anthropological Association (AAA). 1998. *Code of Ethics of the American Anthropological Association.* Approved June 1998. http://www.aaanet.org /committees/ethics/ethcode.htm (accessed June 11, 2009).

Anderson, Barbara A., and Brian D. Silver. 1989. "Demographic Sources of the Changing Composition of the Soviet Union." *Population and Development Review* 15 (4): 609–56.

Anderson, Benedict. 1983. *Imagined Communities: Reflections on the Origin and Spread of Nationalism.* London: Verso.

Anderson, Jon W. 1995. "Rhetorical Objectivity in Malinowski's Argonauts." In *Postmodern Representations: Truth, Power, and Mimesis in the Human Sciences and Public Culture,* edited by Richard Harvey Brown, 80–98. Urbana: University of Illinois Press.

Anzaldúa, Gloria. 1987. *Borderlands/La Frontera*. San Francisco: Spinsters/Aunt Lute.

Appadurai, Arjun. 1988. "Putting Hierarchy in Its Place." *Cultural Anthropology* 3 (1): 36–49.

———. 1996. *Modernity at Large: Cultural Dimensions of Globalization*. Minneapolis: University of Minnesota Press.

Aretxaga, Begoña. 1997. *Shattering Silence: Women, Nationalism, and Political Subjectivity in Northern Ireland*. Princeton: Princeton University Press.

Arutyunov, Sergei A. 1989. *Narody i kultury: Razvitie i vzaimodeistvie*. Moscow: Nauka.

———. 1995. "Etnichnost' kak objektivnaia realnost." *Etnographicheskoye obozreniye* 5: 7–13.

Arutyunov, Sergei A., and Nikolai N. Cheboksarov. 1972. "Peredacha informatsii kak mekhanism sushchestvovania etnosotsialnykh i bilogicheskikh grupp chelovechestva." *Rasy i narody: Vipusk* 2: 8–30.

Asad, Talal, ed. 1973. *Anthropology and the Colonial Encounter*. New York: Humanity Books, an imprint of Prometheus Books.

Asch, Michael, and Marc Pinkoski. 2004. "Anthropology as Science or Politics: Julian Steward and the Doctrine of Terra Nullius." In *Hunter-Gatherers in History, Archaeology, and Anthropology*, edited by Alan Barnard, 187–200. Oxford: Berg Publishers.

Attali, Jacques. 1985. *Noise: The Political Economy of Music*. Minneapolis: University of Minnesota Press.

Austin-Broos, Dianne. 2004. "Anthropology and Indigenous Alterity." *Australian Journal of Anthropology* 15 (2): 213–16.

Ayora-Diaz, Steffan Igor. 1993. *Representations and Occupations: Shepherds' Choices in Sardinia*. PhD diss., McGill University.

———. 2000. "Imagining Authenticity in the Local Medicines of Chiapas, Mexico." *Critique of Anthropology* 20 (2): 173–90.

———. 2003. "Re/creaciones de la comunidad: Espacios translocales en la globalización." *Cuadernos de Bioética* 7 (10): 27–45.

———. 2007. "Consumiendo lo local: Turismo y comida en Yucatán." In *Globalización y consumo de la cultura en Yucatán*, edited by Steffan Igor Ayora-Diaz, 75–107. Mérida: Univeridad Autónoma de Yucatán.

Ayora-Diaz, Steffan Igor, and Gabriela Vargas-Cetina. 2005a. "Globalización y localización: La producción de modernidades locales." In *Modernidades Locales: Hacia una Etnografía del Presente Múltiple*, edited by Steffan Igor Ayora-Diaz and Gabriela Vargas-Cetina, 29–58. Mérida: Universidad Autónoma de Yucatán/ Instituto de Cultura de Yucatán.

———. 2005b. "Romantic Moods: Food, Beer, Music, and the Yucatecan Soul." In *Drinking Cultures,* edited by Thomas Wilson, 155–78. Oxford: Berg.

Bagshaw, Geoffrey C. 2001. "Anthropology and Objectivity in Native Title Proceedings." Paper presented at the conference Expert Evidence in Native Title Court Cases: Issues of Truth, Objectivity, and Expertise, July 6–7, 2001, Adelaide, Australia. *http://www.aas.asn.au/publications/pub_aas.php* (accessed May 14, 2012).

Bailey, Garrick A., ed. 1999. *The Osage and the Invisible World: From the Works of Francis La Flesche.* Norman: University of Oklahoma Press.

Bakhtin, Mikhail. 1981. *The Dialogic Imagination: Four Essays.* Edited by Michael Holquist. Translated by Caryl Emerson and Michael Holquist. Austin: University of Texas Press.

Ball, Patrick. 1999. "Metodologia Intermuestra." In *Memoria del Silencio,* by Comisión de Esclarecimiento Histórico, Anexo III. *http://shr.aaas.org/guatemala/ceh/mds/spanish/anexo3/aaas/aaas.html* (accessed May 11, 2012).

Ball, Patrick, Paul Kobrak, and Herbert F. Spirer, eds. 1999. *State Violence in Guatemala, 1960–1996: A Quantitative Reflection.* Washington, DC: American Association for the Advancement of Science. *http://shr.aaas.org/guatemala/ciidh/qr/english* (accessed June 2, 2012).

Baqueiro Foster, Geronimo. 1970. *La canción popular de Yucatán (1850–1950).* México City: Editorial del Magisterio.

Barney, Ralph A. 1955. "Legal Problems Peculiar to Indian Claims Litigation." *Ethnohistory* 2 (4): 315–25.

Barrett, Richard A. 1984. *Culture and Conduct: An Excursion in Anthropology.* 2nd ed. Belmont, CA: Wadsworth Publishing.

Barrios, Lina. 1996. *La Alcaldía Indígena en Guatemala: Época Colonial (1500–1921).* Guatemala City: Universidad Rafael Landívar, IDIES.

———. 1998a. *La Alcaldía Indígena en Guatemala: De 1821 a la Revolución de 1944.* Guatemala City: Universidad Rafael Landívar, IDIES.

———. 1998b. *La Alcaldía Indígena en Guatemala: De 1944 al presente.* Guatemala City: Universidad Rafael Landívar, IDIES.

Barth, Fredrik, ed. (1969) 1998. *Ethnic Groups and Boundaries.* Prospect Heights, IL: Waveland Press.

Bartók, Béla. (1948) 1979. *Escritos sobre música popular.* CD. De México: Siglo XXI.

Bartra, Roger. 1969. *El modo de producción asiático: Antología de textos sobre problemas de la historia de los países colonials.* Mexico City: ERA.

Basilov, Valery N. 1992. "Etnografia: Est' li u neio buduscheie?" *Etnographicheskoye obozreniye* 4: 3–17.

Bates, Crispin. 1995. "Lost Innocents and the Loss of Innocence: Interpreting Adivasi Movements in South Asia." In *Indigenous Peoples of Asia,* edited by R. H. Barnes, Andrew Gray, and Benedict Kingsbury, 103–20. Ann Arbor: University of Michigan.

Bauman, Toni. 2001. "Shifting Sands: Towards an Anthropological Praxis." *Oceania* 71 (3): 202–25.

Bauman, Zygmut. 2001. *Community: Seeking Safety in an Insecure World.* Oxford: Polity Press.

Beccu, Enea. 2000. *Tra cronaca e storia: Le vicende del patrimonio boschivo della Sardegna.* Cagliari: Carlo Delfino Editore.

Beckett, Jeremy. 2002. "Some Aspects of Continuity and Change among Anthropologists in Australia or 'He-Who-Eats-from-One-Dish-with-Us-with-One-Spoon.'" *Australian Journal of Anthropology* 13 (2): 127–38.

Bell, David, and Gill Valentine. 1997. *Consuming Geographies: We Are What We Eat.* London: Routledge.

Bell, Kathryn. 2003. "Competitors or Companions? Gossip and Storytelling among Political Journalists in Northern Ireland." *Journal of the Society for the Anthropology of Europe* 3 (2): 2–13.

Bellier, Irène. 1997. "The Commission as an Actor: An Anthropologist's View." In *Participation and Policy-Making in the European Union,* edited by Helen Wallace and Alasdair R. Young, 91–111. Oxford: Clarendon Press.

Bellier, Irène, and Thomas M. Wilson, eds. 2000. *An Anthropology of the European Union: Building, Imagining and Experiencing the New Europe.* Oxford: Berg Publishers.

Benedict, Ruth. 1934. *Patterns of Culture.* New York: Houghton Mifflin.

Benhabib, Seyla. 2002. "Citizens, Residents, and Aliens in a Changing World: Political Membership in the Global Era." In *The Postnational Self: Belonging and Identity,* edited by Ulf Hedetoft and Mette Hjort, 85–119. Minneapolis: University of Minnesota Press.

Bennet, Andy, and Kevin Dawe, eds. 2001. *Guitar Cultures.* Oxford and New York: Berg.

Berkhofer, Robert F., Jr. 1978. *The White Man's Indian.* New York: Vintage Books.

Bhabha, Homi. 1994. *The Location of Culture.* London: Routledge.

Bibeau, Giles, and E. E. Corin, eds. 1995. *Beyond Textuality: Asceticism and Violence in Anthropological Interpretation.* Berlin: Walter de Gruyter.

Bodemann, Yark Michal. 1979. *Telemula: Aspects of the Micro-organisation of Backwardness in Central Sardinia.* PhD diss., Brandeis University.

Bond, George C. 1990. "Fieldnotes: Research in Past Occurrences." In *Fieldnotes: The Making of Anthropology,* edited by R. Sanjek, 273–89. Ithaca, NY: Cornell University Press.

Borneman, John, and Nick Fowler. 1997. "Europeanization." *Annual Review of Anthropology* 26: 487–514.

Bourdieu, Pierre. 1977. *Outline of a Theory of Practice.* Cambridge: Cambridge University Press.

———. 1984. *Distinction: A Social Critique of the Judgement of Taste.* Cambridge, MA: Harvard University Press.

———. 1991. *Language and Symbolic Power.* Cambridge, MA: Harvard University Press.

———. 1993. *The Field of Cultural Production.* New York: Columbia University Press.

Bowman, Glenn. 1997. "Identifying versus Identifying with the Other: Reflections on the Sitting of the Subject in Anthropological Discourse." In *After Writing Culture: Epistemology and Praxis in Contemporary Anthropology,* edited by Allison James, Andrew Hockey, and Andrew Dawson, 34–50. London: Routledge.

Braun, Bruce. 2002. *The Intemperate Rainforest: Nature, Culture, and Power on Canada's West Coast.* Minneapolis: University of Minnesota Press.

Brechin, Steven R., Meyer R. Wilshusen, Crystal L. Fortwangler, and Patrick C. West, eds. 2003. *Contested Nature: Promoting International Biodiversity and Social Justice in the Twenty-First Century.* Albany: SUNY Press.

Brillat-Savarin, Anthelme. (1826) 2004. *The Physiology of Taste.* Whitefish, MT: Kessinger Publishing Rare Reprints.

Brockington, Dan. 2002. *Fortress Conservation.* Bloomington: University of Indiana Press.

Bromley, Yulian V. 1981. *Sovremennye Problemy Ethnografii.* Moscow: Nauka.

———. 1983. *Ocherki teorii etnosa.* Moscow: Nauka.

Brosius, J. Peter. 1997. "Endangered Forest, Endangered People: Environmentalist Representations of Indigenous Knowledge." *Human Ecology* 25 (1): 47–69.

Brown, Richard Harvey. 1995. "Postmodern Representation, Postmodern Affirmation." In *Postmodern Representations: Truth, Power, and Mimesis in the Human Sciences and Public Culture,* edited by Richard Harvey Brown, 1–19. Urbana: University of Illinois Press.

Bruner, Edward M. 2005. *Culture on Tour: Ethnographies of Travel.* Chicago: University of Chicago Press.

Brunton, Ron. 1992. "Mining Credibility: Coronation Hill and the Anthropologists." *Anthropology Today* 8 (2): 2–5.

Bryan, Dominic. 2000. *Orange Parades: The Politics of Ritual, Tradition, and Control.* London: Pluto.

Buckley, Anthony D., and Mary C. Kenney. 1995. *Negotiating Identity: Rhetoric, Metaphor, and Social Drama in Northern Ireland.* Washington, DC: Smithsonian.

Bull, Anna Cento. 2000. *Social Identities and Political Cultures in Italy: Catholic, Communist, and "Leghist" Communities between Civicness and Localism.* Oxford: Berg.

Burgos-Debray, Elisabeth. 1984. *I, Rigoberta Menchú: An Indian Woman in Guatemala.* Translated by Ann Wright. London: Verso.

Burke, Paul. 2001. "The Legal Implications of Chapman v Luminis for Anthropological Practice." *http://www.aas.asn.au/publications/pub_aas.php* (accessed June 1, 2012).

Campisi, Jack. 1991. *The Mashpee Indians: Tribe on Trial.* Syracuse, NY: Syracuse University Press.

Campos García, Melchor. 2002. *"Que los yucatecos todos proclamen su independencia": Historia del secesionismo en Yucatán, 1821–1849.* Mérida: Ediciones de la Universidad Autónoma de Yucatán.

Canestrini, Duccio. 2004. *Non sparate sul turista.* Milan: Bollati Boringhieri.

Cardinal, Harold. 1969. *The Unjust Society.* Edmonton, AB: M. G. Hurtig.

Carey, David, Jr. 2004. "Maya Perspectives on the 1991 Referendum in Guatemala." *Latin American Perspectives* 31 (6): 69–95.

Carmack, Robert. 1973. *Quichean Civilization: The Ethnohistoric, Ethnographic, and Archaeological Sources.* Berkeley: University of California Press.

———. 1995. *Rebels of Highland Guatemala: The Quiche-Mayas of Momostenango.* Norman: University of Oklahoma Press.

Carter, Thomas. 2003a. "In the Spirit of the Game? Cricket and Changing Notions of Being British in Northern Ireland." *Journal of the Society for the Anthropology of Europe* 3 (1): 14–26.

———. 2003b. "Violent Pastime(s): On the Commendation and Condemnation of Violence in Belfast." *City and Society* 15 (2): 255–81.

Caso, Alfonso, Silvio Zavala, José Miranda, and Moisés González Navarro. 1981. *La política indigenista en México: Métodos y Resultados.* Mexico City: Secretaría de Educación Pública.

Cassidy, Frank, ed. 1992. *Aboriginal Title in British Columbia: Delgamuukw v. The Queen.* Lantzville, BC: Oolichan Books; and Montreal, PQ: The Institute for Research on Public Policy.

Castañeda, Quetzil E. 1996. *In the Museum of Maya Culture: Touring Chichén Itzá.* Minneapolis: University of Minnesota Press.

Castells, Manuel. 1996. *The Rise of Network Society.* Vol 1: *The Information Age: Economy, Society, and Culture.* Oxford: Blackwell.

Caton, Steven C. 1999. "'Anger Be Now Thy Song': The Anthropology of an Event." The Occasional Papers of the School of Social Science. Harvard University, paper number 5.

Chapin, Mac. 2004. "A Challenge to Conservationists." *Worldwatch Magazine* (November/December): 17–31.

Cheshko, Sergei V. 1988. "Natsional'nyi vopros v SSSR: sovremennoie sostoianie i perspektivy issledovaniia." *Sovetskaia Etnografia* 4: 62–72.

———. 1994. "Chelovek i etnichnost." *Etnographicheskoye obozreniye* 6: 35–50.

———. 1995. "Otvet opponentam." *Etnographicheskoye obozreniye* 5: 11–13.

Chevalier, Michel. 1961. *Society, Manners, and Politics in the United States: Letters on North America.* Edited by J. W. Ward. Ithaca, NY: Cornell University Press.

Clifford, James. 1986a. "Introduction: Partial Truths." In *Writing Culture: The Poetics and Politics of Ethnography,* edited by James Clifford and George E. Marcus, 1–26. Berkeley: University of California Press.

———. 1986b. "On Ethnographic Allegory." In *Writing Culture: The Poetics and Politics of Ethnography,* edited by James Clifford and George E. Marcus, 98–121. Berkeley: University of California Press.

———. 1988. *The Predicament of Culture: Twentieth-Century Ethnography, Literature, and Art.* Cambridge, MA: Harvard University Press.

———. 1997. *Routes: Travel and Translation in the Late Twentieth Century.* Cambridge: Harvard University Press.

Clifford, James, and George E. Marcus, eds. 1986. *Writing Culture: The Poetics and Politics of Ethnography.* Berkeley: University of California Press.

Cohen, Fay G. 1986. *Treaties on Trial: The Continuing Controversy over Northwest Indian Fishing Rights.* Seattle: University of Washington Press.

Cole, Douglas. 1985. *Captured Heritage: The Scramble for Northwest Coast Artifacts.* Seattle: University of Washington Press.

Cole, Jeffrey. 1997. *The New Racism in Europe: A Sicilian Ethnography.* Cambridge: Cambridge University Press.

Collins, Harry, and Trevor Pinch. 1993. *The Golem: What Everyone Should Know about Science.* Cambridge: Cambridge University Press.

Comaroff, John L. 1992. "Of Totemism and Ethnicity." In *Ethnography and the Historical Imagination,* edited by John Comaroff and Jean Comaroff, 49–67. Boulder: Westview Press.

———. 1996. "Ethnicity, Nationalism, and the Politics of Difference in an Age of Revolution." In *The Politics of Difference: Ethnic Premises in a World of Power,* edited by E. N. Wilmsen and P. McAllister, 162–83. Chicago: University of Chicago Press.

Comaroff, John L., and Jean Comaroff. 2009. *Ethnicity, Inc.* Chicago: University of Chicago Press.

Comisión de Esclarecimiento Histórico (CEH). 1999. *Conclusions and Recommendations (English-language summary of Guatemala: Memoria del Silencio).* Guatemala. *http://shr.aaas.org/guatemala/ceh/mds/spanish/toc.html* (accessed May 11, 2012).

Conklin, Beth A. 1997. "Body Paint, Feathers, and VCRS: Aesthetics and Authenticity in Amazonian Activism." *American Ethnologist* 24 (4): 711–37.

———. 2002. "Shamans vs. Pirates in the Amazonian Treasure Chest." *American Anthropologist* 104 (4): 1050–61.

———. 2003. "Speaking Truth to Power." *Anthropology News* 44 (7): 5.

———. 2006. "Environmentalism, Global Community, and the New Indigenism." In *Inclusion and Exclusion in the Global Arena,* edited by Max Kirsch, 161–76. London: Routledge.

Conklin, Beth A., and Laura R. Graham. 1995. "The Shifting Middle Ground: Amazonian Indians and Eco-Politics." *American Anthropologist* 97 (4): 695–710.

Corda, Elettrio. 1985. *La legge e la macchia: Il banditism sardo dal settecento ai giorni nostri.* Milano: Rusconi.

———. 1989. *Storia di Orgosolo: 1937–1953.* Milano: Rusconi.

Cortés Campos, Rocio Leticia. 2004. *La novela histórica de Justo Sierra O'Reilly: La literatura y el poder.* Mérida: Ediciones de la Universidad Autónoma de Yucatán/Instituto de Cultura de Yucatán.

Coumans, Catherine. 2011. "Occupying Spaces of Conflict: Anthropologists, Development NGOs, Responsible Investment, and Mining." *Current Anthropology* 52 (S3): S29–S43.

Cove, John J. 1996. "Playing the Devil's Advocate: Anthropology in Delgamuukw." *PoLAR: The Political and Legal Anthropology Review* 19 (2): 53–57.

Craib, Raymond B. 2004. *Cartographic Mexico: A History of State Fixations and Fugitive Landscapes.* Durham: Duke University Press.

Crapanzano, Vincent. 1986. "Hermes' Dilemma: The Masking of Subversion in Ethnographic Description." In *Writing Culture: The Poetics and Politics of Ethnography,* edited by James Clifford and George E. Marcus, 51–76. Berkeley: University of California Press.

Crehan, Kate. 2002. *Gramsci, Culture, and Anthropology.* Berkeley: University of California Press.

Culhane, Dara. 1998. *The Pleasure of the Crown: Anthropology, Law, and First Nations.* Vancouver, BC: Talonbooks.

Cutler, Robin. 1994. *A Gift from the Past* (video). Washington, DC: Media Resource Associates.

Darder, Antonia, and Rodolfo D. Torres. 1998. "Latinos and Society: Culture, Politics, and Class." In *The Latino Studies Reader: Culture, Economy, and Society,* edited by Antonia Darder and Rodolfo Torres, 3–26. Oxford: Blackwell.

DeHart, Monica. 2010. *Ethnic Entrepreneurs: Identity Politics and Development in Latin America.* Stanford: Stanford University Press.

de la Garza, Rodolfo, Louis DeSipio, F. Chris García, John García, and Angelo Falcón. 1992. *Latino Voices: Mexican, Puerto Rican, and Cuban Perspectives on American Politics.* Boulder: Westview Press.

Deleuze, Gilles, and Fèlix Guattari. 1983. *Anti-Oedipus: Schizophrenia and Capitalism.* Minneapolis: University of Minnesota Press.

Delgado, Celeste Frase, and José Esteban Muñoz, eds. 1997. *Everynight Life: Culture and Dance in Latin/o America.* Durham: Duke University Press.

Deloria, Ella, ed. (1932) 2006. *Dakota Texts.* Lincoln: University of Nebraska Press.

Deloria, Philip. 2004. *Indians in Unexpected Places.* Lawrence: University of Kansas Press.

Deloria, Vine, Jr. (1969) 1988. *Custer Died for Your Sins: An Indian Manifesto.* Norman: University of Oklahoma Press.

DeMallie, Raymond J. 2006. "Introduction to the Bison Books Edition." In *Dakota Texts,* edited by Ella Deloria, v–xix. Lincoln: University of Nebraska Press.

Densmore, Frances. (1918) 1992. *Teton Sioux Music and Culture.* Lincoln: University of Nebraska Press.

Denzin, Norman K. 1995. "The Poststructural Crisis in the Social Sciences: Learning from James Joyce." In *Postmodern Representations: Truth, Power, and Mimesis in the Human Sciences and Public Culture,* edited by Richard Harvey Brown, 38–59. Urbana: University of Illinois Press.

Derrida, Jacques. 1974. *Of Grammatology.* Translated by Gayatri Spivak. Baltimore: Johns Hopkins University Press.

———. 1980. *Writing and Difference.* Chicago: University of Chicago Press. First published 1967.

———. 1995. *Archive Fever. A Freudian Impression.* Translated by Eric Prenowitz. Chicago: University of Chicago Press.

———. 1997. *Monolingualism of the Other: Or the Prosthesis of Origin.* Stanford: Stanford University Press. First published 1996.

———. 2000. *Of Hospitality: Anne Dufourmantelle Invites Jacques Derrida to Respond.* Stanford: Stanford University Press.

Dever, Susan. 2003. *Celluloid Nationalism and Other Melodramas: From Post-revolutionary Mexico to fin de siglo Mexamérica.* Albany: SUNY Press.

Diamond, Stanley, ed. 1980. *Anthropology: Ancestors and Heirs.* The Hague: Mouton.

Díaz Bolio, José. 1998. *Yucatán en el perfil del tiempo.* Compiled by Margarita Díaz de Ponce. Mérida: Ediciones de la Universidad Autónoma de Yucatán, Patronato Pro Historia Peninsular, A. C.

Diener, Paul. 1978. "The Tears of St. Anthony: Ritual and Revolution in Eastern Guatemala." *Latin American Perspectives* 5 (3): 92–116.

Di Leonardo, Micaela. 1984. *The Varieties of Ethnic Experience: Kinship, Class, and Gender among California Italian Americans.* Ithaca, NY: Cornell University Press.

———. 1998. *Exotics at Home: Anthropologies, Others, American Modernity.* Chicago: University of Chicago Press.

Dirlik, Arif. 2001. "Comment on 'Lost Worlds: Environmental Disaster, "Culture Loss" and the Law,' by Stuart Kirsch." *Current Anthropology* 42 (2): 181–82.

Dobyns, Henry F. 1978. "Taking the Witness Stand." In *Applied Anthropology in America,* edited by E. M. Eddy and W. Partidge, 366–82. New York: Columbia University Press.

Donnan, Hastings, and Graham McFarlane, eds. 1997. *Culture and Policy in Northern Ireland.* Belfast: Institute of Irish Studies Press.

Donnan, Hastings, and Mairead O'Brien. 1998. "'Because You Stick Out, You Stand Out': Perceptions of Prejudice among Northern Ireland's Pakistanis." In *Divided Society: Ethnic Minorities and Racism in Northern Ireland,* edited by Paul Hainsworth, 197–221. London: Pluto.

Dove, Michael. 2006. "Indigenous People and Environmental Politics." *Annual Review of Anthropology* 35: 191–208.

Doxtater, Michael G. 2004. "Indigenous Knowledge in the Decolonial Era." *American Indian Quarterly* 28 (3–4): 618–33.

Dreyfus, H. L., and P. Rabinow. 1983. *Michel Foucault: Beyond Structuralism and Hermeneutics.* Chicago: University of Chicago Press.

Drobizheva, Leokadia M. 1985. "Natsional'noie samosoznanie: Bazis obrazovaniia i sotsiokul'turnye stimuli razvitiia." *Sovetskaia Etnografia* 5: 5–23.

———. 1994. "Nationalizm, etnicheskoie samosoznaniie, i konflikty v perekhodnom obschestve." In *Natsional'noie samosoznanie i nationalism v Rossiiskoi Federatsii 1990-kh,* edited by Leokadia M. Drobizheva, 16–47. Moscow.

Dube, Saurabh. 2001. *Sujetos subalternos.* Mexico City: El Colegio de México.

Dueñas Herrera, José Pablo. 1993. *Historia documental del bolero mexicano.* Mexico City: Asociación Mexicana de Estudios Fonográficos, A. C.

Eagleton, Terry. 2003. *After Theory.* New York: Basic Books.

Early, John D. 1982. *The Demographic Structure and Evolution of a Peasant System: The Guatemalan Population.* Gainesville: University of Florida.

Edwards, Caroline, Louise Anderson, and Siobhan McKeering. 2006. "Anthropologists, Lawyers, and Native Title Cases in Australia." *Anthropological Forum* 16 (2): 153–71.

Eggan, Frederick R. 1954. "Social Anthropology and the Method of Controlled Anthropological Comparison." *American Anthropologist* 56: 743–61.

Elias, Norbert, and John L. Scotson. 1994. *The Established and the Outsiders.* London: Sage. First published 1965.

Elias, Peter Douglas. 1993. "Anthropology and Aboriginal Claims Research." In *Anthropology, Public Policy, and Native Peoples in Canada,* edited by Noel Dyck and James B. Waldram, 233–70. Montreal, PQ: McGill-Queens University Press.

Ellen, Roy. 1986. What Black Elk Left Unsaid: On the Illusory Images of Green Primitivism. *Anthropology Today* 2 (6): 8–12.

England, Nora. 2003. "Mayan Language Revival and Revitalization Politics: Linguists and Linguistic Ideologies." *American Anthropologist* 105 (4): 733–43.

Erikson, Patricia Pierce. 1999. "A-Whaling We Will Go: Encounters of Knowledge and Memory at the Makah Cultural and Research Center." *Cultural Anthropology* 14 (4): 556–83.

———. 2005. "'Trends in Image and Design': Reflections on 25 Years of a Tribal Museum Era." *Histories of Anthropology Annual* 1: 271–86.

Erikson, Patricia Pierce, Helma Ward, and Kirk Wachendorf. 2002. *Voices of a Thousand People: The Makah Cultural and Research Center.* Lincoln: University of Nebraska Press.

Errington, Frederick, and Deborah Gewertz. 2004. "Tourism and Anthropology in a Postmodern World." In *Tourists and Tourism: A Reader,* edited by Sharon Bohn Gmelch, 195–217. Long Grove, IL: Waveland Press. Originally published 1989 in *Oceania* 60: 37–54.

Escobar, Arturo. 1992. *Encountering Development: The Making and Unmaking of the Third World.* Princeton, NJ: Princeton University Press.

———. 1995. *Encountering Development: The Making and Unmaking of the Third World.* Princeton: Princeton University.

———. 1998. "Whose Knowledge, Whose Nature? Biodiversity Conservation and the Political Ecology of Movements." *Journal of Political Ecology* 5: 53–80.

Etienne, Mora, and Eleanor B. Leacock. 1980. *Women and Colonization.* New York: Praeger.

Evans-Pritchard, E. E. 1976. *Witchcraft, Magic, and Oracles among the Azande.* Oxford: Clarendon Press.

Fabian, Johannes. 1983. *Time and the Other: How Anthropology Makes Its Object.* New York: Columbia University Press.

———. 1988. *Power and Performance: Ethnographic Explorations through Proverbial Wisdom and the Theatre in Shaba, Zaire.* Madison: University of Wisconsin Press.

———. 2006. "World Anthropologies: Questions." In *World Anthropologies: Disciplinary Transformations within Systems of Power,* edited by Gustavo Lins Ribeiro and Arturo Escobar, 281–95. Oxford: Berg Publishers.

———. 2007. *Memory against Culture: Arguments and Reminders.* Durham and London: Duke University Press.

———. 2008. *Ethnography as Commentary: Writing from the Virtual Archive.* Durham: Duke University Press.

Falla, Ricardo. 1994. *Massacres in the Jungle: Ixcán, Guatemala, 1975–1982.* Boulder, CO: Westview Press.

Favre, Henri. 1996. *El Indigenismo.* Mexico City: Fondo de Cultura Económica.

Feder, Dan. 2001. "No estan solos!" *The Student Underground* (Boston University) 32, April 6, http://bostonunderground.info/old_website/article.php?Issue=32&ArticleID=5 (accessed August 12, 2009).

Feinberg, Benjamin. 2003. *The Devil's Book of Culture: History, Mushrooms, and Caves in Southern Mexico.* Austin: University of Texas Press.

Feldman, Allen. 1991. *Formations of Violence.* Chicago: University of Chicago Press.

Fernández Repetto, Francisco, and Genny Negroe Sierra. 2002. "Estrategias de vigencia de la iglesia católica en Yucatán a mediados del siglo XIX." *Temas Antropológicos* 24 (1): 5–28.

Field, Les W. 1999a. "Complicities and Collaborations: Anthropologists and the Unacknowledged Tribes of California." *Current Anthropology* 40 (2): 193–209.

———. 1999b. *The Grimace of Macho Ratón: Artisans, Identity, and Nation in Late Twentieth-Century Western Nicaragua.* Durham, NC: Duke University Press.

———. 2003. "Unacknowledged Tribes, Dangerous Knowledge: The Muwekma Ohlone and How Indian Identities Are 'Known.'" With the Muwekma Ohlone Tribe. *Wicazo Sa* 18 (2): 79–94.

———. 2008. *Abalone Tales: Collaborative Explorations of Sovereignty and Identity in Native California.* Durham, NC: Duke University Press.

Field, Les, Alan Leventhal, Dolores Sanchez, and Rosemary Cambra. 1992. "A Contemporary Ohlone Tribal Revitalization Movement: A Perspective from the Muwekma Costanoan/Ohlone Indians of the San Francisco Bay Area." *California History* 71 (3): 412–31.

Fischer, Edward F. 1999. "Cultural Logic and Maya Identity." *Current Anthropology* 40 (4): 473–99.

———. 2001. *Cultural Logics and Global Economies: Maya Identity in Thought and Practice.* Austin: University of Texas Press.

Fischer, Edward F., and R. McKenna Brown, eds. 1996. *Maya Cultural Activism in Guatemala.* Austin: University of Texas Press.

Fischer, Michael M. 2003. *Emergent Forms of Life and the Anthropological Voice.* Durham. Duke University Press.

———. 2009. *Anthropological Futures.* Durham. Duke University Press.

Fishman, Joshua. 1966. *Language Loyalty in the United States.* The Hague: Mouton.

Fletcher, Alice, and Francis La Flesche. 1911. *The Omaha Tribe.* Twenty-Seventh Annual Report of the Bureau of American Ethnology. Washington, DC: Government Printing Office.

Flores, Juan. 2000. *From Bomba to Hip Hop: Puerto Rican Culture and Latino Identity.* New York: Columbia University Press.

Forsyth, James. 1992. *A History of the Peoples of Siberia: Russia's North Asian Colony, 1581–1990.* Cambridge: Cambridge University Press.

Forte, Maximilian C., ed. 2010. *Indigenous Cosmopolitans: Transnational and Transcultural Indigeneity in the Twenty-First Century.* New York: Peter Lang.

Foucault, Michel. 1973. *The Order of Things: An Archaeology of the Human Sciences.* New York: Vintage Books.

———. (1978) 1990. *The History of Sexuality.* Vol. 1: *An Introduction.* New York: Vintage Books.

———. (1978) 2000. "Governmentality." In *Power: Essential Works of Foucault, 1954–1984,* edited by James D. Faubion, translated by Robert Hurley and others, 201–22. New York: New Press.

———. 1980. *Power/Knowledge: Selected Interviews and Other Writings, 1972–1977.* 1st American ed. Edited by Colin Gordon. New York: Pantheon.

———. 1984. *The Foucault Reader.* Edited by Paul Rabinow. New York: Pantheon.

Fox, Richard G. 1991. *Recapturing Anthropology: Working in the Present.* Santa Fe, NM: School of American Research Press.

Frazer, George James. 1922. *The Golden Bough: A Study of Magic and Religion.* New York: Macmillan Company.

Friedlander, Judith. 1975. *Being Indian in Hueyapan: A Study of Forced Identity in Contemporary Mexico.* New York: St. Martin's Press.

Friedman, Jonathan. 1994. *Cultural Identity and Global Process.* London: Sage Publications.

———, ed. 2003. *Globalization, the State, and Violence.* Walnut Creek, CA: AltaMira Press.

Gabaccia, Donna R. 1998. *We Are What We Eat: Ethnic Food and the Making of Americans.* Boston: Harvard University Press.

García Bonilla, Roberto. 2001. *Visiones Sonoras: Entrevistas con compositors, solistas y directores.* México: Siglo XXI/CONACULTA.

García de León Griego, Antonio. 2002. *El mar de los deseos: El Caribe hispano musical, Historia y contrapunto.* Mexico City: Siglo XXI Editores, UQRoo, UNESCO.

Geertz, Clifford. 1973. *The Interpretation of Culture.* New York: Basic Books.

———. 1990. *Works and Lives: The Anthropologist as Author.* Stanford: Stanford University Press.

———. 2001. *Available Light: Anthropological Reflections on Philosophical Topics.* Princeton: Princeton University Press.

Gellner, Ernest. 1975. "The Soviet and the Savage." *Current Anthropology* 16 (4): 595–617.

Gerson, Stéphane. 2003. *The Pride of Place: Local Memories and Political Cultures in Nineteenth-Century France.* Ithaca, NY: Cornell University Press.

Giménez, Martha E., Fred A. López III, and Carlos Muñoz Jr. 1992. Introduction to "The Politics of Ethnic Construction: Hispanic, Chicano, Latino . . . ?" *Latin American Perspectives* 19 (4): 3–6.

Giordano, Christian. 1987. "The 'Wine War' between France and Italy: Ethnoanthropological Aspects of the European Community." *Sociologia Ruralis* 27: 56–66.

Giovannetti, Jorge L. 2001. *Sonidos de condena: Sociabilidad, historia y política en la música reggae de Jamaica.* Mexico City: Siglo XXI Editores.

Glaskin, Katie. 2002. *Claiming Country: A Case Study of Historical Legacy and Transition in the Native Title Context.* PhD diss., Australian National University.

———. 2003. "Native Title and the 'Bundle of Rights' Model: Implications for the Recognition of Aboriginal Relations to Country." *Anthropological Forum* 13 (1): 67–88.

———. 2006. "Death and the Person: Reflections on Mortuary Rituals, Transformation, and Ontology in an Aboriginal Society." *Paideuma* 52: 107–26.

———. 2010. "Litigating Native Title: Anthropology in the Court." In *Dilemmas in Applied Native Title Anthropology in Australia,* edited by Toni Bauman, 35–54. Canberra: AIATSIS Native Title Research Unit.

Gleach, Frederic W. 2003. "Theory, Practice, Life: Rethinking Americanist Anthropology for the Twenty-First Century." *Reviews in Anthropology* 32 (3): 191–205.

———. 2005. *Diosa olvidada: Remembering a Latina Pioneer.* Video presentation (29 minutes), 11th Annual Latino Issues Conference, Bowling Green State University, OH.

Gluckman, Max. 1958. *Analysis of a Social Strucure in Zululand.* Manchester, UK: Manchester University Press.

Goertzen, Chris. 1997. *Fiddling for Norway: Revival and Identity.* Chicago: University of Chicago Press.

Goldman, Alvin I. 1986. *Epistemology and Cognition.* Cambridge: Harvard University Press.

Gomes, Laurentino, and Paulo Silber. 1992. "A explosão do instinto selvagem." *Veja* (São Paulo) 25 (24): 68–84.

Gossett, Thomas F. 1997. *Race: The History of an Idea in America.* New York: Oxford University Press.

Gould, Jeffrey. 1998. *To Die in This Way: Nicaraguan Indians and the Myth of Mestizaje, 188–1965.* Durham, NC: Duke University Press.

Grandin, Greg. 2000. *The Blood of Guatemala: A History of Race and Nation.* Durham: Duke University Press.

———. 2004. *The Last Colonial Massacre: Latin America in the Cold War.* Chicago: University of Chicago Press.

Greenwood, Davydd, J. 2008. "Theoretical Research, Applied Research, Action Research: The Institutionalization of Activist Research." In *Engaging Contradictions: Theory, Politics, and Methods of Activist Scholarship,* edited by Charles R. Hale, 319–40. Berkeley: University of California Press.

Grindal, Bruce. 2004. "Do You Really Need It?" *Anthropology News* 45 (9): 19.

Gross, Paul R., and Norman Levitt. 1994. *Higher Superstition: The Academic Left and Its Quarrels with Science.* Baltimore: John Hopkins University Press.

Guha, Ranajit. 1988. "The Prose of Counterinsurgency." In *Selected Subaltern Studies,* edited by Ranajit Guha and Gayatri Chakravorty Spivak, 45–86. Oxford: Oxford University Press.

Gupta, Akhil. 1998. *Postcolonial Developments: Agriculture in the Making of Modern India.* Durham: Duke University Press.

Gupta, Akhil, and James Ferguson, eds. 1997. *Culture, Power, Place: Explorations in Critical Anthropology.* Durham: Duke University Press.

Haenn, Nora. 2005. *Fields of Power, Forests of Discontent: Culture, Conservation, and the State in Mexico.* Tucson: University of Arizona Press.

Hale, Charles. 1994. "Between Ché Guevara and the Pachamama: Mestizos, Indians, and Identity Politics in the Anti-Quincentenary Campaign." *Critique of Anthropology* 14: 9–39.

———. 2006. *Más que un indio: Racial Ambivalence and the Paradox of Neoliberal Multiculturalism in Guatemala.* Santa Fe, NM: School of Advanced Research Press.

Hall, Stuart. 1996. "Introduction: Who Needs 'Identity'?" In *Questions of Cultural Identity,* edited by Stuart Hall and Paul du Gay, 1–17. London: Sage.

Hallowell, A. Irving. 1976. "Ojibwa Ontology, Behavior, and World View." In *Contributions to Anthropology: Selected Papers of A. Irving Hallowell,* edited by Raymond D. Fogelson, 357–59. Chicago: University of Chicago Press.

Hamilton, Annette. 2003. "Beyond Anthropology, Towards Actuality." *Australian Journal of Anthropology* 14 (2): 160–70.

Hansen, Asael T. 1980. "Change and the Class System of Merida, Yucatan, 1875–1935." In *Yucatan: A World Apart,* edited by Edward H. Moseley and Edward D. Terry, 122–41. Tuscaloosa: The University of Alabama Press.

Harkin, Michael. 1995. "Modernist Anthropology and Tourism of the Authentic." *Annals of Tourism Research* 22 (3): 650–70.

Harrington, John P. 1921–1939. "Costanoan Fieldnotes." On microfilm at San Jose State University, New York: Kraus International Publications.

Harrison, Faye V., ed. 1991. *Decolonizing Anthropology: Moving Further toward an Anthropology for Liberation.* Washington, DC: American Anthropological Association.

———. 1995. "The Persistent Power of 'Race' in the Cultural and Political Economy of Racism." *Annual Review of Anthropology* 24: 47–74.

———. 2002. "Unravelling 'Race' for the Twenty-First Century." In *Exotic No More,* edited by Jeremy MacClancy, 145–66. Chicago: University of Chicago Press.

———. 2008. *Outsider Within: Reworking Anthropology in the Global Age.* Urbana: University of Illinois Press.

Hayes, Joy Elizabeth. 2000. *Radio Nation: Communication, Popular Culture, and Nationalism in Mexico, 1920–1950.* Tucson: University of Arizona Press.

Hedetoft, Ulf. 1994. "National Identities and European Integration 'From Below': Bringing People Back In." *Journal of European Integration* 17 (1): 1–28.

Helms, Mary W. 1988. *Ulysses Sail: An Ethnographic Odyssey of Power, Knowledge, and Geographical Distance.* Princeton, NJ: Princeton University Press.

Hendrickson, Carol. 1995. *Weaving Identities: Construction of Dress and Self in a Highland Guatemala Town.* Austin: University of Texas Press.

Henriksen, Georg. 1985. "Anthropologists as Advocates: Promoters of Pluralism or Makers of Clients?" In *Advocacy and Anthropology: First Encounters,* edited by Robert Paine, 119–29. St. John's, Newfoundland: Memorial University Institute of Social and Economic Research.

Heredia, Beatriz, and Rafael De Pau. 2000. *Pepe Domínguez: Un pilar de la canción yucateca.* Mérida: Gobierno del Estado, Instituto de Cultura de Yucatán, Consejo Nacional para la Cultura y las Artes, Dirección General de Culturas Populares, Dirección de Culturas Populares de Yucatán, Programa de Apoyo a las Culturas Municipales y Comunitarias de Yucatán.

Hernández Castillo, Rosalva Aída. 2001. "Between Civil Disobedience and Silent Rejection: Differing Responses by Mam Peasants to the Zapatista Rebellion." *Latin American Perspectives* 28 (2): 98–119.

Hervik, Peter. 2003. *Mayan People within and beyond Boundaries: Social Categories and Lived Identity in Yucatán.* New York: Routledge.

Herzfeld, Michael. 1997. *Cultural Intimacy: Social Poetics in the Nation-State.* London: Routledge.

———. 2002. "Cultural Fundamentalism and the Regimentation of Identity: The Embodiment of Orthodox Values in a Modernist Setting." In *The Postnational Self: Belonging and Identity,* edited by Ulf Hedetoft and Mette Hjort, 198–214. Minneapolis: University of Minnesota Press.

———. 2003. *The Body Impolitic: Artisans and Artifice in the Global Hierarchy of Value.* Chicago: University of Chicago Press.

Hewitt de Alcantara, Cynthia. 1984. *Anthropological Perspectives on Rural Mexican Society.* London: Routledge and Kegan Paul.

Hill, Robert M. 1992. *Colonial Cakchiquels: Highland Maya Adaptations to Spanish Rule, 1600–1700.* New York: Holt, Rinehart, and Winston.

Hinsley, Curtis M. 1981. *The Smithsonian and the American Indian: Making a Moral Anthropology in Victorian America.* Washington, DC: Smithsonian Institution Press.

Hinton, Alexander Laban, ed. 2002. *Annihilating Difference: The Anthropology of Genocide*. Berkeley: University of California Press.

Hispanic Magazine. 2000. http://www.hispanicmagazine.com/2000/dec/Features /latino.html (accessed June 10, 2005).

Hobsbawm, E. J. 1987. *The Age of Empire, 1875–1914*. New York: Pantheon Books.

hooks, bell. 1990. *Yearning: Race, Gender, and Cultural Politics*. Boston: South End Press.

Horsman, Reginald. 1981. *Race and Manifest Destiny: The Origins of American Racial Anglo Saxonism*. Cambridge: Harvard University Press.

Hymes, Dell, ed. (1969) 1974. *Reinventing Anthropology*. New York: Humanities Press.

Igoe, Jim. 2004. *Conservation and Globalization: A Study of National Parks and Indigenous Communities from East Africa to South Dakota*. Stamford, CT: Wadsworth.

Imagine Belfast 2008. 2002. *Imagine Belfast 2008*. Belfast: Imagine Belfast 2008.

Infante Vargas, Lucrecia, and Lourdes Hernández Fuentes. 2000. *Las cocinas del mundo en México: Sabores del mundo árabe*. Mexico City: Clio.

Ingold, Tim. 2000. *The Perception of the Environment: Essays in Livelihood, Dwelling, and Skill*. London: Routledge.

Instituto Nacional de Estadística de la República de Guatemala (INE). 2002. *Municipalidad de Sololá*. Guatemala City: Instituto Nacional de Estadística de la República de Guatemala.

Isaac, Gwyneira. 2007. *Mediating Knowledges: Origins of a Zuni Tribal Museum*. Tucson: University of Arizona Press.

ISR. 2001. "Stop the FTAA." *International Socialist Review* 17 (April–May). *http:// www.isreview.org/issues/17/stop_the_ftaa.shtml* (accessed May 4, 2012).

Jackson, Jean. 1989. "Is There a Way to Talk about Making Culture without Making Enemies?" *Dialectical Anthropology* 14: 127–43.

———. 1990. "I Am a Fieldnote." In *Fieldnotes: The Makings of Anthropology*, edited by Roger Sanjek, 3–33. Ithaca and London: Cornell University Press.

———. 2002. "Caught in the Crossfire: Colombia's Indigenous Peoples in the 1990s." In *The Politics of Ethnicity: Indigenous Peoples in Latin American States*, edited by David Maybury-Lewis, 107–33. Cambridge: Harvard University Press.

Jackson, Jean E., and Kay B. Warren. 2002. Introduction to *Indigenous Movements, Self-Representation, and the State in Latin America*, edited by Jackson and Warren, 1–46. Austin: University of Texas Press.

———. 2005. "Indigenous Movements in Latin America, 1992–2004: Controversies, Ironies, New Directions." *Annual Review of Anthropology* 34: 549–73.

Jacorzynski, Witold, coord. 2006. *Posmodernismo y sus críticos: Discusiones en torno a la antropología posmoderna.* Mexico City: Centro de Investigaciones y Estudios Superiores en Antropología Social.

James, Allison, Jenny Hockey, and Andrew Dawson, eds. 1997. *After Writing Culture: Epistemology and Praxis in Contemporary Anthropology.* ASA Monographs 34. London: Routledge.

Jardow Pedersen, Max. 1999. *La música divina de la selva yucateca.* Mexico City: CONACULTA, Culturas Populares.

Jarman, Neil. 1997. *Material Conflicts: Parades and Visual Displays in Northern Ireland.* Oxford: Berg.

Joseph, Gilbert M. 1980. "Revolution from Without: The Mexican Revolution in Yucatan, 1910–1940." In *Yucatan: A World Apart,* edited by Edward H. Moseley and Edward D. Terry, 142–71. Tuscaloosa: The University of Alabama Press.

Joseph, May. 1999. *Nomadic Identities: The Performance of Citizenship.* Minneapolis: University of Minnesota Press.

Juergensmeyer, Mark. 2002. "The Paradox of Nationalism in a Global World." In *The Postnational Self: Belonging and Identity,* edited by Ulf Hedetoft and Mette Hjort, 3–17. Minneapolis: University of Minnesota Press.

Kahn, Douglas. 2001. *Noise, Water, Meat: A History of Sound in the Arts.* Cambridge: MIT Press.

Kampwirth, Karen. 2003. "Arnoldo Alemán Takes on the NGOs: Antifeminism and the New Populism in Nicaragua." *Latin American Politics and Society* 45 (2): 133–58.

Kandel, Randy Frances, ed. 1992. *Double Vision: Anthropologists at Law.* National Association for the Practice of Anthropology Bulletin 11. Washington, DC: American Anthropological Association.

Kant, Immanuel. (1978) 1996. *Anthropology from a Pragmatic Point of View.* Carbondale: Southern Illinois University Press.

Kaplan, Caren. 1996. *Questions of Travel: Postmodern Discourses of Displacement.* Durham: Duke University Press.

Kaptain, Laurence D. 1992. *"The Wood That Sings": The Marimba in Chiapas, Mexico.* Everret and Philadelphia: Honeyrock.

Karlsson, Bengt G. 2006. "Indigenous Natures: Forest and Community Dynamics in Meghalaya, North-East India." In *Ecological Nationalisms,* edited by Gunnel Cederlöf and K. Sivaramakrishnan, 170–98. Seattle: University of Washington Press.

Karp, Ivan, and Steven D. Levine, eds. 1991. *Exhibiting Cultures: The Poetics and Politics of Museum Display.* Washington, DC: Smithsonian Institution Press.

Karttunen, Frances. 1994. *Between Worlds: Interpreters, Guides, and Survivors.* New Brunswick, NJ: Rutgers University Press.

Kearney, Michael. 2004. *Changing Fields of Anthropology: From Local to Global.* Lanham, MD: Rowman and Littlefield Publishers.

Keen, Ian. 1992. "Undermining Credibility: Advocacy and Objectivity in the Coronation Hill Debate." *Anthropology Today* 8 (2): 6–9.

———. 1999. "The Scientific Attitude in Applied Anthropology." In *Applied Anthropology in Australasia,* edited by Sandy Toussaint and Jim Taylor, 27–59. Perth: University of Western Australia Press.

Kelleher, William. 2003. *The Troubles in Ballybogoin: Memory and Identity in Northern Ireland.* Ann Arbor: University of Michigan Press.

Kertzer, David. 1996. *Politics and Symbols: The Italian Communist Party and the Fall of Communism.* New Haven: Yale University Press.

Kidwell, Clara Sue. 1992. "Indian Women as Cultural Mediators." *Ethnohistory* 39 (2): 97–107.

Kirk, Ruth, and Richard D. Daugherty. 1974. *Hunters of the Whale: An Adventure of Northwest Coast Archaeology.* New York: William Morrow.

Kirsch, Max, ed. 2006. *Inclusion and Exclusion in the Global Arena.* New York: Routledge.

Kirsch, Stuart. 2006. *Reverse Anthropology: Indigenous Analysis of Social and Environmental Relations in New Guinea.* Stanford: Stanford University Press.

Kirshenblatt-Gimblett, Barbara. 1998. *Destination Culture: Tourism, Museums, and Heritage.* Berkeley: University of California Press.

Kohli, Martin. 2000. "The Battlegrounds of European Identity." *European Societies* 2 (2): 113–37.

Kolpakov, Evgenii M. 1995. "Etnos i etnichnst." *Etnographicheskoye obozreniye* 5: 13–28.

Kondo, Dorinne K. 1990. *Crafting Selves: Power, Gender, and Identity in a Japanese Workplace.* Chicago: University of Chicago Press.

Kozlov, Viktor I. 1967. "O poniatii etnicheskoie soobschestvo." *Sovetskaia Etnografiia* 2: 100–112.

———. 1974. "Problema etnicheskogo samosoznaniia i eio mesto v teorii etnosa." *Sovetskaia Etnografiia* 2: 24–38.

———. 1992. "Sredi etnografii, etnologiii i zhizni." *Etnographicheskoye obozreniye* 3: 3–14.

———. 1995. "Problematika 'etnichnosti.'" *Etnographicheskoye obozreniye* 4: 3–15.

Kramer, Lawrence. 1995. *Classical Music and Postmodern Knowledge.* Berkeley: University of California Press.

Krech, Shephard. 1999. *The Ecological Indian: Myth and History.* New York: Norton.

Kroeber, Alfred. 1925. *Handbook of the Indians of California.* New York: Dover.

Kroeber, Karl, and Clifton B. Kroeber, eds. 2003. *Ishi in Three Centuries.* Lincoln: University of Nebraska Press.

Kroeber, Theodora. 1961. *Ishi in Two Worlds: A Biography of the Last Wild Indian in North America.* Berkeley: University of California Press.

Kroskrity, Paul V. 2000. "Language Ideologies in the Expression and Representation of Arizona Tewa Ethnic Identity." In *Regimes of Language: Ideologies, Polities, and Identities,* edited by Paul V. Kroskrity, 329–59. Santa Fe, NM: School of American Research Press.

Kushner, Pavel I. 1949. *Natsionalnoie samosoznanie kak etnicheskii opredelitel.* Moscow: Kratkie soobschenia Instituta etnografii.

Landry, Charles. 1999. "The Role of Culture in Remaking Cities." In *City Visions: Imagining Place, Enfranchising People,* edited by Frank Gaffikin and Mike Morrissey, 151–63. London: Pluto.

Laó-Montes, Agustín, and Arlene Dávila, eds. 2001. *Mambo Montage: The Latinization of New York.* New York: Columbia University Press.

La Rusic, Ignatius. 1985. "Expert Witness?" In *Advocacy and Anthropology: First Encounters,* edited by Robert Paine, 23–27. St. John's, Newfoundland: Memorial University Institute of Social and Economic Research.

Latour, Bruno. 1987. *Science in Action: How to Follow Scientists and Engineers through Society.* Cambridge, MA: Harvard University Press.

———. 1999. *Pandora's Hope: Essays on the Reality of Science Studies.* Cambridge, MA: Harvard University Press.

Lauria-Perricelli, Antonio. 1989. "*A Study in Historical and Critical Anthropology: The Making of 'The People of Puerto Rico.'* " PhD diss., New School for Social Research.

Leach, E. R. 1961. *Rethinking Anthropology.* London: London School of Economics.

Leacock, Eleanor Burke, ed. 1973. *The Culture of Poverty: A Critique.* New York: Simon and Schuster.

Lebedeva, Nadezhda M. 1993. *Sotsialnaia psykhologiia etnicheskikh migratsii.* Moscow: National State University-School of Economics.

LeGalès, Patrick. 1999. "Is Political Economy Still Relevant to Study the Culturalization of Cities?" *European Urban and Regional Studies* 6 (4): 293–302.

Li, Tania. 2000. "Articulating Indigenous Identity in Indonesia: Resource Politics and the Tribal Slot." *Comparative Studies in Society and History* 42 (1): 149–79.

———. 2007. *The Will to Improve: Governmentality, Development, and the Practice of Politics.* Durham: Duke University Press.

Lee, Richard, and Megan Biesele. 2002. "Local Cultures and Global Systems: The Ju/Hoansi–!Kung and Their Ethnographers Fifty Years On." In *Chronicling*

Cultures: Long-Term Field Research in Anthropology, edited by Robert V. Kemper and Anya Peterson Royce, 160–90. Blue Ridge Summit, PA: Altamira Press.

Legorreta Díaz, Maria del Carmen. 1999. "La autonomía como reivindicación indígena?" *Leviatán* (Madrid) 76: 139–59.

Le Pichon, Alain, and Letizia Caronia, eds. 1991. *Sguardi Venuti da Lontano: Un'Indagine di Transcultura.* Milán: Bompiani.

Leventhal, Alan, Les Field, Hank Alvarez, and Rosemary Cambra. 1994. "The Ohlone: Back from Extinction." In *The Ohlone Past and Present: Native Americans of the San Francisco Bay Region,* edited by Lowell Bean, 297–336. Menlo Park, CA: Ballena Press.

Levi, Jerome M., and Bartholomew Dean. 2003. Introduction to *At the Risk of Being Heard: Identity, Indigenous Rights, and Postcolonial States,* edited by Bartholomew Dean and Jerome M. Levi, 1–41. Ann Arbor: University of Michigan Press.

Leyva Solano, Xóchitl. 2001. "Regional, Communal, and Organizational Transformations in Las Cañadas." *Latin American Perspectives* 28 (2): 20–44.

Lightfoot, Kent G. 2005. *Indians, Missionaries, and Merchants: The Legacy of Colonial Encounters on the California Frontiers.* Berkeley: University of California Press.

Lins Ribeiro, Gustavo, and Arturo Escobar, eds. 2006. *World Anthropologies: Disciplinary Transformations within Systems of Power.* Oxford and New York: Berg.

Lippard, Lucy, ed. 1992. *Partial Recall: With Essays on Photographs of Native North Americans.* New York: New Press.

Löfgren, Orvar. 2002a. "The Nationalization of Anxieties: A History of Border Crossings." In *The Postnational Self: Belonging and Identity,* edited by Ulf Hedetoft and Mette Hjort, 250–74. Minneapolis: University of Minnesota Press.

———. 2002b. *On Holiday: A History of Vacationing.* Berkeley: University of California Press.

Long-Solis, Janet, and Luis Alberto Vargas. 2005. *Food Culture in Mexico.* Westport, CT: Greenwood Press.

López de Jesús Lara, Ivette. 2003. *Encuentros sincopados: El Caribe contemporáneo a través de sus practices musicales.* Mexico City: Siglo XXI Editores.

Lowe, Celia. 2006. *Wild Profusion: Biodiversity Conservation in an Indonesian Archipelago.* Princeton: Princeton University Press.

Lyotard, Jean Francois. 1984. *The Postmodern Condition: A Report on Knowledge.* Minneapolis: University of Minnesota Press. First published 1979.

Macdonald, Gaynor. 2001. "Does 'Culture' Have 'History'? Thinking about Continuity and Change in Central NSW." *Aboriginal History* 25: 176–99.

Macintyre, Martha. 2005. "Taking Care of Culture: Consultancy, Anthropology, and Gender Issues." In *Anthropology and Consultancy: Issues and Debates,* edited by Pamela J. Stewart and Andrew Strathern, 124–38. Oxford: Berghahn Books.

Maddock, Kenneth. 1990. "Involved Anthropologists." In *We Are Here: Politics of Aboriginal Land Tenure,* edited by Edwin N. Wilmsen, 155–76. Berkeley: University of California Press.

Manuel, Peter. 1988. *Popular Musics of the Non-Western World.* New York: Oxford University Press.

Manz, Beatriz. 2002. "Terror, Grief, and Recovery: Genocidal Trauma in a Mayan Village in Guatemala." In *Annihilating Difference: The Anthropology of Genocide,* edited by Alexander Laban Hinton, 292–309. Berkeley: University of California Press.

———. 2004. *Paradise in Ashes: A Guatemalan Journey of Courage, Terror, and Hope.* Berkeley: University of California Press.

Marable, Manning. 2000. "Beyond Racial Identity Politics: Toward a Liberation Theory for Multicultural Democracy." In *Critical Race Theory: The Cutting Edge,* edited by R. Delgado and J. Stefancic, 448–54. Philadelphia: Temple University Press.

Marcus, George. 1998. "The Once and Future Ethnographic Archive." *History of the Human Sciences* 11 (4): 49–63.

———. 2007. "Anthropology and National Security in the United States: The Controversy at the American Anthropological Association on Anthropological Engagement in the Human Terrain Systems." Lecture delivered at the Facultad de Ciencias Antropológicas of the Universidad Autónoma de Yucatán. Maestros de la Antropología Seminar Series. Mérida, Yucatán, November 17, 2007.

Marcus, George, and Dick Cushman. 1982. "Ethnographies as Texts." *Annual Review of Anthropology* 11: 25–69.

Marcus, George E., and Michael J. Fischer. 1986. *Anthropology as Cultural Critique: An Experimental Moment in the Human Sciences.* Chicago: University of Chicago Press.

Marriott, Alice. 1953. *Greener Fields: Experiencies among the American Indians.* New York: Thomas Y. Crowell.

Martín Alcoff, Linda. 2005. "Latino v. Hispanic: The Politics of Ethnic Names." *Philosophy and Social Criticism* 31 (4): 395–407.

Maxwell, Judith M., and Robert M Hill. 2006. *The Kaqchikel Chronicles.* Austin: University of Texas Press.

Mayén de Castellanos, Guisela. 1986. *Tzute y jerarquía en Sololá.* Guatemala City: Museo Ixchel del Traje Indígena.

McCallum, Cecilia. 1995. "The Veja Payakan." *CVA Newsletter* 2 (94): 2–8.

McConvell, Patrick, Laurent Dousset, and Fiona Powell, eds. 2002. "Kinship and Change in Aboriginal Australia." Special issue of *Anthropological Forum* 12 (2): 137–245.

McDonald, Maryon. 1996. "'Unity in Diversity': Some Tensions in the Construction of Europe." *Social Anthropology* 4: 47–60.

McVeigh, Robbie. 1996. *The Radicalization of Irishness: Racism and Anti-racism in Ireland.* Belfast: Centre for Research and Documentation.

Mead, Margaret. 1935. *Sex and Temperament in Three Primitive Societies.* New York: Harper Collins.

———. 1942. *And Keep Your Powder Dry: An Anthropologist Looks at America.* New York: Morrow.

Medicine, Beatrice. 2001. *Learning to Be an Anthropologist and Remaining "Native": Selected Writings,* edited by Sue-Ellen Jacobs, 3–15. Urbana: University of Illinois Press.

Meloni, Benedetto. 1984. *Famiglie di pastori: Continuità e mutamento in una comunità della Sardegna centrale, 1950–1970.* Istituto Superiore Regionale Etnografico. Nuoro: Rosenberg & Sellier.

Menand, Louis. 2001. *The Metaphysical Club.* New York: Farrar, Straus and Giroux.

Mendoza, Zoila. 2000. *Shaping Society through Dance: Mestizo Ritual Performance in the Peruvian Andes.* Chicago: University of Chicago Press.

———. 2008. *Creating Our Own. Folklore, Performance, and Identity in Cuzco, Peru.* Durham: Duke University Press.

Mennell, Stephen. 1996. *All Manners of Food: Eating and Taste in England and France from the Middle Ages to the Present.* Urbana: University of Illinois Press. First published 1985.

Merlan, Francesca. 2006. "Beyond Tradition." *Asia Pacific Journal of Anthropology* 7 (1): 85–104.

Merriam, C. Hart. 1967. *Ethnographic Notes on California Indian Tribes: Central California Indian Tribes.* University of California Archaeological Survey Reports 68 (3), edited by Robert F. Heizer. Berkeley: University of California Archaeological Research Facility.

Merry, Sally Engle. 2003. "Human Rights Law and the Demonization of Culture (and Anthropology along the Way)." *PoLAR: The Political and Legal Anthropology Review* 26 (1): 55–76.

Miller Chernoff, John. 1981. *African Rhythm and African Sensibility: Aesthetic and Social Action in African Musical Idioms.* Chicago: University of Chicago Press.

Milliken, Randall. 1995. *A Time of Little Choice: The Disintegration of Tribal Culture in the San Francisco Bay Area, 1769–1810.* Menlo Park, CA: Ballena Press.

Mills, Antonia. 1994. *Eagle Down Is Our Law: Witsuwit'en Law, Feasts, and Land Claims.* Vancouver: University of British Columbia Press.

———. 1996. "Problems of Establishing Authority in Testifying on Behalf of the Witsuwit'en." *PoLAR: The Political and Legal Anthropology Review* 19 (2): 39–51.

Milton, Kay. 1993. "Belfast: Whose City?" In *Irish Urban Cultures*, edited by Chris Curtin, Hastings Donnan, and Thomas M. Wilson, 23–37. Belfast: Institute of Irish Studies Press.

Moksnes, Heidi. 2004. "Factionalism and Counterinsurgency in Chiapas: Contextualizing the Acteal Massacre." *European Review of Latin American and Caribbean Studies* 76 (April): 109–17.

Montanari, Massimo. 1999. Introduction to *Food: A Culinary History*, edited by Jean-Luis Flandrin and Massimo Montanari, 165–67. New York: Columbia University Press.

Montejo, Victor. 2004. "Angering the Ancestors: Transnationalism and Economic Transformation of Maya Communities in Western Guatemala." In *Pluralizing Ethnography: Comparison and Representation in Maya Cultures, Histories, and Identities*, edited by John M. Watanabe and Edward F. Fischer, 231–55. Santa Fe, NM: School of American Research.

———. 2005. *Maya Intellectual Renaissance: Identity, Representation, and Leadership*. Austin: University of Texas Press.

Moore, John H. 1987. *The Cheyenne Nation: A Social and Demographic History*. Lincoln: University of Nebraska Press.

Morphy, Howard. 2006. "The Practice of an Expert: Anthropology in Native Title." *Anthropological Forum* 16 (2): 135–51.

Municipalidad Indígena de Sololá (MIS). 1998. *Runuk'elen ri Q'atb'äl Tzij Kaqchikel Tz'oloj Ya' / Autoridad y Gobierno Kaqchikel de Sololá*. Guatemala City: Cholsamaj.

Municipalidad Indígena de Sololá (MIS) and Timothy J. Smith, eds. 2012. *Runuk'elen ri Q'atb'äl Tzij Kaqchikel Tz'oloj Ya' / Autoridad y Gobierno Kaqchikel de Sololá (Versión Kaqchikel-Español)*. Antigua, Guatemala: Editorial Junajpu'.

Muwekma Ohlone Tribe. 2002. "Response to the Department of the Interior, BAR/BIA Proposed Findings." Unpublished document.

Myers, Fred R. 1986. "The Politics of Representation: Anthropological Discourse and Australian Aborigines." *American Ethnologist* 13 (1): 138–53.

Napier, A. David. 2004. "Public Anthropology and the Fall of the House of Ushers." *Anthropology News* 45 (6): 6–7.

Nash, June C. 1981. "Ethnographic Aspects of the World Capitalist System." *Annual Review of Anthropology* 10: 393–423.

———. 1989. *From Tank Town to High Tech: The Clash of Community and Industrial Cycles*. New York: State University of New York Press.

———. 2001. *Mayan Visions: The Quest for Autonomy in an Age of Globalization*. New York: Routledge.

———, ed. 2005. Introduction to *Social Movements: An Anthropological Reader*, 1–26. Malden: Blackwell Press.

———. 2006. "The Limits of Naiveté in Anthropological Fieldwork: The 1954 U.S. Instigated Coup in Guatemala." In *Practicing Ethnography in a Globalizing World: An Anthropological Odyssey,* 105–36. Laman, MD: Altamira Press, a subsidiary of Rowman and Littlefield.

———. 2008. "Cambios paradigmáticos y dialéctica de los movimientos sociales." *Cuadernos de Antropología Social* 28: 7–12.

Nash, June, and Helen Safa. 1976. *Sex and Class in Latin America.* New York: 1976. First published as *La Mujer en America Latina,* Mexico, D.F.: Sep Setentas 1975.

Nash, Manning. 1956. *Machine Age Maya: The Industrialization of a Guatemalan Community.* Washington, DC: American Anthropological Association.

Navarrete Arce, Manuela. 1889. "El sabor de Yucatán. Consejos para la comida y el buen vivir." Typewritten document kindly provided by Dr. Celia Rosado Avilés.

Nelson, Diane. 1999. *A Finger in the Wound: Body Politics in Quincentennial Guatemala.* Berkeley: University of California Press.

———. 2003. "The Maya, 'Race,' and Biopolitical Hopes for Peace in Guatemala." In *Race, Nature, and the Politics of Difference,* edited by Donald S. Moore, Jake Kosek, and Anand Pandian, 122–46. Durham, NC: Duke University Press.

———. 2004. "Anthropologist Discovers Legendary Two-Faced Indian in Guatemala! Margins, the State, and Duplicity in Post-war Guatemala." In *The State and Its Margins: Ethnographies from South Asia, Africa, and Latin America,* edited by Deborah Poole and Veena Das. Santa Fe, NM: School of American Research.

Nesper, Larry. 2002. *The Walleye War: The Struggle for Ojibwe Spearfishing and Treaty Rights.* Lincoln: University of Nebraska Press.

Neumann, Roderick. 1998. *Imposing Wilderness: Struggles over Livelihood and Nature Preservation in Africa.* Berkeley: University of California Press.

Niceforo, Alfredo. (1897) 1977. *La delinquenza in Sardegna.* Cagliari: Della Torre.

Niezen, Ronald. 2003. *The Origins of Indigenism: Human Rights and the Politics of Identity.* Los Angeles: University of California Press.

Noriega, Chon, ed. 1992. *Chicanos and Film: Representation and Resistance.* Minneapolis: University of Minnesota Press.

Ntarangwi, Mwenda. 2010. *Reversed Gaze: An African Ethnography of American Anthropology.* Urbana: University of Illinois Press.

Oboler, Suzanne. 1995. *Ethnic Labels, Latino Lives: Identity and the Politics of (Re)presentation in the United States.* Minneapolis: University of Minneapolis Press.

O'Dowd, Liam. 2002. "The Changing Significance of European Borders." *Regional and Federal Studies* 12 (4): 13–36.

Oficina de Derechos Humanos del Arzobispado de Guatemala (ODHAG). 1998.

Guatemala Nunca Más. Guatemala: Informe Proyecto Interdiocesano de Recuperación de la Memoria Histórica (REMHI).

Olwig, Karen. 1993. *Global Culture, Island Identity: Continuity and Change in the Afro-Caribbean Community of Nevis.* Amsterdam: Harwood.

Ong, Aihwa. 1987. *Spirits of Resistance and Capitalist Discipline: Factory Women in Malaysia.* Albany: State University of New York Press.

Ottenberg, Simon. 1990. "Thirty Years of Fieldnotes: Changing Relationships to the Text." In *Fieldnotes: The Makings of Anthropology,* edited by R. Sanjek, 139–60. Ithaca, NY: Cornell University Press.

Padilla, Félix. 1985. *Latino Ethnic Consciousness: The Case of Mexican Americans and Puerto Ricans in Chicago.* Notre Dame: University of Notre Dame Press.

Paine, Robert. 1996. "In Chief Justice McEachern's Shoes: Anthropology's Ineffectiveness in Court." *PoLAR: The Political and Legal Anthropology Review* 19 (2): 59–70.

Parsons, Elsie Clews. 1936. *Taos Pueblo.* Menasha, WI: George Banta Publishing.

Patterson, Thomas C. 2001. *A Social History of Anthropology in the United States.* Oxford and New York: Berg.

Paz, Octavio. 1962. "Mexican Masks." In *The Labyrinth of Solitude: Life and Thought in Mexico,* translated by Lysander Kemp, 29–46. New York: Grove Press.

Pearson, Noel. 2003. "The High Court's Abandonment of 'the Time-Honoured Methodology of the Common Law' in Its Interpretation of Native Title in *Mirriuwung Gajerrong* and *Yorta Yorta.*" Sir Ninian Stephen Annual Lecture, Law School, University of Newcastle, March 17, Newcastle, Australia.

Pedelty, Mark. 2004. *Musical Ritual in Mexico City: From the Aztec to NAFTA.* Austin: University of Texas Press.

Pels, Peter, and Oscar Salemink. 1999. "Introduction: Locating the Colonial Subjects of Anthropology." In *Colonial Subjects: Essays on the Practical History of Anthropology,* edited by Peter Pels and Oscar Salemink, 1–52. Ann Arbor: University of Michigan Press.

Pérez Sabido, Luis. 2003. *De Guty a Manzanero: 200 boleros yucatecos.* Mérida: Dirección de Desarrollo Cultural del Gobierno del Estado de Yucatán.

Pérez Sabido, Luis, Carlos Medina Hadad, and Rafael De Pau. 2000. *La canción yucateca: Semblanzas y letras.* Mérida: Museo de la Canción Yucateca.

Perley, Bernard C. 2006. "Aboriginality at Large: Varieties of Resistance in Maliseet Language Instruction." *Identities: Global Studies in Culture and Power* 13: 187–208.

———. 2009. "Contingencies of Emergence: Planning Maliseet Language Ideologies." In *Native American Language Ideologies: Language Beliefs, Practices, and*

Struggles in Indian Country, edited by Paul V. Kroskrity and Margaret C. Field, 255–70. Tucson: University of Arizona Press.

———. 2011a. *Defying Maliseet Language Death: Emergent Vitalities of Language, Culture, and Identity in Eastern Canada.* Lincoln: University of Nebraska Press.

———. 2011b. "Language as an Integrated Cultural Resource." In *A Companion to Cultural Resource Management,* edited by Thomas F. King, 203–20. Malden: Wiley-Blackwell.

———. 2012a. "Last Words, Final Thoughts: Collateral Extinctions in Maliseet Language Death." In *The Anthropology of Extinction: Essays on Culture and Species Death,* edited by Genese Marie Sodikoff, 127–42. Bloomington: Indiana University Press.

———. 2012b. "Silence before the Void: Language Extinction, Maliseet Storytelling, and the Semiotics of Survival." In *Telling Stories in the Face of Danger: Language Renewal in Native American Communities,* edited by Paul V. Kroskrity, 184–204. Norman: University of Oklahoma Press.

Peterson, Richard A. 1997. *Creating Country Music: Fabricating Authenticity.* Chicago: University of Chicago Press.

Pimenov, Vladimir V. 1977. *Udmurty: Opyt komponentnogo analiza etnosa.* Leningrad: Nauka.

———. 1988. "Podgotovka professionalnogo ethnografa." *Sovetskaia Etnografiia* 3: 65–72.

Pitarch, Pedro. 2004. "The Zapatistas and the Art of Ventriloquism." *Journal of Human Rights* 3 (3): 291–312.

Ponce de Leon, Juana, ed. 2001. *Our Word Is Our Weapon: Selected Writings/Subcommandante Marcos.* New York: Seven Stories Press.

Posey, Darrell. 1999. *Cultural and Spiritual Values of Biodiversity.* Nairobi: ITP/UNEP.

———. 2004. *Indigenous Knowledge and Ethics.* London and New York: Routledge.

Poster, Mark. 1990. *The Mode of Information: Poststructuralism and Social Context.* Chicago: University of Chicago Press.

Potiguara, Eliane. 1992. "Harvesting What We Plant." *Cultural Survival Quarterly* 16: 46–48.

Povinelli, Elizabeth A. 2002. *The Cunning of Recognition: Indigenous Alterities and the Making of Australian Multiculturalism.* Durham: Duke University Press.

Pratt, Mary Louise. 1986. "Fieldwork in Common Places." In *Writing Culture: The Poetics and Politics of Ethnography,* edited by James Clifford and George E. Marcus, 27–50. Berkeley: University of California Press.

Quigley, Declan. 1997. "Deconstructing Colonial Fictions? Some Conjuring Tricks in the Recent Sociology of India." In *After Writing Culture: Epistemology and Praxis in Contemporary Anthropology,* edited by Allison James, Jenny Hockney, and Andrew Dawson, 103–21. London: Routledge.

Rabinow, Paul, and George E. Marcus. 2008. *Designs for an Anthropology of the Contemporary.* Durham: Duke University Press.

Raffles, Hugh. 2002. *In Amazonia: A Natural History.* Princeton: Princeton University Press.

Ramírez Berg, Charles. 2002. *Latino Images in Film: Stereotypes, Subversion, and Resistance.* Austin: University of Texas Press.

Ramos, Alcida Rita. 1998. *Indigenism: Ethnic Politics in Brazil.* Madison: University of Wisconsin Press.

———. 2000. "Anthropologist as Political Actor: Between Activism and Suspicion." *Journal of Latin American Anthropology* 4 (2): 172–89.

Ranco, Darren. 2005. "Indigenous Peoples, State-Sanctioned Knowledge, and the Politics of Recognition." *American Anthropologist* 107 (4): 708–11.

———. 2006. "The Indian Ecologist and the Politics of Representation: Critiquing the Ecological Indian in the Age of Ecocide." In *Perspectives on the Ecological Indian: Native Americans and the Environment,* edited by Michael Harkin and David Rich Lewis, 32–51. Lincoln: University of Nebraska Press.

Rappaport, Joanne. 2005. *Intercultural Utopias: Public Intellectuals, Cultural Experimentation, and Ethnic Pluralism in Colombia.* Durham, NC: Duke University Press.

Rappaport, Roy. 1999. *Ritual and Religion in the Making of Humanity.* Cambridge, England: Cambridge University Press.

Ray, Christopher. 2001. "Transnational Co-operation between Rural Areas: Elements of a Political Economy of EU Rural Development." *Sociologia Ruralis* 41 (3): 279–95.

Ray, Verne F. 1955. "Anthropology and Indian Claims Litigation: Introduction." *Ethnohistory* 2 (4): 287–91.

Real Academia Española. 1999. *Ortografía de la lengua española.* Madrid: Espasa.

Redfield, Robert. 1930. *Tepoztlan.* Chicago: University of Chicago Press.

———. 1941. *The Folk Culture of Yucatan.* Chicago: University Press.

Regione Autonoma della Sardegna, Assessorato della Difesa dell'Ambiente. 2004. *Atti del convegno Incendi boschivi e rurali in Sardegna. Dall'analisi delle cause alle proposte d'intervento.* Cagliari 14/15 maggio 2004, http://www.regione.sardegna.it/corpoforestale/notizie/convegno_2004.htm (accessed June 17, 2007).

Reynolds, Simon. 1999. *Generation Ecstasy: Into the World of Techno and Rave Culture.* New York: Routledge.

Richards, Michael. 2003. *Atlas Lingüístico de Guatemala.* Guatemala: Secretaría de la Paz, Universidad del Valle de Guatemala, and U.S. Agency for International Development.

Richardson, Miles. 1975. "Anthropologist—The Myth Teller." *American Ethnologist* 2 (3): 517–33.

Ridington, Robin, and Dennis Hastings (In'aska). 1997. *Blessing for a Long Time: The Sacred Pole of the Omaha Tribe.* Lincoln: University of Nebraska Press.

Rigby, Peter, and Peter Sevareid. 1992. "Lawyers, Anthropologists, and the Knowledge of Facts." In *Double Vision: Anthropologists at Law,* edited by Randy Frances Kandel, 5–21. Washington, DC: American Anthropological Association.

Robinson, Michael. 2001. "Disparate Judicial Approaches to the Production of Anthropological Fieldnotes: Observations on the *Daniel* and *Smith* Cases." Paper presented at the conference Expert Evidence in Native Title Court Cases: Issues of Truth, Objectivity, and Expertise, July 6–7, 2001, Adelaide, Australia. *http://www.aas.asn.au/publications/pub_aas.php* (accessed June 2, 2012).

Rodríguez, Gregory. 2009. "The Generic Latino: What Does the Nomination of Sonia Sotomayor Really Say?" *Los Angeles Times,* June 1, http://www.latimes.com/news/opinion/la-oe-rodriguez1-2009jun01,0,5876536.column (accessed June 27, 2009).

Rorty, Richard. 1982. *Philosophy and the Mirror of Nature.* Princeton: Princeton University Press.

Rosado Avilés, Celia Esperanza. 2004. *La novela histórica de Eligio Ancona: Una literatura con múltiples campos de acción.* Mérida: Ediciones de la Universidad Autónoma de Yucatán/Instituto de Cultura de Yucatán.

Rosaldo, Michelle, and Louise Lamphere. 1974. *Women, Culture, and Society.* Stanford: Stanford University Press.

Rosaldo, Renato. 1989. *Culture and Truth: The Remaking of Social Analysis.* Boston: Beacon Press.

Rosello, Mirelle. 2001. *Postcolonial Hospitality: The Immigrant as Guest.* Stanford: Stanford University Press.

Rosen, Lawrence. 1977. "The Anthropologist as Expert Witness." *American Anthropologist* 79 (3): 555–78.

———. 1979. "Response to Stewart." *American Anthropologist* 81 (1): 111–12.

Roth, Christopher F. 2002. "Without Treaty, without Conquest: Indigenous Sovereignty in Post-Delgamuukw British Columbia." *Wicazo Sa Review* 17 (2): 143–65.

Rowland, Ingrid D. 2004. *The Scarith of Scornello: A Tale of Renaissance Forgery.* Chicago: University of Chicago Press.

Ruane, Joseph, and Jennifer Todd. 1996. *The Dynamics of Conflict in Northern Ireland.* Cambridge: Cambridge University Press.

Rugglers, Greg, and Stuart Sahukla, eds. 1996. *Zapatista encuentro: Documents from the 1996 Encounter for Humanity and against Neoliberalism.* New York: Seven Stories Press.

Russian Federation. 2012. "O gosudarstvennykh garantiiakh i kompensatsiakh dlia lits, rabotaiuschikh i prozhivaiuschikh v raionakh Krainego Severa i priravnennykh k nim mestnostiakh." Russian Federation Law No.4520-1 *http://www.referent.ru/1/66971* (accessed May 9, 2012).

Rybakov, Sergei E. 1998. "K voprosy o poniatii 'etnos.'" *Etnographicheskoye obozreniye* 6: 3–15.

———. 2000. "O metodologii issledovaniia etnicheskikh fenomenov." *Etnographicheskoye obozreniye* 5: 3–16.

Sahlins, Marshall. 2005. *Culture in Practice: Selected Essays.* New York: Zone Books.

Sahlins, Peter. 2004. *Unnaturally French: Foreign Citizens in the Old Regime and After.* Ithaca, NY: Cornell University Press.

Samuels, Stephan R., ed. 1991. "Ozette Archaeological Project Research Report I: House Structure and Floor Midden." Washington State University, Department of Anthropology, Reports of Investigations 63. Pullman, WA.

Sanford, Victoria. 2003. *Buried Secrets: Truth and Human Rights in Guatemala.* New York: Palgrave MacMillan.

Sangren, P. Stephen. 1988. "Rhetoric and the Authority of Ethnography: 'Postmodernism' and the Social Reproduction of Texts." *Current Anthropology* 29 (3): 405–35.

Sanjek, Roger, ed. 1990. *Fieldnotes: The Makings of Anthropology.* Ithaca, NY: Cornell University Press.

Santiago-Irizarry, Vilma. 1996. "Culture as Cure." *Cultural Anthropology* 11 (1): 3–24.

———. 2001. *Medicalizing Ethnicity: Constructing Latino Identity in a Psychiatric Setting.* Ithaca, NY: Cornell University Press.

Sapir, Edward. 1927. "The Unconscious Patterning of Behavior in Society." In *The Unconscious: A Symposium,* edited by E. S. Drummer, 114–42. New York: Alfred A. Knopf.

———. 1949. "Culture, Genuine and Spurious." In *Selected Writings of Edward Sapir,* edited by D. Mandelbaum, 308–31. Berkeley: University of California Press.

Schade-Poulsen, Marc. 1999. *The Social Significance of Rai: Men and Popular Music in Algeria.* Austin: University of Texas Press.

Schneider, Jane. 1998. Introduction to *Italy's "Southern Question": Orientalism in One Country,* edited by Jane Schneider, 1–23. Oxford: Berg.

Scholte, Bob. 1972. "Toward a Reflexive and Critical Anthropology." In *Reinventing Anthropology,* edited by Dell Hymes, 430–57. New York: Pantheon Books.

Scott, James C. 1976. *The Moral Economy of the Peasant: Rebellion and Subsistence in Southeast Asia.* New Haven: Yale University Press.

————. 1985. *Weapons of the Weak: Everyday Forms of Peasant Resistance.* New Haven: Yale University Press.

Seeger, Anthony. 2004. *Why Suyá Sing: A Musical Anthropology of an Amazonian People.* Urbana and Chicago: University of Illinois Press.

Seidman, Steven. 1997. *Difference Troubles: Queering Social Theory and Sexual Politics.* Cambridge: Cambridge University Press.

Semionov, Yuri I. 1993. "Etnologiia i gnoseologiia." *Etnographicheskoye obozreniye* 6: 3–21.

————. 1996a. "Obschestvo, strany, narody." *Etnographicheskoye obozreniye* 2: 3–19.

————. 1996b. "Sotsialno-istoricheskiie organismy, etnosy, natsii." *Etnographicheskoye obozreniye* 3: 3–13.

————. 2000. "Etnos, natiia, diaspora." *Etnographicheskoye obozreniye* 2: 64–73.

Shandel, Tom. 1973. *Behind the Masks* (video). Ottawa, ON: National Film Board of Canada.

Shirokogoroff, Sergei. 1923. *Etnos: Issledovanie osnovnykh printsipov etnicheskikh i enograficheskikh yavlenii.* Shanghai.

Shnirelman, Viktor. 2001. *The Value of the Past: Myths, Identity, and Politics in Transcaucasia.* Senri Ethnological Studies, no. 57. Osaka: National Museum of Ethnology.

Shore, Cris. 1993. "Inventing the 'People's Europe': Critical Approaches to European Community 'Cultural Policy.'" *Man* 28: 779–800.

Shorris, Earl. 1992. *Latinos: A Biography of the People.* New York: W. W. Norton and Company.

Shostak, Marjorie. 1981. *Nisa: The Life and Words of a !Kung Woman.* New York: Vintage Books.

Sider, Gerald. 1993. *Living Indian Histories: Lumbee and Tuscarora People in North Carolina.* Cambridge: Cambridge University Press.

Sjøholt, Peter. 1999. "Culture as a Strategic Development Device: The Role of 'European Cities of Culture,' with Particular Reference to Bergen." *European Urban and Regional Studies* 6 (4): 339–47.

Slater, Candace. 2002. *Entangled Edens: Visions of the Amazon.* Berkeley and Los Angeles: University of California Press.

Slezkine, Y. 1994. *Arctic Mirrors: Russia and the Small Peoples of the North.* Ithaca, NY: Cornell University Press.

Sluka, Jeffrey. 1989. *Hearts and Minds, Water and Fish: Support for the IRA and INLA in a Northern Irish Ghetto.* Greenwich: JAI Press.

Smith, Benjamin R., and Frances Morphy, eds. 2007. *The Social Effects of Native Title: Recognition, Translation, Coexistence.* Centre for Aboriginal Economic Policy and Research Monograph 27. Canberra: Australian National University E-Press.

Smith, Carol A. 1991. "Mayan Nationalism." *NACLA Report on the Americas* 25 (3): 29–33.

Smith, Rogers M. 2003. *Stories of Peoplehood: The Politics and Morals of Political Membership.* Cambridge: Cambridge University Press.

Smith, Timothy J. 2002. "Skipping Years and Scribal Errors: Kaqchikel Maya Timekeeping in the Fifteenth, Sixteenth, and Seventeenth Centuries." *Ancient Mesoamerica* 13 (1): 65–76.

———. 2003. "A Tale of Two Governments: Rural Mayan Politics and Competing Democracies in Sololá, Guatemala." PhD diss., State University of New York at Albany.

———. 2006. "Views from the 'South': Intellectual Hegemony and Postmodernism in Latin America." *Reviews in Anthropology* 35 (1): 61–78.

———. 2009. "Democracy Is Dissent: Political Confrontations and Indigenous Mobilization in Sololá." In *Mayas in Postwar Guatemala: Harvest of Violence Revisited,* edited by Walter E. Little and Timothy J. Smith. Tuscaloosa: The University of Alabama Press.

Smith, Timothy J., and Abigail E. Adams, eds. 2011. *After the Coup: An Ethnographic Reframing of Guatemala, 1954.* Urbana: University of Illinois Press.

Smith, Timothy J., and Thomas A. Offit. 2010. "Confronting Violence in Postwar Guatemala." *Journal of Latin American and Caribbean Anthropology* 15 (1): 1–15.

Sokolovskiy, Sergey V. 1993a. "Etnichnost' kak tsennost': Sluchai minoritetov." *Etika Severa* 1: 98–126.

———. 1993b. "Etnograficheskoie issledovanie: Ideal i deistvitelnost." *Etnographicheskoye obozreniye* 2: 3–14; 3: 3–15.

———. 1994. "Etnichnost' kak pamiat." In *Ethnokognitologiia: Podkhody k issledovaniiu etnicheskoi identichnosti,* 9–31. Moscow.

———. 1995a. "Ethnographic Research: Ideals and Reality." *Anthropology and Archeology of Eurasia* 34 (2): 5–38.

———. 1995b. "Ob avtarkii, natsionalisme, i post-Sovietskoi identichnosti." In *Etnometodologiia: Problemy, Podkhody, Kontseptsii,* 2:87–114. Moscow.

———. 2000. "The Construction of 'Indigenousness' in Russian Science, Politics, and Law." *Journal of Legal Pluralism* 45: 91–113.

———. 2001. *Obrazy Drugikh v rossiyskikh nauke, istorii i prave.* Moscow: Put.

Sokolovskiy, Sergey, and Valery Tishkov. 1995. "Ethnicity." In *Encyclopedia for Social and Cultural Anthropology,* edited by Alan Barnard and Jonathan Spencer, 190–93. London: Routledge.

Soldatova, Galina U. 1998. *Psykhologiia mezhetnicheskoi napriazhionnosti.* Moscow: Moskva Smysl.

Sollors, Werner. 1996. *Theories of Ethnicity: A Classical Reader*. New York: New York University Press.

Spivak, Gayatri. 1990. *The Post-colonial Critic: Interviews, Strategies, Dialogues*. New York: Routledge.

———. 1996. "Subaltern Studies: Deconstructing Historiography." In *The Spivak Reader*, edited by D. Landry and G. MacLean, 203–35. London: Routledge.

Stephen, Lynn. 2001. "Gender, Citizenship, and the Politics of Identity." *Latin American Perspectives* 28 (6): 54–69.

Steward, Julian H. 1955. "Theory and Application in Social Science." *Ethnohistory* 2 (4): 292–302.

Stewart, Omer C. 1979. "An Expert Witness Answers Rosen." *American Anthropologist* 81 (1): 108–11.

Stokes, Martin, ed. 1997. *Ethnicity, Identity, and Music: The Musical Construction of Place*. Oxford: Berg.

Stoll, David. 1993. *Between Two Armies in the Ixil Towns of Guatemala*. New York: Columbia University Press.

———. (1999) 2008. *Rigoberta Menchú and the Story of All Poor Guatemalans*. 2nd ed. Boulder, CO: Westview Press.

Suarez Molina, Victor Manuel. 1996. *El español que se habla en Yucatán: Apuntamentos filológicos*. Rev. ed. by Miguel Güemez Pineda. Mérida: Ediciones de la Universidad Autónoma de Yucatán. First published 1945.

Susokolov, A. A. 1990. "Strukturnye faktory samoorganizatsii etnosa." *Rasy i narody*, journal edited by S. Bruk, 20: 5–39.

Sutton, Peter. 1995. "Forensic Anthropology in Australia: Does It Have a Case to Answer?" In *Native Title: Emerging Issues for Research, Policy, and Practice*, edited by Julie Finlayson and Diane Smith, 83–100. Centre for Aboriginal Economic and Policy Research, Research Monograph no. 10. Canberra: Australian National University.

———. 2003. *Native Title in Australia: An Ethnographic Perspective*. Cambridge: Cambridge University Press.

Tapp, Nicholas. 1995. "Minority Nationality in China: Policy and Practice." In *Indigenous Peoples of Asia*, edited by R. H. Barnes, Andrew Gray, and Benedict Kingsbury, 195–220. Ann Arbor: University of Michigan.

Tarrow, Sidney. 1994. *Rebirth or Stagnation? European Studies after 1989*. New York: Social Science Research Council.

Taussig, Michael. 1993. *Mimesis and Alterity: A Particular History of the Senses*. New York: Routledge.

Tax, Sol. 1937. "*Mitla, Town of Souls, and Other Zapoteco-Speaking Pueblos of Oaxaca, Mexico*, by Elsie Clews Parsons, Book Review." *American Sociological Review* 2 (1): 135–36.

Taylor, Clark. 1998. *Return of Guatemala's Refugees: Reweaving the Torn.* Philadelphia: Temple University Press.

Taylor, Liba. 1997. "Update: Better than Batman." *New Internationalist Magazine* 296, www.newint.org.issue296/update.htm (accessed October 29, 2003).

Tedlock, Barbara. 1993. "Mayans and Mayan Studies from 2000 B.C. to A.D. 1992." *Latin American Research Review* 28 (3): 153–73.

Tedlock, Dennis, and Bruce Mannheim. 1996. Introduction to *The Dialogic Emergence of Culture,* edited by Dennis Tedlock and Bruce Mannheim. Urbana: University of Illinois Press.

Terry, Edward Davies. 1980. "A Panorama of Literature in Yucatan." In *Yucatan a World Apart,* edited by Edward H. Moseley and Edward D. Terry, 264–305. Tuscaloosa: University of Alabama Press.

Thom, Brian. 1999. "Rising to the Test: Meeting Lamer's Tests for Aboriginal Rights and Title after Delgamuukw." Paper presented at the 1999 meeting of the Canadian Anthropology Society, Quebec City.

———. 2001a. "Aboriginal Rights and Title in Canada after Delgamuukw: Part One, Oral Traditions and Anthropological Evidence in the Courtroom." *Native Studies Review* 14 (1): 1–26.

———. 2001b. "Aboriginal Rights and Title in Canada after Delgamuukw: Part Two, Anthropological Perspectives on Rights, Tests, Infringement, and Justification." *Native Studies Review* 14 (2): 1–42.

Thomas, Nicholas. 1994. *Colonialism's Culture: Anthropology, Travel, and Government.* Cambridge, UK: Polity Press.

Thompson, E. P. 1975. *Whigs and Hunters: The Origin of the Black Act.* New York: Pantheon Books.

Tilley, Virginia Q. 2002. "New Help or New Hegemony? The Transnational Indigenous Peoples' Movement and 'Being Indian' in El Salvador." *Journal of Latin American Studies* 34: 525–54.

Tishkov, Valery. 1989a. "Glasnost and the Nationalities within the Soviet Union." *Third World Quarterly* 11 (4): 207–20.

———. 1989b. "O novykh podkhodakh v teorii i praktike mezhetnicheskikh otnoshenii." *Sovetskaia Etnografia* 5: 3–15.

———. 1992. "Sovetsakaia etnographia: Preodolenie krizisa." *Etnographicheskoye obozreniye* 1: 5–21.

———. 1993a. "Ethnicnost, natsionalism i gosudarstvo v postkommunisticheskom obschestve." *Voprosy Sotsiologii* 1 (2): 3–32.

———. 1993b. On the Crisis in Soviet Ethnography: Reply to Comments. *Current Anthropology* 34 (3): 275–79.

———. 1997. "O fenomene etnichnosti." *Etnographicheskoye obozreniye* 3: 3–21.

Torgovnick, Tatiana. 1990. *Gone Primitive: Savage Intellects, Modern Lives.* Chicago: University of Chicago Press.

Torres, Gabriel. 1997. *La fuerza de la ironía: Un estudio del poder en la vida cotidiana de los trabajadores tomateros del occidente de México.* Mexico City: Centro de Investigaciones y Estudios Superiores en Antropología Social; Guadalajara: El Colegio de Jalisco.

Trigger, David. 2004. "Anthropology in Native Title Cases: 'Mere Pleading, Expert Opinion or Hearsay'?" In *Crossing Boundaries: Cultural, Legal, Historical, and Practice Issues in Native Title,* edited by Sandy Toussaint, 24–33. Melbourne: Melbourne University Press.

Trouillot, Michel-Rolph. 1995. *Silencing the Past: Power and the Production of History.* Boston: Beacon Press.

Tsing, Anna Lowenhaupt. 2005. *Friction: An Ethnography of Global Connection.* Princeton: Princeton University Press.

Tully, James. 2002. "Reimagining Belonging in Circumstances of Cultural Diversity: A Citizens Approach." In *The Postnational Self: Belonging and Identity,* edited by Ulf Hedetoft and Mette Hjort, 152–77. Minneapolis: University of Minnesota Press.

Turner, Terence S. 1992. "Defiant Images: The Kayapo Appropriation of Video." *Anthropology Today* 8 (6): 5–16.

Turner, Victor. 1982. *From Ritual to Theatre: The Human Seriousness of Play.* New York: Performing Arts Journal Publications.

Tyler, Stephen A. 1986. "Post-Modern Ethnography: From Document of the Occult to Occult Document." In *Writing Culture: The Poetics and Politics of Ethnography,* edited by James Clifford and George E. Marcus, 122–40. Berkeley: University of California Press.

United Nations Conference on Environment and Development (UNCED). 1992. *Report of the United Nations Conference on Environment and Development.* Rio De Janeiro, June 3–14. *http://www.un.org/esa/dsd/resources/res_docukeyconf_eartsumm.shtml* (accessed June 2, 2012).

Urciuoli, Bonnie. 1996. *Exposing Prejudice: Puerto Rican Experiences of Language, Race, and Class.* Boulder, CO: Westview Press.

Van den Berghe, Pierre L. 1981. *The Ethnic Phenomenon.* New York: Elsevier.

Van der Haar, Gemma. 2004. "The Zapatista Uprising and the Struggle for Indigenous Autonomy." *European Review of Latin American and Caribbean Studies* 76 (April): 99–108.

Vargas-Cetina, Gabriela, ed. 1999. *Mirando . . . ¿Hacia afuera? Experiencias de investigación.* Mexico City: Centro de Investigaciones y Estudios Superiores en Antropología Social.

———. 2001. "Postcolonial Sites and Markets." *TAMARA: Journal of Critical Post-modern Organization Science* 1 (3): 68–79.

———. 2003. "Representations of Indigenousness." *Anthropology News* 44 (5): 11–12.

———. 2010. "Imágenes de Yucatán y 'lo yucateco' en textos sobre la canción yucateca, 1944–2007." In *Representaciones culturales: Imágenes e imaginación de lo yucateco,* edited by Steffan Igor Ayora-Diaz and Gabriela Vargas-Cetina, 81–97. Mérida: Ediciones de la Universidad Autónoma de Yucatán.

Viner, Boris E. 1998. "Etnichnost: V poiskakh paradigmy izucheniia." *Etno-graphicheskoye obozreniye* 4: 3–24.

Vogt, Evon. 1994. *Fieldwork among the Maya: Reflections on the Harvard Chiapas Project.* Albuquerque: University of New Mexico Press.

Wade, Peter. 2000. *Music, Race, and Nation: Música Tropical in Colombia.* Chicago: University of Chicago Press.

Waldram, James B., Pat Berringer, and Wayne Warry. 1992. "'Nasty, Brutish, and Short': Anthropology and the Gitksan-Wet'suwet'en Decision." *Canadian Journal of Native Studies* 12 (2): 309–16.

Walley, Christine. 2004. *Rough Waters.* Princeton University Press.

Warman, Arturo, Bonfil Batalla, et al. 1970. *De eso que llaman antropología mexi-cana.* Mexico City: Editorial Nuestro Tiempo.

Warner, W. Lloyd, and Leo Srole. 1945. *The Social Systems of American Ethnic Groups.* Yankee City Series, vol. 3. New Haven: Yale University Press.

Warren, Jonathan W. 2001. *Racial Revolutions: Antiracism and Indian Resurgence in Brazil.* Durham, NC: Duke University Press.

Warren, Kay B. 1989. *Symbolism of Subordination: Indian Identity in a Guatemalan Town.* Austin: University of Texas Press.

———. 1998a. *Indigenous Movements and Their Critics: Pan-Maya Activism in Guate-mala.* Princeton: Princeton University Press.

———. 1998b. "Indigenous Movements as a Challenge to the Unified Social Movement Paradigm for Guatemala." In *Cultures of Politics, Politics of Cul-tures: Re-visioning Latin American Social Movements,* edited by Sonia E. Alvarez, Evelina Dagnino, and Arturo Escobar, 165–95. Boulder, CO: Westview Press.

———. 2002. "Voting against Indigenous Rights in Guatemala: Lessons from the 1999 Referendum." In *Indigenous Movements, Self-Representation, and the State in Latin America,* edited by Kay B. Warren and Jean E. Jackson, 149–80. Austin: University of Texas Press.

Washburn, Wilcomb E. 1989. "Anthropological Advocacy in the Hopi-Navajo Land Dispute." *American Anthropologist* 91 (3): 738–43.

Watanabe, John. 1992. *Maya Saints and Souls in a Changing World.* Austin: Uni-versity of Texas Press.

———. 2000. "Neither as They Imagined nor as Others Intended: Mayas and

Anthropologists in the Highlands of Guatemala since the 1960s." In *Supplement to the Handbook of Middle American Indians, vol. 6: Ethnology,* edited by J. D. Monaghan. Austin: University of Texas Press.

Weber, Eugene. 1979. *Peasants into Frenchmen: The Modernization of Rural France, 1870–1914.* Stanford: Stanford University Press.

Weiner, James F., and Katie Glaskin, eds. 2006. "Custom: Indigenous Tradition and Law in the Twenty-First Century." *Asia-Pacific Journal of Anthropology* (special issue) 7 (1).

———. 2007. *Customary Land Tenure and Registration in Australia and Papua New Guinea: Anthropological Perspectives.* Asia-Pacific Environment Monograph 3. Canberra: ANU E-press.

West, Paige. 2006. *Conservation Is Our Government Now: The Politics of Ecology in Papua New Guinea.* Durham: Duke University Press.

West, Paige, James Igoe, and Dan Brockington. 2006. "Parks and Peoples: The Social Impact of Protected Areas." *Annual Review of Anthropology* 35: 251–77.

Whitaker, Robin. 2008. "Gender and the Politics of Justice in the Northern Ireland Peace Process: Considering Róisín McAliskey." *Identities: Global Studies in Culture and Power* 15 (1): 1–30.

Wilkinson, Daniel. 2002. *Silence on the Mountain: Stories of Terror, Betrayal, and Forgetting in Guatemala.* New York: Houghton Mifflin.

Williams, Patrick. 2000. *Los cíngaros de Hungría y sus músicas.* Madrid: Ediciones Akal.

Williams, Raymond. 1977. *Marxism and Literature.* Oxford: Oxford University Press.

Wilson, Richard. 1995. *Mayan Resurgence in Guatemala: Q'eqchi' Experiences.* Norman: University of Oklahoma Press.

Wilson, Thomas M. 2000. "The Obstacles to European Union Regional Policy in the Northern Ireland Borderlands." *Human Organization* 59 (1): 1–10.

Wilson, Thomas M., and Hastings Donnan. 2006. *The Anthropology of Ireland.* Oxford: Berg.

Wolf, Eric. 1982. *Europe and the Peoples without History.* Berkeley: University of California Press.

Wootten, Hal. 2003. "Conflicting Imperatives: Pursuing Truth in the Courts." In *Proof and Truth: The Humanist as Expert,* edited by Iain McCalman and Ann McGrath, 15–50. Canberra: Australian Academy of the Humanities.

World Commission on Environment and Development. 1987. *Our Common Future.* UN Documents. *http://www.un-documents.net/wced-ocf.htm* (accessed June 2, 2012).

World Music Network. 2002. *The Rough Guide to the Music of Mexico.* CD with booklet. Music compilation by Eduardo Llerenas. Sleeve notes by Mary Farquharson. London: World Music Network.

Wright, Isabel. 1992. "Anthropology and Capital Case Litigation." *National Association for the Practice of Anthropology Bulletin* 11: 29–42.

Wu, Frank H. 2002. *Yellow: Race in America beyond Black and White.* New York: Basic Books.

Yamashita, Shinji, Joseph Bosco, and J. S. Eades, eds. 2004. *The Making of Anthropology in East and Southeast Asia.* Oxford and New York: Berghahn Books.

Zarinov, Igor Yu. 1997. "Istoricheskiie ramki fenomena etnichnosti." *Etnographicheskoye obozreniye* 3: 21–31.

———. 2000. "Vremia iskat' obschii iazyk (problema integratsii razlichnykh etnicheskikh teorii i kontseptsij)." *Etnographicheskoye obozreniye* 2: 3–17.

Zumwalt, Rosemary Lévy. 1992. *Wealth and Rebellion: Elsie Clews Parsons, Anthropologist and Folklorist.* Urbana: University of Illinois Press.

Contributors

Steffan Igor Ayora-Diaz (PhD, 1993, McGill University) is a professor of anthropology at the Autonomous University of Yucatan, Mexico. His research has focused on local people's embodied, *naturalized* knowledge and its relation to everyday practices. He has done research among sheep and goat herders in Highland Sardinia, Italy; among local healers in Chiapas, Mexico; and among restaurant managers and food lovers in Yucatan, Mexico, where he has been studying regional gastronomy and food-related practices since 2001. He has published on Sardinian cultural and sociopolitical practices, on the politics of recognition and representation of local healers in Chiapas, and on the politics of representation in Yucatecan cuisine.

Beth A. Conklin (PhD, 1989, University of California at San Francisco and Berkeley) is a professor of anthropology and the director of Graduate Studies at Vanderbilt University. She is a cultural and medical anthropologist specializing in the ethnology of indigenous peoples of lowland South America (Amazonia). Her research focuses on the anthropology of the body, religion and ritual, cannibalism, death and mourning, disease and healing, and indigenous identity politics. She teaches courses on cultural anthropology, medical anthropology, shamanism, international development, South American Indians, and the anthropology of contemporary issues.

Les W. Field (PhD, 1987, Duke University) is a professor of anthropology at the University of New Mexico. He has done fieldwork among native peoples in California, Nicaragua, Colombia, and Ecuador. His research interests include indigenous identities and ideologies, narrative and memory, nationalist ideologies and the state, local resources and development, and social transformations.

Katie Glaskin (PhD, 2002, Australian National University) is an associate professor in the Department of Anthropology and Sociology at the University of Western Australia. Her work has focused on native title and property relations, tradition and innovation, cosmology, ontology, dreams, and marine tenure among Australian indigenous people.

Frederic W. Gleach (PhD, 1992, University of Chicago) is a senior lecturer and the curator of the anthropology collections at Cornell University. A historical anthropologist and archaeologist, his research revolves around issues of identity and representation and focuses primarily on the Indians of Virginia, on popular culture in Puerto Rico, and on material and visual culture. He also studies the history of anthropology, particularly the Americanist tradition.

Tracey Heatherington (PhD, 2000, Harvard University) is an associate professor of anthropology at the University of Wisconsin–Milwaukee. She has done fieldwork in Italy and Romania. Her research interests include science, culture and the environment, environmentalism and the nation-state, eco-development, resistance, cultural racism, biodiversity conservation, and the process of Europeanization.

June C. Nash (PhD, 1960, University of Chicago) is Distinguished Professor Emerita at the Graduate Center of the City University of New York. Her research has focused on many themes, including modernization, globalization, work, women and feminism, indigenous rebellions, and violence and social movements, mainly in Bolivia and Mexico.

Bernard C. Perley (PhD, 2002, Harvard University) is an associate professor of anthropology at the University of Wisconsin–Milwaukee. His research interests include language ideology, language endangerment, and language revitalization through linguistics, visual anthropology, and practices of intermediality. Through graphic ethnography, he is exploring American Indian studies' perspectives around the repatriation of tangible and intangible properties, aboriginality, and ethnocosmogenesis.

Vilma Santiago-Irizarry (PhD, 1993, New York University) is an associate professor in anthropology at Cornell University. Her research has examined the issues and paradoxes generated in the production and deployment of ethnic constructs, especially in institutional settings, which are then applied toward the maintenance and reproduction of existing structures of inequality. She has engaged in extensive field research in schools, penal institutions, and community-based organizations in New York City; she has also done ethnohistorical research on the Spanish-speaking Caribbean, especially in Cuba and Puerto Rico.

Timothy J. Smith (PhD, 2004, State University of New York–Albany) is an assistant professor in the Department of Anthropology at Appalachian State University. His research covers the anthropology of politics, ethnicity, democracy, and social movements in Latin America, specifically, Guatemala and Mexico. In addition to holding visiting appointments in anthropology at Harvard University, Columbia University, and Princeton University, he has taught social anthropology, humanities, Latin American studies, and linguistics at the University of South Florida, the University of Illinois at Urbana–Champaign, and the University at Albany, SUNY.

Sergey Sokolovskiy (PhD, 1986, Institute of Ethnography of the Academy of Sciences of Moscow) is a full-time principal researcher at the Institute of Ethnology and Anthropology of the Russian Academy of Sciences, in the Department of Ethnic Ecology. His research interests include nomadic, indigenous, and tribal peoples of Russia and Siberia.

David Stoll (PhD, 1992, Stanford University) is a professor of anthropology at Middlebury College. He has done research in Latin America, especially in Guatemala. His work involves debates over representation, authority and identity, and wider debates over political correctness, identity politics, and ideologies of victimization.

Gabriela Vargas-Cetina (PhD, 1994, McGill University) is a professor of anthropology at Universidad Autónoma de Yucatán. She has done fieldwork in Italy (Sardinia), Canada (Alberta), and Mexico (Chiapas and Yucatan) and has published mainly on globalization and cooperatives in Italy and Mexico and on music and dance in Canada and Mexico. Her interests include local organizations, epistemology, globalization, digital media, mobile technologies, and the expressive arts.

Thomas M. Wilson (PhD, 1985, City University of New York) is a professor and the chair of the Anthropology Department at Binghamton University–State University of New York. His research has focused on national identity and nationalism, international borders and frontiers, ethnicity and ethnic conflict, the politics of Europeanization, European integration and supranationalism, and consumer culture. He has conducted field research in Ireland, the United Kingdom, and Hungary.

Index